BLOWOUT!

BLOWOUT!

Sal Castro and
the Chicano Struggle
for Educational Justice

MARIO T. GARCÍA & SAL CASTRO

The University of North Carolina Press
Chapel Hill

© 2011 The University of North Carolina Press

All rights reserved

Manufactured in the United States of America

Set in Arnhem and TheSans

The paper in this book meets the guidelines for permanence and durability of the Committee on Production Guidelines for Book Longevity of the Council on Library Resources.

The University of North Carolina Press has been a member of the Green Press Initiative since 2003.

Library of Congress Cataloging-in-Publication Data

García, Mario T.

Blowout! : Sal Castro and the Chicano struggle for educational justice / Mario T. García and Sal Castro.

   p. cm.

Includes bibliographical references and index.

ISBN 978-0-8078-3448-0 (cloth: alk. paper)

ISBN 978-0-8078-7181-2 (pbk.: alk. paper)

1. Castro, Sal.   2. Hispanic Americans—Education—United States.
3. Hispanic Americans—Civil rights—History—20th century.
4. Educational equalization—United States.   5. Race discrimination—United States. 6. United States—Race relations.
I. Castro, Sal.   II. Title.

LA2317.C36G37 2011

371.829'68073—dc22

[B]   2010032656

cloth   15 14 13 12   5 4 3
paper   15 14 13 12 11   5 4 3 2 1

MIX
Paper from
responsible sources
FSC® C013483

Many Chicanos have long waited for "The Sal Castro Story."
—Professor Rodolfo Acuña

We saw reflected in the world that people thought that something could be done. We felt we had to do what we could with our lives as well. That was a time in 1968.
—Moctesuma Esparza

Change wasn't going to come from within; it had to come from without.
—Paula Crisostomo

Speak truth to power and things will happen.
—John Ortiz

The strike of 1968 went beyond the objectives of [Sal] Castro and others concerned only with improving education. It was the first loud cry for Chicano Power and self-determination, serving as the catalyst for the formation of the Chicano student movement, as well as the larger Chicano Power Movement of which it became the most important sector.
—Professor Carlos Muñoz

The blowouts reflected the opposition to cultural and national oppression.
—Professor Juan Gómez-Quiñones

The students had not only taught their parents about education, they also expanded what civil rights meant in America.
—Henry Cisneros

Whatever else he may be, man is a social and an historical actor who must be understood, if at all, in close and intricate interplay with social and historical structures.
—C. Wright Mills

CONTENTS

ILLUSTRATIONS

ACKNOWLEDGMENTS

I would first like to thank Sal Castro for his support and patience for this project. Sal spent many hours with me as we conducted our interviews, and he provided me with materials from his private collection, including photos. Getting to know Sal Castro very well has been perhaps the most enduring part of this entire process. I also want to thank Elsa Cisneros for her work on Sal's corrections and additions to the manuscript. For granting me additional interviews for this project, I am indebted to Paula Crisostomo, Mita Cuarón, Moctesuma Esparza, Harry Gamboa, Vicki Castro, John Ortiz, Carlos Vásquez, Albert Valencia, Luis Torres, and Raul Ruiz. I want to thank Chuck Grench and the staff at the University of North Carolina Press for sticking with the manuscript while I did the revisions and for their consistent support and editorial assistance. I am very grateful to the two anonymous readers, who fully engaged with the manuscript and who provided excellent suggestions to strengthen it. They both represent what exemplary reviewers should be. I was aided in my work by grants and support from the Academic Senate at the University of California–Santa Barbara; UC MEXUS; and the Chicano Studies Institute. I also benefited from a sabbatical leave in 2006–7 to work on the initial draft of the manuscript. For the permission to use some of the photos in the book, I want to thank Simon Elliot in Special Collections at the University of California–Los Angeles; Christina Rice at the Los Angeles Public Library; Carmen Gamboa; Harry Gamboa; and Paula Crisostomo. I am indebted to Maura Jess in Instructional Development at UCSB, who expertly processed all of the photos for publication and creatively suggested the cover image. Finally, as always, I want to thank my wife, Ellen McCracken, for her love and support, as well as my children, Giuliana and Carlo, for theirs.

Mario T. García

BLOWOUT!

The Sal Castro Story

Mario T. García

I walk into my office building, always a bit anxious before my class. But today will not be any normal lecture. Today we have a very special guest. I know he is already waiting for me, having arrived the previous evening. As I open the door to my building, where I have a first-floor office, sure enough, there he is—bigger than life. He flashes me that wonderful smile and with twinkling eyes prepares to give me a big *abrazo*.

"Sal, so good to see you," I say, as I prepare to be hugged. "Thanks for coming to speak to my class."

"Hey, no problem, Dr. García, glad to do it."

I'm always impressed that he usually addresses me as "Dr. García." He's older than I am but has a teacher's respect for other teachers, as I have for him.

We have to rush to get to my class. Most of the students are already waiting for us, and as we move to the front of the room behind the desk and podium a few more students arrive. I can sense the students observing our guest—checking him out. "So this is Sal Castro," they seem to be thinking.

"Buenos Dias, Good morning." I begin the class with the same salutation I always give. "I'm very pleased and honored to have with us this morning someone who has made history. Very few of us have the opportunity to make history—to bring about important change. Well, Sal Castro has. He is living history. There's no question in my mind that the 1968 walkouts or 'blowouts' in the East Los Angeles schools, when thousands of Chicano students walked out of the schools to protest a history of discrimination and poor schooling, could not have happened without Sal Castro. As one of the few Mexican American teachers in the Eastside public schools, Sal helped to organize the students to challenge their inferior education. He had the courage to do this, as did the students. Very few of us would have the same courage. Sal has been a champion of educational justice for Chicanos for many years. Even though retired since 2003, he's still fighting the good fight. It is a privilege to have him with us today.

"Please join me in giving a big UC Santa Barbara welcome to Mr. Sal Castro!"

How many times have I introduced Sal like this over the last ten years or so, ever since he started speaking to my History of the Chicano Movement class and then to my larger Introduction to Chicano Studies? He comes to do this at least three times a year, including for my summer class. How many times have I heard Sal give his impassioned talk on the blowouts, on the problems of the schools then and now, and on the need to provide an educational experience for Chicano/Latino students that will empower them by giving them a sense of their history, culture, and self-worth? This is serious stuff. But Sal Castro is also a kind of stand-up comedian who integrates wonderful humor into his sober message. He can have me and the students rolling with laughter one minute and then making us feel uneasy as tears come to his eyes as he chokes up when he recalls the courage of his Chicano students in 1968.

I have heard Sal talk—give his stump speech—so many times that I practically know it by heart. I find myself in my own lectures speaking like Sal ("What the hell is going on?"). And well I should. I have been living with his story for some ten years, ever since we started our oral history project, which laid the foundation for this book—Sal's story, his life and struggles in his own words.

The historic Chicano struggle for educational justice forms the backdrop to this text, but this is first and foremost a story of individual historical agency. This means that Sal Castro, through his idealism, commitment, and courage, made history. He is not a victim of history but a maker of history. It is a story of the role of the individual in history. Sal's story reminds us that people make history and that one individual can make a difference. Sal Castro is one of those individuals, and I am honored to present his story.

Who Is Sal Castro?

Sal Castro, although unknown to most Americans and, indeed, to most other Mexican Americans and other Latinos, is a major figure in the Chicano struggle for educational justice in the United States. Educational justice, in turn, has been a centerpiece of the larger Chicano struggle for civil rights. As one of the few Chicano teachers in the L.A. school district in the 1960s, which included the so-called Mexican schools in East L.A., Castro was the indispensable figure in what came to be known as the 1968 blowouts or walkouts by perhaps as many as 20,000 students to protest inferior education in the Eastside schools. It was Sal—as he is popularly called—who, as a playground director in the late 1950s and then as a young teacher in the 1960s, recognized the problems affecting Mexican students in the schools: low expectations by teachers, a stress on vocational rather than an academic curriculum, high drop-out rates, low reading scores, insensitive teachers and counselors, overcrowded classrooms, and lack of ethnic and cultural reinforcement, among many other problems. Castro's own experiences attending public elementary schools in East L.A. during the 1930s and 1940s further added to his understanding that the schools had historically failed in teaching the Mexican American student.

Castro's recognition that the schools were more of a problem than a solution also was influenced by his personal and family history. Born to Mexican immigrant parents in L.A. in 1934, Castro was a by-product of the mass immigration diaspora from Mexico during the first third of the twentieth century. Mexicans, perhaps a million or more, flocked over the border, in search of the many jobs being offered by U.S. railroads, agribusiness, copper mines, and sundry other industries throughout the Southwest. In addition, many were also feeling the ravages of the Mexican Revolution of 1910, Mexico's major civil war.

Yet America's welcome was short-lived, due to the Great Depression of the 1930s and the unfortunate scapegoating of Mexican immigrants as being part of the causes of the mass economic downturn. Other Americans blamed Mexicans for taking badly needed jobs from "real Americans," despite the fact that many Mexicans had lived in the United States for many years and had contributed blood, sweat, and tears to building the country and, certainly in the case of farmworkers, to feeding Americans. Many possessed legal resident status. In addition, many, as in the case of Sal's parents, had U.S.-born children. Despite all of this, close to half a million Mexicans were deported or repatriated to Mexico from the early to the mid-1930s. This included Sal's father, who did not have all of his papers. His mother was not affected, and she stayed in L.A. with her only son, although extensive visits were made to be with his father in Mazatlán. Yet the split in the family produced tensions that led to divorce. This resulted in Castro being raised predominantly by his mother and her extended family in East L.A.

Castro had started his education in Mexico on prolonged visits to his father, but his parents' divorce assured that he would have a U.S. education. These early public school experiences exposed him to various forms of discrimination and racism against students, like himself, of Mexican American background. As a kid, Castro further encountered exclusion in public facilities such as swimming pools and parks. Moreover, in 1943, he personally witnessed the Zoot-Suit Riots, when rampaging American sailors rioted in downtown L.A., attacking Mexican American young men, especially those dressed in the popular zoot-suit or "drapes." As a shoeshine boy in the downtown area, Castro observed these attacks, which left a permanent impression on him.

A few years after his graduation from Cathedral High School, a Catholic institution, in 1952, near the end of the Korean War and after his mother had remarried, Castro was drafted into the U.S. Army. He was not sent to Korea, but Castro in his two years of service experienced further exposure to racism, both in and out of the military, especially in southern states such as Texas, Georgia, Kentucky, and Virginia.

Upon his return from the army, he married and started a family. Wanting more education and a professional job, he attended L.A. City College and later Los Angeles State College (later Cal State, L.A.) where he earned his BA, in 1960. Through working with kids in the public playgrounds to earn money while attending school and through his own research when he worked on his teaching credentials, Sal came to understand many of the obstacles to an equal and good education for Mexican Americans, and these experiences convinced him that he could possibly make a difference by becoming a public high school teacher. At his first regular teaching assignment, at Belmont High School in downtown L.A., Castro attempted to bring about change by helping to empower Mexican American students. After he organized some of the students to campaign for positions on the student council, from which they had been excluded, he learned just how difficult even such modest reforms could be, as he faced opposition from his own school administration. Not wanting an "uppity Mexican" on the staff, the Belmont principal forced a transfer for Castro to Lincoln High School on the east side.

At Lincoln, into the 1960s, Castro continued to learn from his students about the problems in the schools, and at the same time he encouraged the students to begin to empower themselves. Part of this empowerment came as a result of Castro's involvement in the organization of what were initially called the Mexican American Youth Leadership Conferences held at Camp Hess Kramer in the Malibu Mountains. Beginning in 1963, he and other Mexican American conference leaders listened to student complaints about school conditions and developed dialogues with the students about how to change these conditions. Part of this empowerment process involved reinforcing pride in the students' ethnic and cultural backgrounds. These influences, in addition to the political climate of the 1960s involving civil rights, Black Power, the anti–Vietnam War movement, and a general counterculture in the country, all facilitated the rise of a more questioning and critical Chicano Generation by the late 1960s. This new generation of high school students and the small number of Chicano college students, in L.A. and elsewhere, were prepared to try to change the world—or at least their world.

In East L.A., this generation was fortunate to have a role model like Sal Castro. As a teacher, he encouraged his students to think critically, to be proud of themselves, and, most important, to believe in themselves, and that included the idea of going on to college. No other teacher or counselor—or very few—were talking about these ideas. Castro knew that the schools had to be forced to change, not only for his students but also for those who would come after them. But what to do?

By early 1968, Castro had an answer. He would organize or encourage the students to organize, not only at Lincoln but also at the other Eastside schools, a mass action. Influenced by the civil disobedience tactics and mass protests of the black civil rights struggle as well as of the white student demonstrations against the Vietnam War, Castro concluded that a walkout—a strike—of Chicano students, or at least the threat of a walkout, was the only viable strategy to bring about educational change and justice.

Beginning on March 1, 1968—the year of major national and international events and protests—thousands of Chicano students walked out of their schools for an entire week of protests. These actions brought the Eastside schools to a standstill and shocked not only the L.A. board of education and the district school administration but also the rest of the city. No one had seriously considered Chicano issues, and few had thought of Chicanos as part of the civil rights struggles in the country, outside of César Chávez and the farmworkers' movement. Yet here were thousands of young Mexican Americans engaged in such protests. Popularly referred to as the blowouts, the East L.A. walkouts marked the commencement of the urban-based Chicano Movement, a major part of civil rights history, although still even today not fully acknowledged, despite the fact that Hispanics/Latinos (the large majority being Mexican Americans) represent the largest racial minority in the country (over 45 million people).

Could the blowouts—one of the largest mass protests by high school students in U.S. history—have taken place without Sal Castro? No leader is ever completely indispensable, and yet it is my belief that without Castro the walkouts would not have been as widespread and as effective. As a responsible and committed leader, he had the utmost confidence of the students.

They believed in him and he believed in them. Castro gave legitimacy to what the students did. He passed his courage on to them and they, in turn, sustained his courage. Both empowered one another.

Did the blowouts change conditions in the schools? Many of these conditions regrettably still exist, but some reforms did take place—in the curriculum, through initiatives such as Chicano Studies; bilingual education; more Chicanos entering the academic tracks; more going on to college; and more Chicano teachers, counselors, and administrators. But these reforms did not constitute all of the changes. Most significant, a new spirit, a new attitude, a new politics—Chicano Power—in the Chicano community was led by a new generation of activists. This generation—the Chicano Generation—would no longer accept invisibility, irrelevance, marginalization, discrimination, racism, and second-class citizenship. Embracing a new empowered identity and a new sense of their human worth, Chicanos, including many in the larger community, now would not be taken for granted. They would not be denied respect and their rights. They accepted César Chávez's mantra of "*Si Se Puede*" (It Can Be Done), not because they believed they would be granted respect and their rights from the outside, but because they believed that through their struggles they would gain them. They would make history, not someone else.

Sal Castro did not start all of this, but certainly in the case of the blowouts and the Chicano struggle for educational justice, he played a major role. But Castro's place in history is not just because of the blowouts. Indeed, for over four decades and even to this moment, he has continued the struggle for educational justice—as a teacher, as a counselor, and as the driving force behind the revitalization of what are now called the Chicano Youth Leadership Conferences at Camp Hess Kramer. Castro's leadership has touched thousands of students, many of whom have gone on to become major leaders and role models themselves.

So who is Sal Castro? He is a major figure in U.S. educational history, in U.S. civil rights history, and in Chicano history. He is a major American leader and one who deserves just recognition. He deserves his place in the pantheon of key Chicano Movement–era figures such as César Chávez, Dolores Huerta, Ruben Salazar, Bert Corona, Corky Gonzales, and Reis López Tijerina. This is who Sal Castro is and more, as his story will reveal.

Thus this oral history/autobiography focuses on the life and struggles of Castro. The early chapters (chapters 1–3) cover his coming of age years in L.A., including family socialization, schooling, and military service, as a way of gauging why Castro emerged as a key figure and leader of the Chicano

Movement of the late 1960s and early 1970s. Leadership does not emerge in a vacuum. There are elements of a future leader's early life and culture, in addition to personal traits, that help explain this leadership. Castro's early years as a teacher, his initial confrontation with the school system's discriminatory treatment of Chicano students, and, of course, his role in the 1968 blowouts and his subsequent arrest and career reprisals for his involvement in the walkouts are treated in chapters 4–8. Chapters 9–11 detail Castro's additional teaching experiences and championing of Chicano educational justice up to his retirement in 2003. What emerges is a picture of a teacher whose pedagogical values centered on using education to empower students to think for themselves and to be critics of their own education—a teacher who not only taught history but who made history.

The Chicano Movement

Sal Castro's story has to been seen within the context of the Chicano Movement and, indeed, within the wider context of the 1960s social protest movements. These years, beginning with the black civil rights movement led by Dr. Martin Luther King Jr., began more than a decade of intense social protest in the country on several fronts, most prominently in civil rights and through the antiwar protests. An entire new generation of young Americans began questioning the direction of the country, the policies of both Democratic and Republican administrations, and the very nature of the American system. This new generation wanted to know why, despite the wealth and power of the United States, there was still so much poverty, inequality, racism, and sexism and a military-industrial complex that threatened nuclear annihilation and engaged in wars of imperial intervention, such as in Vietnam. Students in particular questioned why their universities, instead of being champions for human rights and a critical consciousness, focused on producing men (and women) to fit into this system without questioning it. Where was the university's sense of humaneness and morality, when it helped to produce weapons of mass destruction? What had happened to the stated American spirit of democratic values?[1]

Such questioning helped to propel social action, what was called the "new insurgency."[2] The Chicano Movement was part of this history, even though its contributions have not been well integrated—or not at all—by the historiography of the 1960s.[3] Reading such texts, one has no sense that the Chicano Movement, or even Chicanos, even existed. Still, the Chicano Movement constituted the largest social protest movement in the history of Mexican

Americans. At no other time in U.S. history had Mexican Americans—now defiantly calling themselves Chicanos, an older immigrant working-class and barrio term—demonstrated in such large numbers for their civil rights and freedom of expression. Such struggles had a larger history, and I and others have documented those of the Mexican American Generation of the 1930s to the 1960s.[4] The Chicano Generation, in turn, expanded and intensified this struggle as never before.

Beginning with the farmworkers' movement for human and civil rights, led by César Chávez and Dolores Huerta in 1965, the evolving Chicano Movement moved from the countryside to the cities, where the majority of Mexicans lived. There, by the late 1960s and early 1970s, the Chicano Movement throughout the Southwest found a number of political fronts: school protests such as the blowouts; the student movement in the universities, including the development of Chicano Studies; the Chicano antiwar movement; welfare rights struggles; the organization of La Raza Unida Party, an independent Chicano political party; the immigrant rights movement; and the origins of Chicana feminism; as well as many other more localized issues in numerous communities.

In addition, the Chicano Movement heavily focused on issues of a new ethnic identity based on the recognition and promotion of the *mestizo* (mixed origins) of Mexicans, especially stressing their indigenous backgrounds and an assertion that Chicanos were native to the Southwest because of the idea that the original homeland of the Aztecs, Aztlán, was to be found in the region. Although the proposal that Aztlán was in the Southwest was problematic or open to challenge, what mattered was that it furthered the concept of Chicanos representing an indigenous people rather than being immigrants. The famous 1969 "El Plan Espiritual de Aztlán," written by the poet Alurista and adopted as the preamble to the larger "Plan de Aztlán" by the first National Chicano Youth Liberation Conference in Denver, which was basically a Chicano Declaration of Independence, states: "We, the Chicano inhabitants and civilizers of the northern land of Aztlán, from whence came our forefathers, reclaiming the land of their birth and consecrating the determination of our people of the sun, declare that the call of our blood is our power, our responsibility, and our inevitable destiny."[5]

The Chicano Generation rallied its new sense of identity around what was referred to as "Chicanismo." This ideology involved various themes and included the following: (1) Chicanos were an indigenous people; (2) Chicanos possessed a historical homeland—Aztlán; (3) this historical homeland at the same time became the lost homeland, due to the U.S. conquest in the

U.S.-Mexico War (1846–48) of what became the Southwest; (4) the concept of *La Raza Nueva*—the born-again Chicano Generation; (5) the centrality of *La Familia*—both personal and communal; (6) *Carnalismo* (brotherhood); (6) the importance of barrio culture; (7) the tradition of a revolutionary heritage; and (8) self-determination, or Chicano Power.

The movement expressed Chicanismo through its more overt political fronts and also through the Chicano Renaissance, an artistic and literary flowering. New Chicano artists and writers, through their murals, poster art, poetry, theater, short stories, novels, essays, journals, and newspapers, conveyed and involved this new identity, based on Chicanos feeling secure and good about their origins, ethnic background, and history. Chicanos struggled not only for their civil rights but also for the right to be themselves.

There is no question about the significance of the Movement in Chicano history. Because of these struggles, it forced the system as never before to recognize Mexican Americans and other Latinos as important political actors and contributors to American society and culture. It further forced the system to open up and reform itself, allowing more Chicanos/Latinos to achieve better and more education; professional and business advances; political mobility; and cultural breakthroughs. Despite many lingering problems and inequities, the major advances that Chicanos/Latinos have made in the post–Chicano Movement years of the last four decades are in one way or another due to the Movement.[6]

Sal Castro and the Mexican Schools

Sal Castro's story and the Chicano struggle for educational justice has to be seen in the context of the historic relationship between the public school system in the Southwest and Mexican Americans. This involves the role of the so-called Mexican schools. Beginning with the first mass immigration of Mexicans into the United States, the public school system, rather than ignoring Mexican American children, established schools within the barrios and rural *colonias* and installed segregated schools, referred to as "Mexican schools." These were particularly pervasive in urban areas such as South El Paso, West San Antonio, and, of course, East Los Angeles. The Mexican schools would come to characterize the public school response to the growing numbers of Mexican immigrants and their Mexican American children. Indeed, these schools affected later generations of Mexican Americans, whether they were children of immigrants or not.[7]

The Mexican schools belied the general American notion that education and schooling could solve social problems. In theory this is true, but not necessarily in practice, especially when racialization is involved. By "racialization," I mean the invention or creation or identification of certain "racial" groups, such as African Americans and Mexican Americans, as racially inferior people. Such racialization has nothing to do with biology and everything to do with political and economic power and the advantages that one ethnic group achieves over another, based on the fallacious argument that there exists in society different identifiable human races and the supposition that some (whites) are "racially" superior and others (people of color) are "racially" inferior. But this is ideology rather than science. It involves what Omi and Winant call "racial formation." "Race has been a matter of *political* contention," they write, adding: "We use the term *racial formation* to refer to the process by which social, economic and political forces determine the content and importance of racial categories."[8] Races are not born; they are formed by dominant white elites to justify the exploitation of nonwhites. This certainly proved to be the case in the Southwest of white Euro-Americans, or Anglos, and subaltern Mexicans.[9]

Racialization played itself out in the Southwest in a variety of ways. Mexicans as immigrant workers in the early twentieth century, for example, were welcomed as a source of cheap labor. Employers hired them into so-called Mexican jobs, jobs premised on racial inferiority, which consigned them to menial physical labor. They were placed in what Rafael Pérez-Torres terms the "racialized body."[10] This is still true today. As racialized cheap labor, Mexicans formed the labor foundation for the extension and maintenance of the railroads in the Southwest and for the growth of the mining industry in places such as southern Arizona, extracting industrial ores such as copper, lead, zinc, and silver. As commercial agriculture bloomed in southern California and south Texas (the so-called Winter Garden), Mexicans then as now represented most of the farmworkers picking the fruits and vegetables to feed a growing urban population in the United States. Moreover, as urbanization affected the region, Mexicans were hired for construction work, as well as for a variety of service labor, including females for domestic work. This exploitation of Mexican workers as cheap labor contributed to the significant economic boom of the Southwest.[11]

Mexican jobs, at the same time, were paid with what were literally called Mexican wages, wages justified by the alleged racial inferiority of Mexicans, the lowest wages paid to workers in the Southwest and paid exclusively to Mexicans. A racialized hierarchy in wages mirrored the racialized hierarchy in jobs. Various Euro-American groups in the region, as documented by the Dillingham Commission in the early twentieth century, received higher wages and Mexicans received the lowest. This extended even to cases in which Mexicans and Euro-Americans performed the same unskilled jobs, such as in the mining industry.[12] Cheap labor and cheap wages made the southwestern labor market an attractive one for industries, businesses, and investors. Employers justified Mexican jobs and Mexican wages by arguing that Mexicans were not capable of performing more skilled labor and thus not deserving of higher wages—of course, a self-serving argument. Ironically, in some urban areas, including Los Angeles, a few Mexicans were hired as skilled workers but still paid a Mexican wage.[13]

The public school system in the Southwest reinforced this racialization. If there were Mexican jobs and Mexican wages, there were also Mexican schools in the Mexican barrios, based on the alleged inferior mental capacities of Mexicans. These schools, as noted by historians such as Gilbert González, served local and regional labor needs by limiting education for Mexican American children in order to ensure a continued pool of cheap labor. As such, Mexican schools possessed various characteristics. For one, they were segregated schools. However, unlike similar schools in the South, including Texas, for black children, which were legally segregated by state laws, the Mexican schools were segregated not by state laws but by local school board decisions. Both, as González correctly maintains, were forms of de jure segregation, not just de facto, and of what Michel Foucault refers to as "dividing practices" aimed at objectifying and dominating particular subjects.[14]

In addition, Mexican schools were limited in the number of grades provided for students. In urban areas, El Paso, for example, Mexican schools provided no more than a sixth-grade education. In rural areas, it was considerably less. Few Mexican Americans in the early twentieth century attended high school.[15] Mexican schools also included a limited and discriminatory curriculum that stressed vocational over academic instruction. In the Eastside schools of Los Angeles, González notes that two high schools, Lincoln and Roosevelt, by 1932 had a high number of vocational schools. They possessed what were called "Class A" vocational courses, in which students were given over four hours of trade instruction and only an hour and a half of academic instruction.[16] Although English and U.S. history were taught, the children were encouraged or forced to work with their hands in shop classes aimed at training and socializing Mexican American students, both boys and girls, as a new generation of cheap and unskilled, or, at best, semi-skilled, labor.[17]

Added to these restrictions to educational mobility was a general sense of low expectations among teachers and principals concerning the educational and mental capacities of the children. Students learned that their teachers expected very little from them, and this for many became a self-fulfilling prophecy. To add insult to injury, the administering of newly developed IQ tests to Mexican Americans only buttressed racist views concerning their abilities—that language and cultural differences, to say nothing of class ones, might produce low test results was not seriously considered. Many teachers and administrators, including school board members, simply concluded that most Mexican American students were either slow learners or stupid.[18]

These Mexican schools unfortunately became fixtures throughout the Southwest. Surprisingly, some Mexican Americans survived rather than simply dropping out of school. And some Mexican American parents and community leaders did not accept this form of segregation and inferior schooling. By the 1930s and before the Chicano Movement, Mexican Americans led by new civil rights organizations such as the League of United Latin American Citizens (LULAC), the School Improvement League in San Antonio, and later the American GI Forum, as well as other groups, launched efforts to do away with the Mexican schools, or at least to provide more and better education in these schools.[19]

Two approaches were taken. One, best exemplified by the School Improvement League, waged protracted grassroots struggles to pressure school boards and school administrations for reforms. A second strategy involved organizations such as LULAC taking legal action to force desegregation. The best-known and most successful victory in this effort came in 1946 in *Mendez v. Westminster* in Orange County, California. Mexican American parents, supported by various civil rights groups, both Mexican American and non–Mexican American, filed suit in federal court against the segregation of Mexican American students. The court ruled that such arbitrary separation, which was often based on language differences, was unconstitutional and a violation of the equal protection clause of the Fourteenth Amendment. Eight years later, in *Hernández v. Texas*, Fourteenth Amendment rights pertaining to Mexican Americans were further advanced when the U.S. Supreme Court ruled that the Fourteenth Amendment applied to groups such as Mexican Americans that possessed a history of discriminatory treatments as a "class apart." Despite these legal breakthroughs, which put the force of law on the Mexican American side, school boards and school administrations throughout the Southwest, including in Los Angeles, despite other federal court actions against Mexican schools, continued the practice of segregating Mexican American students, either in their own schools or in separate classrooms in "integrated" schools. Like the historic *Brown v. Board of Education* in 1954, desegregation for Mexican Americans, as for blacks, was slow in coming and made a mockery of the call for "all deliberate speed."[20]

By the 1960s, when school boards in the Southwest no longer legally maintained separate schools for Mexican Americans, due to geographic concentration and the lack of economic mobility, Mexican Americans continued to live in predominantly Mexican barrios, with their children attending predominantly Mexican American schools. De jure segregation became de facto segregation. Although Mexican Americans now had access to more schooling, including high schools, retarded academic and educational mobility affected possibilities of going to college. Few Mexican American students attended college in 1960, and even fewer graduated from college. The Mexican schools were alive and well into the 1960s.

All of this is a big part of the context for Sal Castro's story and the story of the 1968 blowouts in East Los Angeles. Castro and the students were responding to their immediate conditions and also, consciously and unconsciously, to over half a century of poor schooling and educational apartheid for Mexican Americans. The scene was set for a dramatic confrontation.

Sal Castro as Educational Critic

Besides putting Sal Castro's story in the context of both Chicano and U.S. history, I also want to address his role as a critic of this country's educational system. First of all, Sal Castro can be seen as an educational muckraker who exposed the underside of public education and the myriad problems of the system or systems as they affected racialized and poor student communities. Yet, as a muckraker, Castro did not expose simply for sensational purposes, but rather to bring about change in the schools and to provide better and just educational opportunities for students who had been denied them. Unlike professional educational critics, such as Jonathan Kozol, for example, who have written many books critical of American schools, Castro has not written any exposés. However, in his active role as a teacher over the years, including his involvement in the 1968 blowouts, he has served to publicize and critique school problems. His action as a teacher and leader has been his script. His published life story further serves as a readily available muckraking text.

Let me note five areas in which Castro can be seen as an educational muckraker. The first two areas are intertwined. These involve the themes of inequality and segregation. Public schools are unequal and segregated based largely on race and class. Kozol refers to such an arrangement as "savage," in the sense of the damages that such disparities do to children, especially black and Latino kids, and to the avowed principles of this country. In maintaining such inequalities, Kozol correctly observes that the country has turned its back on the moral if not legal implications of the *Brown Case*, which ruled that segregated schools were inherently unequal. "The dual society, at least in public education," Kozol writes, "seems in general to be unquestioned."[21] Americans accept what Kozol refers to as "ghetto education" as being a permanent American reality.[22] Writing in the early 1990s, Kozol noted that twenty-five years earlier—when Sal Castro first started teaching—the U.S. commissioner of education, Francis Keppel, referred to the nation's schools as a "caste society" that "violates the style of American democracy."[23]

Sal Castro lived such "savage inequalities," not only in his own educational experiences but more significantly when he began teaching in the L.A. schools. Castro, from the very beginning and certainly by 1968, recognized the unequal and segregated conditions of the school system. Schools in East L.A., such as Lincoln, Roosevelt, Garfield, and Wilson, were large and segregated Mexican high schools with all of the inferior and poor conditions associated with these schools. What angered and concerned Castro was that such conditions condemned Chicano students to a limited future as part of the recycled pool of Mexican cheap and unskilled labor. This was Kozol's "savage inequality," East L.A.–style. Through his teaching and his discussions with students, both in the school and at the Hess Kramer conferences, Castro pointed out these unacceptable inequities. But he went one step further as a muckraker—he organized the students to challenge these conditions and to change them. Action for Castro was not just observing but was also reflecting and acting.

Third, Castro was very much aware of how unequal and segregated schools also breed low expectations of students that further sentenced them to a limited future. The issue of low expectations and the lack of encouragement of Chicano students to reinforce a sense of pride and knowledge of their rich ethnic heritage was part of the failure of the schools. Castro was aware—still is—that too many teachers and counselors do not expect much from their Chicano/Latino students, nor do they expect them to go on to a four-year college. They see these students as only capable of finishing high school, if that, and then going to work or at best going on to a community college, where most will not finish and certainly not transfer to a four-year institution. In his educational career, Castro fought against this attitude of what Paul Rabinow calls "normalization," and on his own he struggled to instill in his students pride in themselves by integrating their history and culture into his teaching of U.S. history.[24] He taught Chicano history even before it was taught in universities. Castro also consistently promoted the idea of going to college. "You're going to college," he told his students time and time again. He drummed it into their heads. He did not always succeed, but he did make a difference for some as early as the 1960s. In his teaching as well as in his lecturing throughout California and elsewhere, Sal Castro challenges the low expectations institutionalized in the Mexican schools.

Fourth, Castro focused on the tragic results of unequal and segregated education—low reading scores, high drop-out rates, overcrowded schools, and the notorious tracking system. He criticized the tracking system in the schools that relegated most minority students to vocational classes rather than academic ones. Castro challenged the status quo and the practices of unequal and segregated Mexican schools. The fifty-five demands authored by him and the students during the blowouts addressed some of these issues, including alleviating the crowded conditions, hiring more counselors, eliminating the tracking system, and ending corporal punishment. Moreover, as his story reveals, Castro, starting in the 1960s, did what he personally could to keep kids in school, to call for lower ratios of students to teachers and counselors, and to move Chicano students from the vocational track to the academic one so that they could go on to college.

Finally, Castro provided a voice for the Chicano students. He did this not through written texts, but through his role as a teacher and educational leader. He continues to do so especially now through his life story. Despite the lingering problems in the schools, Castro still sees the potential in the students and in their abilities. He recognizes a common sense of wisdom that minority students have had to develop in their efforts to survive a system that denies them their humanity and their rights as Americans. Sal Castro, because he has lived through all of this, would certainly concur with Kozol: "All our children ought to be allowed a stake in the enormous richness of America. Whether they were born to poor white Appalachians or to wealthy Texans, to poor black people in the Bronx or to rich people in Manhasset or Winnetka, they are all quite wonderful and innocent when they are small. We soil them needlessly."[25]

In all of these issues, Castro, through his initiatives, including the 1968 walkouts, brought to light and into public scrutiny the same problems that educational critics would still write about some years later and that unfortunately still persist. Yet what reforms have taken place and the many more that are needed require muckrakers such as Sal Castro.

Another way of looking at Sal Castro's role in the Chicano struggle for educational justice is as a "subversive teacher." One year after the blowouts, *Teaching as a Subversive Activity*, by Neil Postman and Charles Weingartner, was published.[26] "Subversive teaching" means redefining schools not as centers of received authority and for the socialization of passive citizens, but just the opposite. Teaching should subvert the authoritarian and antidemocratic tendency of schools and instead engage in a critical dialogue with American social values in order to produce an active and progressive citizenry. The schools must become instruments of democratic social change rather than institutions of domination. Schools need to become training centers for subversion—for challenging the status quo and preparing students to change society for the betterment of greater numbers of people, for exploring the idea that only through questioning is society advanced. This pedagogy has not been part of American education. Finally, for teaching to become subversive the role of teachers is critical. Teachers must rethink their role in the educational process in order to produce questioning and independent-thinking students. Teachers, to be real teachers, must be subversive.[27]

Sal Castro became a "subversive teacher." Even as an undergraduate student and later in his teacher credentials program, he pointed out how the schools were failing Mexican American students. He challenged his own professors when they used stereotypes in speaking about Chicanos. As a young teacher and in his first full-time assignment at Belmont High School in downtown L.A., he questioned why the school tracked Mexican students into a nonacademic and noncollege curriculum. He attempted to subvert the status quo by empowering Mexican American students to run as candidates for the student council, which had excluded them. This effort succeeded, even though it cost Castro his position when the principal had him transferred to Lincoln High School.

But Castro would only accelerate his subversive teaching by reaching out to even more Chicano students at Lincoln, encouraging them to question their own education and come to the conclusion that they needed to transform their own school by engaging in a massive walkout. Rather than passive students, Castro produced active and engaged ones that, in his own words, "were out to change the world." He also came to understand that schools are not neutral institutions but rather part of what Louis Althusser called the "ideological state apparatus."[28] Castro recognized that schools aim to socialize students to accept the dominant system and its governing values. In the case of the United States, schools attempt to get students to accept the capitalist system without questioning it or its accompanying class, race, and gender stratifications. This socialization is not necessarily done overtly, and thus the schools possess what Henry Giroux calls a "hidden curriculum," whereby they transmit ruling beliefs indirectly.[29] Castro saw the schools as political institutions—he saw that there is a difference between schooling and education.[30]

Castro recognized that the schools aimed to socialize students into accepting the same subordinate positions in U.S. society that their parents occupied. He knew that the schools, like the police and the legal system, are not neutral. They did not privilege the working class and minority people and students; they privileged the established white order and what it desired out of the Mexican schools. And he certainly identified the "hidden curriculum," especially as a history and government teacher who was charged with passing down the dominant ideology to the students. But, instead, he subverted this curriculum by questioning it and by going outside the texts to discuss "forbidden subjects," such as Chicano history, and questioned the established view of U.S. history by raising issues such as conquest, colonialism, and racism. Foucault wrote: "It seems to me that the real political task in a society such as ours is to criticize the working of institutions which appear to be neutral and independent; to criticize them in such a manner that the political violence which has always exercised itself obscurely through them will be unmasked, so that one can fight them."[31]

Schools represent institutions of ideological control, but they also produce conditions or contradictions that effectively make them sites of resistance. Both domination and opposition exist in the schools.[32] Sal Castro understood and acted on this dialectic. At one level, the schools attempted to track students into adding to the pool of Mexican cheap labor. On the other hand, the schools provided an opening for someone like Castro to put forward a pedagogy of opposition. In this, he did not have to come up with a counterideology; he simply used the system against itself. It preached the American Dream, democracy, individualism, initiative, antiracism, and open opportunities and yet denied them to Chicano students. Castro pointed out these contradictions, not only in ideological terms but also in how the Mexican schools violated all of these principles. The schools provided their own contradictions. In addition, Castro, through organizing the students in the 1968 blowouts, used the schools as further sites of political resistance in the attempt to transform them into true centers of democratic education.

Humans, including students, can change their conditions through a critical consciousness and through action.[33] Sal Castro is the epitome of human and political agency. He knows that people, including Chicanos, can bring about change by organizing, resisting, and transforming. He is the ultimate oppositional intellectual and adherent of the politics of hope. He has passed on to his students a critical perspective, a citizenship education, and civic courage. He took students from symbolic resistance to actual and political resistance through the walkouts.[34] Sal Castro truly believes that people, and students, can make a difference. Sal Castro is a key educational critic of American education and a voice still relevant today.

Sal Castro, Chicano Leadership, and the Individual in History

Much of my work over the years has focused on the role of Chicano leadership in history. I have always been fascinated with the role of leaders in history and the role of people in making history. Theories and political ideas do not make history—people do. I am also interested in seeing history beyond mass and obscure social movements. I am interested in individuals who emerge as leaders and help make social change. I do not dissociate individuals from mass movements, but I do believe that such movements need key and courageous leaders. These have included a range of figures, whose stories I have told, such as Bert Corona, Josefina Fierro, Ignacio López, Raymond Telles, Ruben Salazar, Frances Esquibel Tywoniak, Luis Leal, César Chávez, Dolores Huerta, Fray Angélico Chávez, Cleofas Calleros, Alonso Perales, Richard Cruz, Father Juan Romero, Father Luis Quihuis, Father Virgilio Elizondo, Father Luis Olivares, Raul Ruiz, María Elena Gaitán, and Rosalio Muñoz.[35] I am honored to add Sal Castro to this list. In fact, I would go further and suggest that to the pantheon of major Chicano Movement leaders—César Chávez, Dolores Huerta, Reies López Tijerina, Rodolfo "Corky" Gonzales, and José Angel Gutiérrez—I would add Sal Castro. Chávez and Dolores Huerta led the historic farmworkers' struggle; Tijerina led the land grant movement in New Mexico; Gonzales led the new youth movement; and Gutiérrez led the Raza Unida Party. Many other leaders, both men and women, emerged in the Chicano Movement, but these are without question the most notable, both in their time and in Chicano history. I believe that Sal Castro's name should be part of this group. Castro was the leader of a mass student movement that some scholars suggest actually began the urban Chicano Movement and that influenced the student movement and the struggle for educational justice throughout the Southwest. It is time that he received his due recognition.

Sal Castro, the *Testimonio*, and Oral History

In my career, I have done many oral histories of key Chicano subjects. These histories represent what in Latin America are referred to as *testimonios*. The *testimonio*, as I discussed in my oral history of Bert Corona, a major twentieth-century Chicano labor and community leader, is unlike the classic autobiographical testimony, which is an individual project written by the subject. A *testimonio* is an oral history conducted by a subject and an interlocutor. In the Latin American context, the *testimonio* developed out of the more recent (1960s and on) political struggles by the peoples of that region to achieve liberation from political and military dictatorships and U.S. imperialism and neocolonialism. The *testimonios* were liberationist texts seen as a tool of those struggles and to further encourage them. A *testimonio* text is founded in oral history and done at the initiative of a journalist or scholar who produces the text. Influenced by this genre, as well as by the increased use of oral history by other historians of minorities and working-class people in the United States, I have employed oral history in many of my studies and have produced several *testimonios*: my work on Corona; the coming-of-age story of Frances Esquibel Tywoniak; the life and scholarly career of Professor Luis Leal, a pioneer in Mexican/Chicano literary studies; the religious and spiritual life of Father Virgil Cordano of the Santa Barbara Mission; the role of community priests such as Father Juan Romero, Father Luis Quihuis, and Father Virgilio Elizondo; the contribution of key Chicano Movement activists in Los Angeles such as Raul Ruiz, María Elena Gaitán, and Rosalio Muñoz; and now Sal Castro.[36] Someone has referred to me as the Studs Terkel of Chicano history, and I consider that to be an honor. Ever since I was a young child at St. Patrick's Elementary School in El Paso, I have found myself drawn to biographies, and I feel privileged to have helped developed the field of biography and the *testimonio* as part of Chicano historiography.

I have usually described in the introductions to these previous studies my methodology in producing my *testimonios*. In the case of the Sal Castro story, I first conceptualized it when I began inviting Castro to speak to my newly developed course on the history of the Chicano Movement in the late 1990s. It did not take me long to imagine doing his life story, especially with the drama of the 1968 blowouts. I knew the importance of this episode in

Chicano history and the key role that Castro played in it. On one of his first visits, I spent time with him taping a summary of his life and role in the walkouts. Soon thereafter, I approached him about doing a more systematic oral history project over a period of time. He, without hesitation, graciously agreed. We began our in-depth interviews in the summer of 2001 and proceeded chronologically. In fact, we did several interviews in a few days. Castro is a natural storyteller. He has great command of memory but also an oral style that combines facts with passion and wonderful humor. Castro tells his stories with no reservations, in both English and Spanish, with colorful colloquialisms and cuss words. But that's Sal Castro—bigger than life. I have tried to remain true in the text to this ingratiating oral tradition.

He came up to the University of California at Santa Barbara from his home in Los Angeles to speak to my classes, and we used these occasions to continue our interviews. Working in this deliberate fashion and not rushing the interviews, we completed the project over an almost ten-year period. I apologize to Sal for taking so long, but it was unavoidable, given my other ongoing research as well as my teaching duties.

As we conducted the interviews, I had the audiotapes transcribed by my longtime professional transcriber, Darla McDavid. I taped Castro for approximately fifty hours, resulting in several hundred pages of transcription.

The next phase was to begin writing the narrative, using the transcripts as my field notes or archival notes because they represent both. Finally, on a yearlong sabbatical beginning in the fall of 2006, I focused on writing Castro's *testimonio*. My wife, Professor Ellen McCracken, who was also on sabbatical that fall, and I drove to Santa Fe and spent a delightful two and a half months working there. In my case, this involved writing the initial draft of Castro's story. I first organized the transcripts to correspond to my perceived chapters, which covered the logical chronology of Castro's experiences. I then went over the chapter transcripts as I listened to the corresponding tapes in order to immerse myself once again in Castro's storytelling and his voice. I found myself thoroughly enjoying reliving the interviews. I laughed plenty at rehearing Sal's *chistes* (jokes) and his humorous stories. I was again moved when silence appeared in the tapes as he choked up in remembering the courage and daring of his "kids"—the blowout generation. From time to time he would jump back and forth in his narrative, and my task was to reorganize the material to conform to my chapters—probably the most difficult part of the process. In most oral histories there is not always a seamless narrative told by the subject—and this was certainly true in Castro's case. The blowout chapters took the longest, due to the amount of material. I expressed a sigh of relief and joy when I finished writing the last chapter the week we drove back to Santa Barbara, in mid-December.

Upon returning to Santa Barbara, and over the next several months, I revised the narrative and checked facts with Castro. But in this phase, I also did more. My previous *testimonios* are seamless narratives of my subjects, but I decided to include other voices in this story, especially in the key chapters about the blowouts. I felt that doing additional interviews, especially with a few of the students and others involved in the walkouts, and including portions of these interviews within the text would add to Castro's own narrative and provide more context to the story. I also searched for additional materials about the walkouts and other phases of Castro's life, such as newspaper sources, including the Chicano Movement press, the transcripts of the East L.A. 13 grand jury inquiry, other studies, including autobiographies that have been done that include discussion of the walkouts, and the 1996 documentary *Taking Back the Schools* about the blowouts, produced by Susan Racho. This additional material is sometimes contained in the extensive notes, especially in the chapters covering the blowouts and their aftermath. I would draw the readers' attention to the rich information contained in the notes.

The inserts, somewhat reminiscent of John Dos Passos's "newsreels" in his trilogy *U.S.A.*, as well as of the more recent oral history of Stokely Carmichael, the 1960s Black Power leader, written by Ekwueme Michael Thelwell, are set off in the text in italics so that the reader is aware of the intervention of these other voices or mini-texts.[37] These inserts give the narrative a collective voice, which is especially appropriate for the blowouts. At one point in the writing stage, Castro mentioned to me that he did not want to come across in his *testimonio* as being the center of everything and that he wanted to convey that many others, certainly the high school and college students, were indispensable to the struggle. I agree, even though I maintain that the walkouts would not have happened without Castro. Nevertheless, Sal is absolutely correct that many other activists had the courage and leadership to make the blowouts the success that they were. By adding some of their voices, the published text contributes to this acknowledgment.

In my 1994 *testimonio* of Bert Corona, I observed that this type of oral history represents a dual authorship, involving the subject and me. In the case of Sal Castro's *testimonio*, I have to amend this by noting that this particular text represents a collective authorship—the collective self—in keeping with the tradition of the *testimonio*, which stresses collective struggles for liberation. This certainly is the case in the Sal Castro story. At the same time, I have tried to limit the number of inserts in order not to disrupt Castro's own voice.

Oral History, *Testimonio*, and Authorship

Finally, a word on authorship is appropriate. This is a complicated issue, due to the nature of oral history/*testimonio* and the relationship between interviewer and subject, with no uniform agreement. Some oral histories carry the name of the historian as the author, and some use both names—the subject's and the historian's. A distinguished example of the former is Nell Painter's oral history of the black Communist leader Hosea Hudson, which lists Painter's name as the author.[38] I have used both formats. In my oral history of Bert Corona, longtime Chicano community and labor organizer, *Memories of Chicano History: The Life and Narrative of Bert Corona*, I am listed as the author and Corona's name is prominent in the title. My coming-of-age oral history of Frances Esquibel Tywoniak, *Migrant Daughter: Coming of Age as a Mexican American Woman*, lists Tywoniak and me as coauthors.

So how did I differentiate between these two formats? In the Corona text, besides initiating the project, I did the interviews, arranged for the transcriptions, and wrote the entire manuscript, including the several drafts. Corona was not involved in any of the post-interview phase. As an activist, he simply did not have the time. It was hard enough for him to make time for the interviews, and I very much appreciated his support at that level. Bert read the final draft and verbally approved it with no changes. He agreed on the title and on my being listed as the author. The two reviewers for the University of California Press never raised the issue of authorship, nor did the press itself. In the published and very supportive reviews of the book, I do not recall a single critic raising a question about authorship.

My relationship with Esquibel Tywoniak—Fran—was much different. I initiated the project, conducted the interviews, and arranged for the transcriptions. But Fran went over all of the transcripts and made additions and deletions—especially additions, as other memories came to her as she read the transcripts. She also went over each manuscript draft and made additional changes, including rewriting and even correcting some of my own writing, as the good English teacher that she was for many years. She was truly a coauthor in every sense of the term.

Sal Castro's case is more like the Corona one. Sal read the submitted manuscript, made certain factual corrections and additions, and approved it, including having my name listed as the author with his name in the title. But what differentiates the Castro text from the Corona one are the additional oral histories that I conducted, which provide a collective voice to the *testimonio*, and the primary archival sources that I integrated into the text.

The issue of authorship in a complicated text like an oral history/*testimonio* is an important one, and, given the different views on this issue, I feel it is important to explain this aspect of the text. However, after much deliberation and the persuasive argument by one of the readers of the manuscript, I decided to include Castro's name as a coauthor. Clearly, there would be no book without Sal Castro. The bottom line is the historical significance of Sal Castro and the blowouts to Chicano history and to the history of the United States. I am grateful and honored to present this story.

Sal Castro An Oral History

ONE

Born in East L.A.

My mother, Carmen Buruel, who was more important to me than my father only because I spent more time with her, was born in the border town of Nogales, Sonora, in the north of Mexico. Her family, the Buruels, were *norteños*. The name Buruel is French, but I don't know the history of how my mother's family got the name. Despite the French connection, they were totally *mexicanos*. Her father, my maternal grandfather, earned his living as a blacksmith during the period of the Mexican Revolution of 1910. In fact, he became caught in the middle of this tragic civil war. The *federales*, the right-wing antirevolutionary forces, believed that he was shoeing horses for the revolutionaries, while the rebels believed he was doing it for the *federales*. It became an impossible situation, and so my grandfather fled with his family, including his youngest daughter, my mother, across the border, an imaginary line in the desert dividing Mexico and the United States. They sought refuge in Nogales, Arizona, the border counterpart to the other Nogales. From there, they went to Tucson, and some, including my mother, eventually went to Los Angeles.

My mother was the youngest of five sisters. One of them, Tía Lola, had already married in the Mexican Nogales and had her own family. She and her family, after they came to *el otro lado* (the other side), decided to go to Los Angeles. They brought with them my mother and one of the other younger sisters, Tía Lupe. One of Tía Lola's sons, Johnny Pérez, would later fight in World War II as a U.S. Marine and was a hero in the battles of Guadalcanal and Iwo Jima. My mother and her family moved into a home on First and Boyle in the Boyle Heights area of East L.A.

My mother had a limited education, although probably more than other Mexican immigrants of that time, especially girls. Her older sisters had to work, but she got the opportunity to attend school both in Mexico and in the United States. In Los Angeles, she attended junior high at Central High School, which had a combined junior and senior high. At the time, Central was located where the L.A. board of education offices were on Grand Avenue.

She went there for a year and then went to work while still living with Tía Lola. She started at a laundry.

My father, Salvador Castro, whose name I bear, was not a major influence on my life. Unlike my mother, who was from northern Mexico, he was born in Mazatlán along the semitropical Pacific Coast. His family was a bit better off, since my paternal grandfather was a pharmacist. Still, during the revolution, the family fell on hard times. My father told me that as a young boy he had to go to the military *cuartel* (garrison) every day with a bucket in hand and wait in line for the daily rations of rice and beans that the *federales* would give to the families. Then he would take the bucket home to share with the family. My father and his siblings apparently received more education than my mother's family. He attended *preparatoria* and received a high school education. Also, unlike my mother's family, he didn't leave Mexico until sometime in the 1920s. After his father died, he migrated across the border legally with his cousin Armando Torres, who became quite prominent later in business with Young's Market Company, which still exists. My father got a job as a baker's helper. He and his cousin, like my mother and many other Mexican immigrants, also lived in East L.A. around First Street and Rowan Avenue in Boyle Heights.

My mother told me that she met my father at a dance. It must have been around 1930 or 1931. He was a couple of years older. You never ask your parents, and certainly not your mother, how old they are. They married soon after they met in a Catholic ceremony. She was nineteen. They stayed in Boyle Heights, where they made preparations to buy the home they were renting. My father continued to work at the bakery, and my mother worked at the laundry and later in a sewing factory or sweatshop. I was born on October 25, 1933, at Alta Vista Maternity Hospital on Eagle Street, right in the middle of the Great Depression. I was a Depression baby. At that time, my parents lived on Hubbard Avenue, still in the Heights. I literally was born in East L.A.!

The Deportations

With the Depression came tremendous pressures on the Mexican-origin population, especially in L.A., where thousands now lived. Many, like my parents, were immigrants, but many others, like me, had been born in the United States. We became part of the Mexican American Generation.[1] Still, many non-Mexicans or whites began to blame *mexicanos* for the Depression and for taking jobs from "real Americans." They used many of the same

Sal Castro at eight months with his parents, Salvador and Carmen Castro. Courtesy Sal Castro Personal Collection.

arguments that, regrettably, you still hear today—that the immigrants are illegal, that they produce crime and health problems, and that they don't really want to become Americans. All of this is baloney. It's baloney now and it was baloney then. Hell, my family worked hard in this country, and many, like my cousins and later myself, served this country in the military.

But these counterarguments fell on deaf ears. Thousands of Mexicans, about half a million, were deported or "repatriated," a nice-sounding word that still forced you out, but under the guise that you "voluntarily" agreed to return to Mexico. Many of these people were not "illegal," including thousands of U.S.-born children, who were swept out with their immigrant parents.

LA OPINIÓN: "*11 Mexicanos presos en un aparatoso raid a La Placita*" [11 Mexicans Arrested in a Spectacular Raid at La Placita][2]

Los Angeles Times: "Greatly are conditions in Southern California affected by the Immigration Service. Laxly directed, it would mean more unemployment, more undesirable aliens, more temptation to American law breakers and more spreaders of disease and pernicious habits than we could endure. Unfeelingly administered, it would bring about many lawful inhumanities. The problem of handling it so that the law is respected, the public served and the individual helped, if possible, is one which calls for the judgment of Solomon.

"Last month this district deported more than 150 aliens who had no right here. It also scared away a great many, probably several times as many as it was necessary to arrest and deport. And it helped a few who were technically subject to deportation, but were valuable residents to straighten out their affairs so that both the law and their private welfare could be served."[3]

My parents were affected by all of this. Both had entered the U.S. legally, but my father's temporary visa had expired, and, as a result, immigration officials apprehended him when they raided his bakery. They gave him a one-way ticket to Mexico, and no one cared about the family he left behind. My mother averted this same fate because she had a renewable regular visa. Every six months she had to travel back across the border to renew it at an American consulate. My father became quite angry about his deportation and at the United States. He vowed never to return to this country for the way he was treated. At the same time, he decided that my mother and I would remain and instead visit him for extended periods. They deported my father in 1935. I once asked my mother about this, and I think she said that they put him on a bus and send him to Nogales, Arizona, where he was forced back across the border. My parents never talked much about this trying experience. I think that they felt embarrassed by it more than anything else.[4]

Upon his return to Mazatlán, my father got a good job as an administrator, ironically, with Wells Fargo Express, an American company. His return began a litany of travels for my mother and me, at least every six months, that coincided with my mother renewing her visa. I was only about two when these trips began. We traveled by trains, which fascinated me. I loved trains and still do. My old man had a train pass because of his Wells Fargo job, and we took advantage of this free transportation. We usually went from L.A. to Nogales either by train or bus and then by train to Mazatlán.

So for the next three years or so, my mother and I trekked down to Mazatlán, sometimes staying several months. On one trip, I got the German measles and almost died, or so I'm told. They quarantined me, and I couldn't make the return trip with mother, who had to return after a certain date, according to her visa regulations. I stayed with my father and my aunt. This was when I was about five or six and ready to start school. But because I couldn't get back to L.A., I began school in Mazatlán, where I went to the

Sal Castro at age two.
Courtesy Sal Castro
Personal Collection.

first grade at a little private school run by two sisters, where I learned to read and write in Spanish. I already spoke Spanish. I remember especially learning Mexican history and about historical figures such as Cuauhtemoc, the Aztec leader who resisted the Spanish conquest, and about *Los Niños Heroes*, the young military cadets who centuries later resisted the U.S. invasion of Mexico City in 1848. This history really excited me; it was part of my history. Perhaps that's why I became a history teacher. I always tried to incorporate some of this history for my mostly Chicano high school students so that they could be proud of their historical heritage.

I also had an opportunity to learn other Mexican cultural traditions, such as learning how to dance the *Jarabe Tapatio* at Tía Lupita Castro's dance studio. She ran a small dance studio in Mazatlán and she taught me this famous folk dance.

But there were also sad moments in Mazatlán. My mother gave birth there to a baby boy whom my parents named David. Apparently my mother developed some kind of fever during her pregnancy, and this affected the baby, who was born quite weak. He only survived six months. The death of my brother meant that I would grow up with no siblings, something that I missed very much. David's death also further stressed relations between my parents. As a little kid I knew little about this, but it seems that after my father's deportation my parent's marriage began to deteriorate. The commuting from L.A. also didn't help matters. My father wanted my mother to relocate to Mazatlán, but she didn't want to because of her family in L.A. Finally, they divorced. I don't know who initiated it. Perhaps both just came to the same conclusion. I was about ten when this happened and already back living permanently in California. It was tough on me. Divorce is terrible, especially on the children. I know, because I later also divorced with kids. I always felt that if my brother, David, had lived dealing with my parent's divorce would have been better. You can fight off the hurt amongst your siblings. But being alone, this was tough.

Growing Up in East L.A.

Since we permanently returned to East L.A. after I went to first grade in Mexico, I started my U.S. school experience at Belvedere Elementary School, which was on First Street and Rowan Avenue. However, my English wasn't so hot. I knew more Spanish.

"Sit in the corner until you learn English," my teacher put me down.

This was just one of the many putdowns I encountered at this school. I remember once that the school district dentist wanted to pull out two of my baby teeth one day before lunch.

"Why don't you wait until after lunch so I can eat?"

Those bastards pulled the teeth. So here I was. I couldn't eat anything, not even a banana—*cabrónes* (bastards)!

In the fourth grade, my mother transferred me to Rowan Elementary School. I could speak good English by then. But I remember that they were giving out musical instruments in order to form a band. I wanted to play the trumpet and asked my teacher if I could.

"No," she said.

"Why not?"

"Because your lips are too big."

"Well what about the saxophone?"

"No, your lips are still too big."

Sal Castro at First Communion, age nine. Courtesy Sal Castro Personal Collection.

Instead, they gave the instruments mostly to the *gavachitos* (white kids). The teachers were too much.

I had another difficulty at that school, when my mother requested permission for me to leave early some days so I could go to catechism classes at our Catholic Church, The Resurrection, in preparation for my First Communion. My teacher refused to allow me to do this. I think this was one of the first times that I witnessed my mother's strength and courage, which influenced my own development. She spoke English well and went and confronted my teacher.

"My son is going to go to his catechism class."

"Mrs. Castro, if you take Sal out of school for this, we might not take him back."

"You will accept him back or I'm going to go to your boss."

She took me out and I went back to school with no problems. I was proud as hell of my mother. She was a fighter. I think I got my fighting spirit from both my mother and my father. Not only was my mother a fighter, but my father did time in a Mazatlán prison for trying to organize the railroad workers there.

It was also at Rowan Elementary that I went from being Salvador to Sal. I was always getting into fights with the so-called White Russian kids there.[5] They used to call me "sourdough." So I started punching them out and they punched back. My mother had to come in to talk to the principal about my fighting in school. After my mother learned that all this had to do with my name, she, not the principal or my teacher, decided that in order to try to avoid further problems I now be called "Sal." "Sal, *esta bien* [it's fine]," she told me. "Sal" was better than "sourdough."

Part of my adjustment to American schooling had to do with the fact that I had learned in Mexico already much about the history of Mexico, including about the rich indigenous cultures such as the Aztecs, Mayans, and Olmecas. I had a sense of my Mexican identity, including being able to speak Spanish. I knew a language going into Belvedere Elementary; it might not have been English initially, but I knew a language—Spanish. That's why I used to get pissed when the teacher couldn't understand me. I used to think the teacher was dumb that she couldn't do this. I didn't think I was dumb because I couldn't understand her. After all, I was the kid and she was the adult. Why couldn't she understand me? The key for me, unlike some of the other Mexican kids, was that I had already developed this pride inside of me. I knew I was a worthwhile person.

But my experience was and is different from a lot of other Chicano kids when they first start school and don't understand what's going on due to the language difference. They feel awkward and insecure. I tell a story about Juanito, a mythical young Chicano student. Juanito, in his kindergarten or first-grade class, can't understand a thing the teacher is saying in English. The teacher says: "Children, today is the first day of your educational life. You're going to learn how to read, write, and sing, and we're going to play games; isn't that wonderful?"

Juanito is saying to himself, "What is this lady talking about. She looks like a chicken. And I need to go to the bathroom. How do I say this?"

"*Señora*," Juanito bravely says, "*tengo que ir al baño.*"

"I understand," the teacher responds; "what's your name?"

Somehow Juanito figures out that the teacher wants to know his name.

"*Juan, Señora*," he says; "*pero tengo que ir al baño.*"

"I understand all that, Juan," the teacher says, "but we're going to call you John. Class repeat after me. This boy's name is John."

Poor Juanito—he had just entered the school and already they had baptized him within thirty seconds.

The teacher went on: "Yes, I understand that John needs to go to the restroom. Spanish is a great language; it's one of the romance languages, like French and Italian. Class repeat after me. 'Please leave Spanish at home.' We're here to learn English. This is America. Let's tell John how he can make a request next time when he wants to go to the restroom. 'I need to go to the restroom.' That's the way. All right, John, go to the restroom."

And here's Juanito. *"No señora, ya paso* [I already went]." He went all over the floor. The kid had peed in his pants because the teacher wanted to teach him how to say it in English. That's traumatic as hell. That's what happens to a lot of kids. It would be cool if the teacher spoke Spanish, or an Asian language if a lot of the kids were Japanese, Chinese, or Vietnamese. But let's learn these other languages. If you're a doctor, you're sure as hell going to know what's wrong with your patients if it means learning another language. Aren't we supposed to be professionals as educators?

When we returned to L.A. and after my mother divorced my father, we lived with my Tía Lola. Her husband had died not too long before. She had several kids, but they were much older than me. Most still lived at home since they weren't married. We later also lived with my Tío Chente and my Tía Lupe. Living with Tía Lola was quite a trip, since it was a large family in a small house. There's a Woody Allen film called *Radio Days* that shows an extended Jewish family living in small quarters. That's how we and most other Mexican families lived during World War II. Everyone lived together because of the housing shortage. Tía Lola's house on Sixth Street is still there. It had two bedrooms, one big living room, and a front room, besides the kitchen and one bathroom. In one of the bedrooms in one bed Tía Lola slept with my cousin Mary. In the same room in another bed my mother and my Tía Matilde slept. Then on a cot in the same room my cousins Estella and Armida slept together. In the second bedroom, my cousins Johnny, Hector, Carlos, and I shared the space. When I got too big, they threw me out and put me in the front room. It was like Grand Central Station. The only way to get out was when you married.

Since my cousins were older, I couldn't play with them, but they still took me places. Hector worked changing records in jukeboxes, and during the summer I'd help him. That's when my liking for music began. Hector later served in Korea. Of course, I played with the neighborhood kids. We played baseball with a tennis ball out on the street. We'd climb the fence of Stevenson Junior High and play football in its field. They wouldn't let us in because we were elementary students. I don't remember playing other sports such as basketball too much. We also played softball, and this actually led to my first public protest. We played on a street, where we constantly hit the ball into this lady's backyard. This pissed her off, and one time she refused to return our ball. This got us mad, and so we started protesting in front of her house. We even made picket signs. The *L.A. Examiner* found out about this and covered the story. My mother cut out the clipping, which I still have. I think we finally got our ball back.

Although we had family meals, we all couldn't eat together because there were too many of us. Instead, we ate in *tandas* or in turns. The older ones ate first. I ate in the third *tanda*. Tía Lola and a couple of her daughters did all of the cooking. We always ate Mexican food. Since the family was from Sonora, they made those huge tortillas *de harina* (wheat), typical of Sonora-style cuisine. They would stretch them out and cook them on the top of a large empty gasoline can that had been redone by one of my cousins into a *comal* (cooking surface). In those days, officials rationed butter, and so we couldn't spread it on the hot tortillas. Instead, we used some kind of synthetic stuff that was called "nuco." As one of my chores, I had to make it. They made me wash my hands, including my fingernails. Then I'd get this white substance that looked like cheese, but it wasn't. After I chopped it into pieces I'd put a little orange powder in it and mixed it up until it turned yellow like butter. This was "nuco" and it tasted like "nuco."

At home, Spanish predominated. At school, of course, I spoke English, as well as on the streets with my friends. In fact, language was a generational thing. My mother and her sisters spoke mostly Spanish, while my cousins and I spoke mostly English, except at home when we addressed the elders in Spanish. I don't remember my cousins, especially the boys, speaking too much Spanish unless they had to. My girl cousins spoke a bit more Spanish since they had more work to do at home. I remember that when I went out with my cousin Hector to change the jukeboxes his Spanish was not as good as mine.

My mother was religious in a traditional sense, but not excessively. We went to Mass, although not necessarily each Sunday. But we did go. She wanted to keep up this practice. Resurrection Church continued to be our parish. Although it was in Boyle Heights, it was not totally just Mexican parishioners who went there. There were some "White Russian" Catholics. At Tía Lola's house, there were also some religious figures, such as Our Lady of Guadalupe and the crucifix, along with *velas* (candles). We celebrated saints' days along with birthdays in the Mexican tradition. Since I was born on the feast day of San Salvador, I got cheated out of two celebrations. My mother's feast day, on the other hand, was Our Lady of Mt. Carmel, and so we celebrated both that feast and her birthday. After awhile, I started remembering the Mt. Carmel date more than her birthday. Increasingly, we celebrated Christmas in the more American way and received presents from Santa Claus. I'd leave cookies for him.

East L.A., including Boyle Heights, was certainly more Mexican by the 1940s, but there was also still evidence of an earlier ethnic diversity. Our neighborhood, for example, was quite mixed. Besides Mexicans, there were *judíos* (Jewish people) and Russians. As one of my first little jobs as a kid, I collected rags and empty bottles for this guy who had a horse-drawn cart. He was a Jewish dude with a black coat, black hat, and a beard. I didn't know at the time that he was Jewish. I just knew that he dressed different. He paid me five cents a week to gather bottles from backyards or wherever and bring them to him. He especially prized big beer bottles.

Jews and Russians also lived in the same streets as we did. My Tía Lola's house was a two-story one. We lived downstairs, and upstairs lived a Mr. Stolberg, a German who owned the property. He got along famously with my aunt who by this time was a widower. She couldn't speak English and he couldn't speak Spanish, but they used to sit in my tía's kitchen and converse for hours while drinking coffee. "Blah, blah, blah," I remember their "conversations." I didn't know what the hell they were talking about. I don't think that they knew either. I just recall Mr. Stolberg's thick German accent when he spoke his bad English. My cousins used to make fun of my aunt about her relationship with our German neighbor. They'd tease her that she was going to marry him, which she didn't. In fact, she never remarried.

My public schools also reflected the same ethnic mixture. We all got along well together, except that the White Russians used to get more favors from the teachers, or so it seemed like when they handed out the musical instruments.

We didn't use the term "Chicano" then. I didn't do so until the 1960s. Until then, I and my family, along with others in East L.A., called ourselves Mexicans or *mexicanos*.

I wasn't too aware either of discrimination against Mexicans in East L.A., outside of what I now recognize as such in the schools. However, one of the first occasions when I experienced discrimination was when we visited relatives in Phoenix. We went to see my Uncle George Sesma and his family. He was real *güero* (blonde) and had served in World War I. He took us to a Fourth of July picnic for veterans, and we got the cold shoulder from the other vets. "Who are these Mexicans spoiling our party?" they seemed to be saying. I just remember the eerie feeling that all eyes were on us because they didn't think we belonged there. What the hell is a Mexican doing at a Fourth of July picnic?

The fact is, as I tell students today, we as Mexican Americans or Latinos have every right to celebrate this holiday and every other U.S. holiday. We've been fighting for this country ever since the American Revolution, when Spanish troops from Mexico aided George Washington and the American revolutionaries against Great Britain. Since then we've fought in every one of this country's wars, including the Civil War and on both sides. This includes the Spanish American War, World War I and World War II, and the subsequent conflicts, including Vietnam and the recent ones in Iraq and Afghanistan. We've shed plenty of blood for this land.

One area in L.A. that discriminated against Mexicans involved the public swimming pools. As a kid, I wasn't fully aware of this, but it affected me nevertheless. When we moved to West L.A., I and my friends would go to the public swimming pool on Vermont and Beverly, but, and this is the kicker, we could only attend on Wednesday nights during the summer. This was the day and time that they admitted Mexicans, "chinos" (Asians), and blacks, because the next day they cleaned the pool. Apparently, the same thing was going on in other parts of the city. Public parks in areas outside of East L.A. also frowned on Mexicans and other minorities going there. Mexicans, for example, shied away from Griffith Park, one of the largest parks in the city, because hostile whites harassed them. If Mexicans went to one of these public parks and started listening to Mexican music on the radio, the whites would call the cops to stop this or the whites would forcibly escort the Mexicans out of the park while the cops just stood around.

To compensate for this discrimination and exclusion in swimming pools and parks, Mexicans, including my family, went to what was called Marrano Beach. It was located by the San Gabriel River on the extreme edge of East L.A. close to Monterey Park and Montebello. *Marrano* means pig in Spanish, but the people called it Marrano Beach because it was just a big hole in the ground filled with water that resembled a pig trough. It wasn't a regular pool, but everyone, including me, learned how to swim there. I don't think they even threw disinfectants in the hole. Why there wasn't an epidemic of polio there, I don't know. It must have been infested with all kinds of things—oil, bacteria, carcinogens, and who knows what else. People also picnicked there. Singing groups entertained on weekends for dancing, and beer was sold. In fact, one of my uncles sponsored some of this entertainment. People came from all over. I even sold *raspadas* (snow cones) at the "beach" as a kid.

As a young kid growing up during World War II, I have some memories of that "great war." I remember listening to the reports on D-Day on the radio and the voice of President Franklin Roosevelt. Everything was rationed during the war, and you had to use ration books to purchase various items. I accompanied my Tía Matilde to get our books for the family every month. Each book had a number of stamps that you used to buy certain products, such as meat, sugar, shoes, and gasoline. The public schools distributed the ration books, and so I was the little dude at about age eight or nine who translated for my aunt on these occasions.

I also remember going to one of my friends' homes and finding him crying up a storm.

"I can't come out because my cousin died," he told me.

His cousin had gotten killed in the army. Many families in our neighborhood experienced the same tragic news. I began to see these little American flags with a blue star in the middle on people's windows. This meant that their sons or daughters were in the military. Some of these flags, however, had a yellow star, which meant that your son had been killed in the war. Some homes displayed both kinds.

One of the things I remember when living by Breed Street School was Japanese families living there. To us Mexicans, they were all *chinitos* (a generic but benign term we used for all Asians). I knew this one Japanese American kid who went to my school. He was the only one that had an electric train in our barrio. After school sometimes, my friends and I would go to his house. His mother wouldn't let us in, but we could go to the backyard and look in the back window while her son ran the train around the table for us. This was great to watch. One day we showed up and no one was there. They were gone. The house had been cleaned out in one day. I learned later that they were part of the unjust internment of the Japanese along the Pacific Coast during the war. Others feared that after Pearl Harbor the Japanese people might be subversives and traitors, although no evidence of this was ever shown. But they were "guilty by birth." Many of them lost their homes and businesses. It wasn't until the 1980s that the U.S. government finally and formally apologized for this injustice and actually provided reparations for survivors of this ordeal.

Zoot-Suit Riots

One of my other little jobs as a kid was shining shoes. In fact, the ragman was the one who told me that if I built a shoeshine box and got some shoeshine stuff I could make some money on weekends working downtown. So I followed his advice, with my mother's approval. Little did I know what this would get me into. I took the streetcar downtown every weekend and staked out my place at the corner of Seventh and Broadway, right by the Clifton Cafeteria. This was one of the busiest intersections. It was 1943. On one of those Saturday afternoons in the first week of June all hell broke loose. This was the commencement of what came to be known as the Zoot-Suit Riots. I was ten years old.

I remember big crowds and cops standing around. These were motorcycle cops. They had long leather boots and military caps. There were sailors attacking Chicanos. The cops just stood around, not even attempting to break up the attacks. They just let the sailors, who outnumbered the Chicanos, go at it. Some of the Chicanos wore the infamous zoot-suits, but many others didn't. The general impression is that tensions between sailors stationed in L.A. and the so-called zoot-suitors or *pachucos* (street dudes) had been building up by 1943, and this finally broke out in the riots. This is partly true, but I witnessed that all Chicanos were being attacked, not just those with drapes (zoot-suits) or recognizable as *pachucos*. All Chicanos seemed fair game. I saw fistfights but no weapons used, such as guns or knives. I did see some sailors using pieces of wood as weapons. I was just a kid, so the sailors left me alone, but I was scared. After a few minutes, I picked up my shoeshine box and got out of there. The riots, themselves, lasted for several days.

LOS ANGELES TIMES: "Zoot Suitors Learn Lesson in Fights with Servicemen"
"Those gamin dandies, the zoot suitors, having learned a great moral lesson from servicemen, mostly sailors, who took over their instruction three days ago, are staying home nights. . . .

"The officers have directed some 200 extra police and 100 deputies who for the last 72 hours maintained vigils at widely scattered points in the eastern sections of the city during a long series of more or less bloody encounters between gangs of zooters and servicemen.

"Strife between the two factions arose as a result of beatings of individual sailors by juvenile street bands and, in two cases, assaults on women relatives of servicemen.

"These attacks by zooters occurred over a period of several days."[6]

Eventually city officials imposed a curfew, not on the sailors but on the Mexican community. We had to be inside our houses by 9 P.M. I also heard that machine guns and sandbags had been placed in front of city hall. The curfew also led to tragedy. One Chicano kid that I knew from Belvedere Elementary went to get a loaf of bread after curfew and went through an alley to avoid detection. The cops shot him in the back and killed him. He was twelve years old. The whole neighborhood was up in arms about it, but nothing came of it.

Later that December, at my school, my third-grade class had to perform a children's play called *The Toy Soldier*. We had to dress up as sailors. The sailors are jumping the Mexicans just about everyday, and now we were supposed to dress like sailors? I didn't want to go to school that day dressed as a sailor. Hell no! This was callousness and stupidity on the part of the teachers. But even though my mother felt fear, confusion, and anxiety about the riots, she made me go and participate in the play. The irony of all this didn't affect me until later in life. My cousin Dofi was killed in Romania while in the Army Air Force. My cousin Johnny Pérez served in the Pacific and saw action at Guadalcanal and Iwo Jima. More than half a million other Chicanos served in World War II, many receiving Congressional Medals of Honor as well as other citations for bravery, and yet others in the military were attacking Chicanos in the streets of Los Angeles. What the hell is going on?

Many years later, I was appalled at the lack of awareness of the Mexican American contribution to the war, as well as other later conflicts. In 1998, Tom Brokaw published his best-selling *The Greatest Generation*, a series of essays on American combat soldiers in World War II. I couldn't believe that not a single Mexican American was included. Brokaw wrote about one Spanish-surnamed veteran who is an American Indian. Did Brokaw or his publisher not know or wonder if Mexican Americans had also fought in the war? I wrote to Brokaw, whom I knew, about this, but he never responded, in spite of the fact that in 1970 when he was a rookie reporter for KNBC, I was also working there trying to put together a documentary on Mexican Americans. I also took him to East L.A. (City Terrace) to pick up photos of the sheriffs pointing their guns into the Silver Dollar Café, where Ruben Salazar, a *Los Angeles Times* and KMEX reporter, had been killed two days before (see chapter 9). He was very grateful for these photos and was going to be able to scoop the other news media on the story; unfortunately, his producer did not allow him to show the photos on Tom's newscast. I guess Tom has a short memory of his experience with Mexican Americans in Los Angeles. He even forgot about having employed a student of mine from North Hollywood High, who happened to be Mexican American, as his kid's babysitter. I even had him come to speak to my North Hollywood students.

Then, in 1999, Steven Spielberg produced and directed his film *Saving Private Ryan*, about D-Day, which also omitted any reference to the large number of Mexican American soldiers involved in that heroic battle. I was so angered that I sat down and wrote to Spielberg:

> After viewing the film "Saving Private Ryan," I was struck by a glaring omission. The omission was the lack of Mexican-American soldiers being portrayed in the movie. Mexican-Americans fought and died in huge numbers at the landing at Normandy and behind the lines 82nd and 101st Airborne Division drops just prior to the landings. The definitive book on D-Day by Stephen Ambrose and the Raul Morín book *Among the Valiant* both give the Mexican-American soldiers their due. It wasn't by coincidence or affirmative action that there was a Mexican-American character in the 1949 World War II movie "Battleground" [Ricardo Montalban] about the exploits of the 101st Airborne. The omission of Mexican-Americans calls into question the credibility of the realism in your film.
>
> Mexican-Americans have won more Congressional Medals of Honor than any other minority group. . . . They have fought and died in every major war including the Civil War, the Spanish-American War, World War I, World War II, the Korean War, and Viet Nam. This is a group of men who have put their lives on the line for a country that did not and does not value them as equal citizens. The five Sullivan brothers are undoubtedly the seed for "Saving Private Ryan." The Castro-Vara family from San Antonio, Texas, had six sons in World War II. . . .
>
> Your films all have a theme of respect and dignity. Please extend that respect and dignity to a community that is crying out for its heroes to be acknowledged and validated. If the opening scene of the film was actually the Normandy Memorial Cemetery, the cross next to the Tom Hanks character reads Pfc. Mike Martínez.[7]

Like Brokaw, Spielberg never replied to me.

This neglect of the Mexican American contributions to World War II unfortunately continues. I was equally shocked to see very recently that Ken Burns, the highly praised documentary filmmaker, had a new documentary on World War II veterans, but, like Brokaw and Spielberg, he omits Mexican Americans. I have also written to him about this. Burns, in reacting to some of this criticism, has said that his film is not about ethnic groups but looks at various communities and how young men from these locations participated in the war. One of these communities is Sacramento (a Spanish-surnamed city). You can't tell me that Burns couldn't find one Mexican American World War II vet in Sacramento to interview! No wonder our kids still have no sense of their place in American history.

After the Zoot-Suit Riots, I never returned to shine shoes downtown. I also never told my mother that I was there when the riots broke out.

My Mother Remarries

In 1945, when I was about eleven or twelve years old, my mother remarried. Her new husband and my stepfather was a man by the name of Antonio Zapata. He had been a Merchant Marine in World War II. I'm not sure how my mother met him. He worked as a display case maker and then decided to start his own shoe repair shop. I didn't like him. I didn't want my mother to remarry—perhaps that's true of all divorced kids. It had nothing to do with my father, whom I had very little contact with by now. He also remarried and had several other children. I know nothing about these half brothers and sisters in Mexico. But there was nothing I could do about all this. I wanted to remain living with my aunts and cousins.

My mother and Antonio did not marry in the Church since they were both divorced. My stepfather had children from his first marriage. He and my mother later had one child, my half brother, Tony Zapata, who went on to become a documentary film cameraman and won several Oscars and Emmys. Following their marriage, they decided to move out of East L.A. and cross the Los Angeles River and rent a house in East Hollywood near Vermont and Sunset Boulevard. This was totally new territory for me. I had never been in this part of L.A. It was *gavacholandia*—it was all white as far as I could see. I was the only Mexican in my new school, Micheltorena Elementary on Sunset Boulevard.

All of these changes were traumatic for me. I had been taken out of my security zone of living with my extended family in a familiar neighborhood. On top of this, I didn't have a very good relationship with my stepfather. He was a tough dude. He was very strict, very Catholic, and abusive. Although I wasn't his blood son, he disciplined me as if I was. I'll never forget how he wouldn't let me play baseball on weekends later on when I went to Catholic school. I was the best player on my team. That sounds pretentious, but it's true. We went to the Catholic Youth Organization (CYO) championship, which was scheduled for a weekend. The old man said that I couldn't go because I had to work at his shop. I could fix shoes at twelve years old.

"What's all this crap about baseball?" he said.

I told the Sister Superior that I couldn't play in the championship.

"The team needs you," she replied.

"But my father won't let me, Sister."

"How about if I ask Father Tom to talk to your father?"

"I don't think it's gonna do any good, Sister, but go ahead."

But deep inside of me, I really didn't want Father Tom, who was the priest assigned to the school, to go see my stepfather. I knew that he still wouldn't let me play and probably would hit me or try to hit me after the priest left. He was very Catholic, but when Father Tom arrived to see him and tried to convince him to let me play, he threw the priest out of his shop. Religion didn't help in this case.

My stepfather was abusive to me in this way, but also to my mother. It was more verbal than physical. I never saw him hit her, but he might have. I intervened to try to stop this and to defend my mother, but this would only make things worse. These were not easy years for me.

Entertainment, Chicano Style

As a kid, I especially came to appreciate both Mexican and U.S. music. There were several Spanish-language radio stations in L.A., but the one I listened to the most came from Rosarito, just south of Tijuana in Baja California. They had good djs and played the songs of Pedro Infante, Jorge Negrete, Mariachi Vargas, Luis Pérez-Mesa, and many others. When I babysat with my baby stepbrother in the afternoons, I'd tune in that station. I also had a record collection. My cousin Hector, since he serviced jukeboxes, had a lot of records that couldn't be used any more on the sides played after they got worn, so he gave these to me. On the unused side, I could listen to a variety of pre–rock and roll music, especially rhythm and blues and jazz with singers such as Billy Eckstein, Ella Fitzgerald, Sarah Vaughn, and Dinah Washington. Some of the records contained Mexican music. I liked both kinds. To me the crossover was just natural.

I also loved to go to movies. I started going to see them in Mazatlán. In the theaters, besides the films, they would have a variety show with singers and comedians. One of these comedians was an up-and-coming one by the name of Cantinflas, who would go on to become Mexico's greatest comic and appeared in numerous films. On one of our return trips from seeing my father, my mother and I actually met Cantinflas on the train. When the train stopped for people to have a meal at a roadside restaurant, we sat at one of the tables, and to our surprise Cantinflas sat next to us. Although he was a comedian, he remained very quiet. He also was on the way to Los Angeles.

In L.A., as I grew up, I often saw Cantinflas's films, as well as others from Mexico's Golden Age of the 1940s and 1950s. These included great stars such as Dolores Del Rio, Jorge Negrete, and, of course, the great Pedro Infante. I would see these films at the Million Dollar Theater, the California, and the Mason, all downtown theaters catering to Mexican audiences. They were located either on Broadway or on Main Street. But I also loved U.S. films and would see these at the Warner Brothers Theater on Seventh and Hill, the Orpheum, or the Los Angeles Theater. I remember being at the United Artist Theater on Broadway watching the film *Wilson* about President Woodrow Wilson. People thought I was crazy going to see the movie since little kids weren't supposed to be interested in such films, but only in cartoons or Superman. But I liked going to see it on my own. In fact, at the theater, some old ladies there who might have been contemporaries of Wilson actually asked me why I was there.

"What are you doing sitting there by yourself? What are you doing here watching this movie?"

I don't know whether they were surprised at a young kid seeing the movie or because they never expected to see a Mexican at a film about an American president. Who the hell knows?

Besides going to the big and elaborate downtown theaters, I also went to neighborhood theaters in East L.A., such as the Jewel, the Unique, and the Vern.

I'd go to see all of these movies mostly by myself. I knew my way around downtown. I was a pretty shifty little guy. I was precocious and didn't need adults to usher me into shows.

Growing up, television was just starting after the war, but it was too expensive for most people to own a set, including my family. Instead, we'd go at night to stores that sold TVs and watch athletic events such as prizefighting, wrestling, and college football games. They'd keep the TVs on at night, even though the store was closed, so people could watch from the outside. You couldn't hear anything, but you could see the black-and-white images. I saw one of the Rose Bowls like this when Illinois or Michigan beat the hell out of USC or UCLA. I also liked to see boxing matches on TV outside the stores and later around 1950 when we got a set. I especially liked to see the fights because I used to sell *Ring Magazine* at the Olympic Auditorium where they staged live fights. I did this when I was in eighth grade through high school. This gave me some money, since my stepfather didn't pay me for working in his shoe shop, and supplemented my earnings when later I worked in high school as a shipping clerk at a sewing factory. The fights at the Olympic would be on Tuesday and Thursday evenings. Since I sold the magazine, I got in free and could enjoy the matches. My favorite boxers were Art Aragón, Carlos Chávez, Willie Pep, Sandy Sadler, Enrique Polaños, Jimmy Carter, and Rocky Graziano. I also got to see the great Sugar Ray Robinson in an exhibition match. Many Mexicans, along with whites, attended the fights, including Hollywood stars. I sold *Ring* to Bob Hope, Al Jolson, and Tony Curtis. The magazine sold for twenty-five cents, and I got to keep a portion of this.

A Catholic Education

After we moved out of East L.A., my mother decided to put me in Catholic school. I don't think this had anything to do with religion per se, but more because she believed that I needed the discipline. I wasn't a bad boy. I never got into gangs or crime or anything like that. But I could get rowdy at times and get into mischief, especially at school. It really had a lot to do with the fact that I was fun loving. On top of this, I always seemed to challenge authority, even as a young kid. I don't know whether some of my rebelliousness had to do with being a product of a broken family. Perhaps, I don't know.

I first attended Our Lady of Loretto, which was close to our home in East Hollywood. It was near Belmont High School at Belmont and Temple. This was the beginning of my Catholic school education. I spent six years in public schools and six years in Catholic schools. I liked being in the parochial schools, starting with Loretto. The nuns seemed much nicer than my public school teachers. They were Notre Dame nuns, or sisters, as they're called today. In those years, they still wore their habits all in black. I especially liked Sister Mary Gregory. I started at Loretto in 1946. I had completed sixth grade in public school but had to repeat it at Loretto. I'm not sure why this was, but it didn't seem to matter to me. The school was predominantly white, although some other Mexicans also attended.

Loretto also meant playing baseball and serving as an altar boy. This was the only time I was an altar boy. In fact, I received a special distinction of being one of two sixth graders chosen to serve as altar boys for the eighth-grade graduation Mass. This was a big deal, because, in addition to serving Mass and carrying the crucifix, you also got to go to the banquet and eat with the graduates. So that I would look nice at this event, my stepfather gave me a haircut. Instead of paying for a barber, he cut my hair. He wasn't very good at it. But this time it was even worse. He cut it so badly—*trasquilado* and-a-half—that the priest at the church, after seeing me, sent me home. I didn't get to participate in the ceremony.

Despite this unfortunate incident, I liked Loretto, but I only stayed there for a year. My parents moved further south, to the area near Pico and Vermont, where my stepfather set up his shoe repair shop. So they transferred me to St. Thomas the Apostle School, which was close to Loyola High School, one of the more prestigious Catholic high schools. I attended seventh and eighth grades at St. Thomas under the Immaculate Heart nuns. Fewer Chicanos attended here, and so it was an even whiter school. But ethnicity wasn't something I dwelled on at this time. I knew I was Mexican, but I didn't wear it on my sleeve. The other kids, as I look back on it now, were of Irish, Italian, and possibly French descent. They represented the gamut of white Catholic kids.

The nuns provided us a rigorous and good education. I responded well and did better academically than I had in public schools. The nuns could also be very strict. My seventh-grade teacher was nasty. But eighth grade proved to be better, and I have fond memories of my teacher, Sister Mary Theresa. She was very good and encouraging. In fact, I accomplished what not too many other students at St. Thomas had done—I successfully passed the entrance exam to Loyola High. My teachers made a big deal about it.

Despite the discipline, I was still *travieso* (mischievous). I didn't get into too much trouble, but once I got caught smoking with a couple of other guys. Today there's a church, St. Sophia's Cathedral, right on the lot across from St. Thomas. In those days, it was just a vacant lot. These two other students and I dug a hole there big enough to hold us. We then gathered some palm tree branches and laid them over the hole. In the hole, we smoked. I don't know how we didn't get killed, because the branches were all dried out and could have easily caught fire with us in the hole. We might have been burned to death. Fortunately, or unfortunately, depending on how you saw it, the nuns saw the smoke from our cigarettes coming out of the branches and found us. They suspended us for a few days. My parents really gave it to me.

In any event, I finished the eighth grade and graduated in 1948.

Although I had been accepted into Loyola, I didn't go there. The tuition was too high, and my parents couldn't afford it. Instead, they sent me to Cathedral High School, run by the Christian Brothers, where the cost was lower. One of my cousins had gone there, so my mother felt it was a good place for me. Cathedral was adjacent to Chinatown. I studied there from 1948 to 1952. We called the brothers "the purple feet," because they had a winery in Napa, Christian Brother's Wine, and there was a myth that they spent their summers up there squeezing the grapes with their feet in the barrels! Of course, we never called them "purple feet" to their faces.

Unlike in today's Catholic schools where the majority of teachers are laypeople, that was not the case at Cathedral in my time. Most of them were brothers with a few lay ones. The brothers were strict, but you got along with them. There was give-and-take. All of the brothers were of white European backgrounds, including the one Spaniard, Brother Julian. The lay teachers also were all white.

By contrast, Mexicans composed more than half of the student body. The rest were whites, with a few *morenitos* (blacks). The kids came from all over the city. Some came from the Lincoln Heights area where Chicanos still lived alongside Italian Americans. The few black kids came from South Central. Some of the other Chicanos came from other parts of East L.A. and from as far east as Highland Park. I was an oddity, as a Chicano from West L.A. Of course, this was west only in that we lived just west of the Los Angeles River. It wasn't West L.A. as in the more middle-class Wilshire Boulevard corridor. The white students were of Irish, Italian, and German backgrounds and came from different neighborhoods of the city, but mostly from the western sections of the city.

But everyone pretty much got along well. I became aware of some ethnic tension once when I supported a good friend of mine, Duffy, for student body president. In fact, I served as his campaign manager. He was white. I used to help him in Spanish class. His opponent was a Chicano by the name of Lefty Valenzuela. Lefty really threw it at me: "Hey, you as a Mexican should be supporting me!" I shined him off. Duffy was my friend and Lefty wasn't. It was as simple as that. I guess this did reflect some ethnic rivalry. Ethnic consciousness among Chicanos existed, but at a very nonpolitical level. We spoke Spanish at home, or at least varieties of Spanish, and many of us brought our burritos for lunch. "Hey, man, don't you eat anything else?" we'd kid each other.

There was no overt racial discrimination at Cathedral, but there was an academic tracking system that served to reflect ethnic backgrounds. The school had a Latin track and a Spanish track. I don't know why they named these two tracks as such, although it appears that those in the Latin track tended to take Latin as a foreign language and those in the Spanish track took Spanish. More *gavachitos* were on the Latin track and more Chicanos were in the Spanish one. One of the white kids, Duane Hickman, later went on to become famous as "Dobie Gillis" in the TV show by the same name. These tracking systems, as I look back on it, determined to some extent whether you went on to college or not. The Latin track was automatic college prep, but not necessarily the Spanish one. If they found you could take the more advanced classes, they let you; otherwise, you took regular ones such as algebra, geometry, history, and the other required courses. It wasn't that some of these classes weren't college prep, but that they weren't as advanced as those in the Latin track. The brothers placed me in the Spanish track even though I had been admitted to the more prestigious Loyola High School. I have no idea how they determined such placement, but I do know that I and most other Chicanos kids found ourselves in the Spanish track.

The other characteristic of the Spanish track was that it included industrial arts, such as auto shop. More of the Chicano students took these classes. They were optional, but many Chicanos, perhaps believing college was not an option for them, took these classes. I shied away from them. I already worked with my hands in my afternoon job. Why would I want to do more of this at school? I did take one industrial arts class when one of my academic classes was overcrowded and the teacher asked for volunteers to take another class. I foolishly raised my hand to do him a favor and, "orale" (right on), I was put in the auto shop class.

One other aspect to the tracking concerned the lack of college counseling. The brothers never encouraged those of us in the Spanish track to go on to college. The only time I ever heard about going to college was when this guy from Loyola University came around to give us some sort of a sample test for what I guess was his dissertation or MA thesis as a graduate student. Somehow after the test, I found myself talking to him, and he said, "You know what, you could go to college." That's the only time I heard that at Cathedral. Still, overall, I did okay academically. I liked my civics and history classes best. I didn't like English. I was good at math but didn't care for it. I surprised myself that I was doing better than I thought I would do.

Religion, of course, played a central role at Cathedral, both in the curriculum and in the school as a whole. Everyone, irrespective of your track, had to take religion all four years. Every day we prayed the rosary, and the brothers encouraged us to always carry a rosary in our back pockets. For years, even though I was no longer a practicing Catholic, I did so. And every Friday, our teachers escorted us to Mass at the gym. Some guys were very religious, but not all, including myself. I'll never forget, one time in my junior year some guys secretly brought a jug of wine to our Friday Mass and passed it around so that the brothers didn't see what was going on. Some even got a bit drunk. After Mass, those of us who drank the wine were all a bit high. But we didn't get away with it. The brothers found out what we were doing. They busted us. I think they suspended us for a day or so.

But such antics didn't deter the brothers from trying to make us devout Catholics. They would take us on retreats. In my senior year, we went to a retreat house in the mountains near San Diego. They also pushed vocations to the priesthood or brotherhood, but not many of us took these seriously. From my graduation class, I don't think anyone went on to a seminary. Even though Cathedral was a religious school, I also don't think it made us any more religious or Catholic. Today, I'm very critical of the Church, not its teachings, but of the racist priests and bishops, not all but some.

I didn't mind the discipline at school, but what I now see as my rebellious nature still came out and sometimes got me into trouble. Besides the incident of drinking at Mass, the other particular incident of trouble that I remember is when I called one of my teachers a "wop." He was a lay teacher of Italian descent from Chicago and my civics teacher. I felt that he picked on me too much. It's true that I used to clown a lot in his class, but sometimes he accused me of talking when I wasn't. One day I got fed up with this.

"Sal, stop that talking. You want to get into more trouble?" he shouted in front of the class.

"You goddamn wop!" I shouted back.

"Stand up and say that again."

I wasn't going to back down.

"You goddamn wop!"

"You're going to tell the principal what you said."

"Okay."

What I didn't know was that the principal, Brother William, was also Italian—*hijo de la fregada* (son of a bitch)! But I had no choice as my teacher walked me down the corridor to the principal's office.

"Okay," my teacher said, "tell Brother William what you called me."

"I called him a goddamn wop because he accused me of talking when I wasn't."

"Sal," the principal responded, "this is very serious. I want you to come back tomorrow with your mother."

But as Brother William gave me this order, I thought I detected a gleam in his eye. I think that he thought it was funny or not that serious, but, at the same time, he had to back up his teacher. So I went home and told my mother what had happened. She didn't think it was funny and really came down hard on me, as did my stepfather. The next day she accompanied me to school, and we met with Brother William. My mother cried and cried about what I had done and pleaded with him not to kick me out of school. Brother William told my mother that the next time I said something like this, I would be dropped from Cathedral, but that because of her he wouldn't do it this time. I still have a feeling that Brother William wasn't going to kick me out anyway.

Fights would sometimes break out among the students. This wasn't ethnic; it was just arguments between students. I got into one such fight with another Chicano guy. He pushed me in the hall, so I pushed back. I think he was just having fun, but I took it seriously.

"Okay, Sal, we'll settle this after school," he said, now also taking it seriously.

"*Orale, suave* [Right on, fine]," I came back, using *pachuco* talk to agree to fight later.

So we did. But I got caught because we fought too close to school. I got another temporary suspension.

Sports were big at Cathedral, but, even though I was a good baseball player, I didn't play on the regular teams. Not because I didn't want to, but because I had to work after school all four years. I'd occasionally attend the football games, especially the big game against Loyola High School. Most of the time, they'd beat the hell out of us. Although I didn't play on the teams, I did play intramural sports, such as football and softball. I could do this because we played these games at noon. Classes would divide the teams.

Because I worked I also didn't join in extracurricular activities. Other Chicanos did, but I don't recall many of them, for example, being elected to key student council positions.

What I did do was go to the dances, if I wasn't working on Friday nights. The dances were in our gym or at some of the other Catholic high schools such as at St. Joseph's. I particularly remember the dances at St. Joe's, which were held in the basement of the school. The school was located right downtown, on Twelfth and Los Angeles streets. The dances were like out of a scene from *West Side Story*. At all of these events, kids would come from all of the Catholic schools. Since the schools were mostly divided between boys and girls schools, you had to have this mix. Many of the girls came from Bishop Conaty or Sacred Heart. The priests, brothers, and nuns closely supervised us. The lights might be turned down low, but you didn't dare dance too close.

I also don't recall that the brothers counseled us too much if at all about sex education. If they did, I wasn't listening. Things like this you learned from your friends or older siblings.

I'd go to the dances with some of my friends. We either walked or took public transportation. Very few Chicanos had cars, but several of the *gavachitos* did. One of the Chicanos who had a *ramfla* (car) was Ernie Navar. Some of us always tried to get a ride with him. His parents had a grocery store in East L.A. Some guys dated, but I didn't really have a girlfriend in high school. I liked this girl, Louise, but at first I had a problem attracting girlfriends because when I first started high school I had to take my little brother, Tony, from our home in west L.A. over to my aunt's in East L.A. before school every day, either on the streetcar or on the bus. Many of the girls I'd run across at dances or parties came from the barrios and commuted to either Sacred Heart or Conaty on the Westside. So I'd see these girls in the morning waiting for the bus or streetcar, and they would see me with my brother, who was only about three or four at the time. They thought he was my kid, and so either I was married or had gotten a girl into trouble. Of course, none of this was true, but I had to work very hard to overcome this impression.

I finally got a girlfriend when I became a senior. Her name was Annette, and she later became my wife. I met her at one of my cousins' parties. She was a junior at Our Lady of Loretto. I took her to my senior prom, and she invited me to her junior prom. After I graduated, I escorted her to her senior prom. She lived in Echo Park near Belmont High School.

Although I got into some trouble at Cathedral, I didn't ever get into serious problems with the police, even though some of my friends outside of school belonged to gangs. The period before and after the war in L.A. saw the rise of many Chicano gangs, some criminal, but most just young kids needing a sense of belonging and comrades. Some of these included the Clanton, White Fence, Maravilla, El Hoyo, and Florencia gangs. A few of these are still around, of course, regrettably, with many other new ones. The ones that I palled around with belonged to the 32nd Street gang, which was an offshoot of the Clanton gang. I didn't belong to the gang, but I hung around with the members. Like the kids say today, "I'm not a gang member, but I know them." That was me. About eight to twelve *vatos* (dudes), all boys, belonged to it. It was a loose gang, members coming in and out. They initiated you by beating you up. I never got beat up since I wasn't a member, but I witnessed some of these initiations. But drugs weren't used, even *mota* (pot). Drinking, yes. We drank a lot of beer. They also favored a version of the *pachuco* look, including me. This consisted of wearing thick-soled black shoes with tight-cuffed pants. Then we got away from that and started wearing Dickie pants, which were like workmen's kakis. We'd wear them with high-top shoes, or *ruquíto* shoes, as we called them. You'd lace them up to the top like old men's shoes. Then we wore a Sir Guy shirt. They were called this because of the label. They were terrible-looking shirts in hindsight: short-sleeved, pullover shirts and usually checkered. All of the guys by the early 1950s had this look. Everyone wanted to look different, but everyone looked the same. We also wore the famous *pachuco* ducktail haircut all greased up. That's probably why there was an oil shortage. We couldn't go to school looking too *pachuco*, but we could wear the ducktail. This didn't faze the brothers, since no gangs existed at Cathedral. Our schools didn't require uniforms.

Gang activity then, as still today, consisted of protecting your territory or turf and baiting other gangs by "invading" theirs. I'd sometimes go out with the 32nd Street gang when they entered, for example, Lincoln Heights. That was foreign territory. We'd confront the gangs there and get chased out. We'd also go to dances there and try to pick up on the girls from that area as a way of also taunting the gang kids. This sometimes resulted in fights, mostly fisticuffs. Gangs didn't have any real weapons except for occasional switchblades and zip guns. So you'd fight mainly with your fists. It would have to be something very serious or very drunk for someone to pull out a blade. This happened to me once. I tried to take a knife away from a kid who pulled it on another, and I got cut, but not seriously. It's very different now, with gangs using all kinds of firearms, including machine guns.

I'll never forget one time at a dance in Lincoln Heights where I met a girl there and walked her home. Little did I know that a rival gang had attacked my gang friends. Outnumbered, they jumped in their car to get away. I saw them driving by yelling for me to jump in since the other gang was right behind them and would no doubt take it out on me. I said to myself, "*Vamonos a la fregada.* [Let's get the hell out of here.]" I didn't even have a chance to say goodbye to the girl as I chased after the car and just was able to grasp on to one of the windows and get on the running board that cars used to have. I hung on for dear life at fifty miles an hour, while ducking beer bottles being thrown at me. We got out of there just in time.

One of the other things about gangs in my time was that there was a code of ethics. If somebody had really hurt one of your members, such as sending him to the hospital, you wouldn't attack the other gang as a whole. You'd wait, and at the right opportunity you'd attack only the guy who had caused the injury.

Of course, the police harassed the gangs. If they saw you dressed in gang or *pachuco* attire, they'd chase you out. To avoid this, sometimes we'd go to the dances dressed up in suits and ties, although there was still a certain *pachuco* look even to this style. We figured that the cops wouldn't harass us if we looked this way. Sometimes it worked and sometimes it didn't. There still is no love lost between the L.A. police and Chicano kids.

I'll never forget one particular incident with the cops. We were out cruising and took up a collection to buy beer. In those days, beer didn't come in small bottles. You had to buy quarts of beer. It was also a lot cheaper this way. So we got a case of quarts. All of a sudden as we're cruising, we see flashing police car lights coming down fast on us. We, of course, thought they were chasing us, so we started to throw the quarts of beer out of the car windows, since we were underage and didn't want to get arrested. I was driving shotgun and just throwing out one bottle after another. We had just finished getting rid of the last bottle when the cops reached us, but to our surprise just passed us up. "*Pendejos*" (idiots), I said to the other guys, "they were after someone else!" We went back to retrieve the bottles, but they were all a broken mess.

My association with the 32nd Street gang came to an end, however, when they attended a dance at St. Joseph's Catholic School and stole the money that students had paid to enter. They jumped the chaperone priest and took the cash. I said to myself, "This is too much for me." So I stopped hanging around with them, and it was just as well. I could have gotten into some serious trouble if I hadn't.

Working

I think what also helped me in staying out of big trouble was that I worked through high school. I had worked in junior high with my stepfather, and I continued to do so in my freshman year. But he never paid me, arguing that since he helped pay my tuition, he didn't have to give me a salary. I disagreed with this and decided to find another job. The only advantage of working at the shoe repair shop was that it was on the corner of Pico and Harvard, almost next door to Bishop Conaty Catholic Girls School, and so I could check out the girls after school.

I missed seeing the girls but got a job at the Swede Blouse Company, the garment factory where my Tía Matilde worked. I worked every afternoon after school and on Saturdays for a few hours and, of course, got paid. It was a sweatshop, and I worked as a shipping clerk's assistant, sweeping the floors, and doing whatever else my supervisor wanted. I called myself a "go-fer," which meant "go for this" and "go for that"—whatever my boss wanted.

Graduation

Finally, in 1952, I graduated from Cathedral. I had my ups and downs at the school but on the whole had a good experience and a good education. I came to admire and respect the brothers, or most of them. At our senior banquet, I felt moved to stand up and say: "I probably have been in more hot water in this school than any of you guys, but yet I wish I was a freshman today. It was fun and I'll miss Cathedral."

We graduated at the Wilshire Ebell Theater on Wilshire Boulevard. Earlier we had a Mass in our gym, officiated by some monsignor. I don't remember a lot about my graduation day except congratulating my classmates and promising to stay in touch, which I mostly didn't. Many of them, especially the Chicanos, were all excited about going into the military. I don't know why, because the Korean War was still going on hot and heavy and a lot of Chicanos were getting killed or wounded. But some of the seniors were gung ho. A few had already in their senior year joined the 40th National Guard, which had its headquarters at the armory in Elysian Park.

"Sal, why don't you join us?" they asked me; "you can get $18 a week for serving."

"That's not bad bread," I responded; "but I can make more money on Saturdays at my job than going with you clowns and marching around."

As soon as they graduated, some of these guys in the National Guard got called up for duty in Korea.

EASTSIDE SUN: "Bodies of Three More ELA [East Los Angeles] Heroes Back from Korean War."[8]

After graduation, I tried to go to some of my class reunions, but I stopped after learning that some of my teachers, such as Brother William, Brother Julian, and Brother Steve, had tragically died in a car accident up in Napa. I cried when I heard this and still cry when I think of them. I'm not afraid to cry. It's part of who I am. I cry when I remember, and I'm thankful that I can still cry. After this, I stopped going to reunions. Besides, my own life was now drastically changing.

TWO

Veterano

After I graduated, I continued to work at the sewing factory. I didn't know what else to do. I also had a feeling that I would soon be drafted, and so I should just stick around until that happened. I signed up for the draft right after graduation. I could have waited a bit to do this, but I figured the sooner they drafted me the sooner I'd get it over with. And sure enough, one day I opened up a letter that read: "Greetings from the President of the United States." This was President Eisenhower and it was August 1953. I didn't have a problem with the draft. Nobody had told me that if I attended college I wouldn't get drafted. I had some thoughts of going to college and, in fact, took the entrance exam at USC. I passed it. One of my aunts lived close to the campus, and I thought if I went there I could live with her and she might even help me financially. But the tuition was way too high. I had also heard about the G.I. Bill and that if you went into the military the government would pay your college. So that was an option. I also wasn't too concerned about being sent to the Korean War since it seemed to be winding down.

Soon I received another letter from my draft board. It informed me that I had to take my physical exam in preparation for going into the military. It also told me to bring with me my "toilet articles." I thought this was funny because I didn't know what toilet articles were. On the assigned day, I went down to the Mode O'Day Building on Washington and Figueroa. It was a garment factory, but the Selective Service or the draft board occupied the bottom floor. It was a Monday or Tuesday morning, and I entered the place with my little shopping bag filled with what I determined were toilet articles. I discovered then that this was going to be the first of two physicals. A month later, I would take another one just to confirm the results of the first. Once in the building, they started to shout orders at you as if you were already in the military. I undressed to my shorts and doctors began to poke me everywhere. I passed both physicals. In fact, after the second one, I took the Pledge of Allegiance to the United States and to the Constitution and I was ready to be shipped out. The Greyhound buses were right there. That's it. Off to basic training, in my case to Fort Ord near Monterey. I remember that we stopped at the Santa Barbara depot for lunch.

All of this happened rather quickly. One day I was a civilian, and the next I was in the army. My parents accepted my being drafted, or they had resigned themselves to it. Being in the military was not foreign to my family. Several cousins had served in World War II, including one, Dofi Anchondo, who got killed. He got blown out of a plane over Romania. He had some education, which allowed him to enter the Army Air Force, which didn't accept you if you didn't have a certain amount of schooling. Dofi became a navigator on a B-24 and flew missions bombing the Romanian fuel storage sites controlled by the Germans. These bombing runs incurred many U.S. casualties. Dofi was one of them. I remember seeing him in his uniform before he left. He looked like a general. I was still only a kid when my aunt gave Dofi a going-away party. She also blessed him before he left. This was the last time we all saw him. The next thing we knew there was a telegram. He was killed. I also remember my other cousin, Johnny Pérez, being drafted. He came back after his basic training in the Marines at Camp Pendleton and brought me some Hershey bars. You couldn't buy Hershey's or any other chocolates like Baby Ruth or, everyone's favorite, O'Henry's because of rationing. It was Johnny who went on to perform heroic deeds in the Pacific. He died a few years ago, and I submitted his name for the new World War II memorial in Washington, D.C. My younger cousin, Hector, joined the Marines a couple of years before I got drafted. He saw service in Korea and was part of General MacArthur's bold behind-the-front-lines landing at Inchon.

So military service was very much a part of my family tradition, which is why my mother, in particular, seemed resigned to my going. My stepfather had been in the Merchant Marines during World War II, and he thought it was a good idea for me to get drafted.

Before I left, I foolishly promised my girlfriend, Annette, that I would return and marry her. This was crazy because I was much too young to think of marriage, but I thought it was part of my machismo to hold on to my girlfriend. I came to regret this, as did she.

Fort Ord

After I arrived at Fort Ord, one of the first things I took was a language test. I had heard that if you passed it, you could be admitted into the Monterey Foreign Language School and work in intelligence. I passed the test in Spanish, but only to find out that the army had no need for Spanish speakers in intelligence. Either they already had too many or they didn't consider Spanish-speaking countries a threat. Now if I could speak Russian that would have been another matter.

Basic training involved sixteen weeks of learning how to be a soldier. But we didn't start this training right away because it was done in cycles for different groups of recruits. When we arrived at the base, the groups ahead of us hadn't completed their cycle, and so we just sat around and waited. While we did, our sergeants in Charley Company, 6th Army Division, thought of things for us to do, such as picking up bricks and taking them from here to there, or cleaning some of the training weapons, such as mortars and 50-caliber machine guns, and other crummy jobs.

I made friends with some guys who were as fun loving as I was and a bit rebellious. We came up with various strategies to avoid doing this work. For example, we tried to disappear before roll call. We'd get up earlier than anybody else, eat, and then we'd get our trench coats and lay them down under the barracks because the ground was always wet. We'd lie there until sunrise so we wouldn't have to do duty. Or we'd find any empty barracks and hide there. One time about eight of us snuck into the heating vents on the ceiling of one of the barracks that were just wide enough to hold us. We'd fall asleep there. With all of this weight, I don't know how the whole thing didn't collapse. We were crazy. We did this a few times, but once got caught. The sergeant came in looking around for some of us to do these Mickey Mouse assignments while we hid in the vents. He didn't see us until one of the clowns moved and a penny from his pocket fell out and hit the floor.

"What the hell are you guys doing up there? Get the hell out!"

He gave it to us. We had to clean machine guns all day.

Still another trick we pulled was to dye our uniforms to look like we had already been to Korea and back. We'd get a lot of Clorox and wash our fatigues with it so that they'd become faded and old looking. This way we could hang out at the PX, the army store and concession stand, and blend in with the guys who had actually just returned. The MPs (military police) wouldn't bother us, thinking we were veterans. I also avoided menial work by telling my sergeant that I didn't know how to swim. You had to know how to swim as part of your training. So instead of doing physical training in the hot sun, a few others and I spent the day in the pool.

These tricks, however, only worked for a little while. As soon as our cycle for light weapons infantry training came we had to fall into line with everyone else. You could hear every morning that first month this funny noise with

Sal Castro at basic training, Fort Ord, California, 1953. Courtesy Sal Castro Personal Collection.

a drum, and you didn't know what it was. We sure found out soon enough. This was our early wake-up call. They got us up and ran the hell out of us. They ran us all over the place. Five, six, eight miles with a full field pack. This got you in shape. You lost your entire baby fat.

Basic training was grueling. You had to crawl about 100 yards, carrying your rifle through mud under barbed wire while being shot at by a machine gun. First they shot blanks, but then when you did it again they shot live ammunition. They shot at a level that if you didn't stand up or get on your knees, you wouldn't get hit. But if you did, you'd get mowed down. It was nerve-racking, especially when they shot real bullets. One guy in the cycle before us got killed doing this. Apparently, they hadn't swept the area before the exercise, so as this guy is crawling he runs into a rattlesnake. Not at first seeing the snake, the kid with his rifle slammed the snake, which started coiling to strike. The kid then saw or heard the snake, panicked, sprang up, and got shot by the machine gun. Besides this dangerous practice, we also threw live hand grenades into big iron tanks.

I had never used a rifle or a gun, so all of this was new to me. But I adjusted as if I were John Wayne. It was exciting, even though I was a terrible shot. This wasn't entirely my fault, and this speaks to the snafus of the army. You have to learn how to calibrate the scope of your M-1 rifle so that you can adjust for distance before firing. But what happened to me was that every time that instruction was taking place, I, for who knows what reason, had to pull down KP (kitchen duty). So I never learned how to calibrate, and if I had gone into combat, I wouldn't have hit anything.

Living with other guys in the barracks also took a lot of getting used to. I had lived with a large family, so I was used to not having a lot of privacy. But some things took more getting used to, such as going to the bathroom using the latrines. This consisted of four wooden toilets with no partition and right next to each other. You were literally cheek-to-cheek with the other fellows. But what else could you do? If you ever saw the movie *No Time for Sergeants,* with Andy Griffith, that was the infamous latrine.

Since my group consisted of whites, Chicanos, and blacks, here and there you had some racial tensions. Some of the *morenos* (blacks) sometimes got into it with the whites. I didn't know what triggered these fights, probably racial slurs. I never got into any fights. Some guys probably thought I was a bad *pachuco* and might pull out a knife on them because Chicanos had that reputation, whether true or not.

Life at Fort Ord was isolated. You rarely left the base, and even if you did like going into Monterey, you didn't have much money to do anything. At least at the camp you could see movies and even drink this awful 3.2 beer that gave you a nasty hangover. The food at the fort was okay. It reminded me of the cafeteria food at Cathedral. Once a week, however, we had to eat canned C rations, which were terrible. Sunday dinner was supposed to be better, but all they gave us were cold cuts.

One form of entertainment was a talent show put on by the recruits. At first I wasn't moved to participate in it, until I realized that none of the performances scheduled had anything to do with Mexicans, even though Chicanos composed a quarter to a third of the company. I, along with two other guys, decided to put on a Mexican singing performance. "There's nothing but *gavacho* [white] stuff," we said. "Let's put on some Mexican stuff." One of these guys was Chicano, while the third was a white Mormon whose Spanish was better than mine, and the other was Chicano. I couldn't sing a damn, but we sang songs such as "Malagueña" and a few others. Somewhere along the line I must have had some inner pride in being Mexican, even though I was a little confused about issues of ethnic identity. We could have sung anything else, but here we went with a guitar and Mexican songs. The Mormon kid actually played the guitar, with me as the lead singer because I knew the words better. It was terrible, but the audience appreciated our effort and gave us a big round of applause. I have a picture of our Mexican Trio with my high school rosary hanging from my back pocket, which I used for good luck in hitting the high notes.

My Army Experience

From Fort Ord, we were all sent to different locations. I was ordered to Fort Jackson, South Carolina. From Jackson, which just served as a reception center, I then went to Fort Benning, Georgia, with the 508th Airborne Regimental Combat Team. Later, I got sent to Fort Campbell, Kentucky. I saw a good deal of the South as I traveled by army convoy. It was green and lush. Others and I kept moving around because after the Korean War they didn't seem to know what to do with us. I thought I might be sent to Germany, only to discover that I didn't have enough time left in the army for this assignment. I never left the states. My final destination in all this moving around was Fort Eustis in Virginia, where I spent the rest of my time in the transportation corps. This is where the trucks, jeeps, diesels, and other vehicles were serviced. I initially directed traffic of convoys going here and everywhere. I did a few other things, such as cleaning the colonel's PT boat, which he used for recreation. I always found it filled with empty liquor bottles. Fortunately, I got out of these assignments and became the company mail clerk because I could type. In addition, I received additional training to become the company projectionist. I showed movies to the guys during maneuvers.

One advantage of being at Fort Eustis was being able to visit places such as Washington, D.C., and Williamsburg. This is where I started to seriously think about going to college. Some of our guys in my unit had been in college and for various reasons had dropped out and were drafted. One had attended Duke and another Ohio State. I thought to myself, "These guys all went to college, but they put on their pants one leg at a time like I do. So if they can go to college so can I." I was also impressed when they put on their Ivy League clothes and visited nearby schools such as William and Mary. I started becoming a little embarrassed because I didn't have preppy clothes. I got to visit that school and loved the college atmosphere, which I had never experienced before. If I hadn't promised to go back to L.A. and marry my girlfriend, I think I might have stayed in the East and gone to a school like William and Mary.

Although I got along pretty well in the army, there did occur one incident that hurt my standing. This was at Fort Eustis. I was in a truck helping to move some trash cans when all of a sudden this captain appears out of nowhere and orders us to stop. Our driver slammed on the brakes, and all of the cans spilled out.

"You goddamn asshole," I yelled at the captain.

I got disciplined by receiving what is called an Article 15, which puts a disciplinary mark in your file. Besides being restricted to base for a couple of weeks, I also never received a promotion from PFC to corporal. But I didn't care; the guy was an asshole.

I also learned a lot about racism during my stint in the army. I'll never forget flying into Atlanta and seeing at the airport and later at the bus depot separate bathrooms for whites and blacks. At each place they had four separate kinds of bathrooms: one for white men, one for white women, one for "colored" men, and one for "colored" women. This was in addition to separate drinking fountains for whites and blacks. This was all brand-new to me. Later at Fort Eustis when I went into town with my black and Puerto Rican soldier friends and went to some Mickey Mouse restaurant, they wouldn't serve them and me because I was with them. We had to go to the back of the place to get our food from a window. We couldn't eat inside. However, when I would go to the same restaurants with my white buddies, including some Italian Americans, we went through the front entrance with no problems. This was all part of the old South. As I traveled through Georgia, I saw nice schools for whites and dilapidated ones for blacks. I witnessed Jim Crow firsthand.

I wasn't immune to direct racism myself. On my flight from Los Angeles to Fort Jackson, I had a layover at the Dallas airport. I had my uniform on, and when you come out of basic training you look like a general. They give you your shooting badge, one for marksmen, all that stuff. Even if you couldn't shoot straight, like me, they still gave you those badges. I also had a blue cord, which meant I was an infantry rifleman. On top of this, I had my army tags with the crossed rifles and the U.S.A. shield, as well as other symbols of my unit. I had a nice hat with a blue trim, which also indicated that I was in the infantry. I looked the part. I go over to the restaurant, and the sons of bitches there wouldn't serve me! They still remembered the Alamo. The waitress came over, gave me a look, and walked away. I thought maybe she had other customers to first attend to. But then a white couple moved in next to me at the counter, and right away she got them water and a menu. It still didn't dawn on me what was happening. Then these other whites came and sat on the other side of me, and she immediately served them. Finally, I realized that I wasn't going to be served. Here I was in a U.S. Army uniform, not the Mexican army, and I still couldn't get a meal in Dallas. What the hell is going on? I was pissed but decided not to make an incident of it. I just left, but I didn't forget it. I thought all of this was chicken shit.

Race affected me in the army also in that I hung around with many of the black soldiers. This may have had to do with race issues, but more directly with music. I liked the same music that they did. I also came to like very much Latino or salsa music that I had more exposure to in the East. Before I went into the army, I actually went to a concert in L.A. at the Zenda Ballroom with the great Tito Puente and the great Tito Rodríguez on the same bill. A year and a half later, in New York City, after I'm in the service, I went to the Palladium with my Puerto Rican *camaradas* (friends) from the army, and who is playing? Tito Puente and Tito Rodríguez! The only difference was that instead of the place being filled with Chicanos, it was now filled with Puerto Ricans. This was *cultura Latina*, but a little different, because the Puerto Rican style of dance was a little different. After the dance, my friends asked me if I wanted to go to have *menudo*.

"Right, get down, let's go have some *menudo*," I replied, already with my mouth watering for the Mexican tripe soup.

But when they brought the *menudo* to me, I said, "Hey, man, this is *cocido* [meat stew]."

It was totally different. It was Puerto Rican *menudo*, but not the kind I had at home. *Menudo* to them was called *mondongo*.

One other incident at Fort Eustis that I'll never forget was my experience with moonshine whiskey. There was this one white kid that literally the first shoes he ever wore were in the army. He used to go on leave sometimes and come back in a pickup truck full of moonshine and sell it. His old man probably made it. We mixed the moonshine with grapefruit or orange juice. It packed quite a wallop. Even worse was when we drank what was called G.I.

gin. This was codeine cough medicine mixed with juice. Talk about a *cruda* (hangover).

During my time in the service, I returned home only twice. I went back after basic training very briefly and then again later when I was stationed at Fort Eustis. I enjoyed being back home and being with my family. On both occasions, I also saw my girlfriend. The second time I formally proposed to her—like a *pendejo* (idiot). I told her that after my discharge we would get married. My parents didn't take this too well. Neither did hers. Both thought that we were too young to get married. They were right. They should have stopped us.

After twenty-two months in the army, I was discharged in 1955. I should have been in for an entire two years, but they let me leave early. At one point, I had considered making the army my career, especially in my fantasy if I could become a helicopter pilot, but this thought didn't last too long, especially when I read the news about possible other military conflicts that might result in the United States going to war again. I left as a PFC because of that Chapter 15 incident. If it hadn't been for that, I might have even become a sergeant. They were passing out stripes all over the place. Several guys that started with me became sergeants. The army liked me. I was a fun-loving guy, but that incident messed me up.

Like everyone else who goes into the service at a young age, I came back changed. You have to, even though I wasn't in combat. You learn to fend for yourself. I got a larger appreciation of the country, its vastness and differences. Most important, I returned with a sense that I could go to college, because of my acquaintances with college boys in the army. I had heard about the G.I. Bill, and I was determined to go to college. That would be the next step in my life.

Coming Home

When I came back to L.A., I needed a job. I wanted to go to college, but I first needed to start working, especially since I was engaged to get married. My future father-in-law stepped in and arranged to get me a job as a busboy at the Sheraton Townhouse Hotel on Wilshire Boulevard. He had worked in the restaurant business and became the business representative with the waiters' union. I had never done such work, and it seemed a comedown for a veteran, but I was getting married, so I had no choice.

The fact was that even though I had gotten engaged while in the service,

I was beginning to have second thoughts about getting married. I had matured in the army, and I wanted to do something with my life, including going back to school. But I felt trapped. I had gotten my discharge in June 1955, and my marriage was scheduled for August.

"Why don't we wait until I start college and then we can get married?" I asked Annette.

"No," she responded, "the invitations are already printed. We can't postpone it. Besides all of my girlfriends are getting married and I don't want to be the one left behind."

"Left behind!" I thought. "You're only nineteen!"

I felt like the train was leaving the station and I had to get on it or rather off it. Her family had already arranged for the big wedding, even though they didn't really care for me. They thought their daughter was marrying down. They were middle-class Mexican Americans, and I was working class. I found out later that they really wanted Annette to go to college and not get married. But they didn't want to disappoint their daughter either. Looking back, I wish her parents had stopped the train and cancelled the wedding. It would have been so much better.

My wedding took place on August 27, 1955. I was twenty-two years old. That morning of the wedding after I put on my rented tuxedo, my mother knelt me down at the door of our house and gave me the *bendición* (blessing). I didn't want to get up. I didn't want to go to the church and get married. I wanted to stay there. My knees didn't want to lift me up. I could see, perhaps in hindsight, that the marriage wasn't going to last. I didn't know how many guys get cold feet like this. I guess a lot.

Somehow I got to the church at Our Lady of Loretto. I had gone to its elementary school for one year, and Annette had graduated from its high school. It was a big wedding with lots of people from both sides of the families. I chose for my best man Richie Solis, a friend of mine from Cathedral, but who had dropped out of school. I helped get him a job before I went into the service. He had wanted to go into the navy, but he had high blood pressure. It didn't help him any in taking his physical when the night before we went out drinking with some other guys. The alcohol only increased his blood pressure more, and he flunked the physical. They told him to return in a month, but the night before we again got drunk and he failed again. He never made it into the navy.

I don't remember much about my wedding. I guess I've blanked it out of my mind. I just know that I felt numb all the way through it. It was just something I had to go through with. It was now for *la familia*. It's what I had to do. It's no fun being at your own wedding with everyone staring at you. It's more fun just going to a wedding, drinking and having a good time.

Annette's parents arranged for the reception at the Bases Hall on Vermont in East Hollywood. What I found ironic was that some of the Mexican waiters and bartenders were some of the same guys that I worked with as busboys at the Sheraton. They were moonlighting. A string orchestra played. We left right after the reception for our honeymoon in Santa Barbara. We spent a couple of days at a beachfront motel and then returned. We couldn't afford a longer trip.

We moved into a little one-bedroom apartment on Sunset Boulevard. Annette and I had made an agreement that after we married I would go on to college although still work. I dreamed of attending Cal (University of California at Berkeley), UCLA, or USC. I think I could have gotten in except for the expenses. I had access to the G.I. Bill, but the problem was that, unlike after World War II, the benefits for veterans in the 1950s, including Korean War vets, had been cut. The money from the feds would not be enough to cover my costs at these schools. I had no choice but to start at L.A. City College.

In the meantime, I had to work. I continued for a period of time as a busboy but knew that I would have to find a better-paying job, or at least a series of better-paying jobs. However, while I still worked at the hotel, I got to talking with many of the Mexican immigrants who also worked there. They didn't have papers and were scared, because beginning in 1954 the immigration people started what they called Operation Wetback, which apprehended thousands of undocumented immigrants in the Southwest and deported them to Mexico. Some of these apprehensions and raids into businesses suspected of employing immigrants had taken place in L.A. I sympathized with them since my own father had been deported in the 1930s. My sympathy was put to the test when they raided our hotel. In a split second, I decided to experience what my fellow workers were going to go through. Even though I was a U.S. citizen and Korean War veteran, I guess I wanted to support them and stand with them.

As agents entered the hotel and panic ensued among the immigrant workers, I quickly put my wallet with my driver's license under the bar. I followed some of the employees who ran and hid in the large kitchen refrigerator. We huddled there for a good half hour and started getting very cold. In a way, we were relieved when they discovered us. They opened the door and started frisking us. They then began to arrest the workers. Before they took me away, our manager showed up and said: "Wait, you can't take him," pointing at me, "he's a U.S. citizen and a veteran."

If he hadn't intervened, I might have gone with the others on the waiting bus to be deported. I was prepared to do that to see what was happening. It would be similar to what happens to Cheech Marin in his 1980s film *Born in East L.A.* My plan—such as it was—was to go through all this and then at the last minute identify myself and try to notify the press of what was happening and how even U.S. citizens were being caught in this dragnet. I guess I saw myself as a rabble-rouser even then. I was still *tapado* (naive) about politics, especially ethnic politics, but I had experienced racism and discrimination, and what was happening to the immigrants was part of this. At the same time, my political vision was clouded then because part of me was self-blaming. In other words, the reason why Mexicans were discriminated against was our fault. It was a sort of weird mind-set in those days.

Following this experience, I decided to move on and get another job. Prior to going into the military, I had worked a bit at Bullock's department store, and I remember admiring the sales guys, who wore nice suits. "I'd like to do that," I thought to myself. So I went to the Bullock's on Wilshire and applied for a job as a salesman. The only thing they could offer me was to work as a stock boy. I was disappointed, but because I needed a job, I took it. I soon realized that there was a caste system at Bullock's and at the other big department stores. Only whites worked as sales clerks. Mexicans were either stock boys or some were allowed to run the elevators. *Chinitos* (Asians) also worked as stock clerks. Finally, blacks labored in the restaurant's kitchen.

The job at Bullock's was only part-time, so I had to look for additional employment. A friend of mine mentioned that there was an opening for a part-time playground director at Echo Park. I applied and got hired. But my two jobs still didn't provide enough since the pay was low. I went back and got my old high school job as a shipping clerk at the sewing factory. During this period, I held down three part-time jobs, which together gave me full-time employment. My wife helped out by working with her father as a clerk at the waiters' union.

All of these jobs increased in importance as the babies started coming. Within a year of our marriage, my first son, Gilbert, was born, and two years later, my second son, Jim, came along. Annette stopped working when she had the babies but went back to work afterward. I didn't want her to work once we had the kids; that's why I had all these jobs—so she could stay at home. But she wanted to work. She wasn't cut out to only stay home.

Sometime after the birth of my first son, we went to a wedding in San

Diego accompanied by my mother-in-law. I'll never forget this, because of the incident of racism that we encountered. Our baby was suffering from colic, so my mother-in-law suggested we stop and get some warm milk for him so he would stop crying. I got off at San Juan Capistrano at a roadside restaurant. As a matter of fact, it's still there. We walked in all dressed up for the wedding with our crying baby. The white hostess took one look at me and said: "The kitchen's closed." What? It's Saturday morning and the place is full? What the hell is going on? I didn't say this because of my mother-in-law and did everything to restrain myself. We left. However, on our return, I insisted on stopping at the same restaurant. I had a couple of beers under my belt and was still angry over what had happened earlier. I walk in and get the same treatment, but this time from a waitress.

"The restaurant is closed," she said, even though it was only about 6 P.M.

"You sons of bitches," I yelled at her, and loud enough for all the people in the place to hear. "My ancestors built that church across the street and founded this town and you sons of bitches won't serve me?"

I got that off my chest and we left. But I never forgot these examples of racism.

Of my different jobs, the one I enjoyed the most was working with the *chavalitos* (little kids) at the playground after they got out of school. It was a form of child care until their working parents could pick them up. This is what I liked to do. "This is fun," I said to myself. I must have talked a lot to myself then. "This isn't work." In fact, I soon left my other jobs as additional playground openings developed with the city. These included being assistant director at Echo Park and Elysian Park. I got another part-time job, this time with L.A. city schools Youth Services as director at Solano Avenue School in Elysian Park near what would later become Dodger Stadium. Still later, I was a playground director at Tenth Street School in downtown L.A.[1] This was as close as you could get to *West Side Story*. It's about three blocks from where the Staples Center is today. Most of the kids at the playgrounds, especially at Tenth Street, were Mexicans, except for a few blacks and whites.

College Man

Despite the fact that I was married, beginning a family, and working my different jobs, I was still determined to go to college. I started at L.A. City College in 1955. I also applied for the G.I. Bill and received $175 a month, which helped a great deal. It paid for my tuition and books. When classes started,

I put in a full day. I took classes in the morning and early afternoon and then went off to work. As I moved to mostly working in the playgrounds, that gave me a bit more stability. I liked going to City College, which was on Vermont Avenue and had been the original campus of UCLA much earlier. Back then it looked like a real college campus. It had ivy-covered walls. A number of films sometimes used it to portray college scenes. The first time I went there, I expected to run into Shirley Temple or Mickey Rooney. It was also predominantly white, with a few Mexicans and blacks. I don't think I ever saw any Asians. It's changed a lot since and become much more urbanized and crowded and composed mostly of Latinos.

When I entered City College, I had thoughts of going into business as a career, so I put down Business Administration and Audio Engineering as my major. I took classes in economics and finance, but also in U.S. history and political science. I soon discovered that the business economics classes bored me, while the history and political science ones fascinated me. I had a wonderful old socialist professor who taught one of my U.S. history classes and who was quite critical of various aspects of this history. I wasn't as aware of it then, but my professor's perspectives were risky at that time, due to McCarthyism and the so-called Red Scare. I learned much from him, including the notion of not just accepting the standard view of our history. I later tried to pass this on to my students. It was around this time as well that I stumbled onto Carey McWilliams's wonderful and pioneering book on Mexican American history, *North from Mexico*.[2] During a break one day at the Echo Park playground, I went into the school's library and was looking around for material on Mexicans. That's when I found McWilliams. I checked it out and read it in a few days. I had never read anything like this that showed that Mexican Americans had a history in the United States and that it went back to the Spanish colonial settlements in the Southwest. This helped me a great deal, as I was struggling then about ethnic identity. Many of McWilliams's themes I would later incorporate also in my teaching. These experiences convinced me to change my major to social sciences.

I felt good about being a college man, but with my family and my jobs, I found it difficult to do my homework and to study for exams. I would do all-nighters and begin studying sometimes at midnight. When I had to take care of the kids to give Annette some time off, I would sometimes wake up with the older child asleep in his high chair and the youngest in my arms. I'd have a bottle in one hand and a book in the other. It was tough. Still, I loved going to school, and especially to the classes I enjoyed the most. Every time I left campus, I regretted it. I wished I could be like some of the other students who could stay and study in the library or engage in sports or extramural activities. I really envied the students who didn't have to work.

The fact was, however, that many other students were in the same boat as I was. I met, for example, a number of vets also on the G.I. Bill at City College. Some of us organized a veterans' fraternity called the Day-O's. We named it after the popular Harry Belafonte song by that title. Even though the school was only a two-year one, it had fraternities and sororities, but they included primarily whites and no vets. We really weren't interested in this kind of college lifestyle, but the reason we started our group was in order to play in an all-fraternity basketball tournament. Some of us were good athletes, and we wanted to compete in intramural basketball but could only do so if we organized a fraternity. The regular fraternities didn't like the idea of a veterans' frat and opposed it. So when they conducted their "rushes," we did the same. We got an old card table and I got a pair of my combat boots, put them on the table, and made a sign, "The Day-O's Sign Up." We signed up a number of vets. These included both whites and some Chicanos. We went on to have a great basketball team and won the fraternity championship. In fact, we played the tournament at the Echo Park School gym where I was the playground director. I'd open it up on Sundays so we could play the games. The president of the college wanted us to become a permanent veterans' fraternity, but we weren't interested in that. We just wanted to play basketball. Besides, the other vets like me were mostly married and had jobs.

Somehow I managed balancing my classes, jobs, and family life and graduated from City College in 1957 with an AA degree. I felt proud of accomplishing this but knew that I needed to continue on to a four-year institution so I could get a BA degree. That was my next step.

From City College, I transferred to L.A. State College, which became Cal State, L.A. It had just started a year before, or it had moved to a new permanent location just above East L.A. It was a new site, but not all of the buildings had been constructed. You still had to attend some classes in Quonset huts. If it rained, you were in trouble. The roads on the campus had not yet been paved, so on a rainy day your car could get stuck in the mud. It was also, like City College, a commuter school. It had no dorms. Everyone drove to their classes and drove right out. I had a jalopy that got me around. I didn't care about the inconveniences; I just felt good about being there.

My wife, however, wasn't too happy. She felt that I should be satisfied with my AA and settle down into a permanent and full-time job. Her parents agreed. They used to call me "college boy." But I didn't care what my in-laws thought; they weren't giving us any financial help anyway. Economically, we still struggled, but I reminded Annette about our prenuptial agreement: we get married, but I go to school. Things were beginning to get tense in our marriage, but we continued. We did move a year later when I became a senior into a rented house with more space for the four of us.

L.A. State, besides being a commuter school, was also a working-class campus. Most students, like myself, and including a number of vets, worked. It was also principally a white campus. There weren't many Mexican Americans or other minorities yet. Today, of course, it is very much a Chicano and minority campus. But not then. In fact, in one of my political science classes, I wrote a paper on Mexicans in the United States. For the paper, I interviewed one of the few Mexican American attorneys in L.A., Carlos Teran, who later became a judge. As part of my interview, I noted the lack of Mexican Americans at L.A. State. I was somewhat taken aback by his reply:

"Listen, there's very few of us who have made it, but that's okay because the fewer of us the greater cut of the pie we get."

I still was a bit *tapado* about politics, but Teran's comments didn't sit too well with me. I decided to interview city councilman Edward Roybal, the only Mexican American on the city council. Roybal wasn't much better. He wasn't any more encouraging about the problems faced by Mexicans. Both of them later changed, to some extent.

Even though I was still somewhat naive about the situation that Mexicans faced in U.S. society, I was beginning to change anyway. One of the motivations for my doing this paper had to do with my increasing work in the playgrounds with the *Chicanitos*. I learned from them about their problems in the schools and reflected back on my own experiences. These kids really disliked school, and yet there were so few of us in the colleges that might help change these conditions. I began to see the extent of the problems. I was also pleased that my professor gave me a pretty good grade. I can't remember whether it was an A or a B.

But that grade was more of an exception. I liked my classes and majored again in social science with a minor in education. However, by now I thought more about teaching, especially in either junior high or high school and thought I could teach at these two levels. I liked most of my classes in history and political science. They stimulated me. But, due to my work schedule, I wasn't able to adequately prepare for exams. I received average grades. I was "gentleman C" and twice was on probation. But I stuck it out.

The classes I didn't particularly care for were the education ones. In these, I began to argue with some of my professors when they referred to Mexican Americans and the schools and I disagreed with them. They saw white, middle-class students as the norm and minority students as deviants. I actually blew up once when one of my professors said in class that the depiction of Latinos—I'm not sure he used this term but it was clear who he was referring to—in the movie *West Side Story*, which had just come out, was accurate. Young Latinos, he believed, such as the Puerto Ricans in the film, tended to be gang members.

"Bullshit." I challenged him right there in class—with the other students stunned that anyone would say this in class, much less take on the professor.

"Bullshit," I repeated. "First of all, *West Side Story* is the figment of the imagination of a white guy. Secondly, if there was a 'West Side Story,' and really dealt with Puerto Ricans, they wouldn't be dancing to that kind of ridiculous music played in the damn movie. What you see is a myth."

This wasn't the first class in education that I spoke out like this. Hell, I wasn't a kid. I was older than most of the other students and a vet to boot. The professors didn't intimidate me. Some of them, to their credit, accepted the criticism, or at least tolerated it. Others, especially the female professors, didn't like it at all. They were more defensive.

I was changing as I got more education and as I became more aware of what was happening in the Mexican American community. For example, my being at L.A. State coincided with the controversy over Chávez Ravine and the coming of the Dodgers to L.A. As part of a deal between the city and the team, the city turned over to the Dodgers a piece of land to build Dodger Stadium close to the downtown area. That was okay, and many welcomed the Dodgers, including myself, because I was a big baseball fan—except that the problem was that a Mexican barrio existed on that property. This was the Palo Verde barrio situated in what was called Chávez Ravine. Not only did Mexicans live there, but also their kids attended Palo Verde Elementary and Solano Avenue Elementary School in that barrio. Other Mexican Americans outside the area began to rally around the Palo Verde community to resist the destruction of their homes and their relocation. I sympathized with this, although I didn't have the time to be part of this protest. But it was an uphill battle against powerful forces. Eventually, the community lost its struggle, and Dodger Stadium was built literally on top of the barrio. Second base is the focal point of where that community existed. I tell students today about this episode and say: "Think about this next time you go to Dodger Stadium and are sitting there enjoying that Dodger Dog."[3]

The other but related thing that was happening that was influencing my consciousness was the construction of all kinds of new freeways, which literally cut apart East L.A. These included the Santa Ana, San Bernardino, Hollywood, and Pomona freeways, which ran through the barrios. What had once been coherent communities now became fragmented. Echo Park was cut up. The freeway went right through one of the playgrounds I used to play in as a kid. Even earlier, my parents had to leave their home on Golden Avenue near downtown when they built the Harbor freeway. These changes and the lack of political power by Mexican Americans to resist them were beginning to motivate me to get involved, somehow.

THREE

Viva Kennedy

Even though I had considered myself *tapado* (naive) in my youth, I was becoming un-*tapado* as time went on. By learning new things at college, by listening to my kids at the playgrounds about their school problems, and by seeing the lack of Mexican American power in the face of urban renewal, I became much more politically conscious. As I underwent these changes, I also recognized that the community needed effective leaders and that I could contribute in this area.

The fact is that I had always been interested in politics, so maybe I wasn't as *tapado* as I thought. Growing up as a kid, I admired FDR and remember listening to his fireside chats on the radio. I remember being saddened by his death. I think I was a Democrat even before I knew it. My uncles born in the United States and who served in World War II and Korea were all Democrats. I began being aware as a Democrat of the Harry Truman campaign in 1948 even though I was only in the eighth grade. And then later, in 1952 while in high school, I avidly followed the national party conventions that nominated for president Adlai Stevenson for the Democrats and General Eisenhower for the Republicans. I was too young to vote that year but did so for the first time in a presidential election in 1956 when I voted for Stevenson. In fact, I watched and listened to Stevenson's acceptance speech at the Democratic convention that year in the hospital where my first son was born. Unfortunately, Stevenson lost again to Eisenhower.

In high school, I began to read some of the newspapers but did so even more after I returned from the service. L.A. had at least three major papers in the 1950s: the *Times*, the *Herald*, and the *Daily News*. I seldom read the *Times* because it was so reactionary. I read the other two, and especially the *Daily News* because it was more liberal. As a kid, I sold these papers.

The Brown Campaign

My big jump into politics, however, came in 1958 while a student at L.A. State. I became involved in Democratic politics, especially as it involved Mexican

Americans. Some Mexican Americans that year organized a campaign in support of the election of Edmund "Pat" Brown for governor. I became part of this effort. I don't recall if we called it the "Viva Brown" campaign or not, but we mobilized on his behalf. Dionicio Morales was a key leader, as was Tony Tijerina. We met in some of the downtown county offices or community agencies in East L.A. I wasn't part of the leadership, but I wanted to help in any way, although my time was restricted because of going to classes and working at the playgrounds. I'd go down to the headquarters and make a few phone calls in Spanish to some of the registered Mexican American voters and encourage them to vote for Brown and the Democratic ticket. I also went into the barrios to register new voters. I found I could reach many Mexican Americans after Sunday Mass. I still think that's a very viable strategy because that's one of the few times that you can contact large numbers of Mexicans.

I also participated in "dirty tricks" in the campaign. Some of us engaged in what was called "snipping." This involved going out and tearing down your opponent's posters and putting up Brown ones. On election day, we tried to jam the Republican headquarters phones. You'd call them up using a public phone and let it ring and just let it keep ringing. This way they couldn't get calls in or out. It was sabotage in a very primitive way, but it worked.

I never personally met Pat Brown at that time, who went on to win the election. But a few years later, after he was no longer governor, I attended a dinner in Beverly Hills that included Brown. I don't recall what the occasion was, but I guess Brown was impressed enough with me that he said, "Goddamn it, why didn't I have you on my staff?" I reminded him that I had been involved in his 1958 campaign. He may have been reflecting on his loss to Ronald Reagan in the 1966 gubernatorial election.

But, in 1958, I wasn't just campaigning for Brown. I and other Mexican Americans were very excited by the one Mexican American candidate running for statewide office, Hank López, a candidate for state treasurer. It would have been a huge political breakthrough if López, an attorney, could have been elected. We had strong hopes, because everything indicated a Democratic year, as voters seemed to be discontented with Republicans all over the country. In fact, López's opponent, the Republican incumbent, was the weakest Republican of all. He was also *muy ruquito* (quite old). But it was not to be, at least for López. Every Democratic candidate for statewide office won except him. It was racism. It was racist on the part of the Democratic Party, which didn't adequately support Hank, and it was racist on the part of many voters who didn't seem to want to vote for a Mexican. This defeat served as a wakeup call for us—*esta feo* (it's ugly), I thought. It indicated the continuing lack of political power and influence by Mexican Americans in California, and elsewhere as well. Mexican American activists expressed concern, anger, and resentment. This reaction led a year or so later to the founding of the Mexican American Political Association (MAPA) by Edward Roybal and Bert Corona. I later joined MAPA as well as LULAC (League of United Latin American Citizens), the oldest Mexican American civil rights organization, but never had the time to be active with them.[1]

Viva Kennedy

We were pissed, but it didn't discourage us from staying politically involved. Two years later, I became even more active in the presidential campaign of Senator John F. Kennedy in California. I joined with other Mexican Americans, not only in California but also throughout the Southwest and Midwest, in the Viva Kennedy movement, an organization that Carlos McCormick, a Chicano from Arizona, had founded. I had been impressed with Kennedy when he almost won the Democratic nomination for vice president in 1956, which I saw on television. When I learned early in 1960 that Mexican Americans led by Carlos McCormick were organizing a specific campaign for Kennedy in the California primary, I knew I wanted to be a part of this. I had seen an article in the paper that an organizing meeting was to be held at an office on First and Soto. I put on a suit and tie and showed up ready to enlist. I think I was the youngest guy there and certainly the best dressed. This was my senior year at L.A. State. This political involvement, however, almost cost me my playground job because I couldn't go to work some evenings when we kept the playground open for kids, because of attending Kennedy meetings. Fortunately, my supervisor turned out to be a Kennedy supporter and covered for me.

Since I attended L.A. State, the Viva Kennedy campaign, which operated under the regular statewide Kennedy operation headed by Jess "Big Daddy" Unruh, assigned me to mobilize support on the campus. He gave me the impressive but lengthy title of Southern California chairman for Students for Viva Kennedy. Since there weren't many Chicanos yet on campus, I promoted Kennedy among all the students. I downplayed the Viva Kennedy stuff. I ran into a particular problem, however, when I discovered that the campus administration didn't permit political posters to be displayed on school grounds. You could have speakers, but no posters. I tried to get around that by using the student council elections that spring to my benefit. I encouraged a *gavachito* (white guy) with the name of Kennedy to run for student body president. This way I could get Kennedy posters on the campus under the guise that they were in support of the student campaign. Unfortunately, this guy turned me down. He would have been a perfect candidate, with red hair and freckles—almost a Kennedy look-alike. But he wouldn't run.

I was able to arrange, however, a speech in favor of Kennedy by Senator Dennis Chávez of New Mexico, the lone Hispanic or Mexican American senator in the U.S. Congress at that time. I had recruited about three other Mexican Americans on campus to work with me, but I was the head *vato* (dude). When we heard that Chávez would be in L.A. campaigning for Kennedy, I contacted Unruh's office and told him we could organize a talk at L.A. State. They agreed. I got around the ban on political posters by giving Chávez's talk some general title that didn't suggest a pro-Kennedy speech. I got away with this. I also got the chair of the political science department to be the principal sponsor of the talk in order to give it more academic legitimacy. Other professors, after I talked with them, agreed to encourage their classes to attend. We had about 400 people at the presentation in one of the campus theaters.

The day of the talk, I and the other Chicano students escorted Chávez on to the campus. He was *muy viejito* then *y no podía ver muy bien* (he was quite old and couldn't see very well). Because of who we were, he got the impression that he would be addressing a predominantly Mexican American audience. I didn't know this as we walked into the auditorium. But I soon realized it when he started to talk: "I'm very honored to be here and to see so many Mexican Americans in attendance. We, as Mexican Americans, have a wonderful opportunity in supporting the candidacy of John Kennedy for President of the United States."

I couldn't believe it—*que chingada* (damn it). Because his eyesight was so bad, Chávez actually believed the place was jam-packed with Chicanos! I think I and the three other students were the only Chicanos there. But, to my relief, the audience was very supportive and receptive to Chávez's speech. He never realized the mistake and I didn't have the nerve to tell him—*pobrecito* (poor guy).

Chávez's speech and the strong turnout for it earned me some brownie points with the Viva Kennedy crowd, now led at the top by city councilman Roybal. We felt even better when Kennedy won the California primary and went on to receive the Democratic Party nomination for president that summer. The Democrats held their convention in L.A., but I didn't attend it or do much work around it. I was also too busy working and being with my family.

I did go over to the Biltmore Hotel, Kennedy headquarters, to pick up some souvenirs.

The fact was that my political work had put some stress on my marriage. My wife did not support what I was doing and felt I was neglecting my family. Even though she and her parents were pro-Kennedy, she thought I was crazy. We argued about this, but I couldn't seem to convince her that what I was doing was important—at least important to me—and that I was not neglecting her or the kids. I worked my tail off for them. But there was no meeting of the minds, and as a concession I curtailed working on the campaign until the fall.

Still, we in the Viva Kennedy movement celebrated the senator's victory, but we also knew that we couldn't rest on our laurels. The real campaign now loomed ahead, as did election day in November. We had to get the vote out.

That fall we geared up again. We pretty much did the same thing we did for the primary: registering voters, putting up posters, going house to house handing out fliers, radio spots, and whatever else we could do to motivate Mexican Americans to vote. Actually, they didn't need much motivation, because many, as we observed in the primary, were becoming devoted to JFK. Mexican Americans were further impressed to vote for Kennedy because of the efforts of his wife, Jacqueline Kennedy, to specifically reach out to us. She didn't visit East L.A., but she cut radio ads in Spanish that Mexican stations in L.A. and elsewhere broadcast. I thought her Spanish was pretty good, even though it seemed to have a French accent.

Of course, we realized that motivation would not be enough. We had to organize to get people to the polls. We also continued, or at least I did, snipping or dirty tricks. This is interesting and ironic because we did this against the master of dirty tricks, Richard Nixon, the vice president and Kennedy's opponent. We pulled down Nixon posters and tried to jam his L.A. headquarters phones. Every time I called one of those lines, there was a busy signal, so somebody else was doing the job. The Nixon people retaliated by doing some of these things to us as well.

This election, of course, was highlighted by the first-ever TV debates. I, along with millions, watched them. Being a Kennedy supporter, I naturally was biased and thought he won. But others believed that on points Nixon won, especially if you listened to the debates on radio. But image was the key, and there was no contest between the handsome and youthful-looking JFK and Nixon with his five o'clock shadow.

Because of my work during the primary, they gave me a responsible role in the biggest effort on behalf of Kennedy during his visit to L.A., just prior to the election. As part of the day's events, Kennedy would attend a luncheon at the Olvera Street plaza, to be attended by Mexican American leaders as well as various other dignitaries such as Governor Brown. My job was to ensure that we had the biggest crowd possible there. Kennedy was not scheduled to speak, but we wanted to impress him and the media with a large Mexican turnout.

Prior to that day, those of us at the Viva Kennedy campaign made announcements all over the place. We did this through posters, radio spots, and just cruising through East L.A. and with a sound system calling people's attention to the event: "*Vengán a recibir al Señador Kennedy.* [Come and meet the candidate, Senator Kennedy.]"

Our efforts added to the emotional response by Mexican Americans to Kennedy. They especially embraced him due to his Catholicism, which made them identify with him due to their own strong Catholic background. They saw in him the same underdog quality that they themselves embodied. I'll never forget how Kennedy took on the allegations that his religion would interfere with his role as president because, so the charges went, his first loyalty might be to the pope. He blew the issue out of the water when he said something to the effect that "I did not lose my right to be president the day I was baptized." I'll never forget that nor did many other Mexican American Catholics.

Those old enough to remember also saw in Kennedy the same charisma of FDR, whom many Mexican Americans had strongly supported. They felt, as did other minorities and working people during the Depression, that Roosevelt felt their pain. They believed that JFK did also. For all of these reasons, and others, we had no trouble selling Kennedy in the barrios.

Kennedy's schedule that day was hectic. After arriving at the L.A. airport early in the morning, he spoke at the Beverly Hilton Hotel, then at the University of Southern California. I attended that rally and passed out Viva Kennedy buttons and posters. He then went to another rally, this time in the garment district. From there his motorcade took him into Olvera Street, where I, along with many other Mexican Americans, waited for him.[2]

I and my cousin, Sam Frias, also a college student, couldn't believe the response. Olvera Street, the birthplace of Mexican L.A., was packed with Mexicans. It was wall-to-wall or shoulder-to-shoulder *mexicanos*. I had never seen so many people in the plaza. You couldn't move. In fact, the crowds for Kennedy that morning all the way from the airport had been unbelievable.

My special role at the luncheon was to make sure that Kennedy and his people got into the Casa Avila, an old adobe building, where the lunch was to be held. Many of the invitees were already inside, but we had to escort Kennedy into the structure. I was all decked out that day. I may have been the only brown face with the then-popular Ivy League suit on. I also had a huge Kennedy button on and some other badges indicating that I was a campaign worker. To my surprise and honor, Kennedy shook my hand that day. He came my way as he exited his car and there I was with my Ivy League suit and my Kennedy button.

"Thank you very much," he said to me. "Good to see you," as he shook my hand.

I don't think I said anything to him. I was probably stunned. JFK was like a rock star. You were just in awe.

As Kennedy lunched inside, the crowd remained outside and continued to swell.

"Kennedy, Kennedy," they began to shout.

Soon they were pressing on the building itself and even shaking it. I don't know how security allowed them, but they did.

"Kennedy, Kennedy," they continued as they moved in.

The Casa Avila was this rickety oldest adobe in L.A. that had not been refurbished. It must have been almost 200 years old. I tried to calm the crowd down by telling them in both English and Spanish that they could see and hear Senator Kennedy that evening at a rally at East L.A. College. But this didn't do any good. They wanted him to come out and address them. As they pressed on the building, the old adobe started to rock as if experiencing a mild earthquake.

"Kennedy, Kennedy," the crowd yelled even louder.

A campaign aide poked his head out and asked me: "What the hell is going on?"

"They want him to come out and say a few words."

"Tell them that he'll be at East L.A. College later."

"No, they want him right now."

To my further surprise, the next thing I see is Kennedy coming to the porch. As he did, the several thousand outside clapped and raised their voices again.

"Kennedy, Kennedy," and this time you also heard, "Viva Kennedy! Viva Kennedy!"

And so Kennedy raised his arms and hands out to quiet them, and when they did so, he says in a loud voice, "*Viver!*"

That's all he said: "*Viver!*"

What he meant to say, of course, was "*Viva!*" but with his New England accent it came out "*Viver!*"

The people went wild. As far as they were concerned, he had spoken Spanish to them. I couldn't believe that I was in the middle of all this. I'll never forget it. I met President Clinton years later in the 1990s, and I guess it was just as rewarding, but meeting and shaking hands with President Kennedy remains one of the most memorable events of my life.

LOS ANGELES TIMES: "200,000 Hail Kennedy on Downtown Route"
"Sen Kennedy disembarked at Olvera Street, symbolic heart of the city's huge Mexican-American colony, and had lunch in the Casa Avila, built in 1818 and said to be the oldest building in Los Angeles.
"Kennedy lunched on a combination Mexican plate and a cola drink, then took a brief rest before getting back in his car."[3]

That day I had also tried to get Kennedy to speak at L.A. State. I approached Roybal about it.

"We can get a huge student turnout there," I enthusiastically told Roybal a couple of weeks prior to the senator's visit.

"That sounds good," he said. "Let me check it with Jessie. I'll call him right now."

Jessie, of course, was Big Daddy Unruh, who was the most powerful figure in Democratic Party circles in California and the head of Kennedy's campaign there. I heard Roybal tell Unruh about my idea, although he didn't mention me by name. But then as Big Daddy reacted, all I heard was Roybal in a low voice say: "Yes, Jessie. No, Jessie. You're right, Jessie. No."

Then he hung up and told me that Unruh didn't think it was a good idea. I didn't argue back, but this only reinforced for me how weak we as Mexican Americans were still politically. We weren't calling the shots; others were. Here was Roybal, the head of the Viva Kennedy campaign, and he couldn't stand up to Unruh.

INSTEAD OF GOING to L.A. State after the lunch, Kennedy went to the South Bay Shopping Center in Redondo Beach. Unruh approved this venue.

I didn't have time to dwell on this because I had to help out with the big rally that evening in the football stadium at East L.A. College scheduled for 7 P.M.[4] The fact that so much of Kennedy's activities that day had a linkage with Mexican Americans, on the other hand, brought to my attention the developing political consciousness of Mexican Americans, especially in national politics, and the latent power involved. The rally wasn't just aimed at

Mexicans, but the fact that it would take place in East L.A. and at a mostly Mexican American campus was significant.

Days prior to the rally, as I had done for the Olvera Street event, I went all over the barrios putting up posters, handing out fliers, and speaking on Spanish-language radio. A guy named Chico Sesma had a very prominent show, and I was able to get on it. My Spanish was okay. Once I started warming up it flowed out. I probably made a few grammatical errors, but I got my points across. I also organized a dance/fund-raiser for the Viva Kennedy campaign and to publicize the East L.A. College rally. Some of the unions helped me in this and let me use one of their halls on South Main Street for the dance. Some of the musicians also helped. Two popular bands, Eddie Cano's and Manny López's, provided the music free. We raised several hundred dollars.

We in the Viva Kennedy group did not plan the college event, but we helped out. Besides my promotional efforts, I was able to arrange for the L.A. State cheerleaders to perform at the rally. We had another incredible turnout. The stadium seated about 20,000, and some 25,000 packed themselves into the seats, with an additional 10 to 15,000 outside the stadium listening to loudspeakers.[5]

My main job that evening was helping out with security. Besides my Ivy League suit and my big Kennedy button, I also wore a variety of security badges so I could get on the field and get close to the speakers' platform. Upon arriving, I first positioned myself there, and, lo and behold, I met Frank Sinatra. He was being escorted up to the platform. He, of course, didn't know who I was, but I had all these badges, so he figured I must be somebody heavy.

"Hi, Frank," I said, as I instantly recognized him. He was already then an icon as a singer and movie star. Growing up in the 1940s, I knew that Sinatra had wide appeal among second-generation Mexican Americans, who loved his singing. So did I.

Sinatra looked at me and shook my hand. I noticed that he was escorting Janet Leigh, a beautiful and popular movie star who appeared in Alfred Hitchcock's movie *Psycho*.

Kennedy's motorcade then came into the stadium and drove around the track. That's when I first saw presidential power. You see all these people stand up and clap and shout support for Kennedy. You see power—people power—being transferred to the candidate. I was also impressed with the number of Mexican Americans there. While many others also attended, I could see a lot of brown faces. Despite the fact that Kennedy was not scheduled to speak until 9 P.M., the crowd waited patiently and with much enthusiasm.

A number of dignitaries spoke first. I don't remember who they were now, but I do recall Adlai Stevenson introducing Kennedy. I didn't meet Stevenson and didn't have contact with Kennedy that evening. They, as the main speakers, the heavies, came in from the back of the platform while I was at the front. I don't remember much about Kennedy's speech. I was also too busy moving around making sure that the exits would be open so his motorcade could take off right away. Another thing some others and I were trying to do was to get the people who had not been able to enter the stadium to break through a fence at one open area and rush onto the field. The platform was at the other end. We thought that this would be a big publicity stunt and with the media in attendance show the enthusiasm of *la gente* (the people), because these were mostly Mexican Americans for Kennedy. But we failed in our efforts. The people shied away from doing this. They thought they might get arrested. As I look back on this, I find it amazing that we thought we could pull this stunt off. Security in those days, even for a presidential candidate, didn't seem to be that strong.

But despite this disappointment, I felt good, not only about the rally but of the entire day. It proved to be a huge success, and I thought we in the Viva Kennedy campaign had made it a success.

Election Day

But we couldn't afford to just rely on the enthusiasm generated by Kennedy's visit. We had to be prepared for anything. I picked up rumors, for example, that the Nixon people were going to station themselves outside of some of the East L.A. precincts on election day and ask people for their IDs. They were going to hassle voters about their citizenship. To counter this, if true, I personally recruited a number of sympathetic L.A. State professors to serve as poll watchers to prevent this. Many actually did so, and we didn't have any problems. That day we also provided rides for anyone who needed them to vote.

Election day saw a large Mexican American turnout. People were really excited about Kennedy. We again felt good about our efforts. After the polls closed, there wasn't much left to do, but I couldn't just go home. Instead, I went to the Viva Kennedy headquarters. When I got there, they were already preparing to go to a big victory party at the Biltmore Hotel, although the results were still coming in. From what I picked up, the election was going to be close. As the night wore on and we decided to stay and watch the TV coverage, it wasn't clear who the winner might be. It didn't look like Kennedy was going to win California. By then, I was quite tired. I had been going since five that morning. Sometime before I went home because I had to go to school and work the next day, the phone rang. It must have been around 10 P.M. I was sitting next to it and picked it up.

"Hello, Viva Kennedy headquarters."

"Yes, this is Jack Kennedy and I'm just calling to thank you and the others for your hard work. I look forward to working with all of you after we take office."

I couldn't believe it. It was JFK. I could distinguish his accent—*que la fregada* (damn it)! All I could think to say was "thank you."

But, before I said anything else, I cupped the receiver and called out, "It's Kennedy; it's Kennedy."

Someone took the phone from me. I don't remember who. I couldn't hear Kennedy, but I learned after he hung up that he wanted from us a list of Mexican Americans that he might consider for his administration. He hadn't even yet won, but he was already planning ahead. Later, after his victory, Roybal and others put together a list and submitted it to Kennedy's advisors. But, sad to say, there was a lot of division about such recommendations and a lot of back stabbing among different Mexican American groups. Eventually, the Kennedy people just threw their hands up and not many Mexican Americans were appointed.[6] Some of the same problems arose much later in the Clinton administration. I don't know and never will if my name was on that list to Kennedy. In all of the exhilaration of the campaign, the thought struck me that it would be fascinating to work in a new Kennedy administration. On the other hand, I certainly wasn't the kind of guy who would lobby for such a thing. I figured that if I worked hard at whatever I did that hopefully some people would appreciate it.

I didn't know that Kennedy had won until the next morning. It was the closest presidential election in history. I felt elated. I kept all of my Kennedy signs and buttons and still have them. That day when I went to work in the playground, the principal of the school, who was also my supervisor, saw me with a Kennedy poster in my car. He was an old socialist and a staunch Democrat.

"Let me have that poster," he said.

"Sure," I replied. I couldn't refuse him because he had let me have time off from my work to do my political activity. He took that poster and went into the supply room, found an old frame, and put the poster into it. He then hung it and put it on the wall next to the main office entrance so that all his teachers and staff could see it. It's possible that he did this to harass some of his teachers who had voted for Nixon.

It was a happy day for all of us who had supported Kennedy. He didn't win California, but that didn't dampen our spirits. Our job had been to get Mexican Americans to vote for JFK, and we did this. We did our part, and we were proud of this.

Kennedy's Legacy

We saw the election of John Kennedy as an important step forward for Mexican Americans. It helped to empower us, even though his administration did not do much concretely for Mexican Americans. Younger Mexican Americans such as myself identified with JFK. He was young and more of our generation. His idealism, or what we took as his idealism, affected us and laid the basis for our further political involvement. To that extent, we have him to thank. Although I came to understand his flaws and limitations, that was not the case in the barrios. Kennedy became a kind of popular saint. You could go into many East L.A. homes and on the *altarcitos* (home altars) you'd find, besides images of the Sacred Heart and Our Lady of Guadalupe, a picture of JFK. That's why his assassination in 1963 was felt so strongly by Mexican Americans. The heart went out in the community.

FOUR

Mr. Castro

Politics was becoming important to me, but I still had school to contend with, besides earning a living for my family. By my senior year (1960–61), I discovered that I wanted to be a teacher. When I entered L.A. State, I thought I might want to be one, but I wasn't fully decided. However, after working more with the kids at the playground, I realized that I enjoyed being with young people and that I could connect with them. They also educated me to their problems in the schools, and I thought if I became a teacher, I could help turn things around. With this goal in mind, I shifted my major to education and took more courses in this area.

My first step in becoming a teacher was when I graduated from L.A. State and received my BA, in 1961. Part of me felt happy and proud. I was the first in my family to receive a college degree. But another part of me saw it in practical terms. College for me was a job. I completed this task—getting my BA—as part of my job. But I still had to keep going. I had to get my teaching credential. For the moment, however, I allowed myself to enjoy the graduation ceremony, which took place in the Hollywood Bowl. Several thousand and I graduated that spring day. My mother joined my wife and my kids there. My mother, of course, was especially proud of me. I'm sure back in the days when she was a single mom that she never dreamed that her son would be a college graduate. I can only imagine what went through her mind that day. If it hadn't been for her concern for my later education, as well as my aunt's concern for my early education in Mazatlán, I'm not sure I would have ever gone to college.

Before I graduated, I applied to the teaching credential program in the School of Education at L.A. State and got admitted. It involved a two-year program, including student teaching. My hope, of course, was to teach in the East L.A. public schools, where the greatest need existed and where few Mexican American teachers were to be found. In these two years, besides classes in educational theory and practicum, I was also able to take some graduate classes in history and political science, since I wanted to be a U.S. history and government high school teacher. I never seriously considered becom-

Sal Castro graduation from Los Angeles State College, 1961. Courtesy Sal Castro Personal Collection.

ing an elementary teacher. I didn't feel I was cut out to work with *chavalitos* (little kids) at that level. At the Tenth Street playground, where I worked, I had more contact with middle school and high school students and felt I could deal better with kids at that age. In fact, in those two years of working on my credential, I found that my preparation for teaching was much more influenced by my work with the playground kids. They taught me more than my professors about conditions in the schools, and they gave me the experience with Chicano students that the School of Education didn't.

On the contrary, my education professors continued to perpetuate the ignorance and stereotypes about Mexican Americans that I had confronted as an undergraduate. They knew so little or nothing about Mexican kids, and yet already they represented a big and growing chunk of the school-age population in the L.A. school district. My professors were way off in approaches to the Chicanos. They didn't know what made them tick. They really didn't. They perpetuated the bullshit that Chicanos were "negative different" rather than "positive different." For them, Mexican American culture hindered Chicanos. They expressed *pendejadas* (stupidities), such as that Chicanos dressed as *pachucos* or *cholos* (street dudes), because that was expressive of Mexican American culture! Where the hell they got that, I don't know. You still hear this kind of nonsense. These were terrible ideas and got away from the fault of the schools themselves in failing to adequately teach Mexicans. Instead, as they had for years, they blamed the Mexican American students, their parents, and their culture for the high drop-out rates, the low reading scores, and for not going on to college. They made the victims into the villains.

I wanted to change all of that. I was a specialist in Mexican kids. I felt that I knew the Mexican kid. I was a Mexican kid myself. I knew their problems.

One of the few opportunities I had in my credential program to really and more adequately study about Mexican Americans and education occurred when I had to produce a lengthy research paper, almost like an MA thesis. I decided to do a comparative paper on Mexican Americans students and Mexican immigrant students. I wanted to find out, and I already had a hunch, which group did better in school. On the surface, one would think U.S.-born students would do better than those born and partially raised in Mexico. I focused on ninth graders. I took on a big task and did interviews in five schools with over 200 kids. Some of the schools like Belvedere and Hollenbeck were on the Eastside, but others were in West L.A. near downtown, which by now had a good number of Mexicans. I didn't have any problems during the interviews or at looking at other school materials. I explained to each of the principals what my research topic was, and they all cooperated. I asked for them to select their top Mexican-origin students for me to interview. I used the term "Mexican American." At this time we didn't use the term "Hispanic" or, as I kiddingly say, "lowspanic."

Besides interviewing the kids, I also got access to their grades. None of the principals balked at this. The ones who gave me some trouble at these schools were some of the few Mexican American teachers there. They were very *tapados*.

"What are you doing here?" they asked me.

They acted with suspicion, as if I were blowing their covers. They didn't want to identify as Mexicans. None of them said, "Hey man, that's a great study." It only reinforced for me the tremendous need for teachers, especially Chicanos, who could identify with their students and really encourage them.

After conducting my research, I discovered that the students born and raised in part in Mexico were performing better in school than the U.S.-

born. This had been my hunch. This had to do, I concluded, with the fact that Mexican-born students came to this country already having had successful learning experiences in their schools, and this helped them do better, despite the language difference. In fact, once they mastered English, they skyrocketed. Second, I proposed that another reason for their success and even leadership, because many of them became student council members, had to do with the fact that having grown up in Mexico, they possessed a strong self-worth and identity as Mexicans. They didn't seem to have the same identity problems and insecurities that the U.S.-born Chicanos possessed that seemed to affect their school work. This particular finding I would take to heart when I began teaching, and I worked to make Chicano students feel good about themselves and their culture by introducing Mexican and Mexican American history into my teaching. That's the cornerstone of early educational success.

I felt proud about this research paper when I presented it to my credentials committee as part of my program. One professor, more liberal, thought it was great, while another, more conservative, didn't think it was all that hot. Still, I got a very good grade. Had I been in an MA program, this would have probably been accepted as my thesis. I wish I had tried to publish it back then. It might have had some impact. I don't even have it anymore. I had stored it, along with other papers, in my mother's garage, but the damn thing burned down along with my papers. We didn't have computers then to better store material. I didn't get an MA but eventually did get my teaching credential.

Student Teaching

But before getting the credential, you had to do practice teaching. They assigned me to Belmont High School, close to the downtown area, for this. Belmont was a huge school, with about 60 percent Mexican American students. A big Japanese American contingent and some blacks and whites rounded out the rest. The principal assigned me to teach a junior U.S. history class that I preferred. I taught only this one class and had a good experience and thought I did a pretty good job, as did the principal. I approached the class with a lot of confidence. I wasn't a spring chicken. I was almost thirty years old and a veteran. In addition, I had already a few years of working with kids in the playgrounds and was used to being around them. That's why I always recommend to college students who are thinking about teaching to start being with kids as soon as possible, such as tutoring or coaching, whatever. I walked into that classroom as if I owned it and almost immediately had the kids on my side. The worst thing is for a new teacher to enter a class shy, retiring, and scared. The kids will immediately pick up on this and make life miserable for you.

Family Troubles and Divorce

I felt good about my student teaching and my work on my credential, but at home things weren't so good. My relationship with Annette was going downhill. I had always feared this, from the moment I got married. Besides the fact that we had different interests, my school and job schedule, in addition to getting involved in politics, didn't help. My playground job at the Tenth Street playground, which I maintained, since this was the only salary I had in addition to the G.I. Bill, kept me out until 9 P.M. each weekday, in addition to a chunk of Saturday. All of these activities kept me away from home and my family a lot. For example, I never watched television during this period. People talk about the Golden Age of TV, but I knew nothing of this. I never saw popular shows such as *Peter Gunn* or *Gun Smoke*, which was all the rage among my peers. Annette also had her own set of friends that she socialized with that didn't include me. We weren't growing together. But it wasn't just my schedule or her's. I wasn't a good boy. I guess my spiritual advisers were Roman Polanski and Woody Allen. I was no *santo*. After seven years of marriage, she initiated the divorce. I didn't necessarily blame her.

Of course, the complication of our divorce, as in many other cases, involved our two boys. Despite my problems as a husband, I felt that I was a good provider and a good parent. In fact, I tried to keep the marriage together because of the kids. I came from a divorced family myself and knew how hard it was on children. I tried to spend as much time as I could with my kids, but it was hard with all of the things I was doing. One boy joined the Cub Scouts, and I went with him to some of these activities. I, along with Annette, attended PTA meetings. Whatever my sons needed, I was there. The little time I had I was with them. I even used to take them to the playground sometimes with me, especially during the summers. In turn, they were very attached to me. I also, along with Annette, tried to give them the best education we could. They started in public schools, but then Annette wanted to transfer them to a Catholic school, St. Francis on Sunset and Micheltorena. I preferred that they go to public schools, because by then I was a big believer in public education. But Annette differed, and I went along with it, even though this further strained our expenses. Despite our differences, Annette and I tried to maintain a sense of family with our kids. We raised them as Catholics, baptizing them, having them make their First Communions, and taking them to Mass each Sunday. Actually, Annette took them most of the time, but periodically I joined them.

Still, despite all of this, Annette felt we couldn't go on and filed for divorce. I didn't contest it. I accepted it, including her having custody of the children. This pained me because it meant I would only see them every other weekend and vacations, and this was hard for me and for them. In addition, I agreed to pay child support, which with my limited income at first was really hard. I could barely make the payments until I started teaching. At the divorce proceedings, I expressed concerns to the judge about the amount of child support he mandated. "But, I'm only a college student," I said.

"That's too bad," he came back; "get a job."

I took that as a challenge, and when I started teaching I actually doubled the child support that I gave to Annette. I did this even though Annette was working first as an Avon saleslady and then as a district manager for the company. Our divorce became final in 1962. We reconciled two years later, but some of the same difficulties in our relationship continued and we permanently divorced in 1967.

In all of this, my mother and stepfather expressed reservations, even though both of them had been divorced in their other marriages. But they shared concerns about their grandchildren. On the other hand, Annette's parents didn't seem as concerned. They had always looked down upon me and perhaps thought their daughter could still find someone better. I was just a college boy to them and not a man of means. I obviously didn't have a good relationship with my in-laws, but, just like the Navajos, you go with the woman's family. During our marriage, I spent more time with them, to my regret, than I did with my mother. That hurt me. The one good thing about my divorce was that I wouldn't have much to do with my in-laws.

My First Teaching Job

Fortunately for my financial pressures as well as for my teaching experience, I started my first regular teaching assignment in the spring of 1963. Washington Junior High in the Pasadena school district needed, in the middle of the school year, a replacement teacher. They inquired at the School of Education at L.A. State if they could recommend someone. To my surprise, they recommended me. Since I had done a good job at Belmont, my professors had confidence in me. "Sal's a cracker jack teacher," they told the principal at Washington Junior High. I, of course, was delighted. I wanted to get my feet wet and start regular teaching. I hadn't quite finished my credential program, so the Pasadena school district gave me an emergency credential. I didn't have much time to prepare, but I jumped right in.

Washington Junior High was not a ghetto school per se, but it was a predominantly minority one. *Morenitos* (blacks) composed about 98 percent of the student body, with a few Asians, Mexicans, and whites. It wasn't a ghetto school, in the sense that the black kids came from working-class and some middle-class families. It represented a stable community, unlike most ghetto or so-called inner city schools, with unstable and broken families, poverty, and lack of employment. I also didn't have major discipline problems, although the influence of the black civil rights movement seemed to be emboldening, and rightfully so, some of the black students. The mostly white teaching staff and white principal didn't seem to know how to handle this.

Although I was more prepared to teach history and social science, they gave me a rather mixed schedule of classes. I had to teach one U.S. history class, two math classes, a business class, and a geography one. I had to really work to prepare these different classes each night. I also found it difficult because of beginning at mid-year, after the kids had gotten used to another teacher. On top of that, because I was a replacement, I didn't have my own room. I shuttled from room to room to teach my classes, rather than having a room of my own with the students coming to me. That meant I had to drag along the various books and materials I needed from class to class. But I didn't complain about this. In fact, I think this actually made me a better teacher because it forced me to adjust and improvise my schedule. Today I hear the teachers' unions insist that all new teachers have their own rooms. Bullshit! If you don't have your own room that's the way it goes. You teach from a cart! You survive better. You become more creative that way than if you're spoon-fed. If you want to be a teacher—a good teacher—you teach under any and all circumstances. I can be a good teacher out in the fields if I have to! I'm a great believer in that. But young teachers today say, "No, I can't do that." *Que la fregada* (that's nonsense).

I think because of my attitude that I did a good job. Again, I went in with a lot of confidence. The kids, despite the fact that I wasn't black, took to me right away. The *morenitos* gravitated to me. The term *morenito* was widely used by Mexican Americans to refer to blacks, but without any derogatory implication. I became a very popular teacher, even considering that they gave me one classroom where they send the problem kids. They called it the "opportunity room." I never understood why they called it this. In my case, the term perhaps applied because I gave these students the opportunity to show that they could do well in school and succeed. I got them to work and to do well. I didn't have a magic wand. I just listened to them, understood their problems, and worked hard to make them feel good about themselves. A kid can't succeed in school if he/she thinks the teacher looks down on them and has no confidence in them. You don't have to be a genius to understand this.

Some of these kids after I left the school came and visited me at the Tenth Street playground to show their appreciation. In fact, the principal and the few black teachers wanted me to stay on permanently. Some of these black teachers were pretty radical, and I made friends with them.

"We need you here," the principal told me. "You can help with our problems."

"I wish I could help you," I told both him and the teachers, "but I have to go to where I can help my own people. My fight is in the barrios in East L.A. You guys take care of business here. The same problems like dropouts exist there. There's few Chicano teachers in the Eastside schools, and if I can get a job there, that's where I need to be."

As I began my teaching career, I couldn't help but also be influenced by the developing black civil rights movement. I, like other Americans, had seen on TV and had read about the marches, sit-ins, and other protests, including the famous march on Washington in 1963, where Dr. Martin Luther King gave his incredible "I Have a Dream" speech. Also, I had not only read some of the speeches of Malcolm X, but I had experienced racism toward blacks when I was stationed in the army in the South. The black civil rights movement inspired me as my own political consciousness developed. But it, at the same time, frustrated me, because I realized, or was beginning to realize, how much further behind Mexican Americans were in comparison to blacks. The more the *morenitos* yelled and raised hell, the further behind we fell on civil rights and educational issues as the nation only focused on blacks. Yet the fact was that the conditions of Mexican Americans were equally as bad or in some cases worse. Our educational situation was terrible. Kids dropped out of school every day. Few Chicanos attended college. By 1964, the Fair Employment Practices Commission (FEPC) reported that less than 1 percent of Mexican American college-age students in California went to college.[1] A professor of education at Occidental College, Paul Sheldon, had pointed this out even before, in a 1959 study on the Los Angeles city schools. The study revealed some startling statistics on how little the schools were meeting the needs of Mexican Americans kids. For his study, the L.A. school district attempted to get Sheldon fired. This was horrible, and yet too many Mexican Americans, including leaders, didn't seem to care. This was spooky. I'd tell people,

"We're in a hell of a crisis and we need to do something about it like the blacks."

"Hey, what crisis?" I'd hear back. "I got a car. I got my own house."

Or I'd go to a social event and start talking to other Mexican Americans about these issues, and they'd shine me off. I'd get into an argument with them. Then they would tell me: "Look, Sal, if you come to a party, don't talk politics. Just have a good time. You're a good dancer, so just dance."

Other Mexican Americans didn't want to talk about these problems, or, worse, they didn't see any problems. They just wanted to hide their heads in the sand. As long as they had a car and a house, they felt everything was fine. They didn't seem to care if Chicano kids didn't finish high school. "That's okay," some would say, "just send the kid over to my place where I work and he can see about getting a job there." People just wanted to survive. They didn't want to make waves.

But unlike some of these Mexican Americans, I was beginning to see things very differently, especially with respect to the need to change conditions in the schools. My main source for learning about these problems continued to be my work with Chicano kids in the playground. Even though I was now beginning to teach full-time, I kept my part-time job at the Tenth Street playground in order to have more income to pay my child support. I worked there from 5 to 9 P.M. I saw more and more frustration in the kids about school as I talked to them one-on-one. Some actually didn't want to talk about their school experiences—that's how bad they were. They didn't want to be reminded.

"Let's just play basketball, coach," they'd say.

Yet their silence only reinforced for me the trauma and bad conditions many of them faced in the schools. When I started teaching, I realized, "Hey, these kids are right. It is terrible for them." All of this began to weigh on me. I felt I had this huge weight on me that seemed to only increase in pressure. It would be 10 pounds, 20 pounds, 50 pounds, 100 pounds on my shoulders. I felt that I had to do something to remove it. I felt that I was ready to go into the Mexican schools, as they had historically been referred to, and begin to change things if I could.

Belmont

I got that chance in the fall of 1963. Belmont High in downtown L.A. had an opening for a social science teacher, and one of my professors recommended me.

"I have the door open for you with the principal," he told me on the phone.

I was delighted, since I had enjoyed my practice teaching at Belmont, and, given the large number of Chicano students there, I felt it was a perfect place for me to start in the L.A. school district. I met with the principal, Mrs. Iona Lord, and she offered me the position. My duties involved teaching U.S. history, world history, and government in the tenth through the twelfth grades. This was right up my alley. I also had my own classroom for the first time.

I still hadn't finished my credentials program, and I now needed a regular credential. What I lacked was one more stint at practice teaching. Fortunately, the school district gave me one credit for my teaching at Washington High for my credential. So when I started at Belmont I was a fully accredited teacher.

I was one of only three other Mexican American teachers at Belmont. The other two, Ralph Poblano and Mary Mend, taught Spanish. Of the two, I got to know Ralph a bit better, although we were very different. He had a silver spoon in his mouth. He never took a risk, which is why he later became a college provost. He was somewhat involved in community affairs, but the *cabrón* (fool) didn't want to rock the boat at school. Mary wasn't much better, but she later became the superintendent of schools in Stockton.

I knew conditions at Belmont from my previous experience, but coming back only confirmed for me some of the problems, especially that Mexican Americans faced. The students, themselves, took to me quickly. I wanted to get them involved in bringing about some changes. I started looking at who was in the student council, for example, and found out that not a single Mexican American student served on it. "Why aren't there Mexican kids in the student council?" I started asking.

Then I discovered that the school had a program where they sent twenty-five of the most capable kids to an advanced English class for college credit at L.A. City College, a short drive from Belmont, and none of them were Mexican Americans. You would think that if the student body was composed of over 60 percent Mexicans/Latinos there would be a few of them among that special group. The same was true in other honors programs. In effect, the Chicanos were being tracked into non–college prep classes and encouraged to take vocational ones. All this didn't surprise me, but it only magnified the

Sal Castro, Belmont High School, 1963. Courtesy Sal Castro Personal Collection.

obstacles to achieving quality education for Mexican Americans in the L.A. schools.[2]

I was able to find out more about these disparities because the principal assigned me to do one period in the attendance office. They had no one there who could speak Spanish, even though the school had many Mexican students with Spanish-speaking parents. I don't know why she didn't ask Ralph or Mary. I translated excuse notes and for parents who came into the office but couldn't speak English. They also didn't have a Spanish-speaking counselor who could communicate with the parents, so Mrs. Lord asked me if I could help out here as well. What could I say, especially as a first-year teacher? I "volunteered" to do this, even though I didn't get paid extra. On the other hand, by working in attendance and counseling, I got an even better understanding of how the school was failing Mexican American students and not effectively dealing with them and their parents. The school approached them as problems rather than as assets. The majority of the mostly white teachers and administrators had low expectations of the students, and so this became a self-fulfilling prophecy. Perhaps they meant well, but they were doing more harm than good. Working in these offices also gave me access to the student files, which provided evidence of the notorious tracking system and of the low performance by Mexican American students.

ALBERT VALENCIA, former Belmont student in the early 1960s: "The teachers and counselors tolerated us, but wondered why we weren't like the white kids. . . .

"My SAT scores were very high. But when I sat down to talk to my counselor, she took out the forms for how to be a body shop worker, a cashier at a market, a security guard, because she said we were all good with our hands."[3]

The only area where the Mexican kids were better represented was on the athletic field, and this involved mostly boys, since girls' sports were almost nonexistent. I actually volunteered some of my time to help with the football team. I gravitated toward sports because that's where the Chicanos were.

Initially, because I was doing all this extra work plus doing well in my classes, the principal expressed pleasure with me, until I started asking questions.

"Why aren't Mexican American students, at least those who are doing well in classes, not allowed to attend the honors program at City College?"

"Why are there no Mexican Americans kids on the student council?"

Mrs. Lord responded in a typical bureaucratic fashion by falling back on the old argument that the school had certain requirements and many times Mexican Americans didn't fit them.

"Yeah, but if you get 60 percent of the student body who are Mexicans," I challenged her, "why haven't they been fulfilling these requirements or why can't they fulfill part of them and still be allowed the opportunity to take advantage of the honors program?"

She called me back one day and said: "Mr. Castro, you're overly sensitive to these issues. The fact is that we have many Mexicans that are doing well in this school. For example, the student who is the head of the ROTC program is excellent. He's probably going to get into West Point."

"Well, I must have missed this kid," I replied. "What's his name?"

"Fernando Chávez," she informed me.

"Fernando Chávez! Mrs. Lord, how many years have you been teaching here? Can't you still not tell the difference between a Mexican kid and a Filipino one? Fernando is Filipino!"

"Well aren't you all pretty much the same?" she defiantly came back.

"Oh my God," I said to myself after this response. "We're in deep trouble here."[4]

At this point, I felt that I had no choice but to begin to confront the racism at the school. The first thing I did was to break through the exclusion of Mexican Americans from the student council. The Chicano kids needed a sense of leadership before other issues could be confronted. If I could help mobilize the latent Mexican power at the school not only would the students become empowered, but also this would help generate the force to change other school conditions.

The first hurdle was to find students who were eligible to run for student government. You had to have a certain grade point average. It wasn't easy, but I found some of these kids who had always been intimidated from running.

"No, Mr. Castro. I don't want to run," they first told me.

"*M'hijo* and *m'hija* [My son and my daughter]," I'd say to them, "it's important that you run. And it's good for your record if you apply to college or try to get a good job."

Eventually I convinced a number of them.

The next step, however, was to get around the teacher who sponsored the student council. He had always found some Mickey Mouse reason or another to disqualify the few Chicanos who wanted to campaign for student council, including those I had selected. I confronted him on this. The guy was from Texas.

"What the hell are you doing? You still remember the Alamo? Every Mexican kid I send to you, you come up with an excuse."

He still wouldn't budge, so I went around him to the vice principal, who proved more understanding, and he cleared the kids to run for office. I didn't see this as doing the students a favor—they had earned the right to compete.

But I also knew that if the Mexican students ran individually they probably wouldn't win or would take votes away from each other. I decided that they would run as a slate, as a political party. One student would campaign for president, another for vice president, another for treasurer, and so on down the line. To organize the party, I invited the kids to meet with me one afternoon at the Tenth Street playground.[5]

To my surprise, some 200 students showed up. I had to open the school auditorium for us to meet. They not only accepted the idea of running a Chicano political party, but they used the occasion as a nominating convention to select those who would run on the ticket and who were eligible to do so. People got up and gave speeches for particular candidates. In this way, the students selected their choices for the different offices. The only one that was chosen by default was that of the candidate for president. The rules for student council elections stipulated that in order to run for president you had to have served at least once on the student council. We had only one such student—a girl—who somehow had gotten through the discriminatory screening process. She was willing to run, and so she automatically became our candidate. At the meeting, the students also selected a name for the party and ticket. In a bold move, they chose to call themselves the TMs, which stood for Tortilla Movement. This was an expression of Chicano power even before there was a Chicano Movement. I had nothing to do with the choice of the name; the students on their own decided. I was proud of them.

ALBERT VALENCIA: "The Tortilla Movement caught on like wildfire."[6]

I then felt that we needed to raise money to help with the campaign. This would be to buy materials for signs and cards to publicize the ticket and the individual candidates. The students didn't have any money, and it was not permitted to hold fund-raisers for student body elections. So I just donated some money and got a few other sympathetic teachers to do the same. But the students also publicized the party in other ways. You'd walk into a classroom and on the corner of the chalkboard you'd see the initials TM or other notes supporting the ticket.

I even arranged to get Eddie Cano and his band to play for a student assembly. Eddie, who had gone to Lincoln High School, was an old friend of mine, and he had helped in the Viva Kennedy campaign. He readily agreed, and the musicians' union even paid him for performing, since we couldn't. Eddie had become very popular, and his song "A Taste of Honey" later became a big hit when recorded by Herb Alpert and the Tijuana Brass. The assembly was for all students to come and enjoy the performance. It had nothing ostensibly to do with the student elections. And yet it had everything to do with them. I had told Eddie about the situation at Belmont and about the TMs. He understood. After playing a few tunes, Eddie concluded his performance by saying: "This next and last song, 'Our Day Will Come,' is dedicated to the TMs. Good luck!"

The Chicano kids went wild. They got the message. I could see the displeasure in Mrs. Lord's face, but there was nothing that she could do about it. The kids hadn't done anything wrong. I hadn't done anything wrong, well not really. If she had a beef, she needed to take it up with Eddie. She didn't.[7]

Election day loomed toward the end of the fall semester. The last thing before balloting was an assembly where each of the candidates for the different offices could make a short speech about why students should vote for them. I thought the TMs could use this opportunity to make their case not only to the majority of Mexican American students on campus, after all this was classic American ethnic politics, but especially to the immigrant kids who still spoke mostly Spanish. I huddled with the TMs before the assembly and told them: "Listen, there's about 400 to 600 kids here that are limited English-speaking, FS, foreign students. Say a few words to them in Spanish after you give your formal speech in English. Say something like *'necesito su apoyo, por favor voten por mí* [I need your support, please vote for me].'"

They also thought this was a good idea. I thought it was perfectly innocent and perfectly political trying to get these kids to vote for the TMs. Well, that's when all hell broke loose. I was not aware that there was a ridiculous school rule that you couldn't speak a "foreign language" on the school stage. Apparently, some kid a few years before who could speak something like ten languages and was running for some student office got up there and proceeded to show off his linguistic abilities for several minutes. To prevent this from happening again, the administration put in this rule. Actually, even if I had known about this, I would have ignored it anyway.[8]

However, the minute our first TM candidate concluded her speech by making her remarks in Spanish, Mrs. Lord immediately jumped on the stage and cancelled the assembly.

"Everyone get back to your classrooms. This assembly is over."

Of course, I was pissed that she did this and that the TMs couldn't finish their speeches. What ever happened to the U.S. Constitution at Belmont? Still, I went back to my class. At the same time, the principal rounded up all of the TM candidates and had them sent to her office. When I got to my room, one of my students told me: "Hey, Mr. Castro, they've got all the TMs in Mrs. Lord's office."

I feared the worst—that these kids might get suspended or even kicked out of school—so I quickly went across the hall and asked another teacher to look after my class for a few minutes. I then raced over to Mrs. Lord's office, bypassed her secretary, and opened the door to the principal's office.

"You kids, get out of this office and go back to class. I'll handle this."

After they left, I slammed the door. Mrs. Lord looked shocked, and I could see she was doing everything to hold back her anger. But I didn't hold back. It was she and I. "What is this for? You know I'm the guy that organized these kids, the guy that got them to do all this. Why are you coming after them? Come after me. They're perfectly innocent. The fact that they haven't been represented in the school, that's not their problem; it's your problem. But right now, I'm the problem. Deal with me, not them."

I don't remember much after my little spiel. I think she said something like, "Well, they violated the rules about speaking a foreign language." *Que fregada*. I think I just left her in her own ignorance and went back to my class.[9]

The next day, she suspended me from teaching. I couldn't even finish the fall semester. Mrs. Lord didn't officially fire me but instead requested that the school district transfer me to another school. I discovered that this was a smart move on her part. By the beginning of December, I was out. Ralph Poblano suggested that I take my case to the Urban Affairs unit of the school district, which dealt with a variety of complaints. I did, but Sam Hammerman of Urban Affairs told me they couldn't do anything for me because even though I was part of the regular faculty at Belmont, as a first-year teacher I was on probation and could legally be dismissed—or in my case transferred without cause. I also had no legal standing because Mrs. Lord hadn't fired me but simply requested a transfer. If she had fired me, I still might have been able to fight on the basis of racial discrimination. But under the circumstances I couldn't.

While Urban Affairs looked at my case, Poblano told Phil Montez, another Mexican American politico in L.A., about me. Phil was a good friend of Ruben Salazar, an up-and-coming reporter for the *Los Angeles Times*, and Phil in turn told Ruben about what had happened to me. Salazar called me for an interview. He wanted to know about my situation at Belmont. Salazar would later blossom as a major reporter covering a range of areas, including Vietnam, Mexico, and the Chicano Movement. He tragically became a Chicano martyr and icon when sheriffs killed him while he covered the historic Chicano anti–Vietnam War moratorium on August 29, 1970, in East Los Angeles. However, my initial impression of Salazar, who became a friend of mine, was that he wasn't as aware of the Mexican American community as he would be in the late 1960s. But he was *buena gente* (a good person) and a damn good reporter. I explained to him about Belmont, and he mentioned it in his article. Even though I put the Belmont incident into the larger context of the school district's discrimination against Mexican American students, he only focused on the language controversy and the prohibition of the use of Spanish. I had hoped he would deal with the larger issues, but at least he brought attention to what had happened at the school.

RUBEN SALAZAR: "Sal Castro, a young teacher who had encouraged the making of the speeches in Spanish 'as educational,' was disappointed that his experiment failed, but did not quit there."[10]

One positive thing that happened as the result of all this was that the TMs were still allowed to participate in the student council election and, to my delight, won every single contest except for president. This represented the first time that Mexican students had achieved effective representation in student government. More important, this process empowered them and other Chicano kids. It laid the basis for future confrontation.

The kids felt bad about what had happened to me. My transfer occurred so fast that they didn't have time to react, and none of the other teachers stepped in to guide them. As a result, no protests took place over my suspension. They invited me, however, later to attend the senior graduation in the spring. Regrettably, this led to another crisis with school officials, who got wind that I would be attending. They feared that a demonstration might ensue, so they requested L.A. police to be in attendance and to prevent me from entering the ceremony. When I walked in with my invitation, a policeman approached me.

"Mr. Castro, I'm sorry, but you can't go in. You're not allowed to be on this campus."

I couldn't believe this, but I didn't make a fuss in order not to spoil the graduation for those who had invited me. I turned around and left.

The irony and funny part of all this is that I was transferred to Lincoln High School. Little did they know, and I didn't know, that this would become the scene of even greater battles that would pose more serious challenges to the school district. But this would come later.

ALBERT VALENCIA: "What Sal Castro taught us was what Emiliano Zapata said— 'It's better to die on your feet then to live on your knees.'"[11]

Political Involvement

In the meantime, I continued to further immerse myself in Democratic Party politics. In 1962 I worked for the reelection of Pat Brown as governor. Two years later, I ran and was elected to the L.A. Central Committee of the party. I competed with a number of other candidates and received more votes than anyone else. I think I ran for this post because a part of me began thinking about more formally entering politics. I even thought I'd in time run for Congress. If I did, I first needed to get my feet wet, and being elected to the Central Committee was one way. Some Democratic elected politicians, such as Assemblyman George Danielson, encouraged me to think about running for elective office. I think I did as well as I did in being elected to the Central Committee because I was beginning to get some name recognition due to what had happened at Belmont and the Salazar write-up. Because I got more votes than some of the other candidates, I should have been named the chair of the committee, but some of the old pros already on it felt I was a rookie, and so they selected someone else.

In addition, I supported the 1964 campaign of Pierre Salinger, who had been President Kennedy's press secretary, for the U.S. Senate from California. Mexican Americans rallied to Salinger because of his connection to JFK, and we organized a Viva Salinger movement. In fact, I became cochair of the L.A. County group. Governor Brown had already appointed Salinger interim senator due to a vacancy in that office. He now sought to be elected outright.

First, we helped in getting Salinger the nomination of the party. This wasn't a problem since he was the incumbent. The real fight came in the general election. His Republican opponent, George Murphy, was a former actor and a racist. He later made a much-quoted remark that the reason many Mexicans were farmworkers "was because they were built close to the ground." He had no understanding of the problems of Mexican Americans and, even worse, no sympathy for our cause. We were as motivated to defeat Murphy as to elect Salinger.

When Salinger campaigned in L.A., we made sure that he spoke to Mexican Americans and visited East Los Angeles. He couldn't speak Spanish, but he would sprinkle in some Spanish terms or phrases in his talks. Like Jacqueline Kennedy, Salinger, who was of French descent, spoke the little Spanish he used with a slight French accent. At one rally in Lincoln Park, I accompanied him on a helicopter and we landed right in the park, where we had mariachis playing. I got some of the Lincoln High School students to distribute bumper stickers at the rallies. As the cars entered the parking area, the kids would ask permission to put the stickers on and did so if the drivers agreed, and most did. I, myself, never spoke at these rallies. I felt more comfortable working behind the scenes.

One event that I'll never forget had to do with my cochair of the Viva Salinger campaign. He owned a restaurant in East L.A. that was a real dive. But he had the nerve to take Salinger there for a lunch meeting with other Mexican American leaders. The place was terrible and the food was just as bad. I remember having to take Salinger's son to the bathroom and feeling embarrassed at how dirty it was. *El vatito se asusto* (the kid got scared) because there were a bunch of drunks in there. I was ready to crawl under the table that day. What the hell are we doing here? There were many other nicer restaurants in East L.A. It was a low point of the campaign.

Maybe this event symbolized the general problems of the Salinger campaign. It wasn't so much our problem as it was the lack of support from the national Democratic Party. That year was also a presidential election year. Lyndon Johnson, who had become president after the assassination of Kennedy, was now running for election in his own right. Mexican Americans throughout the Southwest and elsewhere organized the Viva Johnson campaign in support of LBJ. In California, the Viva Johnson effort existed alongside the Viva Salinger one. But they were two separate movements. The Johnson people did not really support Salinger and only nominally endorsed him. They saw Salinger as a stalking horse for Robert Kennedy, JFK's younger brother, who had been attorney general in the Kennedy administration. There was no love lost between LBJ and Bobby Kennedy. Johnson felt that Bobby didn't really support him and saw him as a usurper of the Kennedy legacy. As a result, the Johnson campaign gave very little money to Salinger for his own campaign. They were willing to risk losing that Senate race to the Republicans because of this animosity. This really disappointed and angered me. How could they possibly want someone like Murphy to win? I didn't have much to do with the Viva Johnson group and, instead, concentrated on Salinger. The result of all this political intrigue was that, while LBJ won a landslide victory, including in California, Salinger went down to defeat. It was a fiasco. The subversion of the Salinger campaign really soured me toward electoral and even Democratic Party politics. After this experience, I didn't even participate very much in the Central Committee, even though I had been elected for a four-year term. I figured there had to be other ways to bring about change.

Camp Hess Kramer Conferences

As I began my career as a public school teacher in the early 1960s, I also came to participate in what became a significant movement to inspire a new generation of Mexican American leaders out of the high schools. It would be a movement that changed my life and that laid the basis for a Chicano confrontation with the school system, which was simmering underneath the surface.

Sometime around 1961, I heard that some Mexican American community leaders had come together to discuss conditions in the schools as they affected Mexican American youth. This wasn't the first time that Mexican Americans in L.A. had expressed such concerns.[12] From high drop-out rates to the lack of matriculation to college, there existed, as I was discovering, a whole range of problems. Some of these were already being publicized by a few scholarly studies. One important one was the so-called Sheldon Report, written by Dr. Paul Sheldon of Occidental College, which among other things documented the 50 percent drop-out rates by Mexican Americans in the L.A. schools.[13] Some of these concerned Mexican American leaders were Dr. Francisco Bravo, Irene Tovar, Phil Montez, and others. Most were small businessmen, and a few were professionals. They organized the Mexican American Education Committee. As I learned more about it, I joined it, although I didn't have the time to be very active in it—but I respected its work. They began to hold discussions with the school board but were only able to get from it the creation of an Urban Affairs committee for the school district. This new unit acted as a liaison between the community and the school board. The board also designed it to serve as a buffer between it and the community. Any community complaint would first go to Urban Affairs.

Recommendations by Mexican American Education Committee, August 15, 1963:

- **That the curriculum take into consideration the needs of the Mexican-American in accordance with his cultural heritage.**
- **That the teaching of Spanish at all levels of instruction be implemented and not restricted to the Junior and Senior High School.**
- **That English and Spanish complement one another as foreign language requirements throughout the elementary level using the basic knowledge of Spanish to advantage in place of a detriment to the children.[14]**

Not satisfied with the board's reaction, the Mexican American Education Committee also discussed with the county board of supervisors the conditions in the schools and the lack of opportunities for Mexican American youth. Out of this, the county established the L.A. County Commission on Human Relations. This commission was not entirely due to the efforts of Mexican Americans, but of the Jewish community's concern about the growing civil rights tensions in the country and in the L.A. area. The Human Relations Commission in turn came up with the idea of organizing a conference to help promote Mexican American youth leadership. Its objectives would be to encourage students to stay in school, do well, and continue on to college. If successful, the conference would be a yearly event. Tobias Kotzin, who owned the Angeles Trouser Factory in L.A., with mostly Mexican American employees, including my own mother, and who served on the commission, provided the initial funding of $4,000 for the conference.[15] Kotzin was also a major leader in the Jewish American community of L.A., and through him, as well as Rabbi Alfred Wolf, the chair of the commission, arrangements were made to hold the first conference at a Jewish summer camp, called Camp Hess Kramer, in the Malibu Mountains off Pacific Coast Highway.

I read in the paper that the commission was seeking volunteers as counselors for the new program. They were looking for adults with experience working with youth. I said, "Hey, I want to belong to that." I figured that with my work at the playgrounds, along with my teaching in the Pasadena schools, I was qualified. So I went to a meeting at the board of supervisors where I learned more about the proposed conference. I liked the intention, applied, and was accepted as one of the first group of counselors. The staff at first was small, about twenty to twenty-five people, and included a few teachers like myself along with some social workers and even some police and county sheriff personnel. All of us were Mexican Americans. Art Almanza from the commission served as the first director. The organizers decided that the first conference would be held in 1963 over the Palm Sunday weekend. The religious connotation was purely coincidental, especially for a Jewish camp, but it was the only time that the camp facilities were available. At first, the conference was called the Spanish-Speaking Youth Leadership Conference but then changed in 1964 to the Mexican American Youth Leadership Conference. Still later, in the 1970s, it underwent another name change—to Chicano Youth Leadership Conference (CYLC), the name it holds to this day.[16]

A few weeks before the conference, the kids who would attend were selected. We as counselors didn't do this but left it up to the principals and teachers at the schools, although members of the Human Relations Commission could also nominate particular students. The school district itself did not officially sponsor the conference.[17] The conference organizers didn't just focus on the Eastside schools, such as Lincoln, Roosevelt, Garfield, or on an inner city school such as Belmont, but also drew from a variety of public schools throughout the county that had important numbers of Mexican Americans. They even selected some students from the Catholic schools. The criteria for choosing the students—and this was true for subsequent students, including those of today—involved not only having good grades but also displaying leadership by being in student government, sports, or in other activities, both on and off the school premises. We didn't select problem kids. We wanted to further develop leadership from students who were already working hard and to encourage them to go on to college. We could only do so much, and I think this was a good decision. The fact was that even these kids had problems. They also faced discrimination in the schools and lack of encouragement from their teachers. I found that they only saw the surface of the problems and didn't know what to do about them.[18]

As the title of the conference indicated, we stressed leadership. For the conference packets that we handed out to the students, we included a statement of purpose, which, in part, read: "The Conference is for the development of youth leadership. It has certain objectives, traditions, and aspirational goals. The theme itself is symbolic of the conference. As you may be aware by now, this conference is a working leadership conference. The objective will repeatedly be stressed throughout, and should strongly be adhered to by all conference participants."[19]

About 100 to 150 students, almost equally distributed between boys and girls and all Chicanos, attended the first conference. There were wall-to-wall Mexicans. Mexicans ran it and Mexicans attended. The students arrived by buses on Friday and left on Sunday. We put them up in the various cabins, separating the boys from the girls. Each cabin had a counselor who stayed with the kids all the time. We also had a structure, which I helped to organize, that we followed and that remained pretty much the pattern throughout the decade and still is the format. After the kids checked in and were assigned to groups with a counselor, we'd have an opening ceremony, with the Pledge of Allegiance and a discussion of the goals of the conference as well as the schedule for the next two days. The first full day on Saturday consisted of several featured speakers, such as Judge Leopoldo Sánchez. Most of these early speakers were moderate, but over time they became more radical. After each speaker, the small groups led by the counselors such as myself engaged in discussion groups about the speaker's remarks and related issues. We also arranged for some workshops. In between talks and discussion sections, there was time for recreation and meals. We wanted to not only keep the kids busy throughout the day but also to even exhaust them in order to keep in check their hormones. Saturday evening we'd have a dance that used to be called a "sock hop," so that they could further get to know each other and enjoy themselves. I eventually became the resident dj for these hops. We strictly supervised all of these activities, and we came down hard on anyone not following the rules.

At the first and even later conferences, I found in my group of students —but this was also true in general—a certain lack of self-esteem and even an inferiority complex among some of the youth. A lot of this had to do with the fact that the schools didn't provide a positive image of Mexican Americans, in history, for example. The schools didn't encourage a self-affirming identity. Instead of promoting the kids to think, they were told what to think. Curiously, I found that at the first conference some of the counselors had the same identity problems, in addition to not having a critical perspective on education and the schools. Some were even "self-haters" who blamed Mexicans for their problems. They weren't "change agents" or risk takers. The early conferences themselves were structured on a very traditional and assimilationist format. Topics discussed included education, civic awareness, acculturation, marriage, and employment. I found myself from the very beginning having to counter these views and providing alternative interpretations to the students as well as building up their opinions of themselves and of their communities.

To further discussion, we included in the students' packets possible questions for reflection. Despite some of my reservations concerning various themes of the initial conferences, at least some of these proposed discussion questions aimed to develop ethnic consciousness or at least explore issues of ethnicity. For example, one question on education was, "Would the teaching of Spanish in the elementary grades be of particular significance?" And another asked, "Do you feel that speaking two languages is a hindrance or an asset?"[20]

My more critical interventions at the start-up conferences didn't come easy and at first I was pretty much alone. I was not the main director and, in fact, never was during the 1960s. I always remained one of the counselors, but always in a very active and involved way—not only with the kids I was in charge of but with as many others as possible. I began to see changes even at the very first conference. First of all, we worked to create an open environment, or what we called a "safe space," to make the kids feel okay to open up and feel confident to speak up. They, of course, were shy about this, but, little by little, at least in my group, they expressed themselves. I found out that many had complaints about their schools. Almost every student complained about their school counselors not paying attention to them, about the disrespect of a lot of teachers toward Mexican American students, about their teachers' lack of knowledge about them and their culture, and about the lack of encouragement to go to college. In this process, I began to see a constructive dialogue between the students and me. My role was not to do all of the talking. It was to initiate the dialogue and comment on the discussion or to direct the discussion in a certain way. I never imposed my views on them. I wanted them to teach themselves and to teach me. All of us would be teachers. I threw something out and let it spin.[21]

VICKI CASTRO, Roosevelt student at 1963 conference: "This is where I got my voice. This is where my passion for justice was born in me. It changed my whole being."[22]

By Sunday, the students talked about what they had gained from the conference. I could see a change in some of them. I could see some of them being more aware. From the time the kids got off the buses on Friday to the Sunday when they left, I witnessed a glimmer—that I and perhaps some of the other counselors had been effective in opening the students' eyes. Above all, I wanted them to first identify their problems at school, recognize the importance of staying in school, begin to be proud of their Mexican background, and commit themselves to go to college. Instead of the problem, they became the solution. These were big goals, and we didn't accomplish them at the first conference, but it was a beginning. In the subsequent gatherings, each year I and other counselors who also were becoming more aware themselves began to make more and more progress with the kids. As I began to teach in the public schools, I was able to bring my skills as a teacher and my greater understanding of the school issues to the annual conferences. I looked forward to them each year and to the challenges they posed. Many students who later became activists in the Chicano Movement first became turned on politically by attending the Camp Hess Kramer conferences. Indeed, one might say that the cradle of the Chicano Movement in L.A. was to be, ironically, found here in the Malibu Mountains.

FIVE

The Mexican Schools

Lincoln High School is an imposing, gothic-style building in the heart of Lincoln Heights on the northern border of what is considered to be generically East L.A.[1] It is just on the other side of the Golden State Freeway, which divides the Eastside from downtown. Little did I know when I walked into the school on a brisk January day in 1964 that within four years I would be at the center of a Chicano student explosion that would send shock waves throughout L.A. and the Southwest and would have national significance. I had a feeling something was inevitable, but I didn't know the direction it would take. I was still a young thirty-one-year-old teacher and eager to change the world.

Lincoln was a classic "Mexican school." This term originated in the early twentieth-century in the Southwest when thousands of Mexican American children, the offspring of the first great wave of Mexican immigrants to cross the border, began to attend U.S. public schools. As they became school age, schools boards throughout the region, including southern California, established separate and segregated schools for Mexicans. They called them "Mexican schools." They not only were segregated, but they were inferior. The children received a limited education with a stress on vocational education, few learning resources such as books, and too many principals and teachers who, besides having no understanding and appreciation for the students' cultural backgrounds, possessed low expectations of the kids. The Mexican schools aimed to socialize and equip these students with just enough skills to enter the low-skilled labor market as replacements for their working-class parents. For years, the public school system, including the L.A. school district, tracked Mexican students to a self-fulfilling prophecy of failure.[2]

This is what Lincoln and the other schools in East L.A. and some in the central downtown district such as Belmont represented. Lincoln had an even larger percentage of Mexican students than Belmont—over 90 percent of the student body, which numbered more than 2,000. The other Eastside high schools were equally Mexican, such as Roosevelt with 83 percent and Wilson with 76 percent.[3] Lincoln had six grades (seven through twelve) because it combined the senior high school with the junior high. The non-Mexicans were some *chinitos* (Asians) and *morenitos* (blacks) and just a few whites. As in Belmont, the reverse was true for the teachers. I was only one of a handful of Mexican American teachers.[4]

As a starting teacher, I got a pretty tough teaching schedule. I had five different subjects and no classroom of my own. The other teachers started calling me the "traveling teacher." I taught U.S. history, government, world geography, and two typing classes. Of these, I taught the geography class and the typing one in the junior high. They kept me very busy so I would stay out of trouble. The principal, George Ingles, of course knew about what had happened at Belmont but was willing to take me. He probably was cautious of what I might do and he would be right, but initially we developed a cordial relationship. After he found out I wasn't out to cut his tail or his horns, we got along pretty good. He even made me athletic director in my second year, after on my own I gravitated to helping out with the jocks. The guy that had the position received a promotion and vacated the job.

"Sal," the principal asked me, "would you be willing to step in as athletic director?"

"Hell, yes," I replied, with no hesitation.

I agreed to do this because I loved sports and liked working with athletes. I also didn't mind that it relieved me of one class and paid me a little extra. I coordinated all of the different teams, all boys at this time; prepared game schedules; arranged for facilities to play games; ordered buses for the teams; arranged teacher supervision for the games; and performed a variety of other tasks. But I enjoyed it and did it from 1965 to 1968. The only problem with the sports program was that even though we had many good Chicano athletes the mostly white coaches never tried to get them college athletic scholarships. They had a mind-set that college coaches weren't interested in Mexican players. As a result, many excellent athletes from Lincoln and other Eastside schools never got a chance to play college ball in football, basketball, baseball, or track.

After about a year or so, I also finally got my own classroom. This made my teaching easier, because I could keep all of my stuff together in one room. I collected for my history and government classes a whole bunch of Chicano pictures showing the history and contributions of Mexicans, as I set out to build up the self-esteem of my students. I even stapled some of these images on the ceiling, because I ran out of room on the walls.

All of this work kept me busy, but I still maintained my after-school job at the Tenth Street School playground to give me additional income, which helped with my child support. I continued to do this, including summers, until 1968, when they forced me out due to the school conflict at Lincoln that year and my role in it.

Conditions at Lincoln

As I settled into teaching at Lincoln, I soon realized the school problems that made it into a "Mexican school." It had all of the trappings that limited educational opportunities for the Mexican students. To begin with, it possessed the notorious tracking system—with a limited college prep curriculum for a few of the kids, mostly the Asians and whites and a few of the Mexican Americans, and the larger regular track, which was not as advanced, didn't encourage going to college, and sponsored vocational education. In fact, Lincoln was called an "industrial arts high school." The boys would be directed into auto shop so they could become good mechanics. The girls would get "secretarial science" or business education. The school possessed a lot of so-called shop classes. In addition to auto shop, there was an electrical shop, machine shop, print shop, and a wood shop.[5] I literally saw boys making coffins. The girls learned how to type and take shorthand. In addition, the girls were encouraged or directed to take sewing and cooking classes in Home Economics. They'd teach the Mexican girls how to make *gavacho* (white) food instead of tamales or *albóndigas* (meat balls). Instead, it was hotcakes and all this other stuff.

One of the serious problems at Lincoln and one that would become a major grievance in time concerned the low reading levels of many of the Mexican students. Undoubtedly, this in part had to do with lack of attention to reading in the barrio elementary schools, but it was also an issue that Lincoln wasn't confronting—and if it was, it wasn't succeeding. I had students who couldn't read at their grade level. I had to make sure that they had a dictionary right next to them so they'd know what the hell the word meant. But this was a constant problem. Someone suggested recruiting college students to volunteer time to help tutor the kids in reading. I had some problems with this.

"Hey," I told our principal, "it's a great idea, but pay them. Why should they volunteer to get our teachers off the hook who aren't teaching these kids how to read?"

He didn't listen to me, and the reading problem continued.[6]

Given the large numbers of students at Lincoln, classrooms tended to be overcrowded. They put about forty kids in a class. The students at the beginning of each semester literally ran to class. What this involved is that the kids would be given their schedules of the classes they had to take, but instead of being assigned to a specific classroom, they were simply told what teachers were teaching which classes and when. "Now run for classes," the office instructed them. They called it "running for classes." The students raced to try to get into the more popular or perhaps easiest teachers' classes. On the first day of class, they'd line up outside of the classrooms, first come, first served. We, as teachers, admitted the first forty students. That's the way the whole schedule was set up. The more popular teachers always had their classes filled and then some. I sometimes had as many as forty-five students in my classes.

One of the major complaints by students who began talking to me concerned the role of counselors. To be fair, they were overworked, as they still are today. Too few counselors and too many students. It was not unusual to have 500 kids assigned to one counselor. You can't do a decent job this way. At some of the other schools, it was just as bad, if not worse. Garfield, for example, had only one college counselor for 4,000 students.[7] On the other hand, the job they did was questionable. "Graduate and get a job," is what they told the Mexican kids. If they encouraged them to go to college, it would only be to a community college. Only a few students might be promoted to go to a four-year school, but a Mexican student had to really shine for this to happen. As far as I know, most counselors were credentialed.

The counselors along with the teachers would also administer achievement tests. They tracked the students based on the results, which in the case of the Chicano students led to them being shuttled into the non–college prep classes and to vocational ones. You rarely saw them in the science classes. It would be mainly the *chinitos* and whites and a small number of Mexicans. The problem with these tests, however—and it's still the same problems with even more tests today, such as the exit exams—is that they are ethnically or racially biased. Tests like this rely on one's experience or what the students have been exposed to, but they take it for granted that all kids have been exposed to the same experiences, and that's not true. The norm for these tests was and still is the white middle class. Those who devise these tests I'm sure are not even conscious of the ethnic/race implications, but because the people who write these tests are from that background that's the way the tests turn out. The result is often disastrous for the minority kids, who, on top of this, come from inadequate elementary schools. The Mexican kids at

Lincoln, for example, weren't exposed to rhymes from King Arthur's court or stuff from Shakespeare that were on the tests. But the *gabachitos* (white kids) were, in other schools. Even things related to geography were and are a problem. Ask Mexican students how many have gone to Yosemite and you won't get too many hands raised. They don't even know where Yosemite is. Basic stuff like this can make a hell of a difference in test scores.

Some years later, I raised hell about the SAT tests. "You have nothing about Mexicans on these tests," I told SAT representatives. So what they did in response, not just to my complaints but to those of other Mexican American teachers, was to simply put in Spanish names sometimes instead of English ones. For example, they'd write: "González hit Rodríguez with a chair. What's the subject of the sentence?" That's how we're now being represented in the SAT. *"No chingen!* [Don't fuck with me!]" The fact is that you test on background. You ask a *gavacho* kid how you make *albóndigas* and he won't know, but that doesn't make him dumb. The same thing with a Chicano student. If he doesn't know where Yosemite is that also doesn't make him dumb.

I had no love for the achievement tests administered at Lincoln because they were just one more way that the Mexican kids were being put down and denied better educational opportunities.

The conditions in the school plus the general history of the Mexican schools led, regrettably and unjustly, to too many teachers at Lincoln and the other Eastside schools having low expectations of the kids. They approached them with the attitude that they were only capable of achieving mediocrity at best. There's nothing worse than teachers with low expectations of their students. The tragedy or crime is that the kids quickly pick up this and it becomes a self-fulfilling prophecy.[8]

Linked to all of this was a general alienation among the large majority of the Mexican American students. This came from all of the problems I've already referred to, but also from the kids being made to feel as strangers in their own school. As in the case with the achievement tests, U.S. public education was basically always aimed at white middle-class kids. When Robert Hutchins, the great educator from the University of Chicago, talked about the "American student," he didn't have in mind black students, much less Mexican ones. History books from elementary schools to colleges only discussed the role of whites in American history. Only until recently have minorities been included in this presentation, and even then not very adequately. It was like the role of minorities was not germane to the American experience. Consequently, when kids, including Mexican ones, very early went to school, they began to feel alien and foreign, right from the get-go. You walked into the classroom and all you'd see were pictures of a bunch of white people.

ROSALINDA MÉNDEZ GONZÁLEZ, student at Lincoln, 1967, statement before the U.S. Commission on Civil Rights: "From the time we first begin attending school, we hear about how great and wonderful our United States is, about our democratic American heritage, but little about our splendid and magnificent Mexican heritage and culture. What little we do learn about Mexicans is how they mercilessly slaughtered the brave Texans at the Alamo, but we never hear about the child heroes of Mexico who courageously threw themselves from the heights of Chapultepec rather than allow themselves and their flag to be captured by the attacking Americans. . . . We look for others like ourselves in these history books, for something to be proud of for being a Mexican, and all we see in books and magazines, films, and T.V. shows are stereotypes of a dark, dirty, smelly man with a tequila bottle in one hand, a dripping taco in the other, a serape around him, and a big sombrero. But we are not the dirty, stinking wino that the Anglo would like to point out as a Mexican."[9]

A kid that walks into a school, and this is basic educational psychology, should have the feeling that he/she can learn. They should have the comfort that they can learn and the positive self-image that they're capable of learning. Most white kids walk in more or less with this attitude. Mexican kids begin with that feeling, but then as they enter the school and see everything foreign around them, they start having self-doubts. When their teachers start talking about things that they're not familiar with, they quickly fall behind the eight ball. From kindergarten on, they start falling behind. They begin to have negative thoughts about themselves. They just keep falling further and further behind, so that by the third grade you can literally walk into an elementary school and see who's going to eventually drop out.

A lot of this had to do with the lack of positive images about Mexicans at Lincoln and other schools. Nowhere did the students learn, for example, about the founders of the cities of the Southwest, like L.A., who were Mexicans. Part of the problem also lay in the universities, where teachers received their education and credentials. As I had discovered at L.A. State, classes did not teach about the history and contributions of Mexican Americans. So teachers came out of those schools and went into teaching, especially at schools such as Lincoln, with no understanding of Chicanos. This just compounded the alienation problem. Teachers walked into the schools with the same stereotypes that I had attempted to counter at the college level. They thought most Mexican kids dropped out of school anyway, got married and had big families, didn't want to go to college, their parents didn't want them to go to college, all of these *pendejadas* (stupidities). It was enough to throw my hands up in frustration.

I'd hear these things in the Lincoln faculty room. Some teachers would say: "These kids, I don't know. I teach them all I can, do everything I can, and then June comes and they all go back to Mexico and forget everything I've taught them."

This was the belittling attitude and thinking of teachers in general. At no time did they think they were hurting the kids by concentrating only on white history. Never did they consider talking about other things, other accomplishments that might better connect with the students. About the only Mexican that the history tests mentioned was Pancho Villa, and then only as a ruthless *bandido* and not the revolutionary that he was. There was no major effort by the teacher to more effectively relate to the background of the kids they taught. For example, a few years later, when I was transferred to North Hollywood High, with mostly white Jewish kids, I made the effort to understand their backgrounds. Students would invite me to a bar mitzvah or other Jewish celebrations, and I'd go. I wanted to know about them and their culture so that I could be more effective with them. I remember one kid's younger brother's bar mitzvah, where everyone there talked about him going to college after high school. They even gave him a gold pen to write his first prescription as a doctor. This kid's only twelve, and they already have ordained him to be a doctor! This was heavy. With us, as Chicanos, the equivalent is our Catholic confirmations. They get 200 of us in church, kneel us down, and then some guy that looks like Superman (the bishop) comes out with a cape and slaps us all and that's the end of that.

By contrast, teachers at Lincoln seemed to never go to anything in East L.A. For one, they didn't live there. As soon as school ended, off they went to wherever they lived. Maybe they'd go to a Mexican restaurant and feel that they had done their penance concerning Mexican culture. But that was about it.

Some teachers would at times even say derogatory comments about the Mexican students. The kids would run to me and report this. I'd go and tell the principal about this, but he wouldn't do anything about it. I even confronted the teachers themselves. I'd tell them to their faces: "What you're saying about these kids is wrong and insulting. If you're not getting through to them, it's because of your attitude. You assume that they can't succeed and that's just wrong."

They didn't like to hear this, but they didn't change. I wasn't a well-liked teacher at Lincoln. Nobody likes a whistle-blower, even if what the teachers were doing was wrong.

This is not to say that there weren't some sympathetic and good teachers at Lincoln. One teacher in particular, Joe McKnight, in early 1968 called attention to the need for reforms in the school. He especially called, in a faculty newsletter, for greater attention to Mexican American culture. If the school failed to carry out changes, Joe feared the consequences of possible student disturbance. Joe prophesized: "There are many angry voices arising in the Eastside, and I, for one, can foresee their voices becoming louder, angrier, and more numerous in the future. We teachers at Lincoln must be prepared to face prospects of student walkouts, picketing, charges of ethnic and race discrimination, civil disobedience. . . . Whether in the end we teachers and administrators become the object of community violence will depend on how responsibly . . . we act. . . . I do not mean only how we listen, but how we act—how we respond."[10]

It was frustrating having to deal with the negative attitudes of teachers and administrators about the Mexican students, not only at Lincoln but also in the school district as a whole. When I first got to Lincoln, for example, I attempted to get the district to support getting the students from the Eastside high schools to go to the Music Center to see a rehearsal of the famous Ballet Folklórico Amalia Hernández from Mexico City. I made the arrangements myself with the Music Center, the Mexican Consulate, the ballet people, and Sol Hurak, the impresario. They all supported the idea. The only trouble I got was from the school district. "We don't think it of that much value and we don't want to waste the buses," was the response from the district. The kids never got to see the rehearsal. I began to see who the enemy was. It was going to take an earthquake to move them.

EDDIE PARDO, student at Garfield: "They [the teachers] aren't aware of the problems in a ghetto. . . . Teachers should be trained in the culture and language of the area that they choose to teach in."[11]

Part of the alienation that Mexican American students experienced at Lincoln also had to do with the language issue. There was no bilingual education when I started at Lincoln, and it wouldn't be until the early 1970s that some of these programs started. It was English only, as it was in all of the schools. There was no sensitivity or understanding of the kid's language background. Some entered being English dominant, but many others were still bilingual, speaking especially Spanish at home, as I did when I was a kid. But those who were totally dominant or fluent in English too often were made by teachers to feel embarrassed about themselves. The fact was that if teachers expected a student entering junior or senior high school to know a thousand words, then the Mexicans qualified, except that it might be 500 words in English and 500 words in Spanish. This is not to say that the student should not become even more proficient in English, but only that it wasn't that the kids were illiterate. On the contrary, many were very literate and effective bilinguals. However, instead of seeing their bilingual abilities as assets, they were looked down upon as problems. There were no attempts to make these students feel good about their language abilities and background.

Ingles, the principal, once came to me and said, "You know what, they're going to stop teaching Spanish at UCLA."

"Why," I responded, not knowing if he was serious or not.

"Yeah, they're doing this because no important documents have ever been written in Spanish."

He was kidding, but it reflected a bad attitude.

I found that even the few other Mexican American teachers weren't addressing the kids in Spanish, if for no other reason than to connect with them and validate their experiences. I did this all the time. I didn't give a damn about the rule that only English could be used in school. I had different ideas about teaching and was always marching to a different drummer.

The worst aspect about the prohibition of Spanish at Lincoln, and at the other schools, was that the students were punished if they were caught speaking it. This, of course, had a long history in the Mexican schools. At Lincoln, kids speaking Spanish were sent to their counselors to be reprimanded. This only made for more alienation.

Adding to the ethnic insecurities of Mexican kids was the almost total lack of attention to their ethnic history and to how Lincoln could help celebrate it. Soon after I got there, I asked the principal if we couldn't do something about celebrating Cinco de Mayo. "Can we even just put something in the school bulletin?"

"No," he sternly rejected my idea, "they're here to learn English and learn American."

To add insult to injury, the school on some occasions limited their studying by shortening class times in order to schedule nonacademic events. For example, in order to raise money for sports and other extracurricular activities, the school showed movies in the auditorium in the afternoon. These would be Westerns, comedies, or musicals such as *West Side Story*. Instead of the kids going to class, teachers escorted them to see the movie, for which they paid a quarter. I didn't have a problem with kids seeing movies or raising funds for the teams, but not when it cut into class time. The kids were having a hard enough time without having to be shortchanged on what education they were receiving.

The unfortunate result of the educational approach to Mexican students at Lincoln and the alienation experienced by them was shocking drop-out rates. Again, this wasn't new to me. I saw this at Belmont, and the Sheldon Report had documented it. Still, it was an indication of the crisis in the Eastside and minority schools. Lincoln had a drop-out rate of 50 percent, the same as at Belmont. The highest drop-out rate was at Garfield High, where almost 60 percent of the students didn't graduate.[12] By comparison, Westside schools had drop-out rates that were much lower.[13] At Lincoln, many of the kids dropped out by the end of the ninth grade or their freshman year. Many did not go on to their sophomore year. At Belmont and then at Lincoln, I got evidence of this when I went through what were called "cum cards." These were the cumulative records of all the students from the time they entered school to when they left or graduated. I was amazed to see how many of the cum cards for the Mexican students stopped at the end of the ninth grade or another grade before graduation. Some of these kids were fourteen or fifteen when they dropped out, and this was against the law. You had to be in school at least until you were sixteen. Truant officers or "hooky cops" tried to get them back, but often without much success. In many cases, they had already been put to work by the old man (their fathers). Others dropped out when they turned sixteen and could legally work.

Parents were also part of the problem. Some erroneously believed that if their children weren't doing well in school, it wasn't the problem of the school or the teachers, but the fact that their kids weren't cut out to be in school. They saw them—especially the boys—as frustrated, and so they figured they might as well just go to work—*que se hagan hombres* (to become men). However, if they could survive until the eleventh grade or junior year, the drop-out rates significantly decreased. These were the survivors. I also observed that immigration status had little to do with drop-out rates. At least in the 1960s, many of the students at Lincoln and, I suspect, at other schools were not immigrant kids, nor were their parents immigrants. They and their parents were U.S.-born Mexican Americans. The high drop-out rates, or what Henry Gutiérrez, a graduate student at the time, calls "push-out rates," had to do with the problems in the schools and continued lack of economic opportunities for most Mexican Americans in Los Angeles.[14]

Teenage pregnancy was an additional problem at Lincoln. Unlike today, when a girl gets pregnant and then after she gives birth she can go back to her high school, that wasn't the case in the 1960s. Then, if kids got pregnant you never saw them again. They were not allowed back into Lincoln. It was like the Scarlet Letter. The few who tried to continue their education while pregnant had to go to St. Anne's School for pregnant girls, where they were sequestered until they gave birth.

The onus on the girls was not fair because nothing happened to the boys who got them pregnant. They just continued in school—business as usual. Part of the problem, as I saw it, was that the school officials and teachers shied away from discussing teen pregnancy in the schools. They never talked about it. "You don't talk about that stuff," was their attitude. They tried to sweep it under the rug. I challenged the principal and the other teachers to address this problem.

"We don't have time to talk about it," they'd say. "I have to cover all this in the curriculum and so I can't talk about it."

It was always referred to as "it."

"You're crazy," I fought back. "They're dropping out because they're getting pregnant. The least you can do is talk about it. If you men aren't comfortable doing this, at least you women should be less disturbed and talk to your girls about it."

"Oh, we can't talk about sex," the female teachers timidly replied. "You need the parents' consent to talk about it."

At least they were willing to use the "s" word. Still, I was as disappointed with them as with the male teachers.

"You're all hiding your heads in the sand."

I sure as hell talked to my students about the perils of teenage pregnancy. I couldn't afford not to. I sometimes started my classes with this subject.

"*No sean pendejas* [Don't be idiots]," I'd tell them, aiming first at the girls. "That's not the thing you want to do. Your parents didn't send you to school to find a husband or for the boys to find a wife. It's ridiculous. Once you get pregnant, it's all over. You can't go back to school. You've lost being a kid. You can't go to dances anymore. You can't do any of this stuff. Do you think that once you have the baby that your parents are going to let you go back to school? You're not getting your independence. It's going to be much worse. Do you really think that the boy is going to marry you? He might come by with child support payments the first couple of months, but after awhile he's going to want something for that child support and you know what that means. If you don't give it up then he won't come up with the money. So you almost become a prostitute for him. Chances are you wind up with a second kid and not married. So think about it before you even think about doing that stuff. If you're so *pendejas* to do it, at least use some kind of birth control or go to the free clinic."

"Oh, no, Mr. Castro, we don't do that stuff," the girls shyly replied.

But I lectured the boys just as hard.

"Don't carry that thing in your wallet for six months and think it's going to work when you use it. It's going to crack up on you and you're going to get the girl pregnant. Then if this happens, what the hell are you going to do about it? Are you going to marry her? And if you don't, how will you afford the child payments? Do you think you'll get a good job as a dropout? Do you think you can afford to think that you'll just drop out, get married, and then your kids will finish school? Bullshit! That's not going to happen. Don't kid yourselves. Getting a girl pregnant isn't being macho; it's stupid—*no sean pendejos* [don't be idiots]."

I was very blunt with them and very open about it and very concerned about them. I think my coming down on them had an effect, at least on my students, but I couldn't reach hundreds of others, at least not by myself.

Although schools like Lincoln blamed parents for not doing more to encourage their kids to stay in school or to help them with their education, the fact was, and still is, that too many Mexican parents and Latino ones today, themselves, don't have much education. In the 1960s, the average education for Mexican Americans was about eight years, and that hasn't changed that much today. But, at the same time, it's always been my belief and impression that most Mexican Americans and Latino parents want their kids to be educated and work to achieve this. Yet poverty and the inability of the schools to overcome the mentality of the Mexican schools works against this. This condition also affected parents at Lincoln. Just a small number attended PTA meetings or met with teachers and counselors. They did come, however, when we had a parents' night. I'd hear these complaints from the administrators and teachers about Mexican parents not caring about the school, and I'd argue back.

"That's nonsense—what parents don't care for their children's education? Why do you assume that Mexican parents are different? But these parents, both of them, are out there working all day and sometimes into the night, six days a week, maybe with two jobs apiece. They're out in Beverly Hills cleaning houses or going somewhere else. How the hell can we expect them after all this to attend a meeting at 3 P.M. or 5 P.M. or even 7 P.M.? Why don't we have these meetings on a Saturday afternoon or, even better, after noon Mass on Sunday? You want parents to come, that's when they'll come. But I don't think you really want the parents here."

They didn't listen. They had their minds made up about Mexicans, and they didn't want to interfere with their weekends.

One of the few programs where many of the Mexican students, but only the boys, seemed to be succeeding, but for all of the wrong reasons, was ROTC and military recruitment. ROTC was very strong at Lincoln and the other Mexican schools. It went hand in hand with an equally strong military recruitment effort at these schools. We might not have many college recruiters coming to Lincoln, but we sure as hell had military recruiters. A lot of our boys thought it was cool to go into ROTC. They had a choice of either PE or ROTC, and many of them chose the military training. It was cool to go marching, get a uniform, and even wear new shoes. They liked to walk around in their uniforms. They also got to do certain duties, such as directing traffic at the school and crowd control at football games, where they got in free.

I didn't have, in general, any particular problem with ROTC—after all I had served in the army. However, the problem was that the military recruiters lied to these kids. They'd tell them, as they still do, "You can be all you want to be in the army." That was and still is bullshit! They'd encourage the kids to go into the military right out of school, with the promise that the military would later pay their college. This usually didn't happen. Or they'd promise that in the service they could learn a bankable skill, but this usually didn't happen either, at least not for the Mexican kids.

On top of all of this, this was wartime—the Vietnam War was heating up big time after 1965. President Johnson, after telling people in the 1964 election that he wasn't a war president—another lie—right after being elected began to send thousands of combat troops to fight a jungle war that they weren't trained for and didn't have the slightest idea of what they were fighting for, nor did most Americans. It, like the recent Iraq war, was a disaster, a fiasco. But Chicano kids, including from Lincoln, were being heavily recruited or quickly drafted after they graduated or dropped out to fight this crazy war. At this time, the military had a draft. That was the problem I had with ROTC and military recruitment at the school. Many of our boys never came back, and those who did were never the same again. They were either physically or emotionally wounded—usually both. Sometime around 1966 or 1967, the school put up a "wall of honor" to honor our boys in the Vietnam War. On one side of the wall were the names and pictures of those who went into the military, and on the other side were the names and photos with gold stars attached to those who had been killed in the war. By 1968, the names on both sides were just about equal. It was tough. I also thought the losses were crazy and ridiculous. The inequality was stark. White college kids got to stay home while Chicanos had to go to Vietnam. That was the worst.[15]

HARRY GAMBOA, a junior at Garfield High School in 1968: "If you look at my high school yearbook, it's like looking at the book of the dead because of Vietnam."[16]

While many of our students, obviously the boys, went into the military, very few—boys and girls—went to college. This just wasn't stressed or encouraged. I constantly tried to reverse this and to encourage the students to think of going to college and to working hard to improve their grades to be able to do so. But I didn't push community college—I pushed UCLA, Cal, USC, and L.A. State, wherever they could get into a four-year school. By 1968, I succeeded in getting some in, but these would usually be those who had been fortunate enough to be the few Mexican students in the honor classes. One of them, Moctesuma Esparza, a very bright and articulate student, went on to UCLA. He was also one of our Camp Hess Kramer kids. I had a much harder time trying to get students from the non–college prep track into college, but I did get a few. This included a kid that I had first met when I was starting to do playground work at Solano Avenue Elementary School near Dodger Stadium. As part of my duties, I coached a baseball team for elementary students. My second baseman was little Chuckie Moreno. I lost contact with Chuckie after this, but when I went to Lincoln I ran into him as a senior. He was a very bright student and one of the few Chicanos in the honors classes and the honors organization, the Knights, which I sponsored. That year, I recruited Chuckie to attend the Camp Hess Kramer conference. This experience turned him on ethnically and politically. He went on to receive a scholarship to Yale University and then achieved a law degree at Stanford. He was one of the first Chicano students at both institutions. I again lost track of Chuckie, but I heard some years later that he was now a prominent attorney. Then, lo and behold, a few years ago, I opened up my *Los Angeles Times* and what do I see: "Carlos Moreno Appointed to the California Supreme Court." I read the headline and saw the accompanying photo and thought, "That's Chuckie Moreno, my second baseman!" I found his number and called him and congratulated him. He has since then been a big supporter of our revived Hess Kramer conferences.

One memorable case of getting one of my students into college involved a very talented girl, Anita Contreras, who, like Esparza and Moreno, was an honor student. She also served as the student body vice president. In her senior year, she applied and received a full scholarship to Occidental College in the Eagle Rock area adjacent to East L.A. Oxy gave her a full ride: tuition, housing, books, etc. The one stipulation involved was that she had to live on campus her first two years. Well, Lincoln received all this as great news, and the principal held up Anita as an example that our Mexican American students were succeeding and going on to college. This wasn't, of course, true, and students such as Anita, Esparza, and Moreno were the exceptions. Anyway, one morning as I walked by the principal's office, I saw Anita in there with her parents, and she was crying. My first thought was that she was in trouble, because her parents were there. So I stuck my head in and said, "Anita, what's wrong?" Mr. Ingles, when he saw me, asked me to come in.

"Mr. Castro," he very formally addressed me, no doubt because the parents were there, "you can speak Spanish can't you?"

"Of course," I said.

"Well, here's the deal. Anita, as you know, has a scholarship to Occidental, but she has to live there at least the first two years. But her parents don't like this. They want her to live at home. They say that because they live close to the school, only about three miles, there's no reason why she shouldn't just commute. Frankly, the father seems especially concerned about Anita getting into trouble if she doesn't live at home. I guess this is a cultural thing about being protective of one's daughter. Can you speak to them?"

"Okay, let me take a chance," I told him.

I then turned to Anita and asked, "How bad do you want to go to Occidental?"

"I want to go, Mr. Castro," and she sobbed even more.

"Okay, how much English do your parents speak?"

"Oh, they don't speak it at all, Mr. Castro."

"Okay, keep a straight face while I talk to your parents."

"*Señores, esta beca que le ofrecen a Anita es una beca federal. Aquí en los Estados Unidos no se juega con el gobierno federal. Si no aceptan esta beca es posible que el gobierno los pueda multar o echarlos en la carcel.* [Mr. and Mrs. Contreras, this scholarship that is being offered to Anita is a federal one.

Here in the United States you don't fool around with the federal government. If you don't accept this scholarship, it's possible that the government can penalize you or even send you to jail.]"

"*O sí, Señor Castro, ahora entedemos. Anita puede ir.* [Oh, yes, Mr. Castro, we understand now. Anita can attend.]"

Anita got to go. She went on to graduate from Oxy, got a Fulbright to do graduate work abroad, got an MA and a PhD, and became a university professor. But Anita was one of the few success stories at Lincoln. In my mind, there was no reason why there couldn't be many more. However, to achieve this, the very nature of the school would have to be confronted.

WITH ALL OF the problems at Lincoln, one would have thought that there would be major discipline problems. In fact, I didn't encounter too much of this, and in general kids behaved well. However, when there would be such trouble, the school allowed, at least for the boys, corporal punishment. The vice principal swatted the boys—and hard. He used a paddle with holes in it so that it wasn't air resistant and he could swing better and harder. I used to hear the whacks all the way down the hall. But the administration discriminated in handing out such punishment. I never heard of a white or Asian kid being swatted, only the Mexicans. While the girls weren't hit, they were suspended if they got into trouble. These types of punishment didn't help with the alienation of a lot of our students.[17]

HARRY GAMBOA, student at Garfield High School: "One teacher nearly choked me to death."[18]

LUIS TORRES, student at Lincoln: "Mr. Lyon was a brute. He would walk up to a student and slap them."[19]

JOHN ORTIZ, student at Garfield: "I hated that school [Garfield]. I begged my mother not to send me there."[20]

At one extreme, a few of our students expressed their alienation by joining gangs. Perhaps about 5 percent of the kids were gang members or hangers on. It's even that way today. But in those days, it had little to do with drugs. It was, as in my youth, more territorial. Today it's all about drugs, which is how these kids get their money.

DESPITE THE CONDITIONS and problems at Lincoln, I welcomed being there. I accepted the challenge, although at first I had no idea of what this would lead to. Mexican kids surrounded me, and this was great, regardless of all the resistance from other teachers and the administration. The administration, beginning with the principal, of course, watched me all the time. They didn't trust me, but that didn't bother me. It's only been since I retired that they're not looking over my shoulder.[21]

My Philosophy of Education

From the moment I arrived at Lincoln, I felt that weight of trying to change conditions for Mexican Americans. I didn't know if I could succeed, but I knew that I had to try. To me, the greatest thing the Mexican students needed was a new positive self-image of themselves. You can't succeed if you don't feel good about yourself. That's just basic psychology. I tried to accomplish this at two levels.

First, in my classes, especially my history ones, I brought in as much as I could of Mexican and Mexican American history. I didn't know much about all this myself, but I learned as I went along. This, in turn, affected my own evolving identity. It wasn't that I had already reached the mountaintop and received the truth. I was learning also, but my own experiences and my gut feeling told me that Mexicans had been put down too often, and we now needed to assert pride in our ethnic background and culture. But my reactions weren't occurring in a vacuum. This was the beginning period, by 1965 and 1966, of the Black Power movement, led by groups such as the Black Panthers who militantly raised the cry of black power—"black is beautiful."

So, in my classes, I talked about the great indigenous civilizations in Mexico, such as the Olmecas and the Aztecas, and of others, such as the Incas in Peru. I taught my students about the major cities that the *indios* built, such as Tenochtitlán, which became Mexico City, and of their advances in science, math, art, agriculture, and mining. I also talked about how the Spanish conquest of Mexico and elsewhere in the Americas produced a mixed or *mestizo* population and how this *mestizaje* was the root of being Mexican. To be *mestizo* was to be part of both the Indian and the Spanish histories. I explained to them how the Spanish/Mexicans or *mestizos* settled the southwest region of what became part of the United States, and that's why cities such as Los Angeles carried Spanish language names. Mexican Americans, I told them, were not strangers or foreigners to L.A. or to the Southwest. We were here first. Then, borrowing from having earlier read McWilliams, *North from Mexico*, I further discussed the contributions of Mexican Americans, including twentieth-century immigrants, to the economy and culture of the

United States. All this was before Chicano Power and Chicano Studies, but it was in that direction. My classes and the students I could reach became a laboratory for awakening a new identity of pride and self-respect.

MOCTESUMA ESPARZA: "Sal Castro out of all the teachers that were there was the only one who was always emphasizing *mexicano* culture and music and stimulating other students to a sense of pride of who they were."[22]

LUIS TORRES: "The classroom experience with Sal Castro was memorable. He didn't shy away at all from having a point of view and expressing it. That point of view was 'know your history and be proud of who you are.' This was like a mantra, and it was a wildly revolutionary notion to us. Nobody else said this. He exuded this feeling that he was one of us and he respected us, and this made a difference for us."[23]

Both in class and outside of it, I also promoted what I now see as my general philosophy of education: making students feel comfortable about themselves and their abilities. I've been compared to Jaime Escalante, the later Latino math teacher at Garfield High who encouraged and got his Latino students to all pass with flying colors the SAT quantitative exams and who Edward James Olmos also made a film about called *Stand and Deliver*. But I would say that Escalante followed me and didn't really focus as much as I did on promoting ethnic self-pride.

My thing was that I expected my students to achieve. There was no reason why they couldn't. I had high expectations of them, and they were going to do it. I constantly and positively motivated them.

"You're going to do term projects just like the kids do in college because you're all going to college. That's the way it goes."

"And you're going to go to the library and do research on a topic in history and you're going to get it done."

"I want you to do well on your exams."

"I want you to take notes and you're going to learn how to take notes because you can do it."

"Nothing says you can't do it. You aren't going to tell me you can't do it because you are going to do it."

This might have been called tough love. But I really did love all of my students, and they were going to succeed.

To expose them to life outside the school and their neighborhoods, I took them on field trips, such as to city hall or the Board of Supervisors.

"You can be sitting right there on the city council or the board. There's nothing you can't do when you work hard. One day some of you will be on the city council and on the board. And guess what? One of you will be the first Mexican American mayor of L.A. since the nineteenth century!"

It was just a constant positive reinforcement—constantly, constantly. Push the hell out of them. Constantly angry with them.

"I don't want to hear that crap that you got a job. Your first responsibility is as a student and that's it. Otherwise, the *gavacho* will have his foot up your ass."

"You want to fight back? You do it with a book. That's your salvation. Salvation is getting an education."

"And don't give me this *pendejada* [crap] about getting married. You're going to first get your education and that means college!"

"The ticket to better things in life isn't just a high school education; it's a college degree. No ifs, ands, or buts about it."

I tried my best and succeeded with some and not with others. The kids responded well to my approach. The ones that complained, I argued with until they came to my way of thinking. But I was one of the few teachers pushing all this. However, by the time they got to me, it was very difficult to convince them that they were college material. By then, they had been told otherwise. "No, you're not going to college," some teachers would tell them. So it was hard. If the whole school had been involved with positive reinforcement, it would have helped. I was no miracle worker, but I felt I was effective to a degree.

I didn't just encourage those in my classes. I tried to reach out to others as well, including the few Mexican students in the honors classes. Moctesuma Esparza, who now is a big movie producer, was one of these. He wasn't in any of my classes, but I talked with him a lot. He and the other Chicanos in the college track, of course, were excellent students, but they were also very *tapados* (naive). They had very little awareness of who they were, yet the school promoted them as future leaders. But I thought, "Wow, what kind of leaders are these kids going to be? These self-haters are going to get a college degree and get the hell out of the community and never help in any way. They're just going to be Spanish surnames on to something else. Who knows, they may even change their last names."

But I didn't give up on these kids either. I talked, for example, to Esparza constantly. I used to see him in the halls, and we'd talk. At first, he'd argue with me. However, he came around, especially after I took him to one of the Camp Hess Kramer conferences in 1967, the year he graduated and then went on to UCLA. Esparza changed, and so did some of the other students who also went on to college by then, but they didn't forget Lincoln and the kids left behind. They would be back and with a vengeance.

Organizing Students

Talking to students was one thing; organizing them, as I had done at Belmont, was another. One of the first things I tried to do was to get more Mexican students to become part of a senior honors club called the Honor Organization of Knights. In fact, the principal assigned me to be the sponsor. Only a small number of Mexican Americans belonged, due to strict academic requirements. Asian Americans represented most of the members. I felt that the requirements unfairly kept out some students who were very capable but didn't quite have the higher GPA to join. I challenged these criteria and argued that if a kid was college-oriented with decent grades, he/she should belong. I nominated various kids, and some more were admitted. I made damn sure that the Knights represented the ethnic composition of the school. In addition, I tried to get the administration to change the name of the Knights to "Caballeros." The principal wouldn't have anything to do with this. "Are you crazy," he said. He was willing to modify the requirements but not the name. He thought it was my way of circumventing the English-only rule at the school! Ironically, after I left Lincoln and went to North Hollywood High, a predominantly white school, I discovered that its honor society was called the Caballeros.

I also encouraged some of the kids, as I had at Belmont, to run for the student council, where Mexican Americans hadn't been fully represented. More of them began to do so, such as Esparza, and got elected. Once we had more of them on the council, I pushed them to promote more Chicano issues to increase ethnic pride and awareness.

"You have to push for more Chicano activities. Don't fall for this crap that we're going to celebrate this and that, but not Mexican stuff. Let's have some Mexican culture here!"

I further promoted integrating Mexican students into the existing clubs and organizations, but I also believed that they needed a specific Mexican American organization. By 1967, some of the few Chicano students in Los Angeles colleges, such as UCLA, USC, L.A. State, and East L.A. College, influenced by the struggle of the farmworkers led by César Chávez, organized the initial Chicano student organizations that became part of the Chicano

Movement. They called the first citywide group UMAS (which stood for the United Mexican American Students). Some of these college students had gone to Lincoln and other Eastside schools. I, working with some of my high school students, organized a UMAS club at Lincoln in the 1967–68 year. "We're going to have a Chicano club," I told them, and by word of mouth this spread. It wasn't hard to put it together. Some of these kids I had also taken to Camp Hess Kramer, where they became more politicized. Al Juárez, a UCLA student, helped me in organizing the UMAS club. Amazingly, the principal approved it. UMAS at Lincoln at first wasn't overtly political, although it stressed ethnic pride. The kids printed some membership cards, which read something like "Proud Mexicans, UMAS." At this time, although some of the kids among themselves used the term "Chicano," an old barrio term, the prevailing term used by both college and high school students was Mexican American. "Chicano," however, within a year or so became the new term of identification. I used all of these terms, including Mexican, depending on the circumstances.

UMAS members met about once a week at lunchtime, and I joined them as their sponsor. About thirty-five students joined the group. At first, it focused on trying to sponsor certain cultural events. We tried to do something for September 16—Mexican Independence Day—but it was hard so early in the school year. We then tried to do something for Cinco de Mayo, but the administration wouldn't support it. The kids did organize a *jamaica*, a Mexican-style bazaar, on campus, and we invited the parents to attend, along with other students. It was pretty successful.

This modest beginning of a Mexican American student organization at Lincoln became very important in creating a new awareness among some of the kids, which laid the basis for increased and more militant activity by 1968. In fact, between the time I arrived in 1964 and 1968, I began to talk with some of the students about my views—that in order for the school to change something had to be done. I expressed my frustration at the problems and the inability of the administration and the teachers to recognize the need for change.

"We're going to do something; we're going to change this thing," I told the students. "I don't know what we're going to do, but we're going to do something."

The kids took this seriously, and the next semester or the next school year, they'd come back and say: "Mr. Castro, when are we going to do that something you said we were going to do?"

The Watts Riot

The growing tensions at Lincoln and at other Eastside schools did not occur, as I've noted, in a vacuum. Civil rights issues, the growth of Black Power, and the beginning influence of César Chávez and the farmworkers' struggle, all contributed to a more politicized climate. However, perhaps the most significant cause of racial tension in L.A. was the so-called Watts Riot of 1965. Watts at the time was mostly black, although today it's becoming more Latino. Following an altercation between the police and some blacks, conditions escalated into urban warfare. Young black men rioted and looted throughout the main commercial streets as thousands of police, National Guard, and regular army troops with tanks entered the area to squash the disturbance. The days of the conflict brought L.A. to a standstill as people watched what was happening on television. If you lived or worked anywhere near Watts, located south of the downtown area, you saw and smelled the smoke from the burning cars and buildings.

I witnessed some of this because of my job at the Tenth Street School playground north of Watts. In fact, a few of the *Chicanitos* from the playground actually went into Watts and looted along with the blacks. Some even tried to disguise themselves as blacks in order to go into the area. They greased up their faces and put black bandanas on and went into the neighborhood. They thought it was fun. They came back carrying TV sets. They even wanted to leave the loot in the playground so they could go back and get some more. I said, "No. Don't bring anything you take from there. Take it home, but I don't want it here."

"Come on, Castro," they appealed to me to change my mind.

"*No la friegen* [Damn it]," I said. "They'll throw me in jail. No way, get rid of the stuff."

I was concerned not only about the kids getting arrested, but also about their lives. The police and army were shooting and killing people in Watts. Not all of the victims were black. Out of the thirty-six or so killed, a few were Mexicans. You could see the violence on television. After conditions quieted, I drove through Watts with my two sons and we saw troops everywhere. Soldiers with rifles patrolled every corner.

Despite what some of the playground kids thought, these were dangerous times. After the riots broke out, I had to drive the principal of the school, Mrs. McFadden, home because she was scared to death. Military officials declared a curfew within a radius that extended and included the Tenth

Street School. Mrs. McFadden, who was white, feared that blacks might attack her.

"Will you give me a ride home, Mr. Castro?" she asked me. "I'm fearful."

"Sure, I'll give you a ride, no problem, don't worry about it."

Despite my chivalry—if that's what it was—a few years later she returned my favor by firing me after my involvement with the student movement at Lincoln in 1968.

Even after the riots, conditions remained tense, especially in Watts. Later that fall, Lincoln kids had to play a football game at Jordan High School in the middle of Watts. It was the first game of the season—a mostly Chicano team against an all-black one. As athletic director, I had to supervise our bus trip into Watts. Although I didn't request it, the National Guard escorted us to the game. The National Guard stationed itself around the field to prevent any disturbance. The Lincoln administration prohibited any of our students, including the cheerleaders, from attending the game. Jordan also banned its students from the game. Only a few parents of the Jordan team attended. It was a weird situation. I don't even remember who won the game. As soon as it was over, we quickly got in the bus and the National Guard escorted us back to Lincoln.

During this time period, I reflected on the meaning of the riots. I didn't support the use of violence, and, in many ways, it was the police and the military that had instigated the violence, although certainly blacks fought back and, of course, looted. I didn't condone this activity. However, one of the lessons I drew from the riots was that these disturbances, including the rioting, brought attention to the *morenitos*. Maybe the tactics used were not what should have happened, but, hell, it was doing a lot of good in focusing on the problems of the blacks. The fear that it generated among whites, including the power elite, led to efforts to deal with those problems. The ends might not have justified the means in this case, but it sure seemed to work. I didn't and don't support violence, but Watts showed me that only dramatic action could capture the attention of officials and the public. Watts also revealed to me again how far behind and how ignored were Mexican Americans and their problems. Racism existed in the barrios as it did in Watts, but no one paid any attention to us. I think that for our students who witnessed Watts and who went to Lincoln after the riots, it impressed on them that any action they might take about school conditions might unleash the police and the military on them. These concerns and even fears hung over us as tensions increased at Lincoln.

SIX

Blowout Part I

"We need to do something dramatic like Watts," I thought to myself follow-ing the riots in Los Angeles. I, of course, didn't support violence, but Watts showed me that only when minorities rebel or publicly resist in such a way to bring attention to their grievances would the rest of society listen. The prob-lem affecting Mexicans in the L.A. schools was so severe and so damaging to our kids that some kind of explosion was needed. I didn't know what this would mean. All I knew was that without some kind of mass protest by the students nothing would change.

It was about this time that my father paid one of his rare visits from Maza-tlán. I had not been very close to him over the years, but he was, after all, my father. One day, during his visit, I told him about all of the problems in the schools and how frustrated I was and how I felt this weight on my shoulders to do something about it. But what?

"*Huelga*," he calmly said to me. "*Huelga*."

"What do you mean, *huelga*? You mean a strike?"

"M'hijo [son], you know that after I went to Mazatlán, I helped to organize the railroad workers. You know that I was thrown in jail for this. But it was only by striking that the workers got changes for themselves. That's the only power that poor people have, to organize and go on strike."

"*Huelga*, strike?" I later thought about what my father had said. "But how would this work with the kids? They're not going to strike. What do they do? They go to school and don't leave or not come to school? How do we work this?"

The Chicano Movement

All this started me thinking about a plan of action, a strategy that could successfully be applied to the schools. I knew for sure that a mass action was needed—something like a strike—but the actual plan was something I started formulating in my mind for the next couple of years. In the mean-time, things were happening in the Chicano community that in different ways inspired me and the students to seriously consider something big. For one, there was the example of César Chávez and the farmworkers. In 1965, César led the farmworkers to strike against grape growers in the San Joaquin Valley. This was the beginning of the Chicano Movement, at least in the rural areas. Those of us in the cities began to hear and read about César. We supported the Mexican American farmworkers in their struggle to achieve dignity and better economic conditions. My family was not of this background, but I could sympathize ethnically and politically with César and the *campesinos* (farmworkers) and their fight in the fields. When César staged the impressive march to Sacramento from Delano, the union's headquarters, in the spring of 1966, I very much wanted to participate but couldn't. I'm sure that this dramatic action also inspired my thinking about what to do in the schools.[1]

I met César for the first time at a MAPA (Mexican American Political Association) meeting in 1965 in Riverside. I had recently joined the group and decided to attend its convention at the Mission Inn. I hadn't realized that César and the farmworkers would be there as well. As I went to a general session on a Saturday morning, all of a sudden I see these guys with red flags with the union's eagle in the center enter the hall shouting "*Huelga, Huelga, Huelga!* [Strike, Strike, Strike!]" Then this little guy—*chaparrito*—gets up and starts talking about the strike. It was César. He wasn't a heavy rapper, but in his quiet and modest way, he exuded a tremendous spirit of commitment and strength. "Damn," I thought, "these guys are organized!"

Although I never visited Delano, I supported the later boycott of grapes and encouraged my students to do likewise. I allowed literature on the boycott to be distributed in my classroom. I didn't bring it in, but some of the kids did. Not many of our students that I can recall actually participated in the boycott, but they were becoming aware of it and of César.

I think that the impact César had on me was that it made me realize his struggle was predominantly in the fields and that his main constituents were farmworkers. That was understandable. This was his fight. But he wasn't talking about people working in factories, sweatshops, and other places where Mexicans worked in the cities and lived in much larger numbers. Somehow the struggle had to also involve the urban barrios. This influenced my thinking about a dramatic action in the schools. There had to be an urban counterpart to César's agricultural struggle.

It was also at this time around 1966 and 1967 that I began to hear about other Chicano struggles. I read about the movement of Reies López Tijerina in New Mexico and his struggle to regain the lands of the poor Hispanos.

Sal Castro and César Chávez, Riverside, California, 1965. Courtesy Sal Castro Personal Collection.

His fiery, evangelistic, and charismatic image made him into an instant media figure. So I knew about him and that this was still another Chicano fighting for his people and bringing awareness to the issues by staging dramatic actions. Then there was Rodolfo "Corky" Gonzales in Denver, who also began to organize young Chicanos. I could more readily identify with Corky because of his urban struggle, including targeting the schools. Both Tijerina and Corky spoke in L.A. when early Chicano students at campuses such as UCLA invited them. I didn't attend, but I knew that they were having an impact.[2]

Because by 1967 there were a few more Chicano college students at UCLA, USC, L.A. State, and East L.A. College, some of whom I knew because they were Lincoln graduates, such as Moctesuma Esparza, but also Al Juárez, Carlos Muñoz, and Carlos Vásquez and others from other high schools, I first began to talk about a serious action in the schools with them. I met with some of these college kids to try to get some of them to volunteer to come back to the schools to help the high school students to read better. As I met with them, I bounced my ideas about the need for something to happen. They responded positively. As products of these schools and survivors of them, they knew the problems and that things couldn't go on as usual.[3]

The Piranya Coffee House

I expanded on my thoughts when some of the college students and a group called Young Citizens for Community Action (YCCA) formed after the 1967 Hess Kramer conference and, led by Vicki Castro and David Sánchez, started the Piranya Coffee House on Olympic Boulevard and Atlantic on the east side. They rented an old abandoned warehouse. Ironically, today it's the site of a fancy Latino restaurant called Tamayo's. I served on the first board of directors of the Piranya, along with Father John Luce, Episcopalian priest from the Church of the Epiphany in Lincoln Heights, who was very active and supportive. They needed adults to help sign for the lease.[4] In those days, everyone had a bohemian coffeehouse, which had been the influence of the earlier beatnik movement of the late 1950s and early 1960s. These coffee-houses were the precursors of Starbucks. Young people sat around drinking coffee and having long intellectual conversations or hearing poets read their stuff. I knew both Vicki and David because both had attended one of the Camp Hess Kramer conferences and were impressive young people. As a result of their experiences at the conference, they became more political.

What also politicized them and some of the others who attended the Piranya was that kitty-corner to it was a highway patrol substation. The officers didn't like young Chicanos congregating right across the street from them. It rubbed them the wrong way to see a bunch of Mexicans out there having a good time. They probably thought these Chicanos were trying to be white. So they started harassing them, going into the Piranya, including raiding the place in the guise of looking for drugs. A few of the kids had pot, but it was not a big-time deal that warranted the harsh and rough tactics of the highway patrol and also the county sheriffs. This harassment had the effect of making the students and young people not only more political, but militant. The YCCA, as a result, became transferred into the Young Chicanos for Community Action, or more popularly known as the Brown Berets. In fact David, as the prime minister of the Berets, and the others made me an honorary Brown Beret.[5]

Despite the problems with the police, the Piranya became a central meeting place for many of the young Chicanos who became activists in the Chicano Movement in L.A. As they became more involved, they invited various political speakers. I think César Chávez spoke, as well as black radicals such as Stokeley Carmichael. They asked me to speak. I talked about the need for a mass action in the schools and I encouraged them to help when it came. I knew even then that if it came to such a protest I would need the college students and the Berets to help with the younger kids. They were developing leaders and I would need them. I concluded by saying: "Hey, stay tuned, because we're going to do something. The kids are going to do something in the schools and we're going to need your help."[6]

PAULA CRISOSTOMO, student at Lincoln: "The Piranya was a fun place for those of us still in high school to go to without our parents around. It attracted kids from all the Eastside schools, so we had an opportunity to meet and share experiences. I'd go on Saturdays either in the afternoon or early evening after getting my parents' permission. The Piranya was called a coffeehouse, but it didn't serve coffee. In fact, nothing was served. It was one large room with some big round tables and chairs and a radio and record player."[7]

Pocho's Progress

I was further motivated to organize the students at Lincoln and possibly other Eastside schools after I read an article in *Time* magazine in its April 28, 1967, edition. It shocked and angered the hell out of me. It was called "Pocho's Progress"—about Mexicans in East Los Angeles. In the first place, the piece used the term *pocho*, which in some circles is considered to be a pejorative term suggesting a Mexican American who has lost his/her culture. Second, the article didn't discuss any progress made by Mexican Americans. Instead, it consisted of one stereotype after another. It was racist. Among other things, the writer described East L.A. in these negative words: "Nowhere is the pocho's plight for potential power more evident than the monotonous sub-scab flatlands of East Los Angeles where 600,000 Mexican Americans live. At the confluence of the swooping freeways the L.A. barrio begins. In tawdry taco joints and rollicking cantinas, the reek of cheap, sweet wine competes with the fumes of frying tortillas. The machine-gun-patter of slang Spanish is counterpointed by the bellow of lurid hot-rods driven by tattooed pachucos."[8]

Son of a bitch, that's how he described us. I remember talking to some of the college students about this and asking them, "Is this you?"[9] But what also pissed me off was that no Mexican American leaders appointed or elected seemed offended or complained. Upset, I went to a meeting of the Mexican American Chamber of Commerce on the east side, and none of the speakers, including this popular radio show guy by the name of Pepe Peña, mentioned the *Time* article. I stood up and said: "Don't you people read? Didn't anyone see that racist article in *Time* about us? Aren't you angry about this? It's an insult to the whole community. Goddamn it! What's it going to take for some of you to do something?"

The article and the passive reaction by community leaders only convinced me that there was no going back. If the adults couldn't or wouldn't lead, then the kids would.[10]

Camp Hess Kramer

In preparing for this mass action by the public high school students, there is no question that the Camp Hess Kramer conferences during the 1960s and especially the 1967 one became the backbone for what was to come. Some of the high school students who attended the conferences and then went on to college were the same college students that I would rely on to help me. Some of the high school students who attended the conference in 1967 and returned for their senior year at the Eastside schools would become leaders in putting together the action.

At all of these conferences, the students continued to share their grievances about the schools. All of them were similar to the conditions at Lincoln. Each conference revealed a growing political and ethnic consciousness among the kids. They began to use the term "Chicano" more and more. This awareness came as a result of their common experiences and the dialogues that went on at the camp. They began to talk about the black civil rights movement, about César Chávez and the farmworkers, and about the Vietnam War. I, as a counselor, encouraged these discussions. I did so not only with my group, but as I table hopped and talked with other students. I also continued to talk about what I did with my Lincoln students concerning about being proud and aware of their ethnic roots and culture, about the history of Mexico and of Chicanos, all these things that they didn't hear in their schools.[11]

The college conference counselors also played a crucial role in this *con-scientización* (conscience building). They were becoming very political and even militant themselves. The conference gave me more opportunity to talk about my ideas with the college students. They were ready to go. Whatever I was going to say, it didn't take much to convince them. By 1967 they had learned about the free speech movement at UC Berkeley and about the anti–Vietnam War protests. They knew about the black freedom marches in the South. They wanted to be in on the action. "How come we haven't done something like this?" they would ask me. They were ready and willing to go, and they helped me socialize this attitude to the high school kids.

The 1967 conference was especially notable because it reflected more and more the politicization of the students, both college and high school. By this time, I was openly discussing with the students the possibility of a dramatic action in the schools. I could see that this appealed to many of them. This growing consciousness was captured in a TV documentary, *Today, Not Mañana*, by KTLA, Channel 5 in Los Angeles. Clete Roberts, a well-known and respected TV reporter, requested permission to do a piece on the conference. We had no problems with this and felt that this would give the conference greater recognition and publicity. Roberts especially focused on capturing some of the dialogue between the kids and their conference counselors and some of the kids' comments at our general session.

Some complained about their school counselors: "They assume you can't take anything more than homemaking and family planning."

One girl said: "How can we as Chicanos find out who we are when our textbooks label Pancho Villa as a criminal?"

And still another girl asserted a developing Chicano Movement theme that came to be called internal colonialism: "When you say we came to America, that's not right because America came to us—we Mexicans were here first."

Impressed by the passion and discontent expressed by the students, Roberts concluded his report by saying: "The main impression we bring back is that of a mood of impatience, a growing sense of urgency. The young Mexican American is tired of waiting for the Promised Land. As one of them told us: 'It must be today, not mañana.'"[12]

Many years later, I was pleased to hear some of our former Camp Hess Kramer students and counselors reflect on what they gained at the conference that motivated them to participate in protesting school conditions. One of the counselors, Vicki Castro, who went on to be elected to the L.A. school board, remembers, "I think that this was the first I have any memory of seeing on a big scope that what I was experiencing in school was happening all over, and to a higher degree of open racism."[13] And Paula Crisostomo adds about her Camp Hess Kramer experience, "I found it safe to say what I believed in and not be criticized. I felt empowered. My world had opened up. I felt validated. I found my voice."[14]

Besides helping to promote a Chicano consciousness at the 1967 conference and of talking about a mass action, I used this occasion to develop an information network. I got as many phone numbers and addresses as I could, knowing that this would be crucial in organizing any protest that would involve kids, not only at Lincoln but throughout the Eastside. This was before e-mail and cell phones, so all I had was a handwritten list of these contacts, but it would come in handy.

I left the 1967 conference that Palm Sunday weekend knowing and feeling assured that the foundation for an action had been laid. The reason why kids were aware is because of the Hess Kramer camp. They knew what the problems were and they knew that sooner or later something was going to happen. All that was now needed was to decide on the protest and to begin to organize it. As I began the new school year for 1967–68, I knew that the time had come.

Excited about the prospects of engaging in protest politics, some of the high school and college students after the 1967 conference drafted a student survey that they planned to distribute in the schools to further document student grievances. This was a questionnaire that they used to interview high school students about conditions in the schools. Vicki Castro, one of the leaders in this effort, recalls that many of these interviews occurred in teen centers sponsored by the War on Poverty of the Johnson administration throughout the Eastside.[15] Paula Crisostomo further adds that she and other high school students distributed the surveys to all of the Eastside schools and that the survey consisted of about ten questions. She believes that several hundred of these surveys were filled out and tabulated by the YCCA.[16]

I had nothing to do with this and, in fact, wasn't even aware that they had done it. Later, they took the results of the survey, which only provided additional evidence of the bad conditions in the schools, to the school district administration and to the school board, which paid no attention to it.[17] Moctesuma Esparza, who was one of the students involved, remembers that the administration and the board "patted us on the back and threw away our survey."[18] This rejection and unsympathetic reaction on the part of officials only served to further encourage the students to protest. The survey also helped in drawing up the demands that we would later present to the board of education. But in the spring of 1967 those demands hadn't been written yet. They were still in my head, although some of those demands had already been written as proposals by the Mexican American Education Committee that I was a member of way back in the early 60s. Those proposals had been presented to the L.A. city board of education. But, as usual, it did nothing.

Nava Campaign

At about the same time as the 1967 Camp Hess Kramer conference, Mexican American electoral politics once again geared up. Mexican American community leaders and grassroots Mexicans had been hungry for some time to elect one of their own to prominent citywide offices. The opportunity to do so arose when Dr. Julian Nava, a professor of history at San Fernando Valley State College (later Cal State at Northridge), announced his candidacy for a seat on the board of education. Nava was a barrio boy, having been raised in East L.A., and he went to Roosevelt High. He encountered some of the same discrimination in the schools as other Mexican Americans. At Roosevelt, they tried to track him into shop classes, but he refused. He forced them to place him in the academic track. He went on to get a BA from Pomona College and then his Ph.D. in Latin American history at Harvard. He used to talk a lot about his Ph.D. from Harvard. He was very bright, articulate, and personable, spoke English very well, and carried himself well, but he was very *tapado* (naive). He didn't seem to be all together Chicano or aware of the problems in the barrio, much less the schools. Despite his barrio background, he had been sheltered from a lot of the bullshit affecting Mexicans.

But Nava perhaps was the only type of Mexican American who could win a citywide election. Unlike today, when the L.A. school board seats are distributed by district, in 1967 a candidate had to be elected by the entire city. This made it difficult for all candidates, but especially for minority ones. You couldn't just expect to be elected by your own people. You had to appeal to all groups in a huge and sprawling city like Los Angeles. Nava's educational background as a Ph.D. and a university professor and his nonethnic politics, including the fact that he was married to a white woman, made him attractive and acceptable to a range of voters, including many whites. At the same time, Mexican Americans were excited about the prospects of electing a Mexican to the school board and so rallied around Nava. Every Mexican American organization endorsed him.

I had never met Nava, but I also supported him and did what I could in his campaign, especially getting the vote out. While I had concerns about him, at the same time I also felt pride that a Mexican might get elected. There was a guy, Henry Calderon, who always ran for whatever office he could. He never won, and it disheartened us. He was a perennial loser. So it was good to see another candidate like Nava. His candidacy gave us renewed hope. As a teacher, I also had expectations that if elected he could be a voice for Mexican Americans on the board that governed the schools and might be able to convey some of the concerns that the students and I had. I talked about his candidacy at the Camp Hess Kramer conference and back at Lincoln with my students. I encouraged them to volunteer for his campaign.

"It's a good thing for you to do. It will really open your eyes to what's going on out there in the community. It will really help you become aware. I'll give you an A on the midterm if you participate."

A few kids took me up on this. Besides a grade, they also learned about electoral politics.

During his campaign, however, Nava didn't talk that much about Mexican American issues or what help he would give to the community with respect to the schools. When he campaigned in East L.A. he reminded people that he had gone to Roosevelt. He did talk about improving reading levels and about doing something about kids not finishing school, but he didn't talk about specific programs. In the white community, he just spoke in generalities, but that seemed to work because, to my surprise but also excitement, he was elected. He did, of course, very well in the Mexican areas, but also in the white ones. He didn't seem threatening to whites, and so many voted for him. Still, I and other Mexican Americans expressed delight at his election and hoped he would go on to champion Mexican American causes.[19] To his credit, later on he did. But, of course, he was only one vote. As I got to know him better, I pushed him in this direction. Before his election, according to Nava, I was B.C.—before Castro—but after the walkouts, which would affect him, I was A.C.—after Castro. If he got on his high horse about his Harvard Ph.D., I'd say to him, "just remember, Julian, how at Roosevelt they wanted to put you into industrial arts."

Early Organizing

Throughout all of this period, I kept hearing my father's advice, "*Huelga, Huelga.*" Although I hadn't yet said the word "strike" to anyone, I had pretty much decided that I would organize a student strike—a *huelga*. But I decided not to use the words "*huelga*" or "strike," which were too labor oriented. I decided that the students, if they were willing, would stage a walkout, not only from Lincoln but also from all of the other Eastside high schools: Roosevelt, Garfield, and Wilson. Belmont might also participate in this. I began to talk to people, including the students, into the fall semester of 1967 and certainly by the beginning of the spring semester in 1968, of a massive walkout that would force school officials, including the board of education, to listen to the students' grievances. I didn't coin the word "blowout." I had never heard of it before. It was some of the students who spontaneously came up with that term during the walkouts. The one in particular was John Ortiz, one of the Garfield High School student leaders.

JOHN ORTIZ: "The term 'blowout' was like an Eastside hipster term; it was a jazz expression. It meant being expressive—you would say of a musician, 'He blew it out.' I improvised using the term to refer to the walkouts. The other kids picked it up, as did the Chicano media."[20]

So the plan was now to inform students and others about the specific idea of a walkout and to begin preparations for it.[21]

By early January of 1968, commencing what *La Raza* newspaper would call the "Year of Decision," I started the actual organizing of the walkouts.[22] I informally met with some potential sympathetic high school teachers at the other schools, such as Tony Ortiz. Some of the college students, like Al Juárez, participated in this. I also took some of my Lincoln students, as seniors, who supported the walkouts to meet at UCLA with the UMAS (United Mexican American Students) group there. Some of the members were Carlos Vásquez, Susan Racho, and Juan Gómez-Quiñones. I think some of the college students that were there from other colleges included Hank López from San Fernando State and Monte Pérez from Golden West College. Moctesuma Esparza, now a leader of UMAS, served as a liaison between it and what I was doing. I told the college kids that if we walked out we would need their help, especially as monitors to help the high school students once they left the schools.

"I need your heads," I told the college students.

"Yeah," they responded, "we can help plan strategy and develop other ideas."

"*No, pendejos* [idiots]," I said, "I need your heads in case the cops come down on the students. I need your heads to get in the way and take the blows in case the cops start swinging their batons to give the kids time to run back to school or to run home, depending on what is closer."

They laughed and understood.[23]

I did the same thing at L.A. State, and there I also met with one of the few Chicano professors on the faculty, Dr. Ralph Guzmán, a political scientist who had participated in a pioneering study of Mexican Americans sponsored by UCLA and the Ford Foundation.[24] Ralph didn't say, "Hey, I'm going to go out on the streets with you guys," but he didn't oppose it and in fact understood why we had to take this action. He would later, in a piece for the *Los Angeles Times*, refer to Chicano activists as "Brown Power: The Gentle

Revolutionaries."[25] I'm not sure just how "gentle" we would be. Faculty like Ralph at first were more cautious, unlike the grad students at L.A. State, like Carlos Muñoz, who was gung ho in support. Carlos recruited other students on his campus to work with us. I also met with other Chicano students at San Fernando State, Long Beach State, East Los Angeles College, and L.A. City College. I even made a visit to USC, Occidental College, and Loyola University.

The Brown Berets, by 1968, led by David Sánchez and Carlos Montes, had already organized. Some were college students and some were not, but they focused on community issues through their educational programs, community newspaper *La Causa*, free breakfast program, health clinic, and monitoring of police abuse. I had already made contacts with them at the Piranya, but I included them now that I had a specific plan.[26] Another important group involved the emerging Chicano underground press such as *La Raza* and *Inside Eastside*. *La Raza*'s publisher and editor was a militant Cuban American, Eliezer Risco, who had worked with the farmworkers before coming to L.A. to start his newspaper in East L.A. I met with him and Raul Ruiz, one of his assistants, and informed them about the walkout idea and that I needed them at the right time to serve as part of my information network to get the word out, especially to the students, about the walkout. They agreed, and Raul, later, after also working with *Inside Eastside*, on his own published another paper called *Chicano Student News*—later called *Chicano Student Movement*—aimed specifically at the high school students. Both papers had high school reporters from the different schools who also helped distribute the paper to the students.[27]

PAULA CRISOSTOMO: "I would bring a whole stack to school and I would give a few to people, and they would pass them out to their friends. And then the school said we couldn't do it anymore, so I'd get to school early and I'd leave them around the campus. I would go into the bathroom and I would put them in the bathroom, the cafeteria, where I knew kids hung out, and I would tell people where they could find them. People would find them, but I wasn't actually distributing."[28]

LUIS TORRES: "*Inside Eastside* was a pivotal publication; it was a catalyst for discussion."[29]

Risco and Raul operated out of the Church of the Epiphany in Lincoln Heights, whose pastor, Father John Luce, supported these activities and let them edit their papers out of his basement. He also provided space for the Berets to meet. Father Luce was a very valuable ally to us, especially since I found it difficult to get Catholic clergy to support our efforts. Because I wanted Mexican parents to think that the Church was supportive, I once asked Father Luce if he didn't mind wearing his priestly collar at our meetings and demonstrations. "I need you to look like a Catholic priest," I told him. Father Luce took this well and complied.

Risco organized some community meetings at the church, where I spoke about the planned action. I didn't hedge my words by this time. I shot real bullets, not blanks. Mainly community people attended, and they seemed ambivalent about my plans. This only confirmed in my mind that it would be the students who would lead the community on the issue of the schools and not the other way around. One teacher from Lincoln, Jessie Franco, attended, and she went and complained to the principal about what I was doing and planning. But I didn't care. I had talked until I was blue in the face of what needed to be done to change the schools to benefit Mexican Americans, and no one at the school listened. "The hell with it," I thought. "Let's go." I was fed up to here, and the pressure within me had to be released. Something had to be done. The schools were hurting too many kids, and this had gone on for several generations. It had to be stopped.

In addition to meeting with these several groups, I also organized an informal working committee. It consisted of some teachers and students from each of the schools. The high school students themselves organized strike committees at Lincoln, Roosevelt, and Garfield.[30] We met at a private residence in the barrio. Each teacher usually brought about five students, as I did. The numbers varied from meeting to meeting. Tony Ortiz brought his Roosevelt students. A Mrs. Washington, a black teacher, from one of the schools also attended but later backed off. Some college students, like Al Juárez and Moctesuma Esparza, also attended. I had about fifty to sixty college students through the various UMAS chapters that I could rely on, and these now included additional schools such as San Fernando State and Long Beach State. Of the high schools kids that came to these meetings, some in the end didn't surface as the key leaders. They supported the walkouts, but as the movement grew, other students emerged as leaders, such as Paula Crisostomo, Freddy Reséndez, and Robert Rodríguez from Lincoln; Mita Cuarón and John Ortiz from Garfield; Tanya Luna Mount, Rita and Kathy Ledesma, Robert Sánchez, and Mario Esparza from Roosevelt. At these meetings, we discussed strategy but also the demands that we would make. The demands included many of the issues that the students had discussed at the Hess Kramer conferences, as well as the problems I had witnessed at Lincoln.

As far as talking to parents, I did a little of this at community meetings,

Paula Crisostomo, Lincoln High School student leader, 1968. Courtesy Paula Crisostomo Personal Collection.

such as at the Euclid Center, at All Nations Church on Soto, and at Our Lady of Lourdes. At these meetings, I only mentioned the need to change conditions in the schools that were holding the kids back. There were rumblings in the community that something was going to happen and about how parents could become involved, not in something like a walkout but in other ways. I didn't discuss with them my idea of a walkout because, whether rightly or wrongly, I feared that they would become afraid and talk their kids out of participating in this. I couldn't afford this. In retrospect, I know I was right. Most parents didn't have the same urgency of the problems as their children had or that I had. They would not have understood the need for a mass protest. I can understand this as a parent myself. I wasn't callous to their feelings, but I knew or felt that only something dramatic such as a walkout could begin to change things. I also feared for the kids, and that's why I took the time to systematically organize the walkouts and make sure that it would be orderly. For the safety of the students, I planned to use the college kids and the Berets as surrogate parents who would be in charge of watching over the students and protecting them against any possible trouble.

The College and Community Organizers

I want to make it very clear that I was not alone in organizing the students in the Eastside schools. I couldn't have done it without the assistance of some of the Chicano college students and some in the community. They were the backbone of the walkouts.[31] Of course, the high school and even junior high school kids were part of this movement. The blowouts were a collective effort. Raul Ruiz, for example, through his publication of *Chicano Student Movement* and *La Raza*, printed large numbers of leaflets about the conditions in the schools. He and his high school helpers distributed them outside of the schools and smuggled them onto the campuses. They also stuck leaflets into the fences surrounding the schools, and sometimes they even broke into the school grounds at night and posted leaflets throughout the halls. In addition, Raul had some of the high school students walk into their classes with leaflets in their books, which they then distributed or left in the restrooms and cafeterias. Vicki Castro from Cal State, L.A., later said: "I remember something that was very important to all of us is that we just didn't want disturbance for disturbance sake. And we were really talking to kids saying, 'We want you to know why you're walking out.' There was a purpose, so that we did meet with groups in the park, in the schools, on the corners, and we tried to say, this is why we're doing this and we need your support."[32]

The Bluff

In planning the walkouts, I kept to myself a deep, dark secret. Yes, I felt that something like the walkouts was needed to shake things up, and I was prepared to go through with it. But what I really wanted was to bluff the school board and school officials. I wanted to use the threat of a mass student civil disobedience as a way of forcing them to listen to the kids and to change their attitudes and practices about our students. I thought that a bluff would be sufficient to achieve our objectives, but I also did fear that if we carried out this protest what might happen to the kids and their safety. In the back of my mind was the Watts Riots and how the police and military came down on blacks with unneeded force that killed and wounded a large number. The last thing I wanted was a similar reaction to the walkouts. Besides the threat of the police, I also worried about the reaction of the gangs in East L.A. if the kids walked out and then, despite our hopes of keeping them organized, spread out into the different barrios and entered gang turf. The gangs might then move in and start hassling the kids and even attack them.

So my hope was to just get the word out that a mass walkout was in the works, as a way of bluffing school officials to fear this action and move to prevent it by negotiating with the students. I even mentioned to my principal that this might be coming down. "You better not get involved, Sal," he warned me. I took it as an implied threat, but smiled at him. I also told the students at the different schools that they should tell their principals that something big like a walkout might occur. But a bluff can only work if people really believe what you're planning on doing is likely to happen. Believing this, I deliberately told no one, including my students, that deep down I hoped we could bluff our way into getting the changes desired. But nothing was guaranteed. It was a bit spooky.

Part of the bluff involved the demands. My idea was to come up with a list of demands that we would first present to the different schools, with a threat of a walkout if they didn't seriously negotiate on them. We would then, assuming the schools went along with discussing the demands, go to the school board and use the same approach. The writing of the demands, however, proved to be time consuming because I had to make sure that we had input from all the schools. The kids in those schools, through my assistance and that of the college students, had organized their own separate strike committees, and they each suggested various demands. As we approached the spring of 1968 we still didn't have a complete list.

I wasn't too worried about this, because my idea was that we wouldn't spring—no pun intended—into action until about May. By then we would have the demands ready and we would approach the schools and the school board. I figured that the threat of a walkout in the late spring would be more effective because it would put pressure on the schools as they got ready for final exams and for graduation. The other factor in planning for a May bluff or possible action was that by May the kids would be very tired of school, and it wouldn't take too much for them to want to leave school. A lot of kids might be failing their classes and looking for places to go. This attitude wasn't entirely the kids' fault, because many teachers stupidly and callously told students who flunked their midterms that there was no way they could pass the class. So they deprived the students of any motivation to continue in these classes. I figured by May we'd have plenty of kids that would walk out. And, of course, May brings even nicer weather to L.A., and I didn't want the walkouts, if they occurred, to be rained out.

As we entered the spring season, in early March, I remained confident that everything was going pretty much as planned and that we would succeed in bluffing the schools. It didn't quite happen this way.

PAULA CRISOSTOMO: "I know tension had heightened, activity had heightened district wide, a lot of schools were talking about it [walking out], everyone knew it was going to happen, everyone was waiting for the sign. But I remember the atmosphere was absolutely tense, I mean it was just electric in school. This had been building for so long, and everyone knew it was going to happen and everyone was just waiting and waiting."[33]

Blowout

One of the Eastside schools that would be involved in the walkouts was Wilson. Some of the students there had been working with me in planning the action. At the same time, school life went on as usual. Students went to classes; they played sports; they went to dances; and they put on plays. The play that some of the kids at Wilson were involved with that spring was *Barefoot in the Park*, a popular Broadway play that had also been made into a film with Jane Fonda and Robert Redford. Wilson also had a very conservative principal by the name of Mr. Donald Skinner.[34] He was so conservative that he wore suspenders and a belt to hold his pants up. No one dressed like that in 1968. It appears that on Thursday, February 28, he went to the final dress rehearsal of the play to give his approval for it to go on that weekend. One of the lines in the play involves the young married couple after they've returned to their New York apartment after their honeymoon. The guy says to his wife: "Shall we go to work today or go back to bed?" When Skinner heard this, he apparently became quite irate and immediately canceled the play. "No, no, this play is not going to be shown here at Wilson," I later heard that he said. He closed the damn play down.

The kids in the play—all Chicanos—were pissed. They had been working hard for weeks and had looked forward to performing. None of these students were part of the Wilson contingent that had been coming to our planning meetings on the walkouts, but they had heard the rumors about the possible protest. So they picked up on this, and that Friday they led other students on a walkout at Wilson. It was a pretty good-size group of perhaps 200. The media picked it up. The students protested the closing of the play, but it coincided with other problems at the school affecting Mexican American students. But Wilson's walkout wasn't part of our plan. It took our organizing committee and me by surprise. I didn't hear about it until after it happened. We hadn't planned on any action this soon, and all of a sudden we have Wilson already walking out. On top of this, there went our bluff. The walkouts had started.[35]

Although I felt that things were getting out of control, I still believed that we might be able to keep things cool at the other schools and hold back the full walkouts until later, giving the bluff still a chance to work.

Monday evening we continued to meet to coordinate the action. Every-thing seemed to be moving smoothly, except that on Tuesday the students at Garfield High also jumped the gun and walked out. The *Los Angeles Times* reported that the principal complained that for more than a week prior to the demonstration leaflets urging the walkout had been circulated. This was the work of the Garfield Strike Committee and possibly some of our col-lege students, the Brown Berets, and the Chicano press.[36] The Chicano press later reported that about 2,000 went out, although my information made me believe that it wasn't as large a demonstration. However, according to John Ortiz, many students who didn't walk out supported the strike.[37] My understanding of the Garfield walkout was that the student leaders there had become tired of waiting for our demands to be presented to the school board.[38] However, it only stressed to me the importance of now definitely going out the next day, and for my committee and me to assert our leader-ship.[39]

MITA CUARÓN, Garfield student: "I remember looking at the clock that morning and then the fire alarm bell went off and we all walked out. I can't remember if we had planned the walkout or if it was spontaneous. In any event, some of us on the strike committee decided that we would stay out and began calling on the students not to return to class. I jumped on top of a car—just like you see the character of Paula in the *Walkout* film—and I had picked up one of those bright red/orange street dividers and began using it as a megaphone. 'Walkout, walkout,' I yelled into it. The police shortly arrived, but I don't remember feeling scared."[40]

What was disturbing about the Garfield walkout and raised possible problems was that the police intervened, declared the walkout an unlawful assembly, and roughed up some of the students.[41] I had feared such police overreaction but was not prepared for it with the spontaneous Garfield walk-out. Henry Gutiérrez, who later was one of the college students who worked on the aftermath of the blowouts, has written the following about the Gar-field incident with the police in very graphic terms:

> At Garfield approximately 2,700 students boycotted classes out of a
> total enrollment of 3,750. The walkout began with about 500 students
> during the noon recess. A telephone bomb threat brought four fire
> trucks to the school. Their arrival created additional excitement when
> the demonstrators believed that the fire hoses would be used on them.
> Striking students lined both sides of the street in front of the school.

Los Angeles police at the Garfield High School walkout, March 5, 1968. Los Angeles Times Photographic Archive, Department of Special Collections, Charles E. Young Research Library, UCLA.

Twenty to thirty sheriff's deputies were on the scene and two students were arrested. There were reports of bottle and can throwing and one automobile window broken. When the students were ordered to disperse they first sat in the street, then got up and started running. The vice principal let students out through the gate, but the sheriff's deputies forced them back into the administration building. The arrival of a TV news vehicle set off additional demonstrations that were again dispersed by the deputies. By shortly after 3 P.M. the students began to disperse.[42]

MITA CUARÓN: "I felt two arms on each side of my body. Grabbed me underneath my arms, pulled me away off from the main line of students. They assumed I was an outsider from the school. We didn't commit a crime. We were protesting."[43]

It was rough at Garfield. John Ortiz recalls seeing a Chicano cop hitting a female student on the head with his billy club. Ortiz also witnessed police snipers on top of the school building, along with at least forty units of deputy sheriffs assembled on the football field.

The walkout at Garfield gave us no choice now but to get back in control and immediately get the other schools to also walk out. I knew it would have to be that very next day. I called an emergency meeting that Tuesday evening at Raul Arreola's house in El Serreno. Raul was an art teacher at one of the

Harry Gamboa Jr. at the Garfield High School walkout, March 5, 1968. © Carmen Gamboa. Courtesy Carmen Gamboa Personal Collection.

schools and prominent in the AFT (American Federation of Teachers). I got the word out to some of the college students, a few of the teachers at the other schools, and a few parents. I deliberately wanted to keep the meeting small in order to make sure that we agreed on a strategy. I also was aware that planning the walkouts and now moving on them might be seen as a conspiracy, and I didn't want to involve too many in this. That's why I didn't invite any high school kids and why at the meeting I isolated the few other teachers and parents in the living room while I and the real "conspirators" met in the kitchen of Raul's house. This was my "kitchen cabinet." Those in the living room talked about how they could support the students *if* they walked out. They never talked that the students *were* going to walk out.

In the kitchen, however, it was another matter. Here we engaged in what Vicki Castro calls "passionate decisions."[44] For us, the kids definitely were going out. With me in the "plot" was a who's who of later key activists and adult leaders: Moctesuma Esparza, Al Juárez, Susan Racho, Carlos Vásquez, Monte Pérez, Hank López, Juan Gómez-Quiñones, and a few others. They all agreed with me that we had no choice now but to get the kids to leave the schools, and that this would start on Wednesday. I assigned different colleges to be responsible for different schools, for the most part. I had always felt that we had to have adults—in this case the college students—to be in charge of the students to ensure order and to prevent any problems. I didn't want any kids going out into the streets without a college student being there. Each one would, in turn, get other college students to help them. In fact, each UMAS group was also assigned to a school. The students from L.A. State and East L.A. College were mostly going to be at Garfield because that was closest to them. The UCLA Chicanos would be at Lincoln, and at Roosevelt would be a contingent from UCLA, L.A. State, USC, and San Fernando Valley College. At Belmont, the students from L.A. City College would be in charge, although I had difficulty reaching them prior to the walkouts. Chicano students from Occidental College would handle Wilson.[45] I divided the college students at our meeting based on which high school they had attended. I gave Lincoln to Esparza, Roosevelt to Juárez, Garfield to Pérez, and so on down the line.

We also got word out to the Brown Berets about our plans, and they agreed to help out with the monitoring of the students, as well as keeping an eye out on possible police abuse if the cops showed up. But I asked them not to wear their paramilitary uniforms this time, in order to not spook the kids. "You can come and help, but remember why you're there. You're there to get in the way in case the cops get nasty. That's your function. But if you come, don't wear your uniforms. Do college boy." "College boy" was the preppy look. The fact was that the high school students trusted the college kids more than they did the Berets, and that's why I wanted the Berets to look like the college students.

Secondly, we began making phone calls to some of the high school students working with us, informing them that Wednesday would be D-Day. They were going out, and they in turn needed to alert as many other students as possible. We contacted students such as Paula Crisostomo, Freddie Resendez, and John Ortiz, among others. We did all this through phone trees. If we had had e-mail that would have helped a great deal, but that hadn't been invented yet. Our plan was that all of the Eastside schools would go out, but that we would also encourage other schools outside of East L.A. to walk out in solidarity. I'm sure some of the kids stayed up late making calls all over.

JOHN ORTIZ, student at Garfield: "The number one issue was unity; we had to be together."[46]

Another thing we had to do was get word to the media that there would be a massive walkout. We didn't know whether it would be massive or not, but we wanted to make sure the media showed up, so we talked in those terms. We were pretty certain that schools like Lincoln, Roosevelt, and Garfield would go out, but beyond that we didn't know. I had assigned Esparza as my communications officer because he was already then interested in the media. To ensure that the media would cover at least Lincoln and Roosevelt, we decided that Lincoln would go out at 10 A.M. that Wednesday, to be followed by Roosevelt at noon. Garfield and Wilson would go out at any time. This would allow the media to cover one school first and then have enough time to cover the other. We especially wanted TV coverage from key stations such as channels 4, 5, and 7. We were savvy enough to know by 1968 that if a protest didn't appear on TV, it didn't happen at all.

This sounded like a good idea, except that Moctesuma, for whatever reason, wasn't paying attention to the time plan. He thought we had decided that both schools would walk out at noon—*pendejo*! Of course, I didn't know this until too late. Esparza did his job by calling the TV stations and other media, but he gave them the wrong time. I still kid Moctesuma about this, but I don't blame him. Events were moving very fast, and it was hectic.

Finally, I got the college students that night to start making signs to give out to the kids as they walked out. These would call attention to their grievances as well as express Chicano pride. Some said: "Education is a right not a privilege;" "Brown is Beautiful;" "Viva La Raza;" "Chicano Power;" "Education not Contempt;" "Ya Basta;" "Educación, Justicia;" "Education Not Eradication;" etc. Some of the high school kids on their own also made signs. All of this would add to the hoped-for TV coverage.[47]

When we finished in the kitchen with our plotting, we informed the others in the living room about the plans and that the students would be walking out Wednesday. They supported our decision, and I encouraged them to be at the schools to show their support for the kids and to help keep control. They agreed and promised to be there and to try to bring other parents.

As the meeting broke up, I had another idea and expressed it to Pat Sánchez, one of the parents.

"Pat, would you do me a favor and bring some *pan dulce* [Mexican sweet bread] to Lincoln tomorrow so as the kids walk out and the TV cameras are rolling, you can pass out the treats to the students. This will show parent and community support."

"Sure, Sal, no problem. I'll be there."

Well, he did show up, but he didn't bring the *pan dulce*. Instead, I saw him outside carrying one of the signs with some radical statement. Poor Pat. The undercover cops filmed him, and later he became one of those indicted for conspiracy to plan the walkouts, yet he had nothing to do with the *mitode* (walkouts). "*Cabrón*," I later kidded Pat, "you were too damn cheap to bring *pan dulce* and that's why you got arrested." Ironically, some of the real conspirators—the kitchen cabinet—such as Al Juárez, Carlos Vásquez, Tony Ortiz, Susan Racho, Juan Gómez-Quiñones, Hank López, and Monte Pérez, were not indicted.[48]

Prior to the Wilson walkout, I had hoped to also get the AFT local in L.A., which represented many of the public school teachers, to agree that if a walkout took place the union would encourage their teachers not to cross the picket line. I hadn't done this as yet, so the Wilson action forced me to quickly arrange a meeting with AFT leaders that Monday afternoon or early evening. They had heard rumors of a possible walkout that spring, so it wasn't completely new to them.

"The kids may be walking out this week," I told them. "They need your help. What will you do? Will you cross their line?"

I couldn't believe the reaction. After going back and forth on the issue, the *cabrones* (bastards) decided to table the issue—*ya ni la friegen* (bullshit).

"Sal, we need more time to discuss this. We'll get back to you as soon as we can."

I'm still waiting today for their decision! They crossed the line.

I knew by Tuesday evening that we were pretty much alone, except for a few supportive teachers and some parents. But we had to go through with it.

I don't think I got much sleep that Tuesday night. I woke up even earlier than usual that morning and got ready to go to school. I didn't think of the historical importance of this day. I just knew that it had to be done. I don't think I even stopped to think about the consequences to my job and whether I could get suspended or even fired. I didn't think about it. I loved being a teacher and didn't want to be anything else, but I guess because I was a teacher I felt I had to do what I had to do for the students and for the students to come.

As I drove into the school parking lot, everything seemed normal as usual.

It was a bit hazy that morning, March 6, as L.A. mornings tend to be, but it proved to be a nice early spring day. "No rain—great!" I said to myself. As I entered the main building, I ran into some of our student organizers.

"Okay, this is it; we're going," I told them.

For weeks, some of them almost every day had been asking me: "Today, Mr. Castro?" Well, this time I said, "Yeah, today."

Instead of going directly to my classroom, I went to see George Ingles, the principal. This was deliberate. I wanted to tell him what was going to happen. I wanted to make sure that he would tell the police that this was going to be a peaceful demonstration and that they should not come on campus. I also wanted him to inform the other school principals to do the same. As he had before, he warned me.

"Sal, don't do this."

"George, I'm going out with the students."

As I left his office and walked to my class, I told other students that we were walking out at 10 A.M.

"Is it true, Mr. Castro? We're going?"

"Yeah, get ready."

They were ready and eager. We had done a good job, thanks to our student leaders as well as the Chicano underground press, of getting the word out. The students in general, of course, knew the problems of the schools. Many had also been with me at Hess Kramer.

My first class that morning was U.S. history, and my second was Guidance, something new I was doing. I didn't talk about the walkout in class because all the students already knew about it. I couldn't do much with them that morning. Their minds were elsewhere. They kept looking at the clock and looking out the windows. Those first two class sessions seemed to take forever. We could have organized the action earlier, but I wanted to wait at Lincoln until ten that morning when all of the students went to homeroom. Teachers took attendance at that time, and this was important because school funding was based on attendance. I wanted to hit the school right in the pocket book by having the kids go out prior to homeroom and before attendance could be taken. Teachers would then have to report all of these absences.

PAULA CRISOSTOMO: "At 9 A.M., while we're sitting in class, we knew it was going to happen."[49]

9:50 A.M. Ring! At first nothing happened. "Am I really going to do this?" one of the students, Pattsi Valdez, later recalled.[50] Then all of a sudden, kids started to go out. I could hear the shuffling in the halls. Some of them went to their lockers, where they had hidden their homemade signs. As students began to exit, some of the college kids and Berets entered the main building and started calling out to the students: "Walk out! Walk out!" I didn't see them, and that had not been part of the plan, so it was spontaneous on their part.[51] Actually, I didn't want the college students and the Berets to go in and do this because I didn't want to spook the kids. The high school students didn't know them, and I was concerned that this might scare them. Some of the Berets, for example, despite my warning, went in with their military-style uniforms, wearing beards, looking like Che Guevara. I wanted the Berets out in the streets to play the tough role if needed with the cops. They and the college students were to be the buffer between the kids and the police. Fortunately, the high school students had it together and walked out on their own without panicking.[52]

I didn't see the college students and the Berets in the halls because my classroom was in the southern end of the campus and not in the main building. Besides, I was busy getting my students out of the school.

As the kids left the buildings, they also shouted, "Walkout! walkout!" They didn't use the term "blowout," or at least I didn't hear it. The origins of the term was at Garfield. When the students walked out that day, one of the students, John Ortiz, started calling out, "Blowout! blowout!" Raul Ruiz recalls that he heard the cry "blowout" at Lincoln.[53] I have no idea where Ortiz got this word, but other students picked it up, as did the media, although not right away, but during the course of that week, and began to refer to the walkouts as the blowouts.

As the bell rang, out they went, out into the street. With their heads held high, with dignity. It was beautiful to be a Chicano that day.[54]

PAULA CRISOSTOMO: "I was very scared and nervous. I didn't know what was going to happen. But when I saw the other students walking out, I began to feel bold and empowered."[55]

I didn't see the college students and the Berets until I hit the sidewalk with my students. Girls were crying, but they bravely walked out.[56] Everyone went out the main door. In a few minutes, almost the entire school was vacated. It was like one of those fire drills. All the kids milled around the sidewalk in the front entrance of the school. Some climbed on top of parked cars. My first concern was, "Where the hell are the TV cameras?" Of course, they weren't there because of Esparza's misinterpretation. My next thought was, "What am I going to do with 2,000 kids?" I had originally planned for the students

Brown Berets. From left to right: Fred López, David Sánchez, Carlos Montes, and Ralph Ramírez. Courtesy Los Angeles Times Photographic Archive, Department of Special Collections, Charles E. Young Research Library, UCLA.

to congregate in the front so the TV people could get their shots. That would be impressive. The TV reporters could then interview some of the student leaders, whom I had prepped about what to say on the reasons for the walkout and about some of the demands: respect by teachers for the students, smaller classes, the need for Mexican American history, etc. But since the media didn't show up, all of this was up in the air. Of course, I didn't know at that time about Esparza's snafu. As I hoped the media would arrive, I told the kids to start marching around the school. We went around and around waiting for the TV. No TV.[57]

While we marched and the kids carried their signs and shouted their slogans, most of the teachers and all of the administrators stayed inside, and some watched from the windows.[58] They hadn't tried to block the students from leaving. They were aware the walkouts were coming; some may not have known it was going to be that day, but they seemed resigned, including Ingles, that they couldn't prevent it. I guess they hoped it would be a one-shot deal, and the kids after an hour or so would return to classes. A few teachers, perhaps ten to fifteen, did walk out with the students. They joined in walking around the school. I was glad to see them and hoped these teachers would continue to support the students.[59]

I found even more amazing that not only had senior high school students

Walkout students at Lincoln High School with Freddy Resendez on top of car, March 6, 1968.
Courtesy Los Angeles Times Photographic Archive, Department of Special Collections,
Charles E. Young Research Library, UCLA.

walked out, but also junior high school ones. I had targeted primarily the older kids for the demonstration and not very much the younger ones. I didn't want to put these *chavalitos* in any jeopardy, but here they were on the sidewalks.

As we marched or walked around the school grounds, I noticed that no police were in sight, although I saw some plainclothes guys with walkie-talkies. I felt relieved about this. I found out later that cops were there but kept out of sight on the periphery of the school. Ingles had alerted them, but to his credit, he had cautioned them about not entering the campus. That was not, however, the case at some of the other schools. The county sheriffs, for example, surrounded Garfield. The Wilson kids had to climb the school fences to get out and had problems with the cops. But the worst conflict with the police came at Roosevelt, which went out as planned at noon. Belmont didn't go out that Wednesday because I hadn't been able to get the city college kids in time to coordinate it. These reports trickled in during the day since we had no direct communications like walkie-talkies, and, of course, cell phones didn't exist then.[60]

MOCTESUMA ESPARZA: "There was this tremendous energy and fervor. There was an excitement that we had pulled it off."[61]

As noted, the walkouts at Roosevelt met with police conflict. It was a totally different scene. The cops, some forty in all, who came from the Hollenbeck station in Boyle Heights, apparently were tougher and meaner compared to the Northeast station by Lincoln.[62] At Roosevelt, the principal there, a guy named Dyer, tried to prevent a walkout by staging a school assembly the first thing that morning. I guess he hoped that by having some of the kids speak there that would defuse the need for a walkout. What he didn't count on was the student council president, a kid named Robert Sánchez, telling me about the assembly the evening before. I told Robert: "Okay, since all the students are going to be at the assembly, you take the microphone from Dyer and say that this meeting is accomplishing nothing and for the students to walk out."

Robert did this, to the apparent shock of the principal, and the students walked out. Some kids had to jump over locked gates in order to get out. But Dyer wasn't through yet. He had notified the cops to be there and to try to prevent the kids from walking out. The Los Angeles police called a tactical alert and came down heavy on some of the students.[63] This proved to be the biggest and most dangerous confrontation with the police. The cops entered the campus wearing their riot gear with batons drawn and tried to push the kids back. They threatened to arrest those climbing the fences.

ROOSEVELT STUDENT: "*Va ver un pedo, a la fregada* [there's going to be shit coming down], start splitting."[64]

Some of the students got out after Vicki Castro, one of our college students and an alumna of Roosevelt, with the help of some of the other college students, tied a rope or chain to the locked gate and to her car and then pulled down the gate. In another account later, Philip Somers, a teacher at Roosevelt, claimed that he saw Carlos Montes of the Brown Berets with a rope that he put around the chain that held one of the gates closed and that he succeeded in snapping the chain and opening the gate.[65] As students scattered down the streets, the cops hit them, including some of the girls, with their batons. They cornered some and ganged up on them as the kids fell down and tried to protect themselves from the blows. They didn't distinguish boys from girls. It was a Rodney King beating.[66] Some kids were cuffed and arrested. They tried to arrest the quarterback of the football team, who tried to break the lock of one of the gates, only to be told by the principal: "We need him; now take it easy; he's our quarterback."[67] The police violence apparently intimidated some of the students into not walking out.

The cops did arrest, however, Raul Ruiz from *Chicano Student News*, who was there taking pictures. They cuffed him, put him in a squad car, and, according to Raul, roughed him up and then released him. The TV crews captured all of this, which made for graphic images on the evening news. Despite this unnecessary violence on the part of the cops, enough Roosevelt students escaped and linked up with us and told us what had happened.[68]

Hazard Park

After about an hour or so and the TV crews still hadn't showed up at Lincoln, I decided that we needed to move out and take our protest to the school board and that might generate the media coverage I wanted. It was too far to walk all the way to the board of education offices downtown, but there was an area office in Hazard Park, about three-quarters of a mile from the school.[69] I told the college students to gather up the kids and start marching to the park, where hopefully we could talk to the area superintendent, Stuart Stengel, if he was there. We left the campus and walked through Lincoln Park. I still didn't see any police along the way. Although some of the kids went home, still several hundred marched, which might have caused some problems, except that some of the students on their own monitored the march. They stopped the students so that cars could cross on Lincoln Park Boulevard, a very busy intersection. The kids were terrific. An ambulance came by, and so they stopped the march to let it pass. The students behaved themselves at the same time they shouted slogans and had a good time. People came out from their homes to see what was happening. It was great to see all of these kids marching, including members of the student council and its president. Even the athletes and members of the ROTC joined us. Anticipating their walking out, their coaches and teachers told them to make sure not to wear their letterman sweaters or jackets or their military insignia. They complied and walked out.

We arrived at the park just around noontime, and to my surprise the reporter and TV crew from Channel 7 met us there.

"What's this all about?" the reporter asked.

I and some students started talking, as all the others surrounded Superintendent Stengel's office. Fortunately, he was in and came out. He tried to speak to the kids, but they drowned him out. The fact was that he alone couldn't do much. I told Esparza to tell the students that we would not negotiate with Stengel. All we wanted was that he facilitate a meeting for the students with the board of education. That was it. So Esparza takes it upon himself to give a speech to this effect. He gets up in front of the students wearing his Lincoln school sweater as if he was still a high school student and tells them what I had said, although he didn't attribute the message to me. Actually, I didn't want Esparza or the college students to speak out that day. I wanted the high school students to do so. But I think the ego of the college kids got the better of them, and so they did most of the talking that day. But this was okay. They said the right things. If they hadn't, I would have stopped them fast. But they followed the party line and that was fine. In fact, they looked good on TV that evening as other TV crews arrived. They looked like high school students. No one could tell the difference.

The only thing we would negotiate with Stengel was for him to agree to walk back to Lincoln with the kids so that the school wouldn't penalize them. He agreed. By this time, the crowd had increased, as students from some of the other schools joined us when they learned somehow that we were at the park. Roosevelt and Wilson kids walked over from their schools since they were closer to Lincoln. The Garfield students came in cars since their school was further. Some of the students went home from the park, but many others returned to the school. I got a ride back, and when I entered the main building I heard Ingles's voice on the intercom saying that this had been a trying day but he hoped that everyone had a good day. I couldn't believe it. He was talking to no one. The school was empty, but he was making a speech to himself.

After I arrived at Lincoln around 1 P.M. and after the students had returned,

Sal Castro with walkout students at Lincoln High School, March 1968. Courtesy Los Angeles Times Photographic Archive, Department of Special Collections, Charles E. Young Research Library, UCLA.

I ran into Arnold Rodríguez, a member of the Urban Affairs office of the school district: "Sal, Stengel wants to talk to you. He's back at his office."[70]

"Great, but all I'm going to tell him is what I'm telling you. We want a meeting with the board. That's it."

Arnold went with me to Stengel's office. The superintendent seemed to see a sinister plot to what had happened that day, so I tried to set him straight: "What the kids did today was honorable. They're trying to make the schools better. They're trying to get smaller classes. They want a better shot at college. They want fewer counselors to student ratios. They want parents from the community to come in and work in the schools. All they really want are community schools. They're giving you some good ideas. There's nothing wrong with what these kids are trying to do."

"But they're breaking the law," he, with irritation in his voice, said.

"Look, get us a meeting with the board. We can stop the walkouts in a second if we get that meeting. That's what they want. They want to negotiate with the board to make some changes."

"It's not in my power." That's all he could tell me.

I walked out, no pun intended, knowing that we would have to raise the ante.

After a long day, I went to have a beer at the Pabst Blue Ribbon Tasting Room, where they gave you free beer right off the tap. I was tired but exhilarated. We had pulled it off. Art Velarde, a teacher at Roosevelt whose students had gone out, met me there, along with Henry Ronquillo, another guy who worked for Urban Affairs. Art was a funny guy. He loved to fool around. You could give him two free tickets to a Dodger game, and instead of using them, he'd give them away and sneak into the park. The thrill for him of going to a ballgame was to sneak in. He had an adult body with a kid's mind. I didn't know Henry that well. He was an ex-jock who had played basketball for the University of Oregon. He taught before joining Urban Affairs as a liaison between the community and the school board. He had heard that the kids were going to walk out, and so he showed up to see what was happening in order to report to the board. Henry was okay. He had been a bit *tapado* when he first started out with Urban Affairs. Vicki Castro, who had gone to Roosevelt and then to L.A. State, some time prior to the walkouts brought Henry to see me. I briefed him on the various problems in the schools, and he seemed sympathetic.

Henry actually proved to be very valuable to me during the protests. He, in fact, became my "deep throat." I passed on to him things I wanted the board to hear, and Henry, in turn, without the board's knowledge, told me how board members were reacting to the crisis. This proved to be a useful exchange. Because I remained fearful of police retaliation, I told Henry about when we next planned another action and for him to pass this information to the board. I intended to make sure that the board knew that our next walkout would also be orderly and peaceful so that they wouldn't overreact and call on the cops to arrest the kids.

Henry reciprocated by telling me certain things about board members that prepared me to rebut their arguments and to better promote the students' case to the media. For example, he told me that at least two deputy superintendents in the city schools did not have administrative credentials, as required of such high officials. To compensate for this, they had gotten friends in the state legislature to arrange emergency credentials for them so that they could get their good-paying jobs. I used this information the very next day when, as part of my ongoing playground job, I had to attend an award ceremony at Toberman Playground in the downtown area. No sooner had I arrived than a TV reporter from Channel 7 with crew in hand stopped me and asked: "Mr. Castro, we understand that one of the demands you're making of the school board is for more Mexican American school administrators, but the board says there aren't many qualified Mexican Americans for these positions. What's your response?"

"Well, that's a good question. But the fact of the matter is that at least one school administrator, Mr. Graham O'Sullivan, does not have a credential. He has an emergency one. So is he qualified? I see no reason why the same procedure can't be done for some Mexican Americans. The board can give them emergency credentials so that they can then have the experience to get a regular one. But to answer directly your question, yes there are many qualified Mexican American teachers who should be principals and vice principals and hold administrative jobs in the district."[71]

Thanks to Henry, I was prepared for this question. I would call him in the middle of the night to tell him our plans and to find out from him what board members were saying. It was a quid pro quo. I still kid Henry about his role as "deep throat."

At the beer garden, we, of course, discussed the walkouts and celebrated their success. This meant that the students from the different schools had walked out in a dramatic act of opposition to the schools, and they did so peacefully and without any major problems, although there was the police action at Roosevelt. This had never before happened in the history of the L.A. schools. I credited this to the courage of the kids themselves. But success was temporary. Our larger goal was to force the school board to negotiate, and by the end of the first day of the walkouts they still refused. We couldn't rest on our laurels.

Assessing the Walkouts

That Wednesday evening, I met only with the high school leaders at the Church of the Epiphany. I wanted to get a sense from them how they felt about the protest. They were on a high. They smelled victory. I could barely contain their enthusiasm and jubilation. This included both boys and girls.

In fact, the girls, like Paula Crisostomo, turned out to be even stronger leaders than the guys.

"Are we going out again tomorrow, Mr. Castro?"

They also expressed their concerns about the role of the Brown Berets. They felt that too many students were getting spooked by the Che Guevara look of the Berets and felt that too many students were not walking out because of that. I promised to speak to the Berets about this.

But I told the students how proud I was of them and that I thought the walkouts had been successful in beginning to bring attention to their issues. But I also had to bring them down to earth. I informed them that the school board had given no indication of meeting with them.

"I want to wait another day before we go out again. I don't want the same schools that walked out today to walk out tomorrow. Belmont will probably do it tomorrow, and that's okay because it couldn't today. But let's wait to see the news coverage tomorrow and see if we get any reaction from the board. In the meantime, we have to finish writing down the demands, so let's work on this now."

What I didn't tell them was that I also was worried about the reaction of their principals and about some of them getting suspended or even kicked out. I waited to see how the schools responded. About 90 percent of the students at Lincoln walked out. At Roosevelt, it was about 60 percent, and at Garfield it was even higher—about 80 percent. Wilson was lower, at about 30 to 50 percent.

Although I could see that the kids really wanted to walk out again the next day, they agreed with me to wait until Friday. So we spent some time trying to conclude the demands. Every student from each of the schools represented had ideas. But I had earlier, when we first started meeting prior to the initial walkout, devised a formula that in making decisions affecting them, including agreeing on the demands, each school would have one vote, even if some schools were larger than others. I wanted equal representation in order to create a spirit of cooperation.

Some of the demands we had already put together, but the students still had other ideas.

"How about covered eating areas outside the cafeteria. Other schools have them."

"That's a good idea," I said. "We should also demand more schools on the east side, and they should be named after Mexican heroes such as Benito Juárez, Emiliano Zapata, and Mariano Vallejo."

"That's good, Mr. Castro," they said as I bounced other ideas off of them.

The fact was that, while the kids had ideas and grievances, I had to guide them in a way to put all of these down in a series of individual demands. With kids you have to do this, otherwise we'd still be writing the demands. We didn't finish that evening, but we made progress. We didn't have access to copying machines or personal computers then, so all of these demands had to be written down longhand on pieces of paper, which I had to make sure I gathered and kept together.

There were a good number of students at our meeting, but I also noticed a few that I hadn't seen before. I didn't think much of it at the time, since we were feeling great about the protest and because we had work to do on the demands. It wasn't until sometime after the walkouts that I realized the police had infiltrated us. They had at least one informer, a kid named Bobby Avila from Wilson, who turned out to be an undercover cop. Not one of us knew. But he was telling the cops about our plans. In retrospect, this explains why we began to see stronger police reaction later that week.

PAULA CRISOSTOMO: "Although the recent HBO film *Walkout* portrays me and Bobby as girlfriend/boyfriend, that isn't true. I knew him but didn't have a personal relationship with him. He came to our meetings, and since he was one of the few students who had a car, he would sometimes give me and others a ride. Although we didn't know he was a cop, we did talk about him behind his back because he dressed strangely. He didn't dress like other Chicano students did. He claimed he was originally from Hawthorne or some other such place and didn't know how to dress like East L.A. boys. He wore tennis shoes that looked like surfer shoes. No one wore tennis shoes then. He wore funny jackets that no respectful Chicano kids from East L.A. would wear in public."[72]

During this week, as well as later, some of the students, especially the females, went around to other non-Eastside schools and organizations to talk about the walkouts. This became crucial in building support for the demonstrations. It involved networking.[73]

Thursday morning, March 7, when I got to Lincoln, everything on the surface appeared normal. Many kids didn't come to school that day. As soon as the students who did go to school that day saw me, not including the leaders, they wanted to know if we were going to walk out again that day.

"Not today," I told them, "maybe tomorrow."

Later that day, as I was getting coffee, a little seventh-grade boy came up to me and said: "Hey Castro, when are we going out again?" This brought tears to my eyes again to see this little kid, not even in high school yet, ready to demonstrate.

But there was a lot more talk among the students about what had happened the day before and much excitement all day. It may have been back to normal for the teachers, but not for the students.

On the other hand, I did notice coldness on the part of most of the other teachers. I ran into Ingles, but we didn't even talk. It appeared to me, however, that he was doing a number on me with the other teachers and trying to isolate me. He wanted them, I guess, to oppose me and what I stood for. Even the AFT people were starting to finger me. I felt that my every move was being reported to the principal—where I went and whom I talked to. Even those teachers and staff whom I thought were my friends seemed to be turning on me. This included the coaches that I worked with as athletic director. I felt like persona non grata.[74] At least Ingles and the other teachers didn't turn this hostility toward the students. There were no reprisals or punishments handed out. How could they? Almost the entire student body had walked out.

Even teaching was hard that day. My students couldn't pay attention to their classes. They were walking on air. I even had kids in my classes that came from other schools. I don't know how they got there. They might have been undercover cops, who knows? Strangers in their own land. But there was no way I couldn't talk about the walkouts in my classes. That's all the kids wanted to hear. I had no problem with this. Here I was a history teacher and my own students had made history.

"Everything went great. I'm very proud of you and it was very brave what you did. It was beautiful to be a Chicano yesterday." As I said this, I choked up and tears came to my eyes. I'm not afraid to cry and often do when I'm moved. But I had no problem with the students seeing me cry. However, I composed myself and continued: "But like I told some of the other students, we're still not finished. We need to get our demands met. I don't have to tell you what the problems are—you know all this. We need more schools; we need to get you into college; we need more and better counselors; we need even better food in the cafeteria. I think we should have your mothers come and cook and get paid for it. The food will get better automatically."

They liked to hear all of this, but I again cautioned them, "Hold on, we're not finished yet."

Although I kept the lid on at Lincoln and the other Eastside schools on Thursday, that wasn't the case at Belmont in the downtown area. There the kids were eager to go out since they hadn't on Wednesday. I knew I couldn't hold them back until Friday. "Go ahead and do it," I told the Belmont kids. The L.A. City College UMAS students had organized the high schoolers, and around lunchtime hundreds walked out.[75] This included not only many of the Chicano students but also many of the whites that still attended the school. In fact, some of the white kids led the action. I didn't go to Belmont, but by noon I had heard about it when some of the Belmont kids came over to Lincoln to tell me.

But unlike the previous day, the cops moved in with force. The principal, Ernest Naumann, a retired navy captain, called them in as he tried to prevent the walkout by going on the intercom and telling the teachers to lock their doors and keep the students inside the classrooms. He testified later that he saw students and nonstudents in the halls yelling, "Walk out, strike, walk out."[76] He said that this occurred at 12:30 P.M. and included men wearing brown berets shouting, "Strike, walk out, we want better food, we want Chicano teachers."[77] However, by then, many of the students had already left and were in the halls. This is where the cops assaulted many of them. They went in with their helmets on and swinging their batons. I have a photo of this. One cop almost hit a young female teacher, thinking she was a student, until the principal rescued her. I still can't understand teachers allowing their students to get assaulted. They just looked out of their classroom door windows and did nothing. This was part of the racism of the schools. The police roughed up the students and arrested two of them, a couple of *gavachitos* (whites). They charged them, I think, with disturbing the peace and resisting arrests. These charges were later dropped. Still, many of the students got out and demonstrated outside the school. We had alerted the media to the possibility of a Belmont walkout, and so they covered it, including the police tactics.

Belmont was rough. I thought that what the principal and the cops did was chicken shit when the students only peacefully protested. Nevertheless, it reinforced in me the dangers involved in engaging in this type of protest. But we couldn't turn back now until we got the response from the school board that we needed.[78]

Although Belmont was the only school scheduled to walk out that Thursday, I found out that some of the Garfield students also demonstrated and that other schools outside of East L.A. also walked out that day. This included some in Montebello, North Hollywood, and San Fernando. There were Chicano kids at these schools, but they also included non-Chicanos as well. Some suffered the same problems as the Eastside schools, but many of the students in these schools walked out in support of the Eastside kids. They had heard about the Wednesday protests, and some probably knew some of the students at Lincoln and the other schools involved. Events now were escalating beyond East L.A., and this was to our advantage because it put additional pressure on the school board and school officials.

The Belmont walkout, despite the police overreaction, signaled another major success in the struggle. At the same time, I was disappointed that the media coverage of the Wednesday protest had been slight, both on TV and in the newspapers. I got the impression that the superintendent's office told the media to sit on the story. The superintendent had an assistant, Bill Rivera, who I suspected he assigned to do this. I later confronted Rivera on this and told him: "Rivera, you're not doing us any good. Change your name!"

What was shown on TV, however—and this might have been the superintendent and Rivera's doings—was an interview with a supposed member of the Lincoln student council conducted by Julian Nava. I had no contact with Nava at this point. What came out on the TV screen that evening was a false statement by one of these Mexican American students that he and other members of the student council did not support the walkouts. But these kids were lying, and they duped Nava, or at least Julian went along with this. The fact was that the real Lincoln student council members had walked out with the other students. They were out in the streets. Those few kids that appeared on TV were ringers—fakes. This really pissed me off—and that Channel 4 carried it without asking others or me for an interview.[79]

The limited media coverage only further convinced me that we had to go out again on Friday and stage an even larger protest involving as many schools as possible.

But what also pissed me off was the almost complete lack of reaction and support from the established Mexican American leadership. They didn't say anything, including Edward Roybal, who by now was a congressman representing parts of East L.A. Judge Leopoldo Sánchez, another prominent figure, didn't say anything, and then Nava did that staged interview. Only later did I hear from some of them. Initially, they seemed stunned, as did many others in the city. However, instead of right away supporting the kids, they reacted with caution.

I had a lot on my mind when I met again that Thursday evening with the student leaders. I don't remember where we met. At this meeting, we had both high school and college students. It was a large gathering, because I felt that if we could pull off a huge series of demonstrations the next day not only would we begin to get more media attention but it might just force the hands of the school board. There was no question at the meeting but that we would walk out again. I made the decision that all Eastside schools would go out at 9 A.M., but this time everyone would march and congregate at Hazard

Park for a rally. In fact, I had pretty much made that decision earlier that day when I went on a radio talk show and encouraged parents in East L.A. to keep their elementary school kids at home on Friday as a way of supporting the walkout, as well as for me to send a signal to the school authorities that we meant business.

We hadn't yet finished the demands, but that wasn't important at the moment.[80] We met late into the night as we made phone calls to get the word out to all the schools, including those outside of East L.A. "We go tomorrow!" Students made more picket signs and we contacted the media. I'm sure I didn't sleep much that week and the following one. It was just one series of meetings and talking on the phone. I was exhausted and began to lose my voice. But my adrenalin and support for the kids kept me going. I have to say that it wasn't just me who felt like this. I'm sure the students, both high school and college, felt the pressure. However, they knew that what they were doing was important and that a lot was riding on them.

SEVEN

Blowout Part II

Friday morning, March 8, came with the threat of rain, and I drove to Lincoln for my eight o'clock class. The kids didn't have to ask me if they were going out; they knew. I could feel the excitement in the air. After I got into my classroom and the students settled down, Ingles came in and asked if he could speak to me in the hallway. I told the kids to read on their own certain pages in their history textbook and went outside, closing the door behind me. I could hear the students starting to talk among themselves, but it was not raucous. In the hallway, another guy, who turned out to be some flunky teacher from the district office, joined Ingles. He seemed to be there as a witness for Ingles, who told me: "Sal, under article [so and so] of the State Educational Code if you walk out with your students, you'll be in violation of the code and guilty of insubordination. Your teaching credential could be in jeopardy."

"*Que la fregada* [Damn it]." Ingles, of course, knew that the students were going out that morning because I had already notified him the previous day, but he felt he needed to exert his authority. To me, it didn't matter.

"Hey, I'm responsible for the kids," I told him, not concerned if the students could hear me inside the classrooms. "I'm not going to stay here in an empty classroom when the kids go out. I'm going with them."

This conversation was later used against me when they tried to take away my credentials. I guess that's why the witness was there.

Testimony of George Ingles to Grand Jury as questioned by Deputy District Attorney Richard W. Hecht:

Q. Let me ask you this. Directing your attention to March 8, 1968, were you at Lincoln High School on that day?

A. Yes, sir.

Q. And sometime during the morning of March 8th, 1968, did you go to see Mr. Castro?

A. Yes, sir.

Q. Approximately what time was it that you went to see him?

A. At approximately 8:45 on that date, I went to Mr. Castro's room.

Q. And would you tell us what happened?

A. And I indicated to him at that time that he was not to leave the campus with the students in any walkout that might be contemplated—I had heard again by rumors that this would be the case "today"—that he belonged on the campus, that he was responsible to his class.

Q. You told him that?

A. Yes, sir.

Q. What did he say, if anything?

A. Well, he said he had an obligation to make to these youngsters, and his obligation was to walk out with them if that was to be the event.[1]

When the 9 A.M. bell rang, the students all started to leave. Some yelled out, "Walkout! Walkout!" and a few even began to shout out, "Blowout! Blowout!" This time the college kids and the Berets didn't enter the building. The high school and junior high schools did it on their own. Everyone, including myself, again went out the main entrance and out into the streets. It seemed even easier the second time. The college kids greeted us outside and handed out the signs from the first demonstration and the ones made the night before.

But unlike Wednesday, we were also greeted by rain. It wasn't pouring but it was slight and steady. It was enough, however, to mess up some of our signs. Some had been made with the kind of paint that's water based, so the lettering began to run. They now looked psychedelic. You couldn't tell what they said. It didn't matter. The media, especially the TV people, were there this time, and that did matter. The police were also there, but in a nonthreatening way. They knew, or maybe I told them, that we were going to march to Hazard Park, and they agreed to escort us there. It became a big parade. They controlled the traffic to allow the kids to cross the streets. They even let me sit on top of an unmarked police car and be driven to the park. As the kids walked on the sidewalks, I passed by on the car with my dark glasses on, waving to the students, who were shouting and happy. I felt like I was the grand marshal of the Rose Parade.[2] I was out there in the rain, my face wet. The kids didn't know it, but I was crying.[3]

Hazard Park Again

After the march, the Lincoln students and I arrived at Hazard Park. We got there about 10 A.M. Some of the kids from other schools had gotten there

Walkout students at Hazard Park, March 8, 1968. Courtesy Los Angeles Times Photographic Archive, Department of Special Collections, Charles E. Young Research Library, UCLA.

earlier, and they welcomed us.[4] Within another forty-five minutes, still additional students showed up from the other schools. TV and print media reporters joined us. The college kids and the Berets monitored the assembled crowd and kept order. Not all of the students from Lincoln and the other schools were present. Many simply went home after they walked out. I estimated anywhere from 500 to 700 students at the park. I had arranged for a portable sound system to be there and had planned an agenda featuring a number of the high school students from the different schools to speak out about the poor conditions in the schools. I hadn't figured for any other speakers, except that one white board member, Dr. Ralph Richardson, requested to address the students. Ed Roybal and Julian Nava also showed to say a few words. They actually had called me the evening before and wanted to meet with me and some of the students in their offices. "No," I said. "You come to the park tomorrow and speak to us there."

Richardson admitted that the walkouts had brought attention to the students' issues: "To the extent that you have dramatized the problems, you have me."[5]

Richardson was a chain smoker, and this only made him appear even more nervous than he probably was anyway. At one point, Moctesuma Esparza,

Sal Castro at walkout rally, Hazard Park, March 8, 1968. Courtesy Sal Castro Personal Collection.

who couldn't help himself, interrupted Richardson and once again emphasized, as part of our game plan, that the students would only negotiate with the full school board. Other students said pretty much the same thing. I was proud of them because it took guts to speak out in public. Henry Gamboa from Garfield took the mike and accused the school board of running away from the students. "They finked out on us," he said, using a popular term of that period.[6] I also told some of the students to call on the parents—and some were at the park—to keep their kids at home on Monday. The students did so, in both English and Spanish. I felt that a boycott of classes on Monday would further put pressure on the board.

PAULA CRISOSTOMO: "I didn't speak at the park. At that time, the boys usually did the public speaking. They were literally the 'front men.' Young women today find this hard to understand, but that's the way it was then. However, while we as girls didn't do much public speaking, we did a lot of the organizing and displayed our leadership in this way."[7]

At the park, Nava said a few words. I don't remember what he said—probably something about the need to resolve the issues by discussion or something like that. Roybal then started to address the students, but while he did,

Walkout rally at Hazard Park, March 8, 1968. Left to right: *school board members Ralph Richardson and Julian Nava; unknown; Congressman Edward Roybal; Lincoln student Robert Rodríguez (on megaphone); and Garfield student Harry Gamboa. Courtesy Los Angeles Times Photographic Archive, Department of Special Collections, Charles E. Young Research Library, UCLA.*

we noticed some of the police coming into the park, closing in on the crowd. The students reacted, and some started to jeer at the police. Roybal picked up this cue and, to his credit, called on the cops to leave. "We don't need the police here," he said. "We can take care of business ourselves." The students shouted in support. I appreciated what Roybal did, but I also wished he had said that on paper to the students and to the community. He didn't want to put anything in writing about supporting what the kids were doing.

I didn't speak and had no intention of doing so. I preferred to remain in the background.

After about an hour or hour and a half, the rally broke up. The rain had let up a bit, and the students left to either go back to their schools or go home. I think many just went home. I went back to Lincoln, but, of course, classes had been cancelled. I went home to rest and then to attend a planned meeting with the students that evening to assess the walkouts. By then, I had heard that besides all of the Eastside schools going out a number of other schools also walked out in support of our students. Not only senior high schools acted, but remarkably also a few junior highs. In all about fifteen schools went out that Friday. That number of fifteen schools would later play a role in charges against me. These included city as well as county schools, all the way from Montebello on the east side of the county to Venice on the west side.[8] White kids walked out in sympathy from schools such as University High and North Hollywood High. I even heard that some elementary students in East L.A. did their version of a walkout. These may have been the younger brothers and sisters of the older kids.

Some of the black schools in Watts also protested. I had actually made contact with some of these schools during that week to see if they would support us. Those schools locked their gates in the morning to keep kids from leaving, but because I still worked at the playground, I had a key that opened up all school gates. Thursday night around 2 or 3 A.M. I drove over to Jefferson and Washington schools and opened up some of the gates in the hope that they wouldn't be locked that morning. Unfortunately, they discovered what I did and changed the locks. The black kids instead staged a sit-in, to not only support us but to complain about their conditions. They soon thereafter had their own walkouts.[9] The following week, several hundred black students walked out of Edison Junior High to protest conditions there.[10] The black student walkouts and sit-ins are part of the blowout story that has not received as much attention. In all, about 20,000 students walked out or protested at their schools that week.[11]

Assessing the Walkouts

I assembled again with our usual group that Friday evening at the home of Mita Cuarón, whose parents were quite active in the community.[12] Some parents also came and met separately to discuss how to further support the kids. I met alone with the students. One of the things we discussed was trying to get public statements of support from key Mexican American officials, such as Congressman Roybal and Judge Sánchez. I even hoped we could get one from César Chávez, if we could contact him. All I wanted was a statement from them saying that what the kids were doing was good. My hopes of getting this were raised when we got a call from both Roybal and Sánchez, who wanted to meet with the students either that evening or Saturday. I didn't take the call, but one of the students did, who then held them on the line until he told me what they wanted.

"No, you guys are holding all the cards," I told the students. "Tell them to come here to talk to you."

So they came. The students, at my urging, pressed them on a public statement. Roybal talked and talked but gave no commitment of a public statement. A student finally cut him off by saying: "No, no. We want you to write a letter saying that we're right."

"Well," a startled Roybal stammered, "my real office is back in Washington, so when I go back I'll send you that statement."

The kids never got it, nor did they get one from Judge Sánchez.

Even though we were disappointed with this reaction, we still felt elated at the walkouts that day. They had exceeded our expectations, although everyone expressed concern about the police violence at Roosevelt on Wednesday and what they did at Belmont on Thursday. We also felt good about the media coverage, especially the TV news that afternoon. At this point, I didn't plan for another walkout. That decision would be made by that Sunday. In the meantime, we planned to work on the class boycott for Monday and hope that all this would force the school board to agree to meet with the students. The one troubling aspect of our Friday evening involved Bobby Avila, the Wilson student and undercover cop who showed up with some other Wilson students. We still didn't know that he was a cop, but he kept pushing for another walkout. Then he said: "Hey, Mr. Castro, let's burn some trash cans tonight on the way out."

I found this off the wall, as did the other students. Burning trash cans wasn't going to get us anywhere. He was clearly a provocateur.

Saturday

I had read that Senator Robert Kennedy was in Delano, and I thought that maybe by some long shot the kids might be able to meet the senator, if he returned to New York by way of Los Angeles. Kennedy was visiting César Chávez and was at his side after César broke his famous twenty-five-day fast by taking Holy Communion with Bobby Kennedy. The only Feds I knew other than Ed Roybal was Dionicio Morales of the Mexican-American Opportunity Foundation (MAOF). So I called his office on Friday afternoon, and he put me through to his associate, Peggy Kidwell, to try and make the contact for us. I didn't know her at the time. I explained to her the situation, and she said she would call me back. She did early Saturday morning and instructed me to bring the kids to the MAOF office, located at that time on Brooklyn Avenue. I then quickly rounded up some of the kids and brought them over.

By now, Kennedy was championing the cause of the farmworkers and Mexican American issues and preparing to run for president. If the kids could meet with him and get a statement of support, that would be a huge breakthrough. I was getting more and more worried about the lack of public support from Mexican American leaders, or any public officials for that matter. Without it, I feared that the walkouts would fail.

I couldn't stay, due to my playground job that day. In the meantime, she had the kids write letters to members of the California congressional delegation and other elected officials asking for their support of their cause. Peggy played the role of teacher and hosted the students that day.

After I left the kids off and before going to the playground, I met with some of the parents that morning, who were beginning to express concerns over reprisals by the schools to their children. In fact, some had gotten calls from the principals that they would have to suspend the students if they continued to support the walkouts. They also threatened some seniors that they would lose their college scholarships if they further protested. They even went so far as to say that they might have to cancel the senior prom. They were hitting hard. I didn't blame the parents for being worried. I tried to allay their fears and expressed great pride in their kids and thanked them for supporting them. I concluded by saying that I hoped that no further walkouts would occur, if the school board agreed to a meeting. I didn't promise that we wouldn't protest again, but I thought I was successful for the moment in assuring them that I didn't think the principals would go through with their threats. "The principals can't do anything to the kids," I assured them; "they're within their rights." I wasn't sure, but I thought to myself that Ingles and the others wouldn't be so stupid as to do this and give us still more grievances to protest against. I also agreed to meet that evening again with some of the parents to see if we couldn't get some church support for the kids.

I had already attempted to get some of the Catholic pastors in East L.A. involved, but they avoided me. I even told the students to see if the priests in their churches might support them, but they got nowhere. One kid, perhaps in frustration, went to his church on Friday before the walkouts and took the banner of Our Lady of Guadalupe from the church and used it in the march to Hazard Park. It was a great image to have and gave the kids a sense that Guadalupe was looking after them. However, when the student returned the banner, the priest had him arrested. Only Father Luce and his associate pastor, Father Roger Wood, from the Epiphany Church openly supported us, and they weren't even Catholic but Episcopalian.

We met that evening at the home of Julia Mount, a longtime Mexican American activist. She had a daughter, Tanya, at Roosevelt. Not that many parents came, but a few came along with some of the students. Since we couldn't get any Catholic clergy to help us, Julia invited two Protestant ministers to join us. One was the Reverend Horacio Quiñones, who had served the

East L.A. community for many years, and the other was the Reverend Vahac Mardirosian, a Tijuana-born Armenian, who had also worked in the Eastside. I wasn't sure of what denominations they represented, perhaps Baptist. Both preachers talked to the students and more or less said that what they were doing was okay because they were standing up for their rights. They reinforced what the students and I had been saying—that the schools were in bad shape, that more counselors were needed, and that the schools had to address the high drop-out rates, among other issues. I had never met the ministers, but they impressed me with their talks. They made the parents feel much better about the walkouts.

Meeting Bobby Kennedy

Some grassroots community leaders that weekend also organized a support rally for the students on Sunday at Obregon Park. These types of community leaders supported us from the beginning; it was the elected Mexican Americans who refused to take a stand. About 500 people, including parents and students, attended. I was surprised to see some Lincoln teachers there. I wasn't sure why they were there, especially since many of them had been avoiding me since the walkouts began.

I don't remember if I was asked to speak or not, but even if I had been, I wouldn't have. I wanted to put forth the kids' leadership and not mine. As I listened to one of the speakers, someone from behind tapped me on the shoulder. It was Peggy from Dionicio Morales's office.

"Sal, round up some of the kids and follow me. Kennedy has agreed to meet with them. See if you can find a photographer to go with us."

I quickly gathered some of the key leaders. About fifteen to eighteen kids in all went. I took some in my car, and Peggy took others. I also got this teacher from Belvedere Junior High named Brostoff to take a few more. I don't remember his first name anymore, but I wanted him to go because he was a photographer. I said to him: "How would you like to meet Bobby Kennedy and take a picture?"

He said, "Yes!"

Peggy told us before we took off that we needed to go to the VIP section of the L.A. airport, where Kennedy would be. She knew the way so she took the lead and I and Brostoff followed. However, we got separated, and I lost them. I thought the VIP section was at the United Airlines terminal, and so my kids and I went there, only to discover that it was at another terminal. Fortunately, Peggy and Brostoff got there. It was a thrill for the students. Paula

Walkout students with Senator Robert Kennedy, Los Angeles, March 10, 1968. Left to right: *John Ortíz, Albert Robles, Eva Esparza, unknown, Freddie Resendez, Paula Crisostomo, Kennedy, Jesse Lara, Harry Gamboa, and Steve Lara. Courtesy Sal Castro Personal Collection.*

Crisostomo, who met with the senator, later told me and the other students that Kennedy was very cordial and supportive. He knew about the demands and said that he supported them because they were justified. According to John Ortiz, one of the students, Kennedy recognized the walkouts as a legitimate tool. After chatting with the kids for over an hour, he agreed to have his picture taken with them by Brostoff. This became the "famous" photo reproduced in the Chicano Movement press with the caption "Outside Agitator?"—the photo shows Kennedy and the students, including Paula, John Ortiz, Freddie Resendez, Cassandra Zacarias, and several others. Harry Gamboa is also seen in the photo holding out his right hand with the peace sign. We tried to get the regular media to print the picture, but nobody picked it up. Either it wasn't news to them or they had been told to cool it on the blowouts.

PAULA CRISOSTOMO: "He shook each of our hands. He raised his fist and said, 'Chicano Power.'"[13]

HARRY GAMBOA: "He was very generous with his words and offered us public support."[14]

A couple of weeks later we were also delighted to receive a telegram from Senator Kennedy addressed to me and "East Los Angeles Chicano Students." It read: "I support fully and wholeheartedly your proposal and efforts to obtain better education for Mexican Americans. *Viva La Raza*."[15]

The kids felt inspired after meeting with Kennedy. Finally a public figure, in this case a major national one, had the guts to publicly endorse their actions. It validated them. It had an impact on the Mexican American community and especially on parents, who now supported their students. It was a moment that none of them has ever forgotten. I'm just sorry I couldn't get some of the other students there.[16]

Meeting with the Board of Education

Events just came, moving fast. To my surprise and delight, later on Sunday afternoon I got home from the airport and after taking some of the kids home the phone rang: "Sal, this is Henry Ronquillo from Urban Affairs. Listen, I have some good news for you. The board has decided to meet with the students and to listen to their issues. They want to meet tomorrow at the regular session in the afternoon. The superintendent and deputy superintendent will also be there. Can you get your kids there?"

"Hell, yes, I can! That's great news, Henry. Tell the board that the students will be there, and thanks for all your help."

We had done it! We had forced the board's hand. But, of course, the next challenge would be to get the board to agree to the demands. With my head spinning, I quickly contacted some of the students and told them the good news and that I wanted to meet with them that evening to discuss the board meeting.

That whole weekend was incredible with everything going on. Since I couldn't use the school as an office, I used my apartment on Eldon Avenue. Here, I and a couple of the college students like Susan Racho set up our blowout office. Susan and some of the other students answered the phone and made appointments for me, including going to different TV stations to be interviewed. When they answered the phone, they did it in such a way as to suggest that we were some big-time organization, which, of course, we weren't. They even made me hot tea because I was losing my voice. These were exciting but exhausting times.

The kids were on another high when we got together. What a day this had been for them. First the rally at Obregon Park showed growing community support. Then the meeting with Senator Kennedy. And now the news that the walkouts had forced the board to meet with them. It was hard to get the students settled down for the meeting. Finally, I got them focused, and I told them what our strategy would be for that meeting.

"First of all, we haven't finished the demands so we can't really present them tomorrow. We have to buy time to do this. But second of all, I think we need to force the board to go to one of our schools and meet with you, your parents, and the community. We need to force them out of their ivory tower and to come over to see the conditions of the schools."

The fact was that you never saw a board member at any of the Eastside schools. The students agreed with this strategy, but now we had to decide what school to propose that they meet with us at. In my mind, it was either Lincoln or Roosevelt. Both had similar problems, although Lincoln had a better physical appearance—only because in 1964 the district had spruced it up when Lady Bird Johnson, the wife of then President Lyndon Johnson, met there with Mrs. López Mateos, the wife of the president of Mexico. They cleaned it up and planted flowers. Maybe for this reason, but also because I was obviously partial to Lincoln, the kids agreed with me that we should propose Lincoln as the meeting site.

I then counseled the students as to what to tell the board. "You tell them that you're not going to give them the demands and discuss them until they agree to go to Lincoln. If they want the demands, fine, but you'll give it to them at Lincoln."

I designated one of the students, Robert Sánchez, the student body president at Roosevelt, to be the main spokesman for the students. Robert wanted to be an actor so I said to him, "Be real dramatic when you tell them what we want. Pretend like you almost have to hold on to the podium because you've been under such pressure. Okay?"

Some of the other students would also speak out, but Robert would be the main voice. I had full confidence in him.

After we had settled on the strategy, I then told the students to spread the word about the breakthrough and about the meeting with the board at 3 P.M. on Monday. "We want to pack the hall with parents and community people, so go home and start calling." I also made a number of calls to the college students and to some of our community supporters. I finally went to bed later that evening with my mind filled with all of these developments. So much had happened in one week. I again didn't get much sleep, as I anticipated the Monday encounter with the board.

We had called on parents to keep their kids at home on Monday, March 11 —high school, junior high, and elementary. But that didn't matter as much, now that the board had agreed to meet with the kids. As word got out of this development, some parents still kept their children home, but others sent them to school. While I had not scheduled any walkouts that day, I later heard that almost 1,500 white kids at Venice High School completely over on the west side walked out in solidarity with us.

The board held their regular weekly meetings on Mondays and Thursdays at their headquarters at 450 North Grand Avenue, just across from the Music Center in downtown Los Angeles. I went to my classes that day and helped inform all of the students about what had happened. Everyone was excited and proud of what they had done. It empowered the kids, and I thanked them for their bravery again. I'm sure I shed tears. Many of the kids wanted to go to the board meeting, but I discouraged this in order to make sure that the available seats would be filled with parents and community people. I felt that such a show of adult support would have a greater impact on board members. They already knew the power of the kids. So only the student walk-out leaders would attend. In fact, many other students also showed up.[17]

For some reason that I can't remember, I showed up late at the meeting. Perhaps I was held up at school or perhaps the traffic was heavy, but for whatever reason, when I arrived at the school district office I ran into a huge crowd of Mexican parents (about 300) and others standing outside the entrance to the building in a patio area. I quickly discovered that there was no longer any more room inside and the fire department wasn't letting anyone else into the hall. The proceedings that had already started were being piped outside to the crowd.

"Sal, Sal, where have you been?" some of the people asked. "You need to be inside."

They started trying to push me inside the meeting. They tried to force open the doors while the firemen on the inside tried to keep us out. So I'm being pushed back and forth. Finally, one of the firemen on the outside grabs me by the tie and pulls me, almost choking me, inside the doors.

Inside, the board meeting had commenced, and I was so proud to see the kids up at the front and having the courage to confront the board by themselves, including the majority of old white dudes on it. I sensed the tension in the air. There were cops all over the place. Some of the old white guys on the board in particular seemed apprehensive and scared. The hall was filled with some 200 brown faces, and the board had never experienced something like this before. They probably thought there was going to be a riot there. In fact, one of these old *vatos* (dudes), a guy by the name of Chambers, startled the whole assembly when he literally pulled a gun out of his brief-case. Chambers was very reactionary; he was to the right of Attila the Hun.

Nothing happened, and I guess Chambers put the gun away. But it showed me how much we had scared the shit out of the board.

I took a seat and watched as Robert Sánchez proceeded to inform the board on behalf of all of the students that had walked out in protest of their inferior education that they would be more than willing to present and discuss their demands, but not there. The board would have to go to Lincoln High School for that. Robert was very dramatic in his presentation but almost too dramatic. After he finished his speech, he fainted and fell to the floor. I immediately reacted and rushed down to him, along with a nurse who was in attendance. She was there officially, perhaps to deal with any heart attacks by the old board members. I suspected that Robert might be acting, but I wasn't sure. As I got to him, he winked at me, and I realized that this was part of his performance. I spontaneously played along with him and turned to the board and said: "You see what you've done."

We got Robert up and sat him down. Some of the other students then got up and one by one supported what Robert had presented. I don't recall any parents or community people speaking, but they might have. I was too focused on the kids to pay much attention to anything else. The board then discussed the students' proposal, but they were very courteous with so many Mexicans in attendance. They also were clearly taken aback concerning the idea of meeting at Lincoln. I'm sure they thought if they didn't give in to the meeting that they might face some kind of rebellion right there and then or that the walkouts might continue. After some three hours, they took a vote, and they agreed by a vote of six to one to the proposal.[18] Only Chambers voted against it. The crowd broke out into a huge round of applause.

The other important thing that the board unanimously agreed to was an amnesty for the kids who had walked out.[19] I don't remember that we pro-posed this at this time, but the board really had no choice since so many kids had walked out. This may have been an effort on the part of board mem-bers to appear conciliatory. Nothing also happened to the student leaders at the different schools. In fact, they treated them with kid gloves because the principals knew that the media was watching. I found out later, how-ever, that some teachers retaliated against some of the students by reducing their grades. As for the students arrested, the police dropped charges, which included trespassing and disturbing the peace, all misdemeanors.[20]

The board dismissed the meeting, and people came up to congratulate the students. We had achieved a significant victory by forcing the board to come to us, to have the guts to go into the Chicano community and to discuss the grievances about the schools. The kids had given a voice to the Chicano community. They had not only empowered themselves but also their parents and the East L.A. community. They had in fact commenced the urban Chicano Movement.

LOS ANGELES TIMES: "School Board Yields on Some Student Points"
"During the discussion, Ray Ceniceros, Garfield High faculty chairman, said, 'We feel disturbed and ashamed that these kids are carrying out our fight. We should have been fighting for these things as teachers and as a community,' he said. 'Apparently we have been using the wrong weapons. These kids found a new weapon —a new monster—the walkout.'"[21]

The EICC

No more walkouts or blowouts occurred in East L.A. following the meeting with the board of education. The meeting at Lincoln was scheduled for March 26. In the meantime, I and the students worked on finalizing the demands. It wasn't so much coming up with more ideas. We knew the issues. We just had to put them into a language that would have an impact. By the time of the Lincoln meeting, we finished them—in all, fifty-five demands—and began to distribute them around to students, parents, the Chicano media, and the establishment media. Although the total demands were fifty-five, the number thirty-eight was the one most used by the media, and this was because the board, itself, only eventually responded to thirty-eight of the demands.[22] We also, shortly before the meeting, sent the board a copy as well. I felt that it would be appropriate for board members to have a chance to examine the demands in the hope that they could respond favorably to all or most of them at the meeting. Some of the key demands included the following:

Compulsory bilingual and bicultural education in all East Los Angeles schools.

Teachers and administrators to receive training in learning Spanish and Mexican cultural heritage.

Teachers and administrators who show any form of prejudice toward students, including failure to recognize cultural traditions, will be transferred.

Textbooks and curriculum should be revised to show Mexican contributions to society, to show injustices they have suffered, and to concentrate on Mexican folklore.

Class size must be reduced so teachers can devote more time to individual students. Team teaching should be used.

Counselor-student ratios must be reduced and counselors must speak Spanish and have a knowledge of Mexican cultural heritage.

Students must not be grouped into slow, average, and rapid ability groups and classes based on the poor tests currently in use that often mistake a language problem with lack of intelligence. A more effective testing system for determining IQ must be developed.

Any teacher with a high percentage of dropouts from his or her classes will be identified to students and the community.

New teachers should be required to live in the community where they teach during their probationary period.

School facilities should be made available for community activities and recreational programs developed for children.

No teacher will be dismissed or transferred because of his or her political and philosophical views.

Community parents will be engaged as teachers' aides.

New high schools in the area must be immediately built, with renaming of existing schools after Mexican and Mexican American heroes to establish community identity.

Corporal punishment, which is carried out only in East Los Angeles schools, should be abolished throughout the district.

Cafeteria menus should have more Mexican dishes, and mothers should be hired as kitchen staff and allowed to help prepare the food.[23]

In the meantime, while the students and I worked on the demands, the adults, through some of the parents and community leaders, began organizing. They established Chicano parent councils in a number of East L.A. high schools, as well as in the San Fernando Valley and in Venice.[24] The media attention to the walkouts and the meeting with the school board helped to legitimize the students' actions and made it easier for parents and community people to get involved. We also began to get expressions of support from groups such as the Mexican American Political Association (MAPA). In fact, I encouraged this because my strategy now was to have the adults take over the fight. It would be too hard for the kids to actually negotiate with the board on the demands, such as the need for more schools, lower class sizes, teacher retraining, and revising textbooks to make sure they presented Mexicans in a much more prominent and positive light. It wasn't practical for the students to do all of this. They couldn't be leaving their schools once or twice a week to meet with the board, and the schools wouldn't allow this anyway. The kids agreed.

"What you need to do now," I also told the student leaders, "is to graduate, since most of you are seniors. You have to pass your tests, and for the schools to get better you have to go to college."

A very powerful outcome of the blowouts was that they also had an effect on the surrounding universities and colleges, and many of them began to more actively recruit Chicano students. Some schools after the demonstrations even sent representatives to talk with some of our students. They were interested in the leadership potential of our students, even if they didn't meet all of the entrance requirements. As a result, a number of our graduating seniors went on to college.

The adults also understood that the students couldn't continue to carry the load, and, to their credit, they stepped up to the plate. Out of that Saturday evening meeting with the parents at Julia Mount's home came the origins of what came to be called the EICC, the Educational Issues Coordinating Committee. This involved some of the parents and community people, such as the Reverend Vahac Mardirosian, the pastor of the Mexican Baptist Church in East L.A., who, along with the Reverend Quiñones, had been at that meeting.[25] A number of community organizations, such as MAPA, the East Los Angeles Improvement Council, the East Los Angeles Democratic Club, and the Mexican-American Opportunity Foundation, also became charter members.[26] Mardirosian even came to me and informed me that his church was prepared to release him to work on these education issues if we wanted him. I said, "That's great. We need you."

But the EICC, which saw itself as now picking up the negotiations with the school board and the school administration, also included the college students. In fact, the college kids proved to be the driving force behind the EICC, although they wisely allowed the others to assume the more public leadership. Mardirosian, for example, became the nominal leader of the group and its principal spokesperson. Still, the college students, such as Juan Gómez-Quiñones, Carlos Vásquez, Jesús Treviño, and others, guided the EICC, since they attended all of the meetings and had a more critical perspective on the schools, in addition to being more politicized. I didn't know Mardirosian very well and so I felt more comfortable with the college students playing an active role. The other thing that concerned me as we began to have more adults and community involvement was how much infiltration by the police, FBI, and even CIA might be involved. I suspected it but didn't have any proof. That's why to me it was important to have some trusted people like the college students around the EICC. At the same time, a few community members expressed some reservations about the role of the college students. One member, Ben Gurule, for example, believed that the students had allowed Mardirosian to become the head of the EICC because they felt that they could control him. In my own mind, I felt that Mardirosian provided effective leadership.[27]

REV. VAHAC MARDIROSIAN: "But now it is up to the adults to take over. We are not going to allow this situation to continue. We are not going to let young people below the age of eighteen to do the work that belongs to us."[28]

At the same time, I continued to meet regularly with the high school students. In fact, we met at the same time as the EICC and at the same location, usually at the Plaza Community Center or the Euclid Community Center.[29] The adults met in one room and the students and I in another. It was not unusual to have 100 people, including many women, at an EICC meeting.[30] This way there was constant contact between both groups. If we needed to pass on something to the EICC, I'd leave our meeting, walk across the hall, and say, "The kids say so and so." This might have been my ideas, but I always put them forth as the students'.

Meeting at Lincoln

The turnout for the meeting with the board at Lincoln was unbelievable. Some 1,200 people, a combination of adults and students, came for the 4 P.M. session.[31] I had never seen so many Mexicans at a school function. Clearly, the walkouts and the kids had inspired the parents and community to become involved. The auditorium only sat 1,000, but it was filled beyond its capacity. The extra 200 had to stand in the back. The mood was jovial, loud, vocal, and boisterous. The board and the school district, undoubtedly leery of what might happen, had ordered tight security, and I identified a number of undercover cops inside the auditorium.

When I entered, what struck me was not only the number of people already there, but the glare of the TV cameras. Almost all of the local stations had sent reporters and crews to cover the event. We, of course, had alerted the media to what I believed was a historic meeting. Never had the board held a session, as far as I knew, outside of its own chambers, and never had they been willing to meet with the Chicano community in East L.A. But one thing disturbed me about the TV coverage. While all of the stations had their crews at the back of the auditorium, only Channel 11 had its cameras and lights on the stage where the board members sat behind tables. They had apparently gotten there earlier than the other stations and took the stage. I had no liking for Channel 11 because one of its main commentators, George Putnam, a very conservative guy, had been lambasting me and the walkouts on his program. He kept calling me a "pinko" and a "borderline Communist." I went up on the stage and told one of the school board staff members to get the TV cameras off the stage. "There'll be no special treatment for Channel 11, and the meeting won't go on until this happens." The guy complied and told the cameramen to get off.

Up on the stage, the board members sat, while in front of them a podium had been set up for the students to present their demands. The audience clapped as the students went onto the stage. I had decided that five students would be on stage with the demands. These included some of our key leaders, such as Paula Crisostomo, Freddie Resendez, John Ortiz, Mita Cuarón, and Robert Rodríguez. But instead of presenting the demands, I planned for each of the students to first introduce themselves and then say: "I am releasing my leadership to Rev. Vahac Mardirosian" or to some of our other designated adult leaders, such as Juan Gómez-Quiñones, Oscar Acosta, Carlos Vásquez, and Professor David Sánchez (not David of the Berets). The adults, in turn, would one by one present the demands to the school board. I thought that this would be symbolic of the student transfer of authority to the EICC. The students did this, to the enthusiastic applause of the audience. The kids then left the stage, and the five adults who replaced them remained. It was the changing of the guard.

As each of the demands were presented, school board members responded to some more than others, such as the need for more Mexican American administrators, bilingual-bicultural education, and a fifth high school on the east side.[32] This is why the meeting lasted for almost four hours. Since board members already had the demands in hand, some of them had pat answers. Although I had my reservations about the board, they weren't all conservatives. It was split fairly evenly between liberals and conservatives. The liberals seemed supportive of the demands. This included Nava, who now had to come out of the closet and became a Mexican representative. The conservatives expressed more reservations and opposition. However, whenever they did so, the audience hissed and booed. Since the board controlled the agenda, they did not permit audience members to make statements, only allowing the students, or in this case their representatives, to speak.

Something that has puzzled me to this day is how our original demands seemed to be altered after we had distributed them to various sources, including the school board. The result was that as the board received comments from these various sources prior to the meeting, they also received different versions of the demands. This made it easier for the board to pick and choose which ones would be easier to respond to. Some of the demands appeared to have been even rewritten by the board to make them sound more fiery and provocative and undoubtedly to make me and the students appear to be "radicals" and for the demands to seem ridiculous. In fact, the original demands were written in much more technical educational language in order to make them understandable to educators. This is why some of the demands discussed by the board were not recognizable to me. Of course, some of the demands discussed that evening were credible. When I realized these changes, I also realized that I was stuck between a rock and a hard place, because to say that these were not the original demands would have really made us look foolish. I had no choice but to accept the demands that surfaced at the board meeting.

I wasn't scheduled to speak and didn't want to in order to put the focus on the students and also on the EICC. But I couldn't contain myself when one of the conservatives, in response to the demand concerning the schools effectively addressing the high drop-out rates, said: "We don't deal with dropouts." When I heard this, I got up from my seat and walked right up to the stage and went to the podium. No one tried to stop me. I was a "big shot" then, I guess. Using the mike, I addressed the board:

> It's not true, and you know it's not true, that you don't address the
> drop-out issue. For example, Garfield High is a 3,500 capacity school
> and yet 50 percent of the kids drop out. Why haven't you made the
> school bigger, or is it that you're allowing for the dropouts by keeping
> the school only at 3,500? If you look at it mathematically, if 1,200 to
> 1,500 freshmen enter each year and they stay, then Garfield would be a
> 5,000 capacity school. Yet you don't have room for 5,000 students. This
> means you're allowing for the high drop-out rates. You're accepting
> them and doing nothing about it, because if you did you would have
> to build a much larger school or add an additional high school in East

L.A., and you obviously don't want to do that. So don't sit there and tell us that you don't deal with dropouts.

I stormed off the stage to much applause and shouting of support.

"You tell them, Sal," I heard someone say.

After my little spiel, I couldn't sit down, so I spent the rest of the meeting walking up and down the aisles.

As the board responded to the demands, they seemed to agree with some and not with others. I didn't expect them at this meeting to have a final deliberation on the demands. This meeting more than anything was theater —drama. I looked on the meeting as an opportunity to air out the problems of the schools, and that we accomplished. We laid out in public the dirty laundry. The acceptance and implementation of the demands I knew would take negotiations between the board and the EICC. My hope was that some of the issues could be agreed to sooner rather than later. I saw no reason why the board couldn't order the hiring right away of more Mexican American teaching assistants. They could also start retraining teachers. Other issues such as the construction of new schools or additions to older schools such as swimming pools, which none of the Eastside high schools had, I knew would take more time and might necessitate the board asking voters to approve new bond issues, especially because they kept saying at the meeting that they didn't have the money to implement many of the demands. "Well, find it," I thought. Many of the demands would take some level of discussion, but at least we had taken the offensive and forced the issues on the board.

The meeting ended with the board making no commitments but agreeing to continue the dialogue. I don't know how the members felt about the meeting, but the students, the parents, and the community people present, including myself, felt very good. We had gotten the board to meet in an unprecedented gathering on the east side. As far as we were concerned, we had won. We felt we had them on the run. We had taken on the second-largest school district in the country and scared them to accept negotiations with the Chicano community. The blowouts may not have changed the hearts and minds of the individual school board members, but more importantly it changed the students and the community. They glimpsed a sense of what power they had. But this new consciousness would be put to the test in the succeeding weeks and months. The walkouts may have ended, but the repercussions of the demonstrations would linger. This would further change my life.[33]

Still, that huge weight that I had felt on me due to all the racism and discrimination that I saw in the schools and in the community had now been lifted with the blowouts. This didn't mean that all of a sudden conditions changed, but it meant that Chicanos, especially the students, were now acting to change all of this. This sense of empowerment is what lifted that weight. I felt more serene. I felt that what I had been put on earth to do I had done at an early age, and I was now very calm. I can't describe it, but it was a very good feeling. I did what I was supposed to do.[34]

VICKI CASTRO: "Sal Castro was a motivator and the most significant adult role [model] at that time."[35]

MITA CUARÓN: "Sal was the catalyst. He was the messenger."[36]

EIGHT

The East L.A. 13

Following the walkouts and the climax of the meeting with the school board at Lincoln High School, it was difficult for the rest of the school year to go back to normal. I found it hard to teach after that and to concentrate, and I think that was true for a lot of the students. It was a bit unsettling. For example, every day I had visitors in my classes who came to meet me or to see if more protests were being planned. These were students from other schools, but who knows—some might have been undercover cops or FBI. As far as my students, including the blowout leaders, were concerned, they remained on a high through the rest of the semester. They believed they had won, and they had. They had become empowered. They walked around on air. Even though no further walkouts occurred, I still met almost every week with the key students at each of the schools. I continued this because I wanted to make sure that there were no reprisals from the schools. Fortunately, at first there were none. They left the kids alone. The principals and the board knew that doing anything to the students would have the community on their backs now that parents and others had become organized through the EICC (Educational Issues Coordinating Committee). They had never seen a community that well organized. This was one of the major effects of the blowouts. The Chicano community in L.A. had risen up in a way not seen before.

The EICC

The EICC picked up from where the students left off. They met weekly at the Euclid Center and people came from all over. Even teachers from the city and county became involved. The people at these meetings now expressed their concerns and even anger at the board and the schools. They realized that the schools, rather than being the solution to Mexican American problems, were in fact part of the problems. The kids had awakened them to this critical perspective, and the adults now moved on it. It became a big thing to be seen at these meetings. Besides providing a forum for the parents to meet and discuss school issues, the EICC, led by Reverend Mardirosian, also came up with strategies to continue the pressure and dialogue with the school board. I think that Mardirosian emerged as an important leader and gave credibility to the committee.

As far as the college students' involvement in the EICC—that continued to an extent, although fewer of these students attended meetings, due to their own classes. I, myself, attended a meeting now and then to keep the group informed about the students and what was happening in the schools. I felt that I needed the parents and community to develop their own leadership without me. The students and I had put the demands in safe hands, and it was time for me to back off. I had opened the door, and now the community had to go through it.

And they did. They met regularly with the board of education. They rehashed the demands and how the board could act on some of them. They also discussed problems at the individual schools. In April, the EICC staged a protest march from La Placita off of Olvera Street to the board of education to express displeasure over the negotiations.[1] The board itself reacted in different ways. If little or no money were involved, they would look into the issues. However, if money was a factor then, as they had already done at the Lincoln meeting, the board hesitated on the excuse of lack of funds. Progress was slow, but the discussions continued into the late spring.

A more empowered community through the EICC also reacted to a racist statement written by Richard Davis, one of the teachers at Lincoln. In a faculty newsletter, Davis wrote: "Most of the Mexican Americans have never had it so good. Before the Spanish came, he was an Indian grubbing in the soil, and after the Spaniards came, he was a slave. It seems to me that America must be a very desirable place, witness the number of 'wetbacks' and migrants both legal and illegal from Mexico."

REV. VAHAC MARDIROSIAN: "We cannot accept as a teacher a person who expresses a contemptuous, bigoted, and ignorant attitude towards the Mexican-American population."[2]

The EICC, along with the Lincoln Heights Parents Council headed by Eva Romero, demanded that Davis be transferred to another school outside of East L.A. and staged a protest by over 200 people in front of the school in May.[3] One way of informing the community of EICC actions was for members to engage in what was referred to as "community walk-throughs," where bilingual teams of two canvassed different parts of the Eastside, informing residents of issues and activities as well as listening to the community.[4] As in the case with the student walkouts, police undercover agents also infiltrated the EICC and tried to incite violence as a way of discrediting the group.[5]

My Personal Life

The blowouts, of course, had an impact on my personal life in various ways. During the period from the initial demonstrations to the Lincoln meeting, I slept very little. Besides all of the meetings and the actual confrontations, I was constantly in demand by the media. I had my fifteen minutes of fame. These included TV, radio, and newspaper interviews. Even *Time* and *Newsweek* asked to interview me but never published a story. I couldn't figure out if they were really reporters or perhaps FBI agents. But I didn't care. I talked to anyone. I didn't have anything to hide. I didn't feel that my students and I had done anything wrong. We might have technically broken the law, but the objective of bringing attention to the injustices in the educational system overshadowed any "illegality."

Besides the media, a number of groups and organizations, especially after the walkouts, invited me to speak to them about the issues. These included parent groups and church ones. Several liberal white Protestant churches in Eagle Rock, North Hollywood, and Pacific Palisades, for example, extended invitations. I also spoke at some black churches. Even the political left sought me out. I didn't know it at the time, but I once spoke at what I call a "swimming pool Communist home" in the rich Bel Air community of West L.A. As part of my remarks, I mentioned that my phone bill had skyrocketed due to all the calls I had to make during the walkouts. After I left, I noticed that in one of my coat pockets a bunch of dollar bills had been stuffed in to the tune of about $200. I had taken my coat off in the house because it had gotten warm, and somebody hung it up for me. People, I guess, felt sorry for me and put money in my pocket. I should have said that my bill was something like $1,000!

I also talked at a gathering sponsored by the *People's World*, the West Coast newspaper of the Communist Party. I didn't know who or what they were, but they were interested in the blowouts, and so I spoke. I didn't know they were reds. Dorothy Healey, a prominent Communist, I later learned, introduced me. After that, I started receiving copies of the paper in my home. That's cool, I thought. Later, when the school district attempted to take away my teaching credential because of the walkouts, one of the things they brought up was that I subscribed to the *People's World*—"*a la fregada* [what nonsense]."

Within my own family, my mother expressed concern about me, although it would be later that she really got worried. In the meantime, I think she was proud of what I was doing and about seeing me on TV. As for my ex-wife and her parents, the walkouts and my role in them only confirmed to them that I was crazy. As far as they were concerned, I lived in another world, like a Martian, because of my ideas that Mexican Americans were getting screwed. They just couldn't understand it. My two sons, on the other hand, were too young to know what was going on. Gilbert was twelve and Jimmy was nine. They weren't really aware of the walkouts, but when I became headline news later they came to understand a bit more. It was hard since I only saw them on weekends, and during the blowouts I couldn't see them. As they've grown up and now as adults they appreciate what I had to do and are proud of what their dad did.

Part of my "celebrity" status involved going places and being recognized. I'd go to a nice restaurant or lounge and people bought me drinks. Ladies wrote their phone numbers on napkins and also bought me drinks. I couldn't drink all the booze they bought. One of these places was the Casa Escobar on La Cienega. They had good chow and music there. I'd walk into big dances at the Paladium and people knew who I was. I didn't see myself as a celebrity and much less as a hero, but I have to admit I enjoyed some of this attention. It certainly livened up my social life. I even got other job offers. Universities such as UCLA and San Fernando State wanted me to consider various positions on their campuses. I was flattered but told them I had no intention of leaving Lincoln.

But there were downsides also to this attention. I started getting death threats after the walkouts. The phone would ring in the middle of the night.

"Hello."

"Castro, you'll be dead by tomorrow," a voice said on the other end.

I received a number of such calls, but I didn't report them because I wasn't too concerned about them. I figured they were sick tricks. I also didn't report them because I was pretty certain the FBI was tapping my phone anyway and so they knew I was getting threats. Every time I picked up the phone I heard a click. Maybe it was the FBI itself that was threatening me. Who knows?

In his own autobiography, Julian Nava claims that he went out of his way to warn me. Julian writes that he became so paranoid that his own phone might be tapped that he once used a public phone to call me and tell me that

I was in danger of being fired except for his intervention and that I was being watched and my phone tapped. He doesn't say who was watching me or tapping my phone. Frankly, I have no memory of Julian's warning. It's possible that he did, but I don't recall this.[6]

It wasn't just phone threats. This crazy right-wing handout called the *Yankee Crier* published a list of people that should be killed or eradicated and included my name. I still have a copy of it. "The ultimate penalty for treason is death," it said. "To live as a traitor is worse than the grave. A nation may forget her patriots but never her traitors."

The only time I worried about one of these death threats was after I got one of those phone calls and the next day I spent the day with my boys. I later that evening dropped them off at their mother's. When I walked back to my car, I had the weirdest feeling that something wasn't right. I thought that if I started my car that it might explode. But after a few minutes I said, "It's just a *pendejada* [idiocy]," and turned the ignition on. Nothing happened, fortunately. Despite these threats, I never seriously considered having like a bodyguard or carrying a gun. I just adjusted to all of this.

The Grand Jury

Sometime into late April and early May, I began to get an inkling that I might be arrested for my role in the walkouts. Some Chicano who worked in the district attorney's office, who had been a speaker at one of our youth conferences and whom I knew, started calling me and suggesting that I go talk to the D.A. (district attorney).

"Why should I do that?" I asked.

"Because we hear there's a chance you might get indicted."

"Well, if they're that *pendejos* [idiotic] to arrest me, we'll get a lot more mileage out of it."

I didn't give the possibility of my being arrested that much thought because I really believed it would backfire on the D.A. if that happened. However, later in May, I heard that a grand jury had started proceedings concerning the blowouts and that it was considering conspiracy charges.[7] I didn't know if they had others or me in mind, but I figured as much. Besides my role in the demonstrations, it flashed on me that perhaps a recent talk show that I was on might have triggered this investigation. Juan Gómez-Quiñones, one of the college students, had a radio program on KPFK, a left radio station, and he interviewed me about the blowouts. I exaggerated as to how well orga- nized we really were. I kept saying to Juan, "We pushed a button and Lincoln went out. We pushed another and Roosevelt went out, etc." I probably made it more sinister that it was. The fact is that we were flying by the seat of our pants that week in March. But this interview was later used against me.[8]

Ironically, I never received a notice to appear before the grand jury and really didn't know much of what was going on in their deliberations or the role of the D.A. in all this. However, this changed on a weekend in May. I can't remember if it was a Saturday or a Sunday. César Chávez was in town, probably campaigning for Robert Kennedy in the California presidential primary scheduled for early June. Julian Nava organized a reception for César at his home in the San Fernando Valley. I was surprised when he invited me, and, of course, I went—*un fregata de gente* (tons of people showed up). Julian had a big backyard where he served food and drinks. This was the first and only time I went to his home. During the reception, a panicky-looking Gómez-Quiñones and Moctesuma Esparza came in—actually they literally ran in. I don't know whether they had been invited or not. They took me aside and told me that they both had been grilled by the grand jury, I think that Friday, and that there was a strong chance that we were all going to be arrested. They spoke only to me, but their voices were loud enough so that other people heard them.

"What are we going to do, Sal?" they anxiously asked me.

"If it happens, it happens," I said, "but that's stupid if they do arrest us because they're going to give us more publicity on the school issues. What the hell are they going to charge us with? We didn't do anything wrong."

"Conspiracy," they replied.

They didn't know who else had been called up by the grand jury or who else might get arrested. They were quite upset, and I got the sense that they seemed to regret not taking an attorney with them to the proceedings —*pendejos!* Of course, I don't know whether that would have helped or not. After they told me this story I myself didn't think that far ahead about getting an attorney. I thought that maybe cooler and smarter heads might prevail. I didn't realize it then but would later that what seemed to be in play in all of this grand jury stuff was that the D.A., Evelle Younger (who I chidingly called "Evil Younger"), was running for reelection on a law-and-order platform and that he could gain political mileage by indicting some of us for the walkouts. In addition, police chief Tom Reddin hated us. Oscar Zeta Acosta, in his novel *The Revolt of the Cockroach People*, about the Chicano Movement in L.A., convincingly argues that the subsequent arrests were part of a strategy by the Republicans to discredit both Senator Robert Kennedy and Senator Eugene McCarthy, battling in the Democratic primary that next Tuesday,

June 4—both had stated support for the blowouts.⁹ This was a heavily politicized time, with the antiwar demonstrations and the rioting throughout the country after the assassination of Martin Luther King in April. Conservative Republicans like Younger were calling for more law and order, and, I guess, we were convenient targets in L.A.

I had no idea of what might happen, and so before I left Nava's house I talked to César about rumors that the others and I might get arrested for the blowouts. I asked, if that happened could we get a statement of support from him and the farmworkers. I'm certain that César agreed, but somehow I think I might have not made as clear as possible what kind of support I would welcome. In any event, we never got that statement, but I think it was a lack of communication on my part, plus the traumatic events that would ensue in early June surrounding the assassination of Robert Kennedy, a close ally of César's.

Arrested

For the next few days, I put out of my mind what had happened at Nava's house. I still didn't think anything would happen. I was thinking more about going to the Lincoln prom on the evening of May 31. I had volunteered to be there as one of the chaperones, and I was excited for our seniors, after all the hard work they had done during the blowouts and the courage they had displayed. I looked forward to the big dance. I even went out and rented a tuxedo. I didn't teach that day because the teachers' union had organized an information meeting about calling for pay increases, and so we all refused to work that day to support the union. Later that day, I had a couple of beers with one of my fellow teachers, Mike Gordon, who had been one of the teachers who supported the walkouts. I then went to pick up my tux and returned to my small apartment on Elden Street near the Pico Union area. I got back to my place about 4 P.M. and was just about to open the door when two guys with suits approached me.

"Mr. Castro, we're from the district attorney's office," they said as they showed me their badges. "You're under arrest. You have the right to remain silent," etc.

"*Ahi que la fregada* [God damn it]," I thought, as I realized I wasn't going to the prom that evening.

As they read me my rights, they handcuffed me behind my back and said they also had a search warrant to investigate my place. They went into my apartment, where they proceeded to look around and take a few things. This included a copy of Mao's little Redbook, which I used as a sample in my U.S. government classes. They also took various papers in my files. Immediately I started thinking of how we could take political advantage of my arrest. It would be like reviving the blowouts and what they stood for, especially since by now interest was waning. My arrest, I thought, would be headline news, and the issues around the walkouts would be back on the front page.[10]

The two detectives who arrested me were both white guys. I heard later from a female deputy sheriff, who now is retired and runs a beach resort in Ensenada, that when the decision to arrest me was made Chicano officers begged off because they didn't want to be involved in arresting me. I don't know how true this is, but that's what I heard.

After the detectives finished going through my place, they escorted me out and put me in their car. I remember sitting in the back seat with my hands cuffed and the two cops in the front. I thought that was strange since usually they have somebody sitting with you. As we drove to the jail, I thought of people looking into the car and seeing me arrested, but it was an unmarked car so nobody would have paid attention. They took me to the county jail that's not too far from Olvera Street. This is the big house, as opposed to the city jail, called the Glass House.[11] The county jail is where they take felons— murderers, robbers, all kinds of criminals are there. In fact, this is the same jail where they kept O. J. Simpson much later.

As soon as we got inside the jail, I felt like a felon by the way they treated me. They took off my handcuffs, booked me, and then made me take off all of my clothes and checked all of my crevices. Then I was ordered to put my clothes on again, and they took me to the "tank." This is a room, not very large, with metal benches bolted to the floor and with vomit all over the floor. You're in the holding tank until you're further processed, and some guys get sick in there. There was a phone, and you could make a collect call. I called my mother and told her that I had been busted and to tell some of my friends.

I was then moved to another room where they gave me a peanut butter sandwich with a glass of orange juice. This was my dinner, since it was now around 6:30 P.M. The bread seemed like it had been there for a couple of days. After my "meal," they once again had me undress, and this time they deloused me with an instrument like a paintbrush. They took my clothes away and gave me instead a pair of what were called "county pants," which were blue Levis and a "county shirt," which is light blue with "County Jail" printed on the back. A blood test followed. I don't know what this exam was all about. This was pre–HIV-AIDS, so it wasn't that. Maybe it was to check to see if I had TB, which I didn't. During all of this, I wasn't alone. Other guys arrested that evening also lined up for the blood test. I guess more people get busted on weekends so the jail gets filled. One of the medics while I waited in line dropped a tray of needles on the floor, picked them up, and still used them. "Oh, shit," I thought, "I hope I don't get some infection." Fortunately, I didn't, or at least it hasn't shown up over all these years.

We were then taken to another place where they gave us a blanket and a mattress but no pillow. During all of this time, I expected to see James Cagney or Humphrey Bogart, because I had seen all of their prison films in the 1940s and 1950s. But this time it was the real thing. They put me in a cell with four other guys, three of them Chicanos, where I would sleep that night. The only problem was that there were only four bunks and these guys already had them. I had no choice but to sleep on the floor. Before we went to sleep we traded stories about what we were in for. One guy was charged with embezzlement. Another had cut his wife's throat, although I didn't find out until the next day. If I had known this, I don't think I would have slept as well as I did that night. I did wake up once when I felt something tickling my nose. It was a goddamn *cucaracha* (cockroach).

The next day, all of the cell doors adjacent to each other automatically opened up at once, just like you see in the movies. Most of the guys in the cells were Chicanos. They took us to breakfast, but by then the others and I arrested were headline news. It turned out that not only had they arrested me, but twelve other guys as well, although I initially wasn't aware of this. Some were actually not physically arrested like me, but only informed to turn themselves in that weekend. They complied. I didn't see any of them my first day in prison. Some of the guys arrested had little to do with the walkouts, but somehow the D.A. fingered them. Somehow, the news of my arrest circulated inside the jail, and some of the others knew that I was there for a political rap. I was a little famous. Inside the prison cafeteria we each got an aluminum tray with a bowl, a cup, and a spoon. They served us gruel, like oatmeal, stale bread, and awful black coffee. That's all you got. As I went through the line. one of the guys serving, who was an inmate, whispered to me, "Let's riot, *vato* [dude]." He knew who I was, and I guess expected me to lead a riot in prison. "I'm in enough trouble already, brother," I thought.

That Saturday, I realized that one of the reasons why the others and I had been arrested that weekend was to prevent us from getting bailed out until Monday. After I returned to my cell, they called me out and told me I had visitors. It turned out to be the president and vice president of the teachers' union.

"Sal, we're sorry you're in here, and we'd like to help out, but we don't have enough money to bail you out."

"Then what the hell are you doing here?" I snapped back.

They left, but the problem was that they had taken up my allotment of one visit per day and I couldn't see anyone else, including my mother, *pobrecita* (poor thing), who after learning I was in jail came by with a little bag containing a toothbrush and some *calzones* (underwear) and socks. She must have thought I was going to San Quentin. They wouldn't let her in, and I only later found out about her visit.

They did let me see Oscar Zeta Acosta, aka the Brown Buffalo, a militant Chicano attorney who apparently was asked by the EICC to represent me, along with ACLU attorneys.[12] I had seen Oscar around but didn't know him very well. He would go on to become well known and a real character in the Chicano Movement and later wrote a couple of books about his involvement and antics. In those days I smoked, so I asked Oscar if he had a cigarette he could give me. He did, but he had to have the guard first inspect it and approve it. I don't know why Oscar even bothered to do this. He could have easily slipped his whole pack to me. After the cigarette exchange, I whispered to him: "Oscar next time buy a whole pack, put it in your coat pocket when you come to see me, and while the guard is not looking, I'll snatch it from you." Next time he came he did have a pack in his pocket, and sure enough, when the guard wasn't looking, I took it from his pocket. But to my surprise, there was only one cigarette in the pack. I said, "*Cabrón barato* [cheapskate], I could have been thrown in solitary confinement for one chicken-shit cigarette."

Oscar told me that they were charging me with conspiracy and that they had arrested others on the same charge and that the formal arraignment would be Monday.

"How much will the bail be?" I asked.

"$12,500," he said.

"What? $12,500!"

Later, when I went back to my cell and told the other guys what my bail was, they just about fell over. "What'd you do, kill someone?" $12,500 was a lot of money in those days, and I would have to come up with 10 percent of it to get bailed out. I found out later that this bail was more than twice the usual amount for assault with a deadly weapon and ten times more than for burglary.[13] They then told me about their bails and their problems with their lawyers. I just listened and felt bad for them, because they were in there knowing they had done something wrong, but I hadn't. I could see the anguish in their faces. I didn't feel bad, because I knew that I hadn't done anything wrong.

The rest of that day consisted of going to lunch and later dinner. I could feel the eyes of the prison guards on me, now that they also knew who I was. Later, in my cell, I kept getting passed notes from other prisoners. They had comments on various things happening in the community. One note, for example, suggested that the logo of the Brown Berets be changed. Some again encouraged me to start a riot in there.

I went through pretty much the same routine on Sunday. I'll never forget the Sunday dinner. I had to pick out *gusanos* (worms) from my salad. The food was pretty crummy, and that's maybe deliberate in order to make sure you don't come back. At least they let me shower that day. Acosta came by again and had more information about the others arrested. He gave me some of the names and that the police has also broken into the *La Raza* office and confiscated much of their material without search warrants.[14] But what I'll never forget about Oscar's visit this time was how he broke down and cried. Here, I'm the one in jail, and my attorney is crying. He was crying because he wasn't getting paid for representing me. I couldn't believe it. Right from there I didn't have too much confidence in Oscar. He was erratic, and I found out later he was a druggy. I was glad that I also had the ACLU lawyers working on my case and those of the others arrested. In *The Revolt of the Cockroach People*, where he writes about the East L.A. 13, Acosta, himself, admitted his own inexperience, as in this passage, where he is talking to the others held in the Glass House: "Look, you guys . . . yeah, I'm a lawyer. I've done a few preliminaries. I've done some divorce work and a few dope cases. . . . I've practiced law for about . . . well, I practiced in Oakland for a few months before I took a vacation."[15]

I didn't know it at the time, but as news of my arrest and that of the others got out, the Chicano community quickly mobilized, and on that weekend about 200 picketed both the police department and the central jail, demanding our release. This demonstration included not only Chicanos but also blacks, including the Black Panthers, and whites, carrying signs that read "Free Our Brothers NOW!" "Freedom Now," and "Justice or RIOT!"[16]

MICHAEL HANNON, attorney: "The demonstration [blowouts] is the poor man's printing press. His right to use it must be as secure as the rich man's right to print his newspaper."[17]

Acosta, in *The Revolt of the Cockroach People*, claims that during one of these demonstrations he gave an impassioned speech about our arrest.

Whether true or not, he did bring out some of the key issues and contradictions of the whole affair:

> The East LA 13 are behind those bars up there. Are they in jail because they rose to speak out against the educational system in this country? Do you think they have been rousted from their offices and their homes like a bunch of criminals simply because they got thousands of Chicanos to walk away from their schools for a few days? Is this government to fall because a small group of men and women have demanded an end to the racist system in the schools? Would the government go to this extreme simply because we want better schools, better teachers, better administrators, because we want the books, the teachers and the materials to reflect our own culture? Are we such a threat just because we have demanded a compliance with the Treaty of Guadalupe Hidalgo [of 1848, ending the U.S.-Mexico War], which provided for a bilingual society? Is there something wrong with speaking Spanish in our schools? But when you stop and think about it, that is exactly why they are in jail on this monstrous prosecution.[18]

The East L.A. 13

On Monday, they got me and others who needed to be arraigned up early around 4:30 A.M. We went down to the bullpen, where they gave us our civilian clothes in exchange for the county jail ones. As we waited there, I glanced over at another adjacent bullpen and noticed Carlos Muñoz, another of the college graduate students who had helped in the blowouts. Carlos, I found out later, had been arrested early Saturday morning, around 2:30 A.M.[19]

"Hey Carlos, what the hell are you doing here? You got busted also?" I called out to him.

We laughed but couldn't really talk.

They took Carlos and me, along with the others, out of the building to a waiting bus to transport us to the Hall of Justice. Inside the bus, they handcuffed both our feet and hands and then attached our cuffs to a long chain that ran down the aisle. After a short ride to the court, they took our handcuffs off both our hands and feet so we could walk off the bus and into the building. They took us down into the basement to another holding tank where lo and behold I saw some of the other guys who had been arrested. This included Esparza. Others arrested included David Sánchez, Carlos Montes, Ralph Ramirez, and Gilbert Cruz Olmeda from the Berets, as well as Eliezer

Risco, Joe Razo, Fred López, Richard Vigil, Henry Gómez, and Pat Sánchez.[20] They had brought these others from the city jail—the Glass House. It was like a big reunion. We hugged and laughed and expressed surprise at our arrests. The others told me that, after their arrest, they had declared a hunger strike until they would be released. They issued the following statement:

> We are behind bars, but those bars are only symbolic of the oppression the Mexican American people have been suffering for over 120 years under Anglo colonization. We are being accused of conspiracy to Disturb the Peace even though there is no proof that we have disturbed the peace in anyway. It is ironic that those arresting us are the same cops that move around East L.A. toting their guns, abusing the constitutional rights of our young *Carnales* [brothers]. We are entering tonight into a Hunger Strike until all twelve of us are free. We will non-violently refuse to accept this farce of justice. We issue a call to La Raza Unida, in the Southwest, to our black brothers, to our Puerto Rican *carnales*, to our Indian brothers, and to all those Anglos who see through the farce of a system that preaches freedom and practices oppression to demonstrate their solidarity.[21]

Being together just fortified us at what we still had to go through. I told everyone that when we walked into the courtroom to plead to the charges that I would walk in last and be the last one to plead to make sure everyone got released. I didn't want to be released if the others weren't. "Either we're all set free," I said, "or we all stay in jail."

They then took us upstairs to the courtroom for our arraignment, all thirteen of us. They kept us together. The judge read off the charges. Each of us was charged with two counts of disturbing the peace and disturbing the peace of the schools. In addition, there were fifteen counts of conspiracy involving those two other charges, for a total of thirty counts, with each count carrying a maximum sentence of five years. If convicted, we faced 150 years in jail! I could have been the Mexican birdman of Alcatraz! The charges themselves were misdemeanors, but since they included conspiracy to commit these misdemeanors they became felonies. The number of fifteen counts was based on the number of schools the D.A. accused us of conspiring to disturb the peace in. It was a hatchet job. Even though the charges were ludicrous, since we were simply engaged in civil disobedience, the irony was that in a sense we were "guilty" of a conspiracy, but a conspiracy to bring social justice to the schools.

The ACLU lawyers, including Abraham Lincoln Wirin, Michael Hannon, and Paul Posner, fortunately were there to represent us.[23] Acosta, for some reason, was not. After the judge read the indictments, we pleaded not guilty to the charges and our lawyers asked the judge to release us on our own recognizance, since none of us had a prior conviction and, they argued, there was no danger of us fleeing. To our delight and perhaps surprise, the judge, while not agreeing, did considerably reduce the bail, to $250, which we were able to post.[24] I later learned that if the judge had not reduced the bail the Kennedy people and the campaign of Senator Eugene McCarthy, also in the Democratic primary, had contributed to our bail fund and we would have been released anyway. Al Juárez, one of our college students, worked in the Kennedy campaign, and I think Al arranged at least for the Kennedy donation.[25] We were then shackled again, returned to the buses, taken back to the jail, and later released that afternoon.

We all hugged each other and celebrated our release, besides thanking our lawyers. However, it was pretty sobering to find no one waiting for us outside the jail—*ni las moscas* (not even the flies). Still, everyone was pretty jovial. The others wanted to go to a restaurant in East L.A. to celebrate further. I didn't go because I had other friends waiting for me. I wanted to go drinking and dancing since I had missed the prom. So the other twelve went their way, and I partied somewhere else. Little did we realize that our fates, of what became the East L.A. 13, would be joined together for the next couple of years as we fought the charges against us. But at least for now we were out of jail.

SAL CASTRO interviewed by *Open City*: "I think my arrest was set up to drive me out of the school system. . . . The experience in jail is an important one we should all have. . . . It's the perfect example of man's inhumanity to man. All of a sudden you are no longer an individual. All your dignity and self respect is taken away. They put you in a blue uniform and you are now just a number in blue. You make no decisions. You're caged up like an animal."[26]

Thrown Out of Class

After I got out of jail, I returned to my classes at Lincoln the following day. Our spring semester didn't end until mid-June. I only missed one day, and that Monday I actually called the school from the holding tank at the Hall of Justice to tell the office to release the substitute teacher because I would return the next day. That evening I partied. I went to some of my favorite clubs such as the Mardi Gras and the Casa Escobar with my girlfriend. I was everywhere and drinking. I nicknamed that drink Chevas Regal Scotch over ice with half-and-half milk "Jail House." *Orale* (right on)! I was a two-fisted drinker. I woke up the next morning with quite a *cruda* (hangover), but I had to go to teach. I didn't even have time to properly shave, so I didn't look very well when I walked into the school.

My head was spinning a bit, but it spun even more as soon as I went into the main office.

"Good morning," I said to the secretary.

Before she could answer, George Ingles, the principal, came flying out of his office.

"Sal, you can't teach."

"George, I know I don't look too good, but I'll be okay."

"No, Sal. I don't mean just today. You can't teach at all for now because under the state education code, you can't be in the classroom because you're an indicted felon. I'm sorry. You need to report to the IMC [Instructional Materials Center] until your case is settled."

George was dead serious. He usually liked to joke, but this was no joke.

"Well, George," I replied, "I think the school district is making it worse on itself because this will have community repercussions."

I couldn't believe what George was telling me. I could accept that someone indicted for beating his wife, for murder, or for a sex offense shouldn't be allowed to teach while under indictment—but for someone like me, whose only "crime" was engaging in a civil rights struggle? I couldn't believe it.

I turned around and left, but in my mind I thought the whole matter would come to a quick resolution and I would be back in class very soon. Rather than go to the IMC, I drove over to one of the Protestant churches a few blocks away where we had sometimes met during the walkouts. I went there because I knew that the Brown Berets were having a press conference to lambaste the police for having arrested David Sánchez, the prime minister of the Berets, and Carlos Montes, the minister of information. I wanted to piggyback off their meeting to tell the press about what Ingles had just told me.

"They won't let me teach; they're throwing me out," I announced as the media people there came over to interview me. This hit the news right away.

The school administration not only retaliated against me but also against some of the kids at Lincoln and at the other schools. Some teachers lowered grades or failed to write letters on behalf of some of the seniors for college

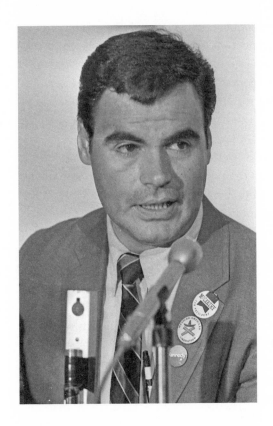

Sal Castro at news conference after release from jail, June 4, 1968. Courtesy Los Angeles Times Photographic Archive, Department of Special Collections, Charles E. Young Research Library, UCLA.

admission. They didn't target all of the kids—but some of the walkout leaders. I felt bad because there wasn't much I could do to help them due to my arrest and then suspension. But the kids hung tough, and they survived these efforts to punish them or to intimidate them.[27]

The Kennedy Assassination

My news, however, was quickly overshadowed by the tragic assassination of Robert Kennedy that same day. That Tuesday was primary day in California. I voted that day for Kennedy. I was a "peacenik" and against the Vietnam War and thought that Senator McCarthy seemed more antiwar than Kennedy, but I voted for Kennedy because it seemed he was going to win—but also because of his support for our students by meeting with them. I was also a big fan of the Kennedys and couldn't bring myself to vote against one of them, especially since I had worked for John Kennedy and had met him.

Later that day, back in my apartment, I got two interesting calls. One was from the campaign staff of Senator McCarthy, who had donated bail money for me. The senator wanted to meet me at his headquarters at the Beverly Hilton Hotel. I thanked the staffer for the senator's generous help and said I would be happy to meet him. Of course, I didn't say I had voted for Kennedy. No sooner had I hung up than the phone rang again. This time it was Kennedy's headquarters.

"Can you come tonight to the Ambassador Hotel? Senator Kennedy would like to meet you and have you at his victory party."

"Of course, I'll be there. Please thank the senator for his support and for his kind invitation. I do have to first go over to Senator McCarthy's hotel because he also donated money for my bail."

"That's fine," the voice on the other line said, "as long as you come by."

Between both Kennedy and McCarthy, they had each donated $10,000 toward my bail. I didn't need it, but I was very thankful to them. I got ready with my girlfriend to go to both hotels wearing a Kennedy button and a McCarthy button on my coat lapel.

We got to the Beverly Hilton probably sometime around nine or ten o'clock. I told the staff in the lobby who I was, and they took my girlfriend and me upstairs to McCarthy's suite. McCarthy was an imposing figure. He was a tall guy. He probably could have played basketball in college.

"I'm Sal Castro, Sir, and thank you very much for your support," I said to McCarthy as we shook hands.

The primary results were beginning to come in on the several TVs in the suite, which showed a Kennedy lead. McCarthy didn't seem too happy, but he was very gracious.

"I support what you're trying to do," he said to me. "Why don't you join us; we're having a buffet supper."

"I'd love to, Senator," I responded with some uneasiness, since I had to tell him about the Kennedy invitation, "but I have to go over to the Ambassador Hotel since Senator Kennedy also donated funds. But thank you very much."

"I understand," he said.

So I took off, and my girlfriend and I got in my car to drive over to the Ambassador. On the way, we heard on the radio that it appeared that Kennedy would win, as he in fact did that evening. We were excited as I parked the car in the hotel lot. They were repairing the hotel at the time, so in order to enter you had to go through the back doors rather than the front ones. We had to walk parallel to the kitchen area, although still outside, to get to the back entrance. The kitchen, of course, would be the site of the assassination.

Before we got to the back entrance, I heard Chinese firecrackers—or what seemed to be Chinese firecrackers—five or six of them.

"Damn," I told my girlfriend, "they're really celebrating."

What I heard were the shots that killed Bobby Kennedy.

I found out later that they wanted me to be up there with Kennedy on the platform with other supporters such as Dolores Huerta, but because of the traffic jam I got there too late for that. They wanted some Mexican Americans up on the stage. Kennedy knew that he had gotten a very large Mexican American vote, was appreciative, and understood that he would need it if he got the Democratic nomination. This was political and I understood it. But what he had done for the students at the time of the blowouts was not political—it was his generosity and genuine support, and I'll always appreciate that tremendously.

We tried to get into the ballroom where the rally was, but couldn't as people streamed out, their faces reflecting the tragedy. I saw Sander Vanocur, an NBC correspondent I had met during the Pierre Salinger campaign, and asked him what was happening.

"They shot him."

"Who?"

"Kennedy."

I couldn't believe it—another Kennedy shot. I choked up. We as Chicanos had big hopes with Bobby Kennedy, perhaps even more than with John Kennedy. Bobby had reached out to César Chávez and the farmworkers, had reached out to us, and he seemed to feel the cause of Chicanos, as well as blacks and other disadvantaged groups.

I also ran into a couple of local reporters from KNX who had covered the walkouts and had been fair in their reporting. They didn't know much more, other than to confirm that apparently Kennedy had been shot after his victory speech and on his way out of the ballroom through the kitchen.

In the meantime, everyone was milling around the back entrance to the hotel. We couldn't leave because the police had quickly surrounded the hotel. While there, I witnessed the police bringing Sirhan Sirhan, the assassin, out of the hotel. He was handcuffed, and right behind him, pounding him on the back, was Big Daddy Jess Unruh, who was Kennedy's campaign manager in California, as he had been for JFK. "You son of a bitch," he was yelling at Sirhan.

We also picked up rumors that a Mexican had killed Kennedy and that it was a Mexican conspiracy. Sirhan looked like a Mexican but was an Arab. Of course, Chicanos are part Arab anyway, since the Arabs had occupied Spain for 800 years. But Sirhan's ethnicity wasn't known immediately, and so all kinds of stories were being spread.

We had to remain at the hotel for quite a while as the cops searched all the cars in the parking lot. I don't think we got out of there until almost 4 A.M. I didn't see when or how they got Kennedy's body out. My biggest regret is that I never got to meet him and to thank him for his support, not only for me but also for the students.

LOS ANGELES TIMES: "Kennedy Shot: Critically Wounded in Head at Victory Fete" "The gunman started firing at point-blank range and Sen. Kennedy didn't have a chance.

"Times photographer-reporter Boris Yaro, who was standing only three feet away from the shooting in the kitchen corridor at the Ambassador, fought back tears as he gave this graphic description of the shooting: 'I was getting ready to shoot a picture and I thought the shots were firecrackers going off. Kennedy backed up against the kitchen freezers as the gunman fired at him at point-blank range. He cringed and threw his hands up over his face. I think five shots were fired.'"[28]

Sit-In at the Board of Education

Even though the Kennedy assassination was crushing, I had to go on to deal with my problems, including the felony indictment over my head and the fact that they wouldn't let me teach. The rationale on this ruling was that an indicted felon should be kept away from children. Yet the irony was that I still continued to work at the Tenth Street School playground with the kids. Apparently, the school administration hadn't caught this. The right hand didn't know what the left hand was doing.

But I resented the restriction at Lincoln. I couldn't even go on the school grounds and had to miss the senior graduation that June. That really hurt, because I missed saying goodbye to all those kids who walked out and had worked with me. Ingles told me that if I showed up, I would be arrested.

PAULA CRISOSTOMO: "I graduated that spring in 1968, but I felt angry that my favorite teacher wasn't allowed to be there. And that really hurt me and I know it hurt him. My God, after 40 years, I'm still crying about this stuff."[29]

That summer, I still had hopes that I could return to Lincoln in the fall. I finished the spring semester at the IMC and continued at the playground. Nothing happened on the felony case on the East L.A. 13 or me, except that we were advised, I think by the ACLU, that in order to fight the conspiracy charges it would be best for each of us to be represented individually rather than as a group. "If you're together," the ACLU stressed, "the conspiracy is obvious." The college students and the Berets didn't have the money for this, so they had to rely on individual ACLU attorneys. I could afford a lawyer, although it would hurt me financially. I told Acosta that I could afford another lawyer so he would be free to help the others. He was too unstable and crazy. Someone, I think Phil Montez, suggested Herman Sillas to represent me. Herman was a young but excellent attorney who helped found MALDEF (the Mexican American Legal Defense and Education Fund). He defended me over the next couple of years as the others and I appealed our indictments on the basis of free speech. For the time being, my legal situation lay in abeyance, but I was still an indicted felon and that was affecting my career.

Although I didn't have anything to do with it that summer, some parents, along with the college students, such as Henry Gutiérrez, began to organize a defense committee on behalf of the East L.A. 13. It was called the Chicano Legal Defense Committee. These were some of the same people who during our short incarceration quickly organized demonstrations outside the Hall of Justice for all of us arrested. They wanted me back in Lincoln that fall. The EICC, of course, led this effort. I became a symbol of the struggle against the school board. They seemed to know something I didn't know as yet, although the handwriting was on the wall. I began getting letters from the school district indicating that I might be transferred to another school.[30]

However, sometime in August, I received another letter, which informed me that I was to report to the Bimini Center in September and that I would be working there during the new school year. This was a decision made by School Superintendent Jack Crowther and sustained by the school board with only Nava dissenting.[31] The Bimini Center, on Vermont and Beverly, did all of the administrative work concerning federal programs in the school. I would be assigned as an audiovisual consultant "evaluating" old movies rather than as a teacher.[32] I found it ironic that the Bimini Center had been built where the old Bimini swimming pool had been located and where as a kid I and other Mexicans were not allowed to swim.

So in early September, when school started, I reported to the Bimini Center. I had no choice. The director was a nice guy and maybe even semisympathetic, but he and the others kept their distance from me. I was like a leper. No one would talk to me or be seen with me. While I remained isolated at the center, events at Lincoln were something else.

Picketing in support of Sal Castro, Lincoln High School, September 16, 1968. Activist attorney and writer Oscar Zeta Acosta is holding the sign that reads "Sal is for you. Are you for him?" Photograph by Myron Dubee. Courtesy Herald Examiner Collection/Los Angeles Public Library.

The group that had formed that summer, including the EICC, to demand that I be reinstated to my teaching position at Lincoln began to publicly protest. On the first day of school, interestingly on September 16, Mexican Independence Day, anywhere between 100 and 300 formed a picket line in front of the school.[33] "We want Castro," they shouted as they carried their picket signs with different slogans for part of the morning. What was heartening was that these were now adults rather than the high school kids doing this. They picketed each day throughout September. The police and undercover cops remained ever vigilant.[34] I actually never saw the demonstrations because I had to be at the Bimini Center and because I was not allowed on the school grounds. I couldn't afford to get busted or get fired, because I still had to make child support.[35]

Besides picketing, the support group also went to the school board meetings to try to get the board to change the ruling that prohibited me from teaching while my indictment was ongoing. The board met twice a week, and so each time the group went to get on the agenda. However, the board, or at least a majority, dug in their heels and refused to change this policy.[36]

Picketing in support of Sal Castro, Lincoln High School, September 1968. Photograph by Myron Dubee. Courtesy Herald Examiner Collection/Los Angeles Public Library.

I had also on my own appealed to the Teachers' Negotiation Council to help me get back to Lincoln.[37] I didn't get very far with it. I don't think they gave a shit about me. Its reaction was that I shouldn't push my case because they believed that I would be allowed to teach at another school and as a result they didn't have to fight my case. "As long as you can still teach somewhere," the union said, "you're not being denied your rights." That was bullshit!

Nothing seemed to be happening, and, in the meantime, I'm still at the Bimini Center. The EICC and the college students began to get frustrated with the school board. As a result, without my knowledge, one afternoon on a Thursday in the last week of September, after a large number attended a board meeting, they decided not to leave.[38] They did a sit-in protest, picking up from the black civil rights protests, which included sin-ins in establishments that wouldn't serve blacks. They told the board that they now constituted the "Free and Liberated Board of Chicano Education" and would remain there until it reinstated me. I don't know whether they planned this protest or it was spontaneous. I have a feeling that it was planned.[39]

I first heard about the sit-in on my way home after working at the playground. I had the car radio on, and when the news came on I heard: "Radical Mexican Americans take over the Board of Education over the Sal Castro issue," or words to that effect. That's me! I quickly changed directions and headed over to the school district office, where the board met.

I went to the entrance of the board room, where I met these two big Chicano guys who were guarding the doors like bouncers. They looked like *Villistas* or *Zapatistas*. They recognized me and welcomed me inside. As soon as I entered, the others—maybe as many as 100 in all—saw me and came up and gave me big *abrazos* (hugs).[41]

"We took over; we took over," they kept saying. "We're going to force them to take you back."

They were excited and empowered about what they had done. The sit-in included mostly the college students. I was proud of them. It took a lot of guts to do this. They were having a good time as well. Someone had a guitar, and they sang songs. They were going to sleep there as well, as part of the protest, and I couldn't bring myself to leave. I felt that if they were doing this for me the least I could do was sit in with them, including sleeping at the board. I had only my playground clothes on and no toothbrush or anything like that, but then neither did anyone else.

I don't know what time I finally fell asleep with all the lights on in the place. We all slept either on the floor, in the auditorium seats, or on a few tables. We used the bathrooms in the building. I didn't sleep very well but got up early, about five in the morning, and left. I went to my apartment, where I showered, changed, and prepared to go to work at the Bimini Center. But that evening, I returned and again spent the night at the board. People didn't necessarily stay there all day, since some had to work or had classes, but some always remained to continue the sit-in.[42] In fact, the board of education even still had some committee meetings there and on the next Monday had their regular board meeting. The Chicanos simply converted from being protestors to being the audience for the meeting and used the occasion to again demand that the board change its policy and, if it didn't, the

Sit-in at the Los Angeles Board of Education, September 26–October 2, 1968. At center is college student Jesús Treviño. Courtesy Los Angeles Times Photographic Archive, Department of Special Collections, Charles E. Young Research Library, UCLA.

sit-in would continue. As the *Chicano Student Movement* newspaper put it: "Never have these white walls absorbed so much brown."[43]

Fortunately, the board was smart enough not to create a worse crisis by calling in the police immediately. I guess they figured that we would soon tire of the circumstances and leave on our own. Consequently, no police entered the building, even though a few lingered outside—but didn't harass as people went in and out.

To feed the protestors, some parents and other adults, especially the *mujeres* (women) brought homemade food. The moment I saw them bringing in food, I felt that we were going to win, with such tremendous support. They kept bringing in tamales, tacos, burritos, and all kinds of other great Mexican food. I had to say, "*Ya no señoras.* [We have enough.]" I think that we all gained weight during the sit-in. By now the board room began to have the beautiful aroma of a Mexican restaurant. It reminded me of the movie *Viva*

Zapata, where you see Zapata and Villa sitting together and all these people bringing them food.

As the days and evenings wore on and almost a week went by, the morale remained high. The college kids, like Raul Ruiz, Rosalinda Mendez, Juan Gómez-Quiñones, Susan Racho, Jesús Treviño, Henry Gutiérrez, Carlos Vásquez, and others discussed strategy and had animated political discussions. At one point we held our own Chicano Board of Education meeting, with me as president of the board, and had Julian Nava explain to us what he was doing to change the board's position. The Chicano board told Julian that he would not be allowed to "come home" unless he made a greater effort to reinstate me.[44] Some of them read, especially for classes. Mariachis came one day and serenaded the protestors.[45] On Sunday, we even had Father John Luce, from the Church of the Epiphany and always a strong supporter, come in and say Mass. He was an Episcopalian priest, while most of us were Catholics, but it was close enough. He gave us Communion using bits of tortillas. It's hard to describe the wonderful spirit in that room. The people there were thoroughly committed, and they were not going to be denied.[46]

The sit-in started on a Thursday and lasted almost a week. The media, of course, covered it, and it became a big political event. However, by the next Wednesday, October 2, the patience of the board ran out, and they asked the police to evict the protestors. In the meantime, a deal was cut—I think by Julian Nava—to have the board put on its agenda my case, in return for the sit-in to end. But not all of the protestors accepted the deal. The police gave everyone a warning and said that if everyone wasn't out by a certain time that evening they would be arrested. Some, like the Reverend Mardirosian, who spent some time in the auditorium, decided that it would be best to leave, while some, mostly college students, defied the police and were arrested.[47]

LOS ANGELES HERALD-EXAMINER: "School Board 'Sit-Ins' Arrested"
"Thirty-five demonstrators who refused to leave the Board of Education offices to enforce a reinstatement of Sal Castro as a teacher at Lincoln High School were arrested peacefully after a weeklong 'sit-in' siege of the education offices.

"Demonstrators were arrested at 10 P.M. after they were given three warnings to leave the building. They were taken outside in the rain and placed in paddy wagons while a group of 100 sympathizers chanted, 'We shall overcome.' Many waved Mexican flags."[48]

I wasn't there at the time of the arrests, because I worked at the playground until 9 P.M. I would have gotten arrested if I had gone to the auditorium earlier. Actually, I had been further delayed because there had been a

Celebration after Sal Castro is reinstated to his teaching position at Lincoln High School, October 3, 1968. Courtesy Los Angeles Times Photographic Archive, Department of Special Collections, Charles E. Young Research Library, UCLA.

gang shooting that evening, not at the playground but in the neighborhood. I stayed later to make sure all the kids went home safely. By the time I got to the board of education, everyone had left. However, I got a call later that everyone and more would be back the next day to confront the board at their regular meeting time to pressure them to reassign me back to Lincoln.

Again because of my playground work, I got to the board meeting late. The first thing I noticed was at least 100 people outside the auditorium who couldn't get in because the inside was filled to capacity of about 200 persons. Somehow I got inside and walked in with my usual playground jacket and clothes. As soon as I entered, the board had finished its deliberation, after several hours on my case, and was prepared to vote. I unfortunately missed some wonderful speeches by community people, including EICC leaders such as Reverend Mardirosian. I listened to them later and saw some clips of these speeches on the late evening TV news.[49]

Sign held by one Castro supporter at meeting: "Sal is for you[;] are you for him?"[50]

REV. VAHAC MARDIROSIAN: "We are here to express to you that in accepting a Mexican teacher who says that it is good to be Mexican, you're also accepting a principle that may govern our city without barbed wire in the middle of the street."[51]

Standing in the back of the place I heard the roll call on the vote: Mr. Gardner; yes; Mrs. Harding; yes; Mr. Nava; yes; Reverend Jones; yes; and so on until the end. The motion to reassign me passed, to our surprise, by a five-to-one vote. Almost immediately, I heard a huge roar and people began clapping. The board, by a strong majority, had reinstated me back to Lincoln. People then realized that I was there, and they hugged me and some guys picked me up and started carrying me on their shoulders around the auditorium. I wasn't a small guy even then, so this was no small effort. Everyone was congratulating me as I pointed to the guys to put me down, but to no success. Others started the rhythmic and prolonged Chicano clap, which began low and then built to a loud climax. It felt great to have all of this community support. I banked on it. Even in the days, especially during the summer, when I felt alone, I also believed that the community would come through, and they did! I was going back to Lincoln, thanks to those who were willing to fight for me and for their rights. I couldn't believe the bold headlines in the *Los Angeles Times* the next day: "Castro Restored to Teaching Job." It was a bigger headline than the one a few years later announcing the end of the Vietnam War.[52]

What we had started with the blowouts in March carried through that October with the sit-in and the decision by the board. The Chicano Movement had commenced in L.A., and the protests around the Eastside schools marked only the beginning.

NINE

Reprisals and Struggles

Being reinstated to Lincoln was a major victory—but a tentative one. For the next few years, I had to constantly battle the school district concerning my role as a teacher. At times, it appeared that I might not be able to survive. There are always repercussions for your actions. The school district was not about to forgive me for my role in the blowouts. I had to be punished and marginalized. I can't say that I didn't think about possible reprisals when I conspired to organize the walkouts. But there are times in one's life when you have to put principles ahead of security or not rocking the boat. I had no regrets for organizing the students—and still do not have. It had to be done. It not only changed my life, but the lives of so many kids who had the courage to act and make history in the process.

Back at Lincoln

The kids, minus the seniors who had graduated, welcomed me back with a lot of excitement at Lincoln. The administration and most of the teachers had the opposite reaction. I had a lot fewer friends among the teachers than before the blowouts and the sit-in. The principal right away attempted to isolate me. He first took away my role as athletic director. That hurt, because I loved that job. Instead, Ingles put me conducting the buses after each school day. On the other hand, he let me teach my regular history and government classes. He also put me to work in the attendance office during the first period of school. Here is where I came to realize later how they were keeping tabs on me.

Since first period attendance meant getting to school early, I just went directly to the attendance office. Before, I would always first go to the main office to sign in, along with the other teachers. I didn't think much of this, because after that first period, I always then went back and signed in myself. But what Ingles was doing as a way of retaliating was to note that I was late to school because I didn't sign in first. He knew damn well that this wasn't true, because I was there in the attendance office. However, without telling me, he kept accumulating a phony record of tardiness on my part, which he later used to transfer me. The fact was that other teachers and administrators did the same thing—they didn't always sign in first when they arrived at school. Ingles was picking on me and looking for anything to still get me out of Lincoln. His later claim that I had been late fifty times was bullshit.

But I didn't know this at first, although I knew Ingles and others were watching me. I had to be sure to dot my i's and cross my t's. But I went on as before, encouraging my students to change the culture of low expectations at the school. One of the things I did was to organize with some of the students a Fiesta de los Barrios where the kids put on Mexican singing and dancing performances for the parents and the community. As part of this event, I helped organize the Lincoln High School Ballet Folklorico Estudiantil. We put the festival on later in the spring, and it was a big success. It also included an art show, with many student and community artists, as well as various other events, including food booths. Several thousand people attended.[1] I didn't know anything about singing and very little about dancing, and so I got a few sympathetic teachers to help, including my former student, Anita Contreras, as well as bringing in some community people to teach the kids. I helped in arranging for the costumes. At first it was difficult to get some of the students involved, but eventually a number of them did and loved it.

The fact that the school allowed this Mexican cultural performance represented one of the results of the blowouts. One of the demands included the need for the schools to recognize and promote cultural diversity, and the fiesta was part of this. In fact, the fiesta itself marked the one-year commemoration of the blowouts. I didn't want to organize something political because the arrest of the East L.A. 13 had cast a certain doubt on what had happened the previous year. Some people figured that if we got arrested, we must have done something wrong. I didn't want to feed these suspicions.

One of the other ways that the school district got back at me was to fire me from my extra playground job. Once they realized that even during my suspension from Lincoln I still worked at the playground, they hit the ceiling. They discovered this when, after the school board reinstated me to Lincoln and it became banner headlines, the *Los Angeles Herald-Examiner* sent a reporter to do a follow-up story on me at the Tenth Street playground. She brought along a photographer, who took pictures of me with the kids. In the article that the paper published they also quoted me as saying—which was true—how ironic it had been that the school district denied me teaching kids while I could still direct them at the playgrounds. "This is the first victory of Mexicans in the Southwest since 1849," I said about the blowouts and the decision to keep me at Lincoln. "It is only very recently that our community has begun to question if all authority is just. Now maybe we can get somewhere."[2]

Unfortunately, the story alerted the superintendent's office that I worked at the playground. The right hand finally found out what the left hand was doing. Even though I had been returned to Lincoln, they still retaliated by firing me from the playground. They picked December of 1968 to do this, hoping that the holidays would distract people from their action, and it did. One evening a guy by the name of Larry Houston from the district showed up with two L.A. city school detectives at the playground.

"Hello, are you Mr. Castro?"

"Yeah."

"It's a pleasure to meet you," he said, as he handed me a letter.

I opened it, and it said in part: "You are hereby terminated as playground director at the Tenth Street School."

The guy then said: "May I please have your keys." So I gave them to him.

"Thank you very much," he said and then extended his hand to shake mine.

"You son of a bitch," I said to his face. "You just fired me, and you want me to shake your hand? The hell with you!"

I was pissed. After all of these years in working the playground and doing a good job, not to mention that the extra pay helped me with child support, this is what I got. They had me. I couldn't appeal this because it wasn't a regular part of my teaching position. But I was pissed, and I realized that it was going to be tough for me from then on with the school district and on me financially.

IT APPEARS AT the same time that some in the non-Mexican community also resented my reinstatement to Lincoln and my role in the blowouts. One person, in a letter to the editor of the student paper at L.A. City College, wrote a very vicious racist attack on me:

> To Sal Castro. . . . The U.S.A. was founded by white people; it is a white society; when you come here you should adjust to it or GET THE HELL OUT!
>
> In its early history, many minorities came, and they put their shoulders to the wheel, and they progressed. If you don't like it here, *GET TO HELL OUT*! You evidently couldn't make it in your own country, or your

adults coulnd't [*sic*], so you think you are going to reach up and take the plums here, but you are not. WE HAVE HAD IT WITH YOU, AND WE WANT TO SAY: SHUT UP, OR GET OUT. No body asked you or yours to come here—why did you come? To get more for yourselves; but you have *to earn it, man, you have to earn it.*

It is up to minorities coming in here to learn English, to adjust to the society if they want to stay; otherwise, go back from whence they come. *We taxpayers have had it from you.* GET OUT! WE ARE ASKING THE IMMIGRATION NOT TO LET ANY MORE OF YOU IN.[3]

Que tapado (what an idiot)! Boy, did this guy show his stupidity.

In the meantime, although I wasn't involved, negotiations between the EICC and the school board continued. It soon became clear that the board had no intentions of accepting many of the demands. They would do only what was easier and not cost very much money. I felt frustrated, but I didn't seriously plan on more walkouts. The first had been hard enough. I also worried more about police violence against the kids. I wanted to avoid this. I didn't want to chance students getting hurt.

Another problem in thinking about additional protests was that the EICC began to lose some of its commitment and energy. In part, this had to do with the college students and other activists turning their attention to other issues of the growing Chicano Movement. Some of this also had to do with the Reverend Mardirosian in a way selling out to the school board. Shortly after the sit-in, I found out that he had accepted a nice cushy job as assistant to the school superintendent at a very substantial salary. He got bought out, and he still has never sent me any contributions for our youth leadership conferences.

This isn't to say that some changes didn't occur. One of the more positive reactions, as I've noted already, is that more and more of the colleges, including Ivy League ones, began to recruit in the Eastside schools and in the Southwest in general. This allowed more of our kids to go on to college, despite the problems in the schools. The colleges took chances on some of our kids through special admissions programs such as the EOP (Educational Opportunities Program) in the UC and Cal State systems through affirmative action. The kids came through by many of them graduating. In addition, the school district hired more Mexican American teachers, including the first crop of principals and vice principals.[4] They even allowed some of the mothers to work in the schools by hiring them as cafeteria and maintenance workers as well as teaching assistants.

As the EICC began to go by the wayside, the board in 1969 established a Mexican American Education Commission composed of thirty-six community people to theoretically advise it on school issues.[5] Some of the initial members included Dr. Rodolfo Acuña, María Baeza, Rosalinda Méndez, Raul Arreola, Marco De León, Monte Pérez, Carlos Vásquez, Henry Gutiérrez, Jesús Treviño, Dr. Francisco Bravo, Raul Ruiz, Esteban Torres, and, of course, Reverend Mardirosian, among others.[6] So there were some reforms, but the over-all picture didn't change that much and wouldn't over the years. This lack of change wasn't necessarily reflective of the Chicano community but of how intransigent and bureaucratic the educational system is and remains.[7]

Working at KNBC

The 1968–69 school year, by comparison with what had happened the previous year, was mild. This didn't mean that the majority of students were any less committed. We continued to take a number of them to the Hess Kramer conferences, where you could see after 1968 the growing political consciousness and militancy among both the high school and college students. But there were no more mass walkouts or arrests during the next school year, with the exception of a walkout at Roosevelt in early 1969 due to a teacher, a Mr. Hogan, calling one of the students a "dirty Mexican." For several days, the EICC picketed the school to demand the teacher's transfer.[8] As far as the East L.A. 13 were concerned, we appealed our indictments, but the slowness of the appeal process dragged on for the next couple of years. We remained indicted felons.

In spite of the way the administration treated me at Lincoln, I enjoyed being again with the students. However, things changed that would affect my status at the school. Sometime, I think in the spring or summer of 1969, I got into some conversations with Julian Nava. We weren't really friends but had developed a professional relationship since the blowouts. I expressed to him a concern I had that on television there was nothing at all about the history of Mexicans in the United States or in Mexico itself. There were some programs coming out on blacks, but never on Chicanos, either nationally or locally.

"Something should be done," I told Nava. "Maybe you could start a project to develop something for television."

Nava apparently took this suggestion seriously, because not too long after this he asked me to meet with him and a guy named Pete Rodríguez from KNBC, the NBC affiliate in Los Angeles. Nava wanted me to talk to Rodríguez about my concerns. I told him about the different contributions of Mexicans to the country and to California, and yet there existed all of these negative stereotypes about Mexicans, such as the famous "Frito Bandido" commercial at the time.

"We need to change these images on TV by showing the real history of *mexicanos*," I said.

"Well," Pete replied, "how would you like to be the executive producer of a program on KNBC that will do this?"

"Me, a producer? I have no TV experience. I'm not the guy you want."

"Yeah, but you've got a lot of ideas, and I think KNBC may be interested in doing something," Rodríguez responded and promised to get back to me.

It turned out that KNBC was up for its license renewal and had to show that it was providing a certain number of hours of local public programs. As a result, they liked Pete's idea of a Chicano program with me as producer. After more discussion with Pete, I agreed to try it out. The only problem was that I would have to commit to working full-time at the station to develop the program. I didn't want to give up teaching, but I finally decided that I had to put my commitment where my mouth was. I could reach more people on TV than I could in the classroom. Still with doubts that I could succeed in this new venture, I requested a leave from Lincoln for the 1969–70 school year to do the TV program. To my surprise, they gave me no difficulty with my request. I think that Ingles and the school district were only too pleased to get rid of me, even for a semester or two.

I surfaced again in the newspapers when the *Los Angeles Times* picked up the story of my TV program when it reported: "Sal Castro, controversial former Lincoln High School teacher, is currently producing a series of television programs entitled 'Chicanos in America.' Castro is filming the series for KNBC and the programs are tentatively slated for showing in January 1971. He is host and coordinator of the series."[9]

So that fall, instead of teaching, I started at KNBC. But from the very beginning, I began to realize that this was a token program and that the station wasn't going to provide many resources. For starters, they wanted me to do the whole job pretty much on my own. They gave me no budget for writers and no technical help for visuals. The only staff they provided was to get me an assistant, Alicia Sandoval. I knew Alicia because she also was a teacher and an officer in the teachers' union, but she didn't have any more TV experience than I did. We did the best we could with what we had.

The first thing I did was to call the show *Chicano: Mexican-American Heritage Series*. But because I had only a shoestring budget, the only thing I could think of was to produce a half-hour program on Chicano Studies in ten installations. I planned to invite various Chicano Studies professors to be on the show. Each one would basically do a lecture, and we would come up with slides and other images to accompany the lectures. Since I didn't have a budget for writers, the professors would have to write their own lecture. I couldn't believe this. How could KNBC call it a first-class production if they couldn't even come up with writers? I got, for example, Dr. Tómas Martínez from Stanford to agree to do a presentation on Chicano stereotypes and Dr. Ernesto Galarza, a longtime labor leader and one of the early Mexican American intellectuals, to do a lecture on Mexican agricultural workers. Other Chicano professors included Federico Sánchez, Carlos Arce, Jaime Sena Rivera, Julian Nava, Paul Sánchez, and Manuel Ramírez.[10] Some of the titles of the shows included "Aztlán;" "Myths of the Southwest;" "Mexican American War Period;" "Spiders in the House;" "Economic Repression of the Chicano;" "Mexican Americans and Education: Quo Vadis America?" "Barrio Life and Cultural Democracy;" and "Stereotyping in the Mass Media."[11] The budget was so low that the program had to be in black and white rather than color.

After almost seven or eight months of planning the program, I had had enough. I could see that the program was not going to be very good because of the lack of real support by the station. I concluded it was destined for failure. On the other hand, some community people got very excited about it. They thought it was a big deal for a show like this to be on TV. I disagreed, given what I knew about KNBC's lack of support.

"It's great, Sal," they said.

"No, it isn't. What's great about it? To die on the set there of a heart attack?"

I got so frustrated working on the show that I had to go have drinks every day across the street. Finally, I just quit. "All this is doing," I told Pete Rodríguez, "is getting an FCC renewal license for KNBC. It's not really serious about doing a quality show." The first ten programs were ready to air when I did this. The station had wanted me to be the narrator of each program, so they instead recruited Frank Cruz, a teacher at Lincoln High who, I think, already worked for KNBC, to be the narrator. Frank had a more positive view of the program and saw it as a pioneering one even before the more famous *Roots* series of the later 1970s, which dealt with the black experience. The producer, Pete Rodríguez, talked me into staying as the executive producer. The title of the program was also changed, to *Chicano: Mexican Heritage*.[12] Rodríguez went on to produce another ten programs, and then, as I feared, KNBC cancelled the show. Frank Cruz and Alicia Sandoval, however, went on to successful media careers.

In a way, I guess, *Chicano* was pathbreaking, because for the first time on L.A. television a specific and positive program on Chicanos aired. The only problem is that few people actually saw it, since it usually ran like around 11 P.M. on Sunday evenings. I felt bad about quitting, because I'm not a quitter, but I wasn't going to be used and jerked around on a Mickey Mouse program. It wasn't like KNBC didn't have the resources to produce a first-rate production, but it instead was just being paternalistic and going through the motions.

Transferred from Lincoln

Although I had gotten a leave for the entire school year 1969–70, I couldn't return to teaching at Lincoln even after I quit at KNBC. Before the school year started in September of 1970, the district administration made the decision to transfer me to another school. Actually, as early as the summer of 1969, I received notification from the school district that I wouldn't be back at Lincoln because of various complaints against me the previous year. Incredibly, they brought forty-six charges of unprofessional conduct, none of which related to the blowouts. I didn't know what the hell they were talking about. I knew that I was being set up. I decided to fight, with my attorney Herman Sillas and a lawyer from the teachers' union, Larry Trigstad. The district, of course, had its own lawyers. We didn't file a lawsuit or anything like that, but I had recourse to an appeal with a formal hearing.

The hearing lasted three weeks and consisted of a board or committee that listened to the pros and the cons. It included a so-called referee, an independent lawyer, two teachers from other schools, and a principal from another school. At the hearing, the school district lawyer brought out these lies and distortions about my record during the 1968–69 year. For one, he used the trumped-up accounts that I had been late to work some fifty times. They actually used the figure of fifty times. The school district knew that this wasn't true because I had been there all those times in the attendance office and then signed in later. But they denied this and insisted that the documents clearly showed that I had not signed in on time when I was supposed to, and therefore I was late all of those times. This was the first main charge.

Then they accused me of falsifying a student's report card. But this wasn't true either. What had happened was that this Chicano kid, who was a good track runner, was in jeopardy of not being able to run track because of his grades. Because he wasn't doing well, they put him in what was called the "opportunity room." You got put in this class if you were in danger of failing your other classes. You didn't get a real grade for the opportunity class. It was just a warehousing of kids. I was in charge of this class. The kid's mother came to see me and told me that her son was going to drop out if he couldn't run track. I certainly didn't want him to drop out, so I put a "C" grade on his opportunity attendance, which meant that he was not in danger of failing his other classes. This was simply a temporary administrative decision, and after he finished the track season, I would put him right back on probation, which I did. I wasn't falsifying his record. I just wanted to keep the kid in school. But, at the hearing, the district accused me of falsifying the record. I disputed this when questioned about it at the hearing.

Two of the people on the hearing board seemed to be leaning on my behalf, but the other two seemed hell-bent to get me. In fact, one actually lied to the lead hearing officer and attorney about this whole issue of my falsifying that student's record. I know this because I was in the cloakroom during a recess period and I overheard this one guy tell the attorney this lie. The lawyer asked him if this change I had made would be a permanent one and thereby get the student off the hook. The teacher said that it would be permanent. That was a lie, but the lawyer believed it, and he turned against me. In the end, the board voted three to two to sustain the district's decision not to keep me at Lincoln but to transfer me to another school.[13] I, of course, was upset, but I had no other appeal, and it would be too expensive to go the legal route. I already had enough legal problems with the East L.A. 13 case. I had no choice but to leave Lincoln. This hurt, given all that had happened at that school. If I'm remembered for anything, it will be what we did at Lincoln and the blowouts. It's part of my life that I'll never forget.[14]

Although the transfer was ordered, I was impressed and thankful for the large community support on my behalf. Besides expression of support by Chicano Movement groups, a number of mainline Mexican American organizations, Mexican American attorneys and educators, as well as sixty-three Lincoln High School parents and community people signed an open letter to Deputy Superintendent Graham Sullivan that was published in the *Eastside Sun* objecting to my transfer. The letter in part read: "The present 'concerted effort' to remove Mr. Sal Castro from Lincoln High School is obviously the result of the defeat suffered by the administrative hierarchy last year following the board's decision to reinstate him there. This conspiracy was initiated following the October 1968 decision."[15]

East L.A. 13

Although I, along with many community people, were upset and even angry over my not being able to remain at Lincoln, one bright spot in 1970 was the vindication of the East L.A. 13 over our roles in the walkouts. I don't want to underestimate this, because frankly I—and I'm sure the others—were concerned about being convicted and what this would do to our lives. Fortunately, we had good lawyers who opposed our indictments. Because of our attorneys, we never went to trial. They, including Herman Sillas and Oscar Acosta, challenged in Superior Court the very process of our charges by the grand jury. They asked questions as to why no Mexican Americans served on the grand jury, including the one that indicted us. It was incredible. Mexican Americans made up about 40 percent of L.A. County, and yet no Mexican Americans for years had been on the jury. How could Mexican Americans receive a fair trial by a jury of their peers?

"Who appoints the grand jury," Oscar Zeta Acosta asked.

"The Superior Court judges," they were told.

So our lawyers put the judges on the stand at one of our appeals.

"Who have you nominated for the grand jury in the last five years?"

They gave names.

"Why have you not nominated anyone of color?"

They didn't know.

"Well, who's your gardener?"

Now they named some Mexican Americans but couldn't explain why they didn't nominate them or, for that matter, any other Mexican Americans. Our attorneys questioned more than thirty judges in the initial hearing in Superior Court.[16]

The challenge of the indictment process was effective in throwing a cloud over our indictments, although initially the lower court that ruled that the exclusion of Mexican Americans from the grand jury was not intentional upheld them.[17] However, in the end, a state appellate court (California Second Appellate Court) in 1970 ruled that the indictments based on the conspiracy charges were illegal because they violated our First Amendment rights of free speech and the right of redress of grievances.[18] After two long years, we were no longer indicted felons. It had not been easy for any of us. I had faith in my attorney, Herman, and I'll always be grateful to him. He did a terrific job, as did the other attorneys, including, to his credit, Acosta. MALDEF, the Mexican American Legal Defense and Education Fund, also came to our assistance and footed almost all of our attorney fees. But I have to admit that I feared I would eventually do time. If this happened or if I couldn't teach, I didn't know how I would help take care of my children. I had nightmares of those bastards sending me to a hard-core maximum-security penitentiary such as Folsom or Soledad. But now it was all over. We had been vindicated for our roles in the blowouts. The system had tried to cut us off and to make lessons of us for what would happen if Chicanos got out of line. But we prevailed.[19]

Ironically, I had been charged with conspiracy, and, as I tell students today, the fact was that I was guilty of this! I had conspired to get the kids to walk out so that they could have a better future, perhaps not for themselves but for their younger brothers and sisters who would come after them. For this, I paraphrase the words of Corky Gonzales's epic poem "I Am Joaquin":

"Here I stand before the Court of Justice guilty for all the glory of my Raza."[20]

North Hollywood High

Despite our legal victory, the school district still refused to reinstate me to Lincoln High School. The problem for the school district and the school board, with the possible exception of Nava, was that they didn't want me in a Mexican school. That's the last thing they wanted. They agreed to not send me to L.A. High but instead assigned me to North Hollywood High, in the spring semester of 1971.[21]

North Hollywood High was, like Lincoln, a very large school of about 2,000 students. The main difference, however, was that the great majority of the kids were white, many of them of Jewish backgrounds. I think the school district wanted to disorient me and discourage me by putting me in a totally different environment. It didn't work. The other teachers put up with me, although the principal, Lloyd Pack, whom I called "Six Pack," was hostile and looked for anything to get rid of me.

But just as I started at North Hollywood, some of the same Chicanos who had protested my exclusion from Lincoln following my arrest organized again, once they realized that I wasn't going to be at Lincoln. This time, instead of picketing at Lincoln, they did so at North Hollywood. In fact, I encouraged them to do so. "Let's scare the hell out of the *gavachos* [whites] by going into their barrios," I said. We were the only Mexicans there. The problem was that North Hollywood was distant from the Eastside, and people began to get tired of going over there. In retrospect, it would have been better if they had picketed at Lincoln. Still, for about a week each school day, about 100 Chicanos demonstrated at North Hollywood. They didn't let them do so in the front of the school but on the side of the main entrance. After about a week, the picketing ended. I didn't blame them for stopping. It was hard on them, and I appreciated their support.[22]

My initial adjustment at North Hollywood had to do with the racial composition. At Washington Junior High in Pasadena I had taught mostly *morenitos* (blacks); at Belmont, there were large numbers of *raza* (Chicanos); and, of course, at Lincoln it was predominantly Mexican. Now, all of a sudden, I'm put into a school that's 95 percent white, many of them Jewish and the children of people in the movie industry. I kidded some of the mostly white students by saying: "I used to pray to people that looked like you"—all those white Jesus and Virgin Mary figures in the Catholic churches on the east side.[23]

But I adjusted and got along very well with my students. The kids took to me. This scared the principal and some of the other teachers. They thought I would fail because I would be out of my element. This was pretty racist when you think about it—the idea that a Chicano teacher couldn't teach white kids. I taught history and government. At the same time, the principal didn't allow me to be the sponsor of any student organization or to coach or help out in any sport. They clearly wanted to isolate me as much as possible and to discourage me.

But it didn't really work. I organized the kids within my classes. For example, one of the key political issues being debated in the early 1970s was giving the vote to eighteen-year-olds. So in my government and history classes, I got the students not only to debate this issue but also to go lobby the congressman from that district to support extending the vote. The war in Vietnam also still raged, and we discussed this in class. I encouraged the students to participate in antiwar rallies in L.A., and many did. It was easier with these kids on Vietnam because they came from liberal Jewish families who also opposed the war. On the other hand, "Six Pack," the principal, didn't like what I was doing. He didn't want politics in his school. In the spring of 1971, some of the kids wanted to attend a national antiwar demonstration in San Francisco. There had been previous such demonstrations in San Francisco, including one in November 1969, where early Chicano antiwar protestors such as Rosalio Muñoz spoke and that helped inspire the large Chicano antiwar moratorium on August 29, 1970.

"If we go can we get class credit, Mr. Castro?"

"Sure, no problem. Go for it."

Besides issues like the war, I also discussed in my classes about conditions in the Chicano barrios and about the Eastside schools. I explained to them about the blowouts. They liked my approach, and so too did their parents. I also brought in guest speakers like Tom Brokaw and Jess Marlow, both news anchors from KNBC. I knew both of them from my stint at the station.

There was one incident that comically almost got me into really hot water. In my twentieth-century U.S. history class, I had the students work on a term paper. One kid comes up to me and says: "My dad has a bunch of stuff on World War II like flags, German helmets, and other things. Can I do my report on the war and the German army?"

Since it was part of World War II, I said, "Hey, no problem."

Besides writing these reports, the students also had to do oral presentations. This same kid, the day before his presentation, comes up again to me and says,

"Mr. Castro, can I come in early tomorrow and put up some of my dad's stuff on the German army for my presentation?"

"Sure, no sweat."

So he comes early the next day before class and starts putting up all of these Nazi flags and banners on the wall. That was okay with me, except that my classroom was right across from the cafeteria, and on this morning the PTA was meeting there. Between my room and the cafeteria there was a big window, so that you could look directly into my room from the cafeteria. So as my class starts and this student begins to make his oral report on the German army, explaining all of the swastikas and flags on the wall, the PTA parents looking in were in a state of shock. What the hell is going on? These are mostly Jewish parents with strong memories of the Holocaust. They rush to Principal "Six Pack" and tell him that I have all of this Nazi stuff in my classroom.

"Isn't he the teacher who caused problems in one of the Eastside schools? What is he teaching our kids?"

The principal panics and calls the area superintendent, who races over. Then all of them go to my class, open the door, and begin to enter, when they hear this kid, who has a German helmet on his head, saying: "My dad was shot in World War II after D-Day, but before he was sent home, he picked up a whole bunch of souvenirs like this helmet and these Nazi flags. Because of him, I've learned about what the Germans did."

This completely deflated what ire the PTA people, the principal, and the superintendent had, and without a word they quietly retreated and gently closed the door. Nothing happened to me about the incident, but I think that it only confirmed on the part of the principal that it was too risky having me around.

I enjoyed very much my students at North Hollywood. Some of them went on to movie careers. I don't remember their names, but I heard this later. One kid whom I do remember is a Japanese American by the name of Desmond Nakano. I guess I influenced him to some extent, because he later became a screenwriter and wrote a script about Chicanos called *Boulevard Nights* about East L.A., which was made into a movie.

Although I couldn't coach or assist in sports, I was able to officiate some games. This included being a timer in track meets. At one meet, I had to be at the top of a ladder so I could better see the runners. When I reached the top, I realized that I had left my chalkboard with the numbers of the runners on it. I foolishly started to jump down to get the board, when in midair I realized that I was going to land right on the board and possibly break it. Rather than doing this, I twisted in the air to avoid it and landed on my back. I felt the pain right away and couldn't finish the meet. My doctor, after taking X-rays, told me I had reinjured my back—the slipped disc. This meant that I couldn't finish the 1971–72 school year because I needed bed rest. I had to be laid up for a couple of months. The principal used this as an excuse to get rid of me. Even though I had to be put on medical leave, he made a big deal about how he needed a full-time teacher and how I had been absent for two months. I wasn't absent, of course, because I was on medical leave, but "Six Pack" made it seem like I was slacking off. That was bullshit, because lots of teachers have accidents, but in my case the principal complained to the superintendent and asked to have me transferred again. He didn't want me back.

Católicos Por La Raza

At the same time that I was working at KNBC, the Chicano Movement was going hot and heavy in L.A. and throughout the Southwest. Picking up from what we had done in the blowouts, other Chicano high school students throughout the Southwest and Midwest also demonstrated against their schools, including using the tactic of walkouts. In addition, college students and young community activists all expressed a growing militancy as part of the new Chicano Generation. Influenced by the Black Power movement, by white student radicals, by the anti–Vietnam War movement, and by the general protest spirit of the 1960s, Chicano activists contributed to the history of mass insurgency, although their contributions, unfortunately, have not been well acknowledged by historians of this era, other than Chicano historians.

One of the early Chicano Movement manifestations in L.A. occurred in the fall of 1969 in protests put on by a group called Católicos Por La Raza (Catholics for the People). They accused the Catholic Church in L.A. of not doing enough to deal with the social problems faced by Chicanos, at the same time that Mexicans constituted a very large percentage of L.A. Archdiocesan Catholics. The Church, led by archconservative Cardinal McIntyre, responded by refusing to dialogue with Católicos.

I wasn't a member of Católicos, but I did attend some of their meetings. I was especially impressed with Richard Cruz, the key leader of the group. He was a smart, articulate, and passionate law student at Loyola University Law School, who, like me, was a graduate of Cathedral High School. Richard did his homework on the Church to document the extraordinary wealth of the Archdiocese at the same time that many Mexican Catholics in L.A. lived in poverty. At one of the meetings I attended, Richard showed reams and reams of paper with all of the properties that the Church owned in L.A. and Orange County. But Católicos didn't just sit around and talk; they acted on their beliefs that the Church had to recommit itself to being a Church of and for the poor.

After Cardinal McIntyre refused to seriously consider a list of demands presented to him by Católicos, Richard and the others organized a mass demonstration against the cardinal at his Christmas Eve midnight Mass at the newly built St. Basil's Church on Wilshire Boulevard. It was at this protest that Católicos, after holding an alternative Mass on the steps of the church, attempted to enter and disrupt the cardinal's Mass in order to read their demands to the mostly white parishioners. As they moved in or tried to move in, they were attacked by county sheriff deputies disguised as ushers, who were soon reinforced by L.A. police. A near riot broke out, both inside and outside the church, with some people—all Chicanos—arrested.

I wasn't at the protest, but I did show up the next morning to help Católicos picket St. Basil's before and after the Christmas Masses. Many other Chicanos and supporters of Católicos also protested on a bright sunny day. The media covered the demonstration, although it remained peaceful. I remember Henry Alfaro, a rookie reporter for Channel 7, KABC, being there and being totally amazed with the protest. Being a classmate of mine from Cathedral, he asked me on the steps of the church, "What's going on?" Henry wasn't too politically savvy yet about the Chicano Movement, and so he had never seen so many *raza* protesting. He soon became more educated about the issues of the Chicano Movement.

I didn't continue with Católicos into 1970, as I had other things to deal with, but I always remained impressed with the group and their leadership. Richard Cruz continued as an angry young man, but yet totally committed to *la causa*. I think the more "no's" he got, the stronger he got. Because of him and Católicos, the Catholic Church in L.A. began to come around. After Cardinal McIntyre retired, or was forced to retire because of the Católicos demonstration, new leadership came in and began to implement certain reforms aimed at making the Church more attentive to the Chicano community. The Church isn't perfect, but since then it has been on the side of the Chicano poor and especially the Latino immigrants. Richard Cruz and Católicos had a lot to do with this. I didn't see Richard much over the next several years, but I know that after he became a practicing attorney he devoted his life to helping Chicanos and other Latinos. He didn't sell out to the establishment. I learned of his untimely death many years later, and I remembered that passion. It's the same passion that I've striven over the years to instill in my students, so that, like Richard, they can go out and change the world.

The Chicano Moratorium

Even more dramatic and powerful was the Chicano antiwar moratorium against the Vietnam War. Many Chicano kids, like the ones at Lincoln, were being drafted in large numbers and many killed or wounded. By 1969, the war had become a major issue for the Chicano Movement, and its leadership came from L.A. Chicanos. What came to be called the National Chicano Anti-War Moratorium Committee organized some of the first antiwar protests in East L.A. The key leader was Rosalio Muñoz, whom I knew from his days at UCLA, where he had served as student body president—the first Chicano ever so elected—in the late 1960s. He was then called Ross. I had met him because from 1968 to 1972 I worked as director of the summer Upward Bound Program at UCLA. We brought in high school kids to take classes on the campus and to get oriented to go to college. I think Rosalio helped us out. He, like Richard Cruz, proved to be an equally committed activist. He was definitely the person behind the moratorium.

Besides the initial antiwar demonstrations in December 1969 and in February 1970, Rosalio and the Moratorium Committee planned for a larger protest, scheduled for August 29, 1970, in East L.A. It would be the biggest antiwar protest during the Vietnam War by any minority community. Over 20,000 people, mostly Chicanos, marched that day.[24]

I attended the first couple of smaller protests. I don't remember speaking at the rallies, but I might have. I also went to some of the meetings of the Moratorium Committee. Most of the members were young college students or graduates such as Rosalio, along with some of the Brown Berets such as David Sánchez. I knew many of them, but I certainly had no intentions of becoming a leader with them. The committee was already in good hands. The few meetings that I attended, everyone seemed to be on the same page. Throughout the months leading to August 29, everyone also worked very hard making preparations and doing all the difficult things for a successful march and rally. I didn't have the time to be involved in all of this, but I did volunteer to be a monitor at the march. Monitors would serve to keep order. No one expected trouble or police violence, but you never knew. The committee encouraged people to bring family members and their children to provide a family atmosphere to the event and to hopefully deter any police intervention.

I'll never forget that day, just as I'll never forget the week of the blowouts. I took my two young sons with me. We arrived early to the staging point at Belvedere Park. It was a very warm day. Early on in the march, I ran into Ruben Salazar. He, of course, had interviewed me back in 1963 for that piece on the schools and Mexican Americans. I didn't see much of him for a few years due to his stint as a foreign correspondent in the Dominican Republic, Vietnam, and Mexico City, where he headed the *LA Times* bureau.[25] After he returned to L.A., around early 1969, to cover the Chicano Movement, I met up with him again. We actually became pretty good friends. We used to go out to drink. I'd meet him at his office in the *Times* building on First and Spring. He and many of the other reporters liked to go to a nearby watering hole called the Redwood to drink after work. Some times we stayed for dinner as well. They had good steaks. Ruben lived in Santa Ana, so he would wait out the traffic at the Redwood.

Ruben had not been in L.A. during the blowouts, so he was interested in learning from me all about what had happened and about my arrest later. He believed that what I and others were doing in trying to change the schools to provide a better learning experience for Chicano kids was of critical importance. That, in addition to the growing Chicano Movement, led him twice to invite me to meet with the *Times* board of editors and to discuss with them my views on the schools, on education, and on the Movement. I was flattered to do so. We met on the top floor of the *Times* building in the penthouse of publisher Henry Chandler Jr. I was impressed that Chandler on both occasions attended. He was interested in what was going on. These were great sessions of discussions, and it was good give and take. They served great food as well, but no booze. I craved having a beer, but they didn't even have one. "This is terrible that you guys don't have booze here," I kidded Ruben on the side. "Make them hurry up so we can go to the Redwood."

At one of these luncheons, someone asked me how circulation could increase in East L.A. "You know what," I said mischievously, "you bring a bunch of trucks and drop your papers off at First and Soto and on Whittier and Indiana, and your circulation will increase immediately." Ruben smiled at this.

As I got to know Ruben better, I could see his political growth since I had first met him. He had gone through a lot in the last few years. His eyes had opened up to the problems of Chicanos. As part of this evolution, Ruben decided to leave the *Times* in early 1970 and accept the position of news director of KMEX, the only Spanish-language TV station in L.A. He felt that this would give him more access to the Mexican American community, especially the Spanish-speaking. KMEX was also offering much more money, and Ruben had to think about his family, including his three young children. Before he made this decision, he talked to me about it. I agreed that it was a good move, but I hated for him to leave the *Times*.

"Don't do that, *mano*," I told him. Ruben loved the term *mano* or *manito*, which was short for brother. I think this came from his El Paso background, where—and in New Mexico—these terms are common. "Why don't you stay part-time with the *Times* and do KMEX also?"

He took my advice and worked out a deal with the paper where he could still write a weekly column in English on Chicanos. These became very influential and gave Ruben a voice in both the English-speaking and Spanish-speaking portions of the Mexican community. His news programs on KMEX also began to cover, much more extensively, Chicano issues, including police abuse in the barrios. He interviewed me a couple of times for the news show. All of this worked out nicely for Ruben.

So when I ran into Ruben at the moratorium, he was symbolically wearing his KMEX hat. His cameraman, a guy named Chapo Gómez, accompanied him. When I saw Ruben, the march had already commenced, and we had just passed St. Alphonsus Church on Atlantic Boulevard, where a Chicano couple had emerged with their whole wedding party from the church following their wedding. They had timed it deliberately to do so to show solidarity with the moratorium. I knew the groom, who went on to be a lawyer. In fact, the couple had invited me to their reception later that afternoon. I saw Ruben about a block or so past the church and told him that the wedding party had joined the march, which would make a great shot. Ruben thanked me for the tip, and he and Chapo went down to film it. I don't know if they filmed it or not, or at least I never saw any footage of it.

As a monitor, I wore a red piece of cloth around my arm to identify me as part of the security. But it was difficult at first for me to serve as a monitor, because I also had to watch my two kids. Somewhere during the march, I asked Mike Gordon, a fellow teacher at Lincoln who was there, if he could take care of them so I could more easily monitor the march. Mike agreed, and we arranged to meet at the gas station at the entrance to Laguna Park, where the rally would take place. Free of the kids, I moved around more easily with the marchers, and I was able to see much more. I saw cops in full uniform on side streets. In fact, I saw what I'm sure were undercover cops throwing smoke bombs and other stuff into the crowd to try to incite the protesters. There's a bridge over Whittier, the main avenue of the march, where the Long Beach freeway goes over the street. It's there that I saw these older-looking whites dressed like *cholos* (street dudes) throwing smoke bombs into the march. They could have been undercover sheriff deputies, FBI, or even CIA. As I look back on it now, I think these cops were rehearsing for eventually breaking up the moratorium. They figured that if Mexicans could pull 20,000 into the streets, what could other antiwar efforts in L.A. do. They weren't going to allow this.

At the end of the march, as people entered Laguna Park, I once again ran into Ruben. He and Chapo were filming the marchers entering the park. Ruben said that after the rally he and Chapo were going down to a bar to get a drink. He invited me. "*Vamos manito echarnos uno o dos.* [Come on, brother, we'll throw down one or two drinks.]" "*Carnal* [brother], I can't," I told him, because I couldn't stay for the rally. I had to drive my kids back to their mother's house and then get ready to go to the wedding reception, which was up in the Montebello hills. The last thing Ruben said to me was to ask for the address of the reception. I gave it to him, and that's the last time I saw him. I left him there chatting with Bob Navarro, another Chicano reporter who worked for Channel 2. If I had stayed and hadn't had my boys with me, I might have wound up at the Silver Dollar Café with Ruben, and who knows what would have happened.

It wasn't until I was at the reception that I learned about the sheriffs entering the park and breaking up the rally. Hundreds of cops with batons and teargas rifles attacked, without cause, the people, beating up many and arresting others. As Chicanos escaped the park, a riot ensued on Whittier Boulevard. Storefronts and police cars were burned. At the reception, we saw clouds of smoke over that part of East L.A. where the demonstration had taken place. We knew something was wrong. Then news reports began to come in over the radio about what had happened. I decided to leave and try to go back to Laguna Park to see the situation. Before I left, the family of the bridegroom gave me a couple of hundred dollars to help in case some of the Chicanos needed bail money. My suit was stuffed with money.

I went home first, to change, and then tried to drive to Laguna Park, but couldn't. The cops had blocked off that whole area of Boyle Heights. I couldn't enter until sometime early that evening. It looked like a war zone, with many cops still lingering. As I drove, I heard on my car radio not only more details of the police attack but one that sent chills through me.

"Ruben Salazar, the news director of KMEX, is reported missing and possibly hurt, according to associates of his."

I thought, "Oh, my God, Ruben."

I didn't know what else to do, so I drove to the moratorium headquarters to see if they had more information on Ruben. There I later met Danny Villanueva, the former Dallas Cowboy place kicker and the station manager of KMEX. I knew Danny from KNBC, where he started as a sports reporter before moving on to KMEX. Danny informed those of us there that Ruben had been killed at the Silver Dollar Café on Whittier Boulevard sometime after the breakup of the rally—that apparently a sheriff deputy had shown up and, without warning, shot one or more teargas projectiles into the bar. One, from all indications, struck Ruben in the head and instantly killed him. When Danny said this, I thought to myself: "I could have been sitting next to Ruben." His death was one of three that afternoon caused by the cops.

I couldn't believe it. All of us were stunned at the news. Danny knew I was friends with Ruben, and he invited me to go with him to Ruben's home and pay our condolences to his wife, Sally. I agreed to do so. We drove most of the way in silence to Santa Ana, both us still shocked at Ruben's death. I knew that Ruben was married to a white lady, but I had never met Sally. When we got there, a few other people were already with her. She seemed very composed. Everyone was, of course, saddened, but Sally was a gracious hostess, and we began to relax a bit and trade favorite stories about Ruben.

The very next day, I got a call at home from Raul Ruiz of *La Raza* magazine.

"Sal, I've got photos of the sheriff with a shotgun aiming into the Silver Dollar Café where Ruben died. I just happened to be right across from the bar and took the shots. It's the sheriff who shot into the bar and probably killed Ruben. You've got connections at KNBC—can you see if they'd be interested in showing the photos?"

Raul called me at KNBC, where I was still working, and I told Raul that I would go over and see Tom Brokaw who, at that time, did the 4 P.M. and 11 P.M. newscasts. I had met Tom at KNBC. Between a commercial break on the afternoon news set, I told Brokaw: "Tom, I have hot photos about the Salazar shooting. Are you interested?"

"Yes, definitely. Can you take me to see the photos?"

"Well, can't you just meet me at *La Raza* magazine's office in East L.A., where the photos are?"

"No, you drive me there."

Brokaw was afraid to go into East L.A. He then said: "Why don't you meet me at Vermont and Hollywood Boulevard and we'll change cars and then you can drive me to the office."

I agreed but thought all this was pretty weird. It was almost like an old World War II movie called *Foreign Intrigue*.

I picked up Brokaw, and we drove to the *La Raza* office. Raul showed us his photos, and Brokaw thought they were great. "I'll use them on the 11 o'clock news." I guess, like Brokaw, I was also a bit paranoid and had arranged for a friend to follow us in a different car and wait while we saw Raul. Later, this friend told me that when Tom and I entered *La Raza* an olive drab telephone van pulled up right in front of my car. All of a sudden an antenna went up. Whoever they were, they were spying on us. Who knows who they were. After all, President Nixon had an enemy's list, and I was on it.

A few days later, I attended Ruben's funeral at Newport Beach, where they buried him. It wasn't a Mexican funeral. It was very formal. I felt a bit hurt that I wasn't able to help carry the casket, while other wannabe friends did. But I shook this off and paid my final respects to my friend. Of course, his death at the moratorium catapulted him to political martyr status for the Chicano Movement, the last thing Ruben would have wanted. He was just a good and sensitive reporter and a great guy to be around. I still miss him.

Some time later, after Ruben was killed, the FBI questioned me about him. They wanted to know about how I knew Ruben, where he lived, and what I knew about rumors of a conspiracy to kill him. I talked with them, but I didn't believe in a conspiracy theory. If someone, including the cops, wanted to kill him, as some Chicano activists believed and still do, it seems to me that it would have been stupid, at least in the way Ruben died. If they wanted to get rid of him, why do it in a way that's going to sensationalize the whole thing? The cops weren't that dumb. If they really wanted to get him, all they needed to do was to kill him on the road going home. That way, anyone could be blamed for it, but not the cops. Now, I'm not justifying what that deputy sheriff did by shooting into the Silver Dollar. That was criminal and callous, because he wouldn't know who he might hit. But if the conspiracy is that the cop knew that Ruben was inside and hoped to kill him, I don't buy that. It's too obvious. The fact is that Ruben wasn't that much of a threat. He wrote provocative articles, but nothing so threatening that the police would have killed him for that. That was my feeling then and my feeling today.

The conspiracy theories, of course, on Ruben's tragic death continue, and they do so because the so-called inquest that was held later in September was a joke. It didn't really investigate anything. It was simply used to get the heat off the cops and unfairly blame the Chicanos for the violence. I saw some of it on TV, but I thought it was a setup from day one.

At the time of the inquest, or shortly before it, the Moratorium Committee staged another march, this time to protest what the cops had done on August 29 and especially to call for justice for Ruben's death. The committee piggybacked off of the annual September 16 parade in East L.A., which drew thousands of people to celebrate Mexican Independence Day. Somehow they got the organizing people to agree that the Moratorium Committee could be part of the parade. They later regretted this. I again attended, but this time I rode in style. Julian Nava was asked to be one of the dignitaries who would ride in a convertible in the parade, with his name on the side of the car. Julian agreed but feared that he might get stoned or something like that. I guess he thought that Chicano militants saw him as part of the establishment and that he would be a convenient target after what had happened at the moratorium. To give him political cover, he invited me to be in his car. I didn't think he would get attacked.

"Julian, don't worry. I'll ride with you. You bring your kids and I'll bring mine."

This made Julian feel better, but he still didn't bring his kids. In a photo of the parade, you can see me with my youngest son, Jimmy, riding in Nava's car. For whatever reason, one large sign on the side of the car read "Sal Castro" while a smaller sign read "Dr. Julian Nava."[26] Behind us in the parade was the moratorium contingent.

Everything went fine at first. However, after the parade concluded, some of the Chicanos who had marched with the Moratorium Committee moved against the cops stationed there, and conflict and violence ensued again. I didn't see the trouble, because as soon as the parade ended and before the clash, I left. The renewed conflict only reflected the increased tensions between the Chicano Movement and the police following the moratorium. Things would never quite be the same again.

Bilingualism, Biculturalism, and the Chicano

In the early 1970s, as I was being bounced from one school to another, I had an opportunity one summer to work on creating new bicultural materials for the newly developing bilingual education programs. The school district hired me to come up with a cultural component. I guess they thought I couldn't cause too much trouble doing this. At the district's expense, I traveled to different California locations to find materials, especially on the early history of Mexicans in California during the colonial, Mexican, and early U.S. periods. This followed from two basic convictions of mine. One, as I tried to do at Lincoln, had to do with instilling ethnic and cultural pride in Mexican students, especially by showing how Mexicans had been important in history and in particular to the history of California. My philosophy was, and is, that in order for kids to learn well they have to feel good, secure, and confident about themselves and about their schools. The second conviction had to do with my view that bilingual education was vacuous if there wasn't a cultural context. If you're going to use Spanish in part to help students adjust to school, then you also need to teach them their culture. You're not going to use Spanish to teach about Plymouth Rock! You could, but it doesn't make much sense. Use Spanish to teach kids about how Mexicans founded Los Angeles.

So, to develop this cultural component, I needed to find and copy records and other materials that could then be transferred into teaching sources. For example, I got access to early L.A. city records. These document the Mexicans who founded and ran the town, first under Spain, then Mexico, and even after the U.S. conquest in 1848. This history could then be written up as part of a teaching plan for the bilingual program, or for any other curriculum for that matter. I found other similar records at the San Diego Historical Society and at the Huntington Library in San Marino. I not only looked for documents but also for photos that could be duplicated and used in classes to show the actual faces of Mexicans in California in these early periods. I also found a lot of material at the Title Insurance Company in L.A., and, in fact, they wanted to donate some of their collection to the city schools. However, when I went to the school district office about this, they complained that it would cost too much to store the materials. I couldn't believe it. Fortunately, I went to see Elizabeth Martínez, who ran the East L.A. Library, and she arranged to host the collection. Later, the L.A. City Library housed the collection.

I also arranged for the school district to purchase a collection of slides on Mexican history, including Pre-Columbian images from one of the major museums in Mexico City. Other materials that I collected included photos of Chicano war heroes, many of them Congressional Medal of Honor winners, as well as images of other Chicano contributors toward the development of the United States as we know it today. All of these materials were then made available to teachers, especially in elementary, middle, and high schools with large percentages of Mexican American students. Regrettably, many teachers didn't take advantage of these teaching aids. I don't understand why, except that many teachers, both Mexican Americans and Anglos, themselves didn't appreciate the importance of this cultural component and the need to validate the students' cultural backgrounds. It was and still is important and a tremendous shot in the arm for kids to know their ancestors' contributions to American history. This includes Mexican American writers of the California state constitution in 1850. Kids need to know that this constitution was written in both English and Spanish. This is just one example of how this new teaching material could contribute to an enriched teaching of U.S. history that would include the Chicano contributions. "All kids should learn this [their history]," I told an *L.A. Times* reporter, "but we want our kids to learn this because they need a positive self image." It would have really juiced up the teaching of American history and the cultural component of bilingual education. However, it died from lack of interest, and as a result the cultural reinforcement in our public schools, such as the L.A. school district and many others as well, still suffers.[27]

More School Transfers

In the summer of 1972, after a year and a half at North Hollywood High, I knew that I wouldn't be going back there. I had no idea where they would assign me next. This bothered me, of course, because I felt more like a substitute teacher than a regular one. But I hung on. Finally, the district notified me that I was being sent to teach at Eagle Rock High School in Northeast L.A. in the fall of 1972. This wasn't too bad, because it was close to East L.A. and, as a result, it was in the process of becoming a more mixed school, as Mexican Americans began moving into the area. The demographics were a bit better for me, but unfortunately not the reaction of the school administration, including Principal Charley Hammer.

Under vigilance and harassment, teaching at that school was not easy, even though I did very well with my students in my usual history and government classes. But as at North Hollywood High, I wasn't allowed to do anything else but teach. They wanted to restrict me as much from contact with the students as possible. Everything I did was monitored. While other teachers walked into classes with cups of coffee, when I did it, they reprimanded me for violating the rule against bringing food into class.

While I had more than enough difficulties with the school administrators at Eagle Rock, I got along pretty well with most of the other teachers. They sympathized with me and saw that I was being scapegoated. As a show of support, they gave me a huge, hand-painted Christmas card with a picture of a Mexican and a burro with a serape with a bull's eye on the back of the Mexican that read "Castro." The faculty was telling me that I was in the principal's bull's eye. I knew that.

But I couldn't take it at Eagle Rock anymore with all of this pressure on me. I went to see the school superintendent, Bill Johnston, whom I actually had a decent relationship with, even though he was part of my being shuttled around to different schools. "If you leave me at Eagle Rock," I told him, "I'm going to hit Hammer. The guy is paranoid and he's on me all the time. I swear one day I'm going to him, so you better get me out of there."

Johnston agreed to transfer me for the second semester in 1973 to Gardena High School. Very few Mexicans attended, while mostly Asians and some blacks composed the student body. The only thing Mexican at this school was that the principal allowed the Chicano club to sell *menudo* (tripe stew) every Friday. One thing I found out at Gardena was that not all Asians represent the "model minority." Some of them had academic problems. However, I didn't have any problems with any of these students and enjoyed teaching them. Still, my reputation followed me, and it went to the extent of the school police attempting to entrap me in a sexual scandal. They planted this pretty little *morenita* in one of my classes. After school, she'd stay around, wanting to help me. I didn't want or need any problems like this. Even if I didn't already have problems with the school district, I wasn't going to go down this road. So every time she wanted to stay I tried to discourage her and always kept my door open. Although she tried to come on to me, after awhile she got discouraged, and then I never saw her again. I assumed that she had dropped out of school.

However, about a year and a half later, I had been hired again during the summer as a playground director at Hollenbeck Junior High School in East L.A. One day I ran into two L.A. school cops, who came around just checking on things. To my surprise, one of them was that little *morenita* girl from Gardena.

"I know you," I said to her.

"No, no, you don't," she, with anxiety, responded and left immediately with her partner.

She knew who I was, and I knew who she was, and that she had been an undercover cop at Gardena. You don't graduate and within a year or so become a school cop. It takes much longer than that. She clearly had been a cop at Gardena and looked young enough to be assigned undercover. There's no question but that her assignment there was to seduce me and then expose me and create a sex scandal that would end my career and probably send me to jail. I'm just glad I didn't give in to temptation.

Busing in L.A.

It was around the early 1970s that the controversy over busing also started. In 1970, a Superior Court judge, Judge Alfred Gitelson, ruled, in a lawsuit against the school board initiated some years earlier by blacks with white liberal support, that the board was guilty of supporting a de facto segregated school system and ordered that this be remedied.[28] It became a huge issue, not only in L.A. but also throughout the country. Liberal whites such as those in the ACLU pushed for busing. They believed it would result in better and more integrated schools. Courts mandated busing as a way of achieving racial integration in the public schools, but they also started firestorms. Many white parents in the Westside and suburban schools in the L.A. school district refused to support busing. They didn't want black and Chicano kids bused into their schools, and they certainly didn't want their kids bused to Mexican and black schools. The issue became further inflamed because it attracted really reactionary types, including the Ku Klux Klan. The opposition resorted to stopping the buses. I thought it was a double standard, that these people disrupted the schools and yet few if any got busted for their actions, while I and the others of the East L.A. 13 got arrested for just trying to improve the schools.

My feelings on busing ironically also caused me to oppose it, but for different reasons. I saw myself as a liberal like the ACLU; in fact, I considered myself a socialist, but on this issue I disagreed with my liberal white friends. I didn't want Chicano kids bused out of their neighborhood schools. What I found was that more capable Chicano students would be bused to predominantly white schools, but that they would face even more alienation and segregation there. They wouldn't be able to shine there and would be overlooked. The whites would look down on them and taunt them. Teachers would remark to each other: "When more than two Mexicans walk into the restroom, follow them because all they're doing is tagging the walls." I actually heard such bullshit. I wanted the Chicano students to stay in their schools, because, despite the problems there, which we hoped to change, at least they could see successful role models among themselves. Chicanos, for example, would be the student body officers, including president. Chicanos would win scholarships to college. Chicanos would be in the AP (Advanced Placement) classes. I didn't kid myself. The blowouts had only begun the process of reforming the Mexican schools, but overall Chicano students would still feel more comfortable there, and more importantly they would achieve more success than in the white schools.

Most Mexican American parents agreed with me. They didn't want their kids all the way out by Santa Monica or way over in the San Fernando Valley. "*Yo no quiero que mis hijos vayan con los gabachos.* [I don't want my children going over with the whites.]" They wanted them close to home, so if anything happened, they could easily get to the schools. The parents had also learned from the blowouts the use of community pressure. They had become hip to this. They recognized that if the community organized and pressured the schools better conditions would result. So they were prepared to fight for better schools on the east side rather than support busing. In fact, I was ready to lie down in front of the buses, like the white parents were doing.

Despite the Mexican American community opposition and the Anglo parents' opposition, busing still took place, even though it soon became a one-way process. Since the white parents had more clout, the district stopped any effort to bus white students to minority schools. At the same time, they bused Chicanos and blacks outside of their neighborhoods. This meant long bus rides on dangerous freeways back and forth. Kids had to get up very early to catch the buses, and if some played sports or participated in other after-school activities, they'd be bused back quite late. Even after the school board dropped the policy of busing for racial integration, they continued busing, as it continues today, on the grounds of minority schools being overcrowded.[29] This is an issue I continued to be concerned about for many years and still am.

I believe that the first generation of Mexican students who were bused in the 1970s paid a very high toll. They suffered because of having to attend white schools, where they weren't wanted. I think we lost a generation of kids who either dropped out or carried psychological scars for years to come. They became very bitter about education. It was tragic.

Defending My Teaching Credential

Besides all of the hassles I had to put up with concerning my teaching after the blowouts, I also had to defend myself when the State Board of Education went after my teaching credential in the early 1970s, because of my indictment as well as the trumped-up complaints about my teaching after the walkouts. I had to go up to a hearing in Sacramento with my attorney, Herman Sillas, to defend myself. At the hearing, they accused me of all kinds of things, and, of course, that I had broken the law, due to my "conspiracy" in the blowouts. This FBI-looking dude read an article by Raul Ruiz that had been published in his paper, *Inside Eastside*, around the time of the blowouts. But Raul screwed me on this one. He never actually interviewed me but instead quoted me as if he had done so. In the article, I come across as Che Guevara, with all of these militant-sounding statements, including lots of cuss words. I cussed, but not as much as Raul suggested in his piece. I didn't blame Raul. We needed that rhetoric in the heat of the movement, and there wasn't time for all of the journalistic niceties. He may have put words in my mouth, and perhaps more militantly than I would have actually said them, but they still conveyed my sentiments about the schools and the need for action to change them. Anyway, the school officials used Raul's article as additional evidence that I should have my credential taken away from me.

But we rebutted all of these arguments, and Herman reminded me that they couldn't convict me if the courts themselves hadn't done so. We won this battle and saved my credential.

Going to Belmont

I felt even better when I got a call from Jim Taylor, the highest-ranking black superintendent in the district.

"Sal, how would you like to teach this coming fall [1973] at Belmont High School?"

"Hey, that's great with me," I said. "It's poetic justice, since they threw me out back in '63."

"Okay, report there in September."

I was on a high. I don't know what strings Jim pulled to get me this assignment, but I couldn't thank him enough. I wasn't going back to Lincoln, but Belmont for all practical matters was a Mexican school and, in fact, one that in the next few years would become a Latino school, as Central Americans began to attend in large numbers. All I cared about was that I would be back teaching the kids that I could best relate to and for whom I had dedicated my teaching career. I was going back to Belmont, where I would spend the rest of my career and where I hoped to make a difference. The blowouts were a memory now, but one that guided me for the rest of my career and my life. Memory was not only the past but also the future.

FRANK DEL OLMO in the *Los Angeles Times*: "Exile Ends for Controversial Teacher"
"The years of exile apparently are over for Sal Castro, the East Los Angeles high school teacher who became the center of controversy five years ago when he made himself an outspoken Chicano advocate. . . .

"Contacted by a reporter recently, he [Castro] would say only that he is 'glad to be back at a school where I feel needed.'

"'This is my area,' said Castro, who was raised in the barrio neighborhood around Belmont.

"'I'm comfortable here,' he said. 'It's like putting on an old favorite suit.'"[30]

TEN

All My Children

In the fall of 1973, I returned to Belmont High, where I had started my permanent teaching career ten years earlier. Although part of me wanted to still be back at Lincoln, another part felt satisfied that I was at least back to a mostly Mexican school. Belmont was not on the east side, but even more so than in 1963 it had all of the characteristics of a Mexican school, including an even larger percentage of Chicano students and soon a growing number of Latino kids.

However, the school did not welcome me with open arms. In fact, the principal, a guy by the name of Ernest Naumann, when he learned that I had been transferred there, immediately moved to block it. He even threatened to quit. When I went to the school a few days before classes started in order to get my classroom in order, I discovered that I had no classroom and that I had not yet been assigned any classes. I knew that this wasn't a mistake. I called Jim Taylor, the assistant superintendent who had assigned me to Belmont, and told him the situation. Taylor was pissed. He right away drove over to Belmont and went directly into the principal's office, slamming the door behind him. I waited outside. Jim was a tall, handsome, and imposing figure. You didn't fool around with him. He read the riot act to Naumann. After about twenty minutes, they both exited, and the principal says to me: "Mr. Castro, you are here to teach history and government and nothing else." Jim shook my hand and gave me a knowing look. He knew it would be rough for me, but he also knew I belonged there. Of course, I knew this too. From the principal on down to the teachers, they treated me as persona non grata, as a leper.

They, including the staff, had been warned about me. One clerk, Miss Bolden, later, after we became friends, even told me, "We thought you had horns by the way the principal described you; we thought you were Satan himself." When I walked into the cafeteria for the first teachers' meeting, I recognized some of the teachers from when I first taught there. This included a basketball coach, who back then had wanted me to be the junior varsity coach, but I couldn't due to my playground job. When I spotted him I went to sit next to him.

"Sorry, Sal, this seat is taken," he said, without shaking my hand.

He and the other teachers obviously didn't want me there. They were all standoffish. This was especially true of the older teachers who remembered me. The new ones didn't know who I was, but they had gotten the word to avoid me. I heard later that Naumann had actually told the other teachers to keep an eye on me and to inform him if I did anything "deviant." This even included when I used the phone in the faculty room.

Conditions at Belmont

In returning to Belmont, I soon discovered that not much had changed. It was still a big school of about 3,000 students, with the large majority being Chicanos and other Latinos. But many of the problems I had observed in 1963 were still there in 1973. These were problems that I would have to deal with, as I didn't back off continuing to challenge the educational system and its discrimination against Mexican and Latino students. I don't mean to imply that some changes hadn't taken place due to the pressures of the Chicano Movement and the blowouts. The discriminatory structure remained, but some of the personnel, including teachers, seemed more willing to promote certain educational opportunities for the kids.

In the first place, the tracking system at Belmont was alive and well. Belmont had three tracks: general education, semi-academic, and college prep. Based on students' cumulative records and testing, counselors placed most of the Chicano students in the general education classes, which were a mixture of basic educational requirements plus so-called industrial classes. A standard class schedule for these kids would be an English class, a math class, P.E., and two industrial classes. As at Lincoln, the boys took auto shop. All Eastside schools, including Belmont, had good auto shops. In fact, many of the teachers had their own cars fixed or serviced there, including tune-ups, or had the oil changed for a minimum price. It was exploitative. The girls, of course, took cooking and sewing, as well as "secretarial science." Belmont even had restaurant management classes, and kids cooked and sold food to the faculty once a week.

The one difference from the past was that, with some pressure, I found I could convince some counselors to allow more Mexican students to move into the more academic and even college prep tracks. I told the students that

Sal Castro teaching at Belmont High School, early 1970s. Courtesy George Rodríguez.

if they wanted to do this to get a note from their parents requesting this and I would then advocate for them. I was pleasantly surprised that some counselors and teachers also supported these transfers. There wasn't the rigid refusal I had seen in the early 1960s. The problem, however, was that this new attitude only benefited a few more students and not the large majority.

As a result, the college prep classes, or what would later be called AP (Advanced Placement) classes, as well as honor classes, still excluded many of the Chicano students. The few white and Asian kids filled most of these classes, with a sprinkling of Chicanos. Still, I tried my best to change this. I went in and raised hell.

"This kid is too bright to even be in my class; he/she belongs in AP," I told one counselor.

"Well, we tried him, but it didn't work out."

"Well, try it again!"

One AP teacher had mostly Asians in his class, with a few Mexicans. However, he had his students meet on Saturdays as well as after school. So if a Chicano kid was in the band or in sports, he/she couldn't be in the class, even if he/she qualified for it. This teacher was very selective of whom he would allow in, and he favored the Asians. Sure he was successful, but that in part had to do with his exclusionary policy. I would have produced nothing but doctors and lawyers if I did the same thing.

My confrontations with teachers repeated many times over my years at Belmont as I tried to change the notorious tracking system.

One curriculum change that I found at Belmont was that the school had started a Chicano Studies class. This, of course, had been one of the blowout demands. The only problem was that it was organized as a basic educational class where they dumped all the expected dropouts. Ms. May Fong was the teacher and doing a good job, but the counselors considered it a dumping ground for kids that they believed were going to drop out of school. After about a year or so, I took over this class and got a few more students to take it. I upgraded the quality of the class and focused on teaching material that would instill ethnic pride and confidence in my students. I did this in all of my classes, but the Chicano Studies one gave me more of an opportunity to do this. But here again I soon had a problem when both the University of California and the California University State systems raised their entrance requirements to focus on certain classes that the students had to take to be admitted.

This forced public schools like Belmont to eliminate many elective classes. My Chicano Studies class was an elective, and even though it wasn't dropped, it meant that I had fewer students, and certainly not the better ones that I had fought hard to recruit into the class. This change even involved classes like California history that I wanted to teach, but since it was an elective and not part of the new college requirements, I wasn't able to offer it. You now needed too much English, too much math, and too much science. I wasn't opposed to this, but not at the expense of a more diverse curriculum, especially for Chicano students, who needed to learn more about their own history and culture.

One of the other demands of the blowouts involved the hiring of more Mexican American teachers and counselors. I found a few more at Belmont this time, but still a relatively small percentage of the staff. Some weren't Mexican Americans but of other Latino extractions. This percentage grew over the next couple of decades. More impressive in 1973 was the number of Mexican *señoras* working in the cafeteria. This was unheard of before and had been a blowout demand. Of course, these hires didn't compensate for the still low number of Mexican American teachers and counselors.

Dropouts continued to be a problem into the 1970s, and Belmont unfortunately had its share. Like most other Mexican schools, the rate was 50 percent. Some schools like Belmont tried to disguise this statistic, as they still try today. What the school did was to put a kid's name that had dropped out into a list for continuation school. The student only had to come in at least once a week, if even that. This way the student was not recorded as a dropout, and this lowered the drop-out rate. It was also done so that the school wouldn't lose its ADA (Average Daily Attendance) money, since school budgets were based on attendance. It was all a bunch of lies, and I told different principals over the years so.

One difference that I noticed from the 1960s at Lincoln was that the kids seemed to be dropping out not only earlier in high school but also later, in the tenth and eleventh grades. Many of the same factors for kids dropping out that existed at Lincoln I also saw at Belmont. One important difference involved some efforts now by the school to try to prevent or cut the drop-out rate. This included what was called the 4-4 program. If a kid was going to drop out for economic reasons, they allowed him/her to take four classes in the morning and then work in the afternoon presumably for four hours. Some students took advantage of this and, as a result, stayed in school and graduated. Unfortunately, some counselors also abused this program, and if they thought a kid was a problem, they channeled them into it so they'd be less of a problem. This affected the student academically, plus stereotyping them as a problem.

One other program that I personally got involved with to prevent dropouts at Belmont was the Academic Support Program. It was a drop-out prevention program, but when it started I said, "Don't call it a drop-out program because drop-out is a stigma. Call it something else." They took my advice and called it the Academic Support Program. Ignacio García, one of our teachers, and who later became principal at Belmont, directed the program, and I was one of the members of the unit, along with Rosa Morley, a Cuban Chinita (Chinese), who later became an assistant principal and later a superintendent. For being in this program, I had a three-course reduced schedule. We weren't paid extra. What we did was to use three class periods—three hours—to schedule meetings with kids whom we identified as potential dropouts based on their records or what we knew of these kids.

We divided the students into three groups: a lower tier of more hard-core students who clearly seemed on the verge of dropping out; a middle group that could go either way; and an upper rung. All of these kids were potential dropouts as far as we estimated. We soon discovered that we couldn't seem to do much with the lowest group. These kids by now were so alienated and so self-defeating and so channeled to drop out by their bad experiences in the school, as well as bad conditions in their homes and neighborhoods, that unless we radically changed all of these conditions, it seemed they were going to drop out. We had much more success with the other two groups. We focused on positive reinforcement to keep them in school.

In addition, I volunteered to extend my drop-out activity by visiting the homes of some of the kids who had recorded large numbers of absences but were not yet officially dropouts. I got paid only mileage for this. Some of these kids were latchkey kids, because their parents worked long hours and sometimes the kids would stay out all night. This meant my going into South-Central L.A., which was in the Belmont jurisdiction. It was a high-poverty area, as it still is today. The poverty was striking. Many families lived in run-down tenements—whole families in a one-bedroom apartment. I saw these conditions when I visited these homes. There would be a little sink and no toilets in most units. Residents had to use a common bathroom to go to the toilet or to shower, one for males and one for females. This made it very dangerous for the women and especially the young girls. I walked into one tenement at 6 P.M. one time and saw a girl holding a bat in the hallway. It turned out she was one of my students—but she wasn't the reason I was there. I had come to interview another kid in her family.

"Are you going out to play ball?" I asked her.

"No," she said, "I'm going to the bathroom."

This was not uncommon in these tenements, for girls and women having to protect themselves from male residents preying on them, especially in the hall bathrooms.

In many of these cases of absent students, their parents weren't even aware that their children weren't going to school. Once I went to a girl's home —*pobrecita* (poor thing)—who also was one of my students. She opened the security window of the door, and I said: "*M'hija*, you haven't been to school for two weeks. What's wrong?"

In a soft voice, she said, "I've been sick, Mr. Castro."

The mother heard this and was shocked. "*¿Qué dijiste? ¿Que no has ido al* *escuela? ¿Por cuantos días, Señor?* [What did you say? You haven't been to school? For how many days, sir?]"

I said, "*Por dos semanas, Señora.* [For two weeks, Madame.]"

She replied, "*Muchas gracias, Señor.*"

She excused herself and closed the door as I left. I could hear her slapping her daughter. The next day, the girl began attending school again.

Teen pregnancy likewise continued as a problem, and it seriously affected Belmont. Many of the girls who got pregnant were in the early grades, like freshmen and sophomores. As I had tried at Lincoln, with little success, I encouraged other teachers to talk about the issue in their classes. But they wouldn't listen and gave the same lame excuses about needing parental permission. I didn't pay attention to this crap, and, as at Lincoln, I talked about it in my classes.

"Stay away from that boyfriend-girlfriend thing. There's no need to get serious with a boy here in high school. Your studies are first. Don't get into that *noviasco* [marriage trip], because once you get serious and then after three months you run out of things to do, what do you do next?"

I couldn't believe it when I saw some of the teachers countering what I was trying to do when they actually had baby showers in the classroom for their pregnant students or students who returned after having their babies! I thought that was wrong. Some of these girls, after giving birth, would come back for their day of glory with their stroller and showing off their baby.

"*Que chulo, que bonito* [How cute, how pretty]," the other girls would say, clearly envious of the new mother. This type of display didn't help us discourage teen pregnancy.

Although girls who got pregnant either dropped out or were encouraged to go to either St. Anne's or McAllister, both schools for pregnant girls, the Belmont administration allowed some of them to resume classes at the school once they gave birth. This was a change from Lincoln. Or they were allowed to come back and graduate from Belmont. I thought this was encouraging them to get pregnant, because they could still do so and graduate.

"At least don't put these girls in the front row," I told the vice principal in charge of graduation; "put them in the back. We don't want to encourage other girls to think it's okay to get pregnant because it's not. It's going to ruin the kid. I feel sorry for the teenager mother, but don't encourage the younger ones."

"Well, it's not so bad," he weakly replied; "look, those girls are graduating so it can't be that bad."

I felt I was walking on eggs. It was a tough situation.

The only thing the school did, and at least it was a step forward, was to provide some sex education into the 1970s. The students could obtain this, but only with their parents' permission. However, these classes only dealt with venereal diseases and had nothing to do with getting pregnant. They deliberately avoided any discussion of birth control.

I disagreed with all of this and in my classes talked about birth control. I got in hot water for this. A later principal, John Howard, a former seminarian who had left the seminary, had a plan to get himself promoted off my back. That wasn't new, of course. He kept writing me up for almost anything he could, because he wanted to become superintendent and figured that if he was able to throw me out of Belmont or get me into serious trouble this would be a feather in his cap. He really thought he had me once when I invited a doctor and a nurse from Children's Hospital to come and speak in my classes about birth control and abortion. I didn't publicize the reason for their coming and instead extended the invitation under the guise that they would speak about careers in medicine. However, Howard got wind of it and prevented them from going to my classes. He confronted them in the main office and raised hell with them.

"How dare you come to speak about such subjects!"

When I saw them in the main office, I apologized to my guests, who were shocked. They didn't expect this kind of reception.

"I'm sorry," I told them. "Let me take the heat. I'll speak to Howard."

They walked out, and I walked into the office and slammed the door shut. I went toe to toe with Howard.

"You had no business inviting them without my permission and especially to talk about those things. I'm calling the superintendent and reporting you. You've gone too far this time."

"*Orale* [Right on]," I said, using some Chicano slang. "Go for it, you son of a bitch, because I'm going to kick your ass."

He got scared. Maybe because I was bigger than him. He didn't call the superintendent, and he didn't report me. He also realized that if he went to his superiors I knew certain things he was doing that he shouldn't be doing. He backed off, but the problem of teen pregnancy continued—and it still does today.

BY THE 1970S AND certainly into the 1980s and, indeed, as long as I was at Belmont until 2003, drugs proved to be a problem. However, it was always a minority of the students, and it had to do not with drug consumption but with drug dealing. The high school students didn't and still don't have the money to buy drugs, so they sell drugs. Seldom did I see a kid loaded at school or in the nurse's office. But they knew how to sell drugs and get others to OD. The students who sold drugs usually sold them to white kids, such as the students at USC. They'd sell the drugs not at Belmont but in the barrios. The college students would come in their SUVs and buy the stuff, usually pot and pills.

Because of the drug dealing, the cops periodically busted kids in the school. This usually involved a narc (cop) posing as a student. The sad thing is that this also involved a lot of entrapment. The narc would ask around as to who could provide drugs, and when a *pendejo* (idiot) student offered, the narc arrested him. A lot of entrapment occurred, because these narcs had to justify their existence. They wouldn't stay around much if they didn't bust students. Sometimes, however, things didn't go as planned by the narcs. There's the example of a female narc who fell in love with one of the students. She had to leave the force.

Connected to the drug problem were the gangs. As in the case at Lincoln, this involved only some of our students, and these were usually ones only affiliated with gangs and not hard-core members. Most of the gangs operated around the periphery of Belmont and certainly in the barrios. If anything, Belmont was a refuge from the gangs. Inside the school, our students felt safe against harassment by the gangs. Compared to our students who sold drugs, the gangs were big-time operators. The more drugs were involved, the more gangs grew and became more violent, as each gang competed against one another and defended their turf. God forbid for a rival gang to try and sell drugs in another gang's territory. To prevent this and to punish those who violated the *placas*, the gang signs of turf possession, the gangs armed themselves to the teeth. No longer did they have minor weapons such as zip guns. They now carried semiautomatic ones.

I frankly don't think we'll ever get rid of drug dealing and the problems they cause both in our schools and in our barrios until we legalize drugs or some drugs. In the meantime, you have dropouts driving around in low rider Mercedes Benzes and SUVs, because they make good money selling drugs. How can you tell these kids not to drop out and stay in school when they say, "I can make five to ten times more money selling drugs than getting a job after graduation." It's a tough situation. There aren't a lot of students who do drugs, but there's enough to cause problems. The gang problem in L.A. is only getting worse. There's more shootings and indiscriminate killings. These kids don't seem to care. They've seen the movie *Scarface*, and they think they're little Al Pacinos acting out the role of kingpin gangsters. It's a big shame, and we've lost many kids due to this problem.

FINALLY, ANOTHER LINGERING problem that existed at Belmont, as it had at Lincoln, was the presence of military recruiters trying to entice the students to enter the military right after graduation rather than going to college. They dangled sign-up bonuses—anything from $1,000 to $3,000. "This will help pay for your senior expenses, and you know how expensive your prom will be. But with the bonus you can rent a nice limo, buy yourself a car, pay for your class ring, and your girlfriend's prom dress. What do you say?" Unfortunately, too many students—*pendejitos* (fools)—bite on the sales job.

It was a constant problem with these recruiters coming around. It didn't help that Belmont had a big ROTC program, as did the other Mexican schools. The recruiters especially went after those kids. The recruiters also asked to come into our classrooms to give their pitch. Many of the teachers foolishly agreed to this, because it meant you didn't have to teach a class that day if you let them come to your class. They also gave you a coffee cup that read "U.S. Army." Unlike those teachers, I tried to keep the recruiters out of my classes as much as possible. I would let them in only under certain conditions. They could only talk about college ROTC or about how students could apply to West Point, Annapolis, or the Air Force Academy. That's the only thing I would let them talk about to my students, because at least it involved going on to college. Unfortunately, this problem of military recruiters on our high school campuses, especially in the minority schools, is still a major issue today, and, as a result, many Chicanos and Latinos are in Iraq and Afghanistan, and many have been killed or severely wounded.

Although many of these problems that I had also encountered at Lincoln spilled over into the 1970s and beyond and many of these are still problems today, still I have to say that, based on the blowout demands, some improvements did occur. More Mexican American and Latino teachers and teacher aids were hired. More Mexican American and Latino counselors served the students. Some Mexican Americans became vice principals and principals. Some even became superintendents, not only locally in California but also throughout the Southwest. Chicano Studies classes and bilingual education now became part of the curriculum. Also more Mexican American and Latino parents became involved in the schools and were less reserved about making complaints. Finally, more Mexican American and Latino students were going to college. So some changes for the better took place, but still always not without struggles and pressures for change. Unfortunately, that's the only way that reforms are accomplished. They don't trickle down from somewhere.

Changing Conditions

One of the positive changes that I witnessed at Belmont was that little by little more Chicano students were going to college. This was different, but what unfortunately remained the same, at least into the 1970s, was that too many academic counselors still didn't encourage students to apply for four-year colleges. At Belmont, the counselors put most of their energies in getting college scholarships for the few Asian students there. If they assisted Chicanos it involved helping them apply for loans. That represented a big difference.

While more Chicanos began to attend college, this was deceiving, because most attended community colleges. The counselors prided themselves on the number going on to the two-year schools, but I thought this was disastrous. Why? Because then as now, most kids that go to a community college never transfer to a four-year institution. The statistics are staggering. Only 1 out of almost 200 Chicanos/Latinos transfer as juniors to four-year schools. It's just a system set up for this failure. Part of the problem, as I saw it then and still see it now, is that many of those kids in the community colleges continue to live at home while going to school. Mexican parents won't believe that the student is really in the library at night studying for an exam. They think he/she is clowning around. On top of this, if they live in a dangerous neighborhood, the parents especially don't want their daughters returning home in a bus at one in the morning. If students continue to live at home, the parents think they're still in high school. They say: "*M'hija*, you're not going to school today, you have to take me to the doctor." This results in the student falling behind and many times dropping out.

On top of this, many community college students work full-time, and this hurts their grades, which, in turn, hurts their ability to transfer to a UC school or even a Cal State one. Most of these students also live at home. That's why I'm a big believer in a kid going away to college, even if it's just across town. Go live there. I'm a big advocate of community colleges having resident dorms, but this always falls on deaf ears.

This question of convincing students to go away to college is one that I've grappled with for years. It's especially a problem for the girls. Parents, especially the fathers, don't want their daughters leaving home to go to college. Girls will tell their parents: "I want to go to a four-year school."

But the parents won't listen to this.

"No, you don't leave this house until you get married. So you'll stay here under this roof and go to the community college."

But the boys also face problems in going away to school. Most of these are self-imposed barriers. They're afraid of college. On the other hand, they're not afraid of the Marines or the army, but they're sure as hell afraid of being in college. They haven't seen anyone in their families in college, but they've seen their big brothers and cousins in the Marines.

I had one guy whom I had got into San Jose State on a football scholarship, but he wouldn't go.

"No, Mr. Castro, it's too far. It's 385 miles away, man."

"But, I hear that instead you want to go into the Marines."

"Yeah, the recruiter said they will send me to Camp Lejeune in North Carolina."

"Camp Lejeune! That's 3,000 miles away. You want to go 3,000 miles to be a Marine, but you won't go 385 miles to go to college?"

Despite all of these hurdles, I, as I did at Lincoln, took it upon myself to encourage as many students as possible to consider and apply to a four-year college. In effect, I became a college counselor, even though I wasn't hired as one, and I sure as hell wasn't getting paid as one. Not only did I talk about college in my classes, but also on my own I arranged for college trips to introduce the students to college life. Most of these kids had never seen a university. They had no idea what it was all about. Arranging for these trips wasn't easy because of the high school bureaucracy. To go on a trip on a school bus, the students had to get permission from all of their teachers. Many of the teachers wouldn't approve this for the Chicano kids. They felt it was a waste of time, since they believed these students weren't college material. To circumvent them, I simply had the kids bring a note from one of their parents giving them permission to go on a day trip. Technically, I wasn't supposed to do this, and I'd get into hot water with the principal. But I did it anyway and got away with it.

For many of the students I took on these trips to UCLA, USC, Cal State, L.A., and up to UC Santa Barbara, it was an eye-opener. For one, they got to see how the other half lives. They got to see the dorms where the students lived and an academic atmosphere they had never been exposed to in their school lives. These trips turned on the *foco* (light) for some of these students. They were now set on going to college.

Besides these trips, I also worked to get scholarships for some of them. Since many of the colleges wouldn't give scholarships to many Chicano students but instead offered loans, I went directly into the private sector. My biggest effort was with the L.A. Dodgers. I went to Peter O'Malley, the owner and president of the Dodgers, and said: "Do you know that Dodger Stadium sits on a former Mexican rancho? Julian Chávez, an early Los Angeles leader who served on the first city council, Board of Supervisors, and still later mayor and judge, owned this rancho. That's why it's called Chávez Ravine. Do you know that many Mexican families were kicked out of Chávez Ravine in order for you to build Dodger Stadium? The least you can do is help us out and fund scholarships for some of our kids to go to college. Can you do this?"

He didn't commit himself right away, but a few days later he called me.

"Mr. Castro, I've got a deal for you that you can't refuse. I'll provide you tickets to some of our games at half price and you can sell them at full price and use the profit for your scholarships."

"Mr. O'Malley, thank you very much. This is very generous of you. But can I ask you one more thing?"

"Sure, what is it?"

"Can I arrange for some musical entertainment prior to the games to draw a crowd?"

"No problem," O'Malley said.

The program was a big success. We called it Chicano Scholarship Night and did it under the auspices of the Association of Mexican-American Educators (AMAE), East Los Angeles Chapter.[1] Joe Kapp, former pro football quarterback and one of the few Chicano pro football players, served as the MC for the pregame program, along with Alicia Sandoval from Channel 11 and myself. We welcomed the crowd and announced the scholarships. Then I got the popular Chicano rock band Tierra to perform, along with the Mariachi Los Camperos, probably the most famous mariachi in the United States. We did the program for two years and raised enough money to provide scholarships to about twenty students to help them go to four-year colleges. The Dodgers wanted me to continue the program, but it just proved to be too hard for me to do by myself. If the school district had helped me, we might have continued it, but the district didn't offer, and it wasn't very farsighted.

We made important strides, beginning after the blowouts, in getting Chicano and other Latino students into college, but it's a struggle that still continues. We're still fighting the low expectations that too many teachers have of our students, as well as the lack of college-educated role models in their families. But we have to do it to avoid the tragedies of kids who don't continue their education. They wind up in dead-end jobs, and most likely their kids will do the same. When I lecture to Chicano Studies classes at universities and to Latino teachers groups, I really push how we have to go out of our way to encourage our students about college:

"Our Mexican and Latino kids are very social. They're always talking about who's taking who to the prom. So counselors and teachers have to get through this and start pulling ears. Because this country is for everyone. Otherwise, you're going to continue to see our people as blue-collar manual laborers. 'Manuel Labor.' Mexican first and last name. We make tremendous checkers at Home Depot. You've seen us there. You see us at Target. We're not the general managers. A kid tells me, 'I'm going to work for McDonalds, Mr. Castro.' I say, 'Okay, but I want you to work as the West Coast regional manager.' Yes, of course. You see we have to almost hit the kids in the head.

"We can do this despite the obstacles, both in our schools and in our families. Let me tell you a funny but important story. I had a girl student who got a scholarship to go to UC Riverside, only fifty miles from L.A. She told me her parents wouldn't let her go. '*M'hija*,' I told her, 'you have to bite the bullet and just tell your parents that you're going.' Well, she did. The night before she was going to leave, the parents, especially the father, got all her clothes and threw them on the porch and said, 'You're no longer our daughter; you're now a woman of the streets because you're leaving home and going to Riverside.' Fortunately for the girl, her brother had just gotten out of the Marines, and he helped her gather her clothes, stuffed them in his Marine duffle bag, and took her the next day to the Greyhound bus station to go to Riverside. That afternoon, the father went to the Rampart's division of the L.A. Police Department and told them that his daughter had run away from home.

"'Any idea where she's gone?' the police asked.

"'Yeah,' the father said, 'she's gone to UC Riverside.'

"'Sir, we don't have time for this.'

"But when this young lady returned home for Thanksgiving, her parents gave her the biggest homecoming in the barrio. The old man now went around bragging about her. '*M'hija va a UC Riverside.* [My daughter goes to UC Riverside.]'

"So what was all the hassle for?

"It can be done. *Sí se puede!* That young Chicana over there at Home Depot could be the next Chicana astronaut like Ellen Ochoa. But she won't because she's a checker at Home Depot. Think of all the talent we're losing. If our ancestors, the Mayas, the Olmecas, and the Aztecas, were good enough to be the first scientists, the first great mathematicians and astronomers of the Western Hemisphere, who's to stop us now? But we've all got to work at getting our kids educated and into college in large numbers. We can't afford not to."

At the same time that I and a few other teachers and counselors at Belmont worked hard to get our students into college, conditions always seemed to be against us. By the late 1970s, for example, and certainly by the election of Ronald Reagan as president in 1980, the political climate began to change, especially with respect to civil rights and affirmative action. In California, the *Bakke* decision in 1978, when the U.S. Supreme Court addressed the legality of affirmative action programs based on race, highlighted this conservative shift. The court didn't rule out race as a consideration to remedy discrimination, but it did begin to marginalize it by deciding that it could not be the only factor. The *Bakke* decision affected more the colleges and professional schools, and in California many Chicano students rallied against it. But some high school students, including at Belmont, also reacted to *Bakke*. Some of our more active students, including student council types, organized protests on the campus and participated in college-sponsored ones. They opposed *Bakke* because they felt that what little opening there was to get into college through affirmative action programs might now be completely closed. I, of course, for the same reasons opposed *Bakke* and encouraged my students to protest.

Yet *Bakke* did not prove to be the main obstacle against minority college admissions, as colleges were able to accommodate to the ruling and yet still practice affirmative action. What hurt more, as previously noted, were the higher and more stringent entrance requirements adopted by both the UC and Cal State systems by the late 1970s. In inner-city schools, including Belmont, with a dearth of honors and AP classes or the more demanding classes now required for college admissions, these new regulations hit hard. To get into one of these colleges, our students had to do so much more writing, math, science, and many more recommendations from teachers and counselors. It just became harder for the kids to make it.

But it wasn't just this new academic pressure that affected our students; it was also that, unlike the suburban high school kids, ours had to work to aid their families. This took a toll not only in getting into college, but also just in doing well at Belmont. I don't know how some survived. Belmont students faced the additional disadvantage that they had to find work outside of their neighborhoods, where few jobs for kids were available. As a result, some commuted after school all the way to Beverly Hills or Santa Monica, many miles by bus. They worked as shipping clerks, busboys, janitors, store clerks, and in other forms of low-skilled jobs. The need to work, plus the time spent in commuting, really cut into their homework time. Some wouldn't get back home until nine or ten at night and then had to be at school by 7:30 the next morning. It was a vicious cycle of future failure. You could just see it. It's amazing that some overcame these hurdles and still succeeded and went on to college. But for every one that did, several more fell by the wayside.

ONE OF THE NEW CONDITIONS that I faced at Belmont had to do with the influx of new Mexican and Latino immigrants. By the early 1980s, we witnessed a new wave of Mexican immigrants into L.A. due to the peso devaluation in Mexico and the economic depression that followed. In addition, a wave of Cuban refugees—the Marielitos—fled the island, and a number migrated all the way to L.A. Finally, thousands of Central American refugees escaped the raging civil wars, especially in El Salvador and Nicaragua, but also in Guatemala and Honduras. Many of the Central Americans settled in areas close to Belmont, such as the Pico Union area. Some of these immigrants/refugees came or later sent for their high school–age children, who attended Belmont.

These students and their parents, besides facing language and cultural differences, also faced severe economic handicaps. Most were poor people, and this poverty affected their living conditions in the tenements. I saw a lot of this in my role in the drop-out prevention program when I visited many of these families.

I'll never forget one encounter with a Salvadoran mother whose son had gotten into a gang. I went to her home to try to get her help on getting this kid back into school. "*Señora*" (I spoke in Spanish), "your son is in danger. He's running around with a gang that's selling drugs and he could get killed. Perhaps you'd better think of returning to El Salvador to protect him."

"Oh, no," she said, "if we return he'll get killed there."

"*Señora*," I replied, "*mejor que lo maten alla por una causa. Aquí lo matan por andar de pendejo.* [Madame, it's better that he is killed for a cause there. Here he'll be killed for being an idiot.]"

All this led to adjustment problems in the school. Many of these new immigrant students had to take ESL classes to learn English. The language issue set back many of them, which influenced dropouts. Those who came already knowing some English obviously adapted the best. As far as the teachers were concerned, all of these new students were "Mexicans." They made no distinctions between the different Latino students that we now had by the 1980s. I knew the difference and adjusted by toning down my emphasis on Mexican American issues and attempting to develop a kind of broader Latino outreach to all of these kids. What I didn't change was my constant theme of telling all of these new students that they too could succeed and that they should be proud of their particular backgrounds.

Although the Latino students by and large got along well, they still, of course, had a connection to their ethnic backgrounds. Just as I had done with the Chicanos, I wanted to help the new students also feel good about themselves and supported their efforts to form school clubs representing these new backgrounds. The Cuban students, for example, started a Cuban club. I helped them in this. I knew a record store, Musica Latina, owned by a Cuban family, that was willing to donate records and prizes to the club. The Cuban students celebrated their own ethnic holidays. The one group that didn't do this was the Salvadorans. We had a few Salvadoran teachers, and I tried to get them to develop a similar program for the Salvadoran students, but it didn't pan out. To compensate for this, as well as to bring the different Latino students together, I helped organize a *Día de la Raza* celebration to replace Columbus Day in October.

As new immigrants began arriving, unfortunately anti-immigrant feelings in L.A. and elsewhere sprang up during the 1970s and continued to escalate until today. These views were not only anti-immigrant but also anti-Latino. Many whites and even some other minorities began to fear a "Latino invasion." This was bullshit, but it affected relationships in L.A., including our students. I, of course, was familiar with anti-immigrant sentiment, since my own father had been deported in the 1930s. We felt these rising tensions at Belmont, since many of our immigrant students, both Mexican and Central American, were undocumented, as were their parents. Efforts to deny sanctuary to Salvadorans in the 1980s only added to these pressures.[2]

Immigrant raids and roundups by federal officials accompanied anti-immigrant hysteria. This affected the attendance by immigrant students. As raids increased, attendance dropped. When they subsided, the kids returned to school. It was very unsettling. I talked about these issues in my classes and encouraged the students to stay in school and that no one was going to raid the school. In fact, the immigration people, the INS, never did go into the school. On the other hand, I heard of incidents in some schools where some teachers actually fingered kids that were undocumented. Students naively told their teachers about their status. The INS then arrested them and their parents at home.

MY OWN PERSONAL CONDITION at Belmont went through ups and downs, a lot of this depending on the different principals I had to deal with. At first, these guys kept a close eye on me. One of them, Ron Oswald, actually believed that I was a Communist because of my involvement in the blow-outs. To him, no one in their right mind would do what I had done unless you were a Communist.

But the worst principal I had to contend with was John Howard, who came down on me for bringing in that doctor and nurse to speak about birth control and abortion to my students. But that was only one run-in of many I had with him, especially since he was out to get me fired. This never happened because I had the goods on him. I went and met with Assistant Superintendent Dan Issac.

"Dan, check on the money at Belmont. Howard is cheating you. He holds these three-day carnivals and pockets the money. I think he uses it to have some of his flunkies not teach and instead be part of the entourage that always accompanies him. Then there's the use of the vending machines. There are eight vending machines, and the money isn't being turned in. Howard is also taking this. On top of this, the guy is having a love tryst with some of the female teachers in his office, including on Saturdays. The custodians say he's too cheap to go to a motel to cheat on his wife. The custodians have to clean up after him. He's also promoting some of his girlfriends ahead of other teachers. One of his lovers with little experience is now a vice principal."

I laid it all out to Issac, who checked it out and discovered that what I had told him was true. Howard wanted me fired. Instead, he got fired.

Eventually, they replaced Howard with a Latina, a Cuban American by the name of Martha Bin. She, at first, was suspicious of me. I think she somehow linked me with Fidel Castro because of my surname. She was part of the anti-Fidel Cubans who had fled after the Cuban Revolution of 1959. Martha also watched me like a hawk. During this time and, in fact, since the blow-outs, I was in demand a lot to give talks, especially to Latino teacher groups, and I always did so. Some of these invitations involved my having to get excused from some of my classes. I never had a problem with this until Bin became principal. At first she wanted me to do this only on my own time, meaning after school or during a period when I didn't teach. After awhile,

Sal Castro at Belmont High School, late 1980s or early 1990s. Courtesy Sal Castro Personal Collection.

she told me I couldn't leave the campus unless I got permission from the superintendent.

"But I'm doing it on my own time, as you said," I told her.

"No, you can't leave campus from now on. I'm ordering you to obey me."

About a month later, a community group called Padres de la Communidad honored me by giving me an award as Teacher of the Year. So I asked the principal if I could attend the ceremony, since it was a lunchtime affair.

"No, remember our agreement that you were not to leave campus without permission from the superintendent."

"I never agreed to that, but, okay, let's have it your way," I said.

But I wasn't going to let her get away with this. I called Bill Anton, one of the assistant superintendents, and talked to his secretary, Rosie, who was always friendly to me.

"Rosie, this group is giving me an award, and Bin won't let me go. Tell Anton."

Bill Anton was a good guy and never accepted all of the suspicions and accusations about me. He understood what I was fighting for and supported me in his own way. He did it on this occasion. Later that day, Mrs. Bin asked to see me in her office.

"Mr. Castro, I have a note from Superintendent Anton and it says: 'Mr. Castro will go to the meeting of the Padres de la Communidad in my name and represent me. William Anton, Assistant Superintendent.'"

From then on, Martha Bin completely changed. She knew that I would challenge her, but eventually we became close and great friends. My life got much better at Belmont. In fact, the last years of the 1980s and into the 1990s were up years for me. Finally, I had a series of principals—all Latinos—who recognized and supported my work with the students. They gave me breathing space. I could be totally myself without having to look over my shoulder. It was a relief to me.

New Crises

Although my teaching situation at Belmont by the early 1990s became more relaxed and less pressured, at the same time new political crises in both L.A. and California affected the school. The first of these was the outbreak of the so-called L.A. Riots in late spring of 1992. The disturbances centered in South-Central L.A. were triggered off by the exoneration of LAPD cops who had severely beaten up Rodney King, a black person, a beating that a witness captured on video. News of the court decision sent waves of young black men into the streets, breaking into family stores mostly owned by Asians and violent assaults on white motorists. Police and National Guard units moved in to quiet the riots, reminiscent of Watts in 1965. Latinos, mostly Central Americans, unfortunately, who lived in the area, joined in the looting and disturbances. The recorded scene of Latinos coming out of stores looting boxes of Pampers became part of the fixed images of the crisis.

Some politicians and intellectuals referred to the disturbances as a rebellion.[3] I don't agree with this view about a resistance movement tied to the L.A. riots. Maybe so, in the case of blacks, but not with the Latinos. For the Latinos, it was mostly a "me too" reaction. They weren't participating as a result of the King acquittal. Most didn't even know who Rodney King was. They saw an opportunity to see what they could get, once the stores were being looted. It reminded me of what some of the Mexican kids, including some of my playground ones, had done during the Watts Riots, when they went into the area to loot. Many Latino kids participated in all of this, but they were mainly Salvadoran and Central Americans along streets such as Alvarado and Third. The police arrested some of them, but I didn't think many of them were from Belmont. It's possible, since Belmont at that time had 3,500 students, but I wasn't aware of any of our students being arrested.

I saw the extent of the riots with fires raging, when on that day they started I had to drive on the freeway to speak at another school and I passed the South-Central area.

Despite the disturbances in these neighborhoods close to Belmont, we kept the school opened. We didn't want our students out in the streets. Most, in fact, attended. We also had Belmont opened to host many hundreds of elementary Latino students whose schools had to close because they were right in the middle of the violence. Many of these kids walked over with their teachers, and we accommodated them as best we could. Belmont for several days served as a safety zone for these kids. Some of us stayed at the school well into the evening with the elementary children until their parents came by for them. While the L.A. riots were seen by the media and whites in L.A. as a black thing, it at the same time brought some attention to the growing Latino population in areas that had been predominantly black in earlier years. Latino L.A. into the 1990s would become more and more visible.

More significant to the Latino community was Proposition 187, in 1994, which denied various forms of public assistance to undocumented immigrants in California, including public education to the children of the undocumented. Prop 187 symbolized the hysteria over "illegal immigration" and its exploitation by conservative Republican politicians, such as then-governor Pete Wilson. It was not only dangerous but also ridiculous, especially with respect to the schools. It would make teachers like myself into enforcers of immigration laws, in that we would be responsible for fingering undocumented students or the children of the undocumented. It was a bunch of racist crap and was fortunately later declared unconstitutional and, in my opinion, against the Treaty of Guadalupe Hidalgo (1848), which protected the rights of Mexicans after the United States conquered the Southwest from Mexico. Some teachers at Belmont agreed with me, but others didn't and expressed resentment toward the students. I argued with them.

"You're cutting your nose to spite your face," I told them. "These people [the undocumented] are paying your salaries. We've got more teachers here because we've got a lot of kids. These kids are paying your salary whether they're documented or not because our salaries are based on ADA [attendance]. We're not supposed to ask where they're coming from. How come we're only singling out the Spanish surnames? There's Asian kids that are undocumented, like the Vietnamese and Koreans, but nobody's asking them anything."

I, of course, talked about Prop 187 in my classes and expressed my views.

"Teachers aren't supposed to be gatekeepers," I said. So too did many of the students. The undocumented kids opposed it but didn't know what to do. They feared for themselves and their parents. To their credit, the U.S.-born Latinos also rejected the proposition. Although they were citizens, many of them had undocumented parents and would be affected if the proposition passed. They also were less afraid of the *"migra* [immigration officials]," because at least as U.S. citizens they couldn't be deported.

Many in the Chicano/Latino communities likewise opposed Prop 187 and organized mass protests against it. Similar to the more recent demonstrations against proposed anti-immigrant legislation, thousands participated in California, including in L.A., which witnessed the largest marches and rallies in the history of Latinos in the city. As in the 2006 demonstrations, high school students in 1994 also marched in protest. At Belmont and many of the other inner-city schools, Latino students staged their versions of the 1968 walkouts. They walked out to protest Prop 187. The main difference from 1968 was that the school administration approved of their going out. As they left, the gates of the school opened so that the students could leave, demonstrate downtown, and return later to school. Of the many who walked out, I would say that the majority were U.S.-born, but also included were many undocumented kids as well.

In these walkouts, I played a much more subdued role than I had in 1968. I encouraged the students to demonstrate, but many were self-motivated, given the threat of the proposition. My main role was to supervise the students who left school. Mrs. Bin asked me to do this. "Sal, go out there and help protect the kids." I wanted to make sure that the students not do anything crazy and that they be safe. Knowing the emotions around the proposition and the proponents' racist accusations—that the undocumented and their children were somehow un-American and anti-American—I made sure that our kids carried as many U.S. flags as I could get. I went into every classroom and borrowed the flags and gave them to the students. I even put one flag on my pickup truck so that I could lead the march from Belmont.

About 400 students left the campus and went downtown. I wanted them to go to the state building, since the proposition was a state measure, but when we linked up with the other marchers, the people in charge of the march moved everyone toward the more recognizable city hall. There, different speakers addressed the huge crowd, including some of the Chicano city council members, such as Richard Alarcón. After the rally, we returned to Belmont, where the school cafeteria had kept lunches available for the students. I very much appreciated the supportive attitude of our administration and couldn't help but contrast it with the more hostile one in 1968 at Lincoln.

Prop 187 unfortunately passed, but the Latino population in L.A., including the students, had shown that they weren't going to roll over and instead fought against anti-immigrant and anti-Latino movements. However, as I suspected, a federal court decreed Prop 187 unconstitutional on the grounds that only the federal government could regulate immigration, and not the states. The mass demonstrations in 1994 became the models for the even larger and national demonstrations in 2006.

Two years after Prop 187, the voters in California approved still another racist law, Prop 209, which did away with affirmative action in state institutions. This didn't affect the public schools such as Belmont, since affirmative action had no role at this level. With close to 80 percent or more Latino students by 1996, the school was a de facto affirmative action school, for what little that meant. Where it hurt was in making it even more difficult for our students to get into a good four-year state university. Not only did they have to meet increasingly stringent UC and Cal State requirements, but also now special action programs based on affirmative action were either eliminated or scaled back. I used to get some students into these schools by writing letters noting that, while their grades should be higher, in my opinion, they were college capable, and this worked. After Prop 209, this became much more difficult. As a result, more of our students, if they went to college at all, entered the community colleges, with the problems I've already addressed.

What bothered me also about Prop 209 was the insensitivity and selfishness displayed by many whites over who got to go to good colleges. All many white voters were concerned about was, Can my kid get into Berkeley or UCLA?—even if it meant denying minority kids access to these schools. They were concerned about their children, but they sure as hell weren't concerned about ours. While Prop 209 has not significantly reduced the number of Latino students in the UC system, for example, and, in fact, at some campuses the numbers have increased, much of this reflects demographics more than a real willingness to diversify. What's worse is the number of those who can't get in to the UC or Cal State systems that are being rerouted to the community colleges. This continued low-expectation attitude toward Chicano/ Latino students is unfortunately still alive and well, but, at the same time, this only reinforces and reenergizes my will to fight against this in any way I can. I am always telling my children—my students—"You can get to college; you can achieve your goals; don't let anyone make you feel you can't."

To add insult to injury, in 1998 the anti-immigrant and anti-Latino movement expressed itself again in still another statewide proposition, Prop 227. This aimed at eliminating bilingual education in the public schools. Bilingual programs had been instituted after federal legislation mandated them in the public schools in the late 1960s and provided funds for such programs aimed at helping non–English-speaking students entering the schools. It was patterned after some successful bilingual programs in Florida with the children of Cuban exiles. California started implementing bilingual education by the early 1970s. From the beginning, bilingual ed was mired in political and educational controversy, pitting its supporters against opponents who believed that bilingual ed supported ethnic separatism.

I always thought that the notion of bilingual ed fostering ethnic separatism was nonsense. We supported bilingual ed as part of the blowout demands, but this had nothing to do with ethnic separatism. The walkouts were an American experience aimed at forcing the schools to integrate Mexican American students into the full-fledged academic tracks that would lead to success rather than failure.

Nevertheless, bilingual ed represented a political football for over two decades, culminating in Prop 227, which the voters of California strongly approved, effectively eliminating the formal program. However, it left open the option that if parents petitioned for bilingual ed for their children, the schools could provide it on a minimal basis. Since most parents, especially immigrant ones, wouldn't even know of this option, it didn't really matter.

Many Latinos rallied against Prop 227, as they had on Prop 187. But the opposition wasn't as intense as on the immigration issue. The fact was that many Latinos, themselves, possessed split opinions on bilingual ed. Many immigrant parents opposed it, because they wanted their kids to learn English as quickly as possible and saw bilingual ed as retarding this process. This was only partly true. However, you could assemble studies supporting the idea that bilingual ed facilitated the learning of English and studies that argued that it didn't. This split, which also affected the Latino community, influenced the political reaction to Prop 227. Students, certainly public high school ones such as at Belmont, did not protest or walk out on this issue.

I didn't like Prop 227, because it originated from the same racists who had promoted Prop 187 and Prop 209. On the other hand, I was not a supporter of the way bilingual ed had evolved in the schools. Initially, I endorsed it because it linked language issues with cultural ones. It recognized that bilingual ed would only succeed if, in the process of transitioning from Spanish to English or securing both languages, the student also received a positive reinforcement of his/her cultural background. It's what was referred to as bilingual-bicultural education. Many Spanish-speaking kids, for example, entered the schools insecure and afraid due to the language and cultural differences. Bilingual ed would cushion this transition by making the kid feel more secure, by receiving some of his early education in the language he was familiar with and by initiating a positive validation of his cultural heritage. The whole philosophy was based on the idea that, in order for a student to succeed in school, he or she had to possess a secure identity. Give the child early success.

I endorsed this, and that's why, in the early 1970s, I worked in the L.A. school district to develop the cultural component of bilingual education. As mentioned, I researched and acquired a great deal of information and learning materials on the role of Mexicans in the history of California. If Mexican American students were taught early on that their ancestors in the state were just as important as George Washington, they would develop a balanced, positive, and secure identity that would work against any feelings of inferiority or identity crisis. I always believed this and in my teaching stressed cultural enrichment. That was at the core of my educational philosophy. But it's also a very American philosophy of education. It's American Education 101. Teaching about George Washington and the cherry tree is cultural enrichment for whites. I have no problem with this but want to expand it to include the culture and history of Mexican Americans so that they won't feel left out.

Sad to say, it didn't work out this way. The focus of bilingual ed programs became centered on language and marginalized the cultural component. Much of the material I had acquired was never utilized. When voters in California passed Prop 13 in 1978, which reduced property taxes, thereby sharply cutting into school budgets, what little was left of the cultural component of bilingual ed met its final death. It certainly meant the death of the concept of bilingual/bicultural education.

So I didn't shed too many tears when Prop 227 passed. The fact was that even what passed as bilingual ed was problematic, in my opinion. The proof of this was that many of those involved in the program didn't take it seriously. For example, many teachers got into the program not because they were committed to it but because they received an extra salary stipend. Many of these teachers didn't even know Spanish or didn't even bother to learn it. It also amazed me that I could not have taught bilingual ed, because, as the system was set up, I was not "qualified" to teach it. Spanish-speaking teaching aides did most of the Spanish used in their classes. When you have the aide doing the actual teaching, it's a half-ass program. That was okay to an extent, but if the students realize that the main teacher can't communicate in Spanish, they're not going to take that teacher seriously, so the crucial tie between teacher and student fails. This was part of the problem with bilingual ed. Instead of eliminating these programs, I would have returned them to the original vision of language acquisition and transition with cultural enrichment.

As far as English-only or English immersion is concerned, that became the focus after Prop 227 passed. I have serious doubts if there is no cultural reinforcement. The student might learn English faster this way, but if in the process there is no support of his cultural heritage, the kid will be stripped not only of his family language but of his family culture. The result will be an insecure child who feels inadequate compared to white kids. If he doesn't know his cultural history to reinforce his new American identity, he/she will become a potential self-hater.

Over the years, I worked to counter this lack of cultural enrichment in our schools by introducing Chicano history and Chicano Studies into my teaching so that my Chicano/Latino students, at least in high school, could have a better sense of the contributions of Mexicans and other Latinos to the United States. Knowing this, they hopefully would develop a more positive image of themselves. This drove my educational approach. Unfortunately, not all teachers in the schools felt as I did, including even new ones coming into schools such as Belmont. When I retired in 2003, my classes were taken over by a young Latina teacher just out of college. Before I left, she came by to see me and to check out my classroom, which was filled with all kinds of materials, including images related to Chicano/Latino history. I had pictures of César Chávez, Dolores Huerta, Emiliano Zapata, Mariano Vallejo, Antonio Coronel—all significant people in this history. She looked around and said: "Mr. Castro, could you before you leave take down all of this stuff. I think it's distracting to the students."

I don't remember what my response was, but I know I felt disappointed and maybe even a bit pissed off. I thought to myself that we're in an even more horrible state in public education if this young Latina teacher doesn't know what this stuff is all about or doesn't have the curiosity to ask what it is. I felt very discouraged. I was shocked that young teachers, including Latino ones, are so ill trained and ill prepared. What am I leaving my kids to?

New Latino Leadership

In the many years that I taught at Belmont, I've seen both continuation of problems but also changes. One important change has been the electoral success of Latino politicians. When I think back to 1968, at the time of the blowouts, when we had only a handful of elected officials such as Ed Roybal and Julian Nava, to today, when we have many more including Antonio Villaraigosa, one of my former students at Camp Hess Kramer and now mayor of Los Angeles, it's been an impressive change. There's no question but that the Chicano Movement, including the blowouts, helped ignite these changes. It was the political struggles associated with the Chicano Movement that forced the system to open up to Chicano/Latino political representation. The politicians of today owe a great debt to this legacy. But it's not an easy road. Once you get into politics there's all kinds of compromises and efforts to get you to sell your soul for political contributions. Our Latino elected leaders struggle against this. Some are able to deal with it; others succumb to it. Term limits in California politics don't help. As soon as you get elected, you're already looking toward what other office you'll run for once you get termed out. Money, of course, is at the root of many of these problems. To run for office, even for the school board, in L.A. means you have to have a good war chest.

As you move up the electoral ladder, you need even more money. This is where the seduction takes place. Special interests or the corporate elite come to you and offer to bankroll your campaign if you later remember who your friends are. It's difficult for politicians, including Latino ones, to look the other way. Soon they forget their Latino constituents and pay more attention to those who paid their campaign bills. I don't say that all of our Latino politicians are like this, and many of them have continued the struggle to uplift their communities. I'm proud to know many of them and to have had some of them as former students or former graduates of Hess Kramer. I invite some of them to return to the annual conference and hold them up as role models for our kids. But I also want to serve as a reminder to the politicos of where they came from and where their responsibilities lie. The kids during the blowouts displayed much courage and commitment, and this is what I want our Latino politicians to display as well.

Through most of my years at Belmont, Chicano influence on the board of education and the school bureaucracy varied. Julian Nava, of course, had been elected prior to the blowouts, and even though he started *tapado* (naive), he grew in that position and played an important role, both during and after the walkouts, in articulating our demands and concerns. He remained on the board well into the 1970s, until President Jimmy Carter appointed him as ambassador to Mexico, in 1979. Another Chicano, Larry González, succeeded Nava and also did a good job. After Larry stepped down, later in the 1980s, Vicki Castro was elected. Vicki had been one of the college students who helped out in the blowouts. At the time, she attended L.A. State and she was a graduate of Roosevelt High. Her election represented a kind of vindication of what we had done in 1968. She had been with us protesting against the school board, and now she was on the board! Vicki's election was important, but the problem still remained that we seemed to be able to elect only one Latino to the board, despite the fact that, by the time of Vicki's election, Latino students represented the large majority of public school students. At-large elections for the board, however, were no longer the problem, since this had been eliminated by the time of Vicki's campaign. The problem now was that most of the Latino electorate for the school board was heavily concentrated in only one district. This became a safe Latino seat, but we were gerrymandered out of a few more seats.

More significant than the one sole Latino representative on the school board was the work of the Mexican American Education Commission, which had been set up by the board after the blowouts to advise the board on Mexican American issues. This hadn't been one of our demands, but we accepted it. The idea for it had come out of the discussions between the EICC (Educational Issues Coordinating Committee) and the board. The board also set up similar commissions for blacks and Asians. The only problem I had with the commission was that I wasn't selected to be on it when it started. I was still too much of a "hot potato." I did, however, serve on it years later until it was killed off.

The commission, to its credit, over the years that it functioned, brought pressure to bear on the board, as well as serving as a liaison with the Latino community. Board members selected commission members. The commission, for example, had the power to recommend people for appointments as principals and vice principals. It also advocated for so-called battlefield commissions, which allowed certain people to receive special credentials to serve as principals and vice principals. This is how more Latinos received administrative appointments. They still had to go back to college to work on an administrative credential while they served in these positions, but it got them in the door. In addition, Latinos, if they had complaints about the schools, could go directly to the commission or commission members to voice their issue, without having to fight the school bureaucracy.

Unfortunately, the school board disbanded the commission, along with the other ethnic ones, by the late 1990s. In the case of the Mexican American Education Commission, it got embroiled in local Latino politics, which led to some Latino politicians pulling the rug out from under it. On top of this, the new superintendent, Roy Romer, at that time did not want competing power in these commissions and recommended that they be eliminated. Regrettably, the board caved in to his demand.

Demographics and political changes also led, by the late 1990s, to the selection of two Latinos to serve in the position of superintendent of schools. Bill Anton, who didn't emphasize his Latino roots, was the first, and Rubén Zacarias was the second. When Anton became superintendent, he was the first Mexican American to hold that position since Antonio Coronel in 1850. I saw this selection as a vindication of the blowouts and our demand for a greater voice in the running of the schools. Both Anton and Zacarias were decent guys and good administrators. They didn't see their roles as being political or playing political games. This, however, proved to be their downfalls. The running of a school district as large as that of L.A. means huge budgets. In fact, its budget is larger than the budgets of some countries. I'm not just referring to teachers' salaries and the operating budget for the schools. I mean the large contracts that the superintendent and the board give to private corporations to provide a whole range of services to the district, including contracts for building and maintaining schools. It's a multibillion-dollar arrangement. The superintendent is right in the middle of all this.

Both Anton and Zacarias received pressures, not only from lobbyists for these private interests but from the mayor, at that time Richard Riordan, himself a rich businessman. Riordan wanted to make sure that some of his corporate friends got these contracts. When Anton and Zacarias didn't play ball, Riordan, in turn, pressured the board to remove them. Regrettably, as part of all this political intrigue and hardball, most Latino politicos didn't speak out for Anton and Zacarias. Riordan, who is a crooked son of a bitch, intimidated them. More recently, longtime school administrator Rubén Cortines has been appointed school superintendent. I hope that he will have the ability to deal with this pressure, and I hope that our Latino politicians will stand up for him. We can't afford to play politics with our kids' education.

Future Leaders

I saw leadership emerge among the students in 1968, and it's a quality that I continue to nurture among students and young people. Many of those students, both high school and college ones, have gone on to important professional and community positions. Progressive leadership is a lot of what I talk about when I'm invited to speak to college classes and student gatherings. This is part of what I say:

> You have a responsibility. Kids in 1968 and in the Chicano Movement risked their lives to get you a college education. Make damn sure they didn't risk their lives in vain. People actually died in the streets raising hell. People lost careers to make sure that college doors were open to you to get an education. You owe the community a responsibility. Let's get away from that crap that Reagan started in the 1980s —the me-only thing. What's in it for me. We have to go beyond the crap that's shown on TV that only reinforces that selfish individualism.
>
> You have to go back to the kind of sense of community that we saw in 1968 and in the Movement. I don't want to idolize or romanticize those experiences and those years. There were plenty of problems and contradictions then, but on the whole we had common goals and we were struggling for the common good. That's what we still need today. But we need this from you. Your responsibility is to complete your education and then provide the leadership needed in our communities. I'm not asking you to go back to the barrio. But I am asking you to have the awareness and the courage—as did the kids in 1968—to stand up for what is right and just and speak out on behalf of those still left behind. This is responsible leadership, and you can and should do this.

ELEVEN

Education Today and Legacies

In my years as a public school teacher, I have encountered a variety of educational issues and problems that I have had to address. This is no less true at the end of my teaching career as it was at the beginning. I remain concerned because many contemporary educational issues continue to negatively impact Latino students. As a former teacher and a citizen, I have strong views about the following issues that face our students and community today. I address these in no particular order of importance. They are all critical topics.

Educational Issues

First of all, there is the recent obsession with testing our students to gauge educational progress. I have always had strong reservations about the objectivity and fairness of testing, as applied to minority students such as Latinos. I have just as many reservations today to the even-larger number of tests being administered.

There are several problems concerning all of this emphasis on testing. For one, the teachers now just teach to the tests. All they're concerned about is that their students do well in the tests. They know that their teaching positions may be on the line if their students don't pass the tests, and so their concerns are first and foremost to protect their jobs. In addition, by teaching to the tests, the teachers abandon any educational or cultural enrichment in their classes. If, for example, they know that very little in the tests will include questions on Latinos then they won't add material in their classes on Latinos, even in schools that are predominantly Latino. This is a crime! Teachers need to be sensitive to the backgrounds of their students, and the tests that are still heavily premised on the white experience, especially the verbal sections, don't help in this.

To boot, the teacher then is pulled out of the class one day a week for in-service training concerning the tests. So the kids suffer more because they're now deprived of their regular teacher once a week and have to deal with a substitute teacher. On top of this, their regular schedule is shortened, and they get out of school after lunch. The fact is that in-service training isn't worth a damn. This, more than anything, pushed me to retire—having to attend these stupid sessions while taking me away from my kids.

This pressure on the teachers to reorient their teaching to the tests is compounded by the pressure on principals, who are also being evaluated on how well their schools perform on the tests. If the scores don't go up they not only get their budgets cut but they may also lose their jobs. So they're part of the problem as well, because they in turn put pressure on their teachers to focus on the tests rather than on a more comprehensive approach to teaching. Remember that teaching is an art, not a science. The No Child Left Behind law didn't help one bit, because it only added even more pressure on test scores while providing very little money for teacher training on testing. Testing, testing, testing. Scores, scores, and more scores. This seems to be the only thing the educational bureaucracy and most of the public and media are interested in. But what about smaller classes? What about more and sensitive academic counselors? Somehow we've lost sight of what is really needed to achieve success in education, including positioning our students at the center of the schools.

For a short while, there was a stress on smaller classes in California, especially in the elementary schools, and the target was twenty students to one teacher. But this didn't last long, and the size of classes today has gone up again. The concept was good, but to reach this goal you needed to have more teachers, and the state didn't provide enough money to do this. Everyone wants positive educational results, but no one wants to pay for this. But there's no free lunch. We're not spending enough for education. There must be a gargantuan effort to get taxpayers to accept larger taxes for education. All developed countries spend much more per capita for education that we do. A first-class education should be offered to all children from kindergarten through twelfth grade, and college opportunity for all youngsters should be guaranteed, in order for us to maintain our leadership in a changing world.

In the high schools, especially in the inner-city ones, the reduction in class sizes never kicked in anyway. When I left Belmont in 2003, I was still teaching classes of about forty or forty-five. I didn't mind it because at least I knew I could reach all of these kids. But this wasn't true in other classes. Some teachers reduced their classes by kicking students out if they had a few too many absences or they didn't turn in some assignments. "Don't bother to come back to class," they'd tell these students. Or, if they didn't kick them out, they'd refuse to teach them by having them spend the entire class session with their heads down on their desks. Those kicked out would wander the halls or simply drop out. I rescued some of them by putting them into my classes and adding extra chairs and at least teaching them something.

FRANK DEL OLMO in the *Los Angeles Times*: "He [Sal Castro] is not an educational theorist. His reply to all the 'highfalutin' proposals for improving public education is simple as befits a front-line teacher. 'Give every teacher fewer kids per class and you'll get better teaching. Assign fewer students per counselor and you'll get better counseling.'"[1]

In the debate over educational results today, provisional teachers who don't yet have their full teaching credentials have, in my opinion, been scapegoated. Critics point to the large numbers of noncredentialed teachers, for example, in the inner-city schools, as proof of the problems of these schools. But some of these teachers aren't the problem. I've seen many good noncredentialed teachers at Belmont and other schools while seeing many bad credentialed teachers. The key to successful teaching is conveying to your students that they can succeed. I don't care if you have an emergency credential, but if you know that the child can succeed and you're willing to nurture that child and go that extra mile, you're a great teacher. Having a credential has nothing to do with this approach. There are probably college seniors in a Chicano Studies class today that could do a better job than some credentialed *bofos* (idiots) teaching at Belmont.

We have good teachers and we have bad teachers in our public schools today, but the only way we're going to get more and better teachers is if we raise salaries. You can get all the committed and culturally sensitive teachers you want and that I want, but you're not going to keep them unless we raise their salaries. It takes about twenty years to finally achieve a professional salary in keeping with a teacher's education, but by then it's too late. By then, we've already lost many good teachers who can't afford to stay in teaching, especially after they start their own families.

We're bilingual when it comes to teachers' salaries. We speak from both sides of our mouths. We talk a good game when it comes to education. We say it's the cornerstone of democracy. But then we're not willing to pay for it. We saw that when California voters passed Prop 13. This refusal to pay adequately for education is also racist. Many whites know that they can afford to send their kids to private schools, while minorities populate the pubic schools. In the 1950s, when the majority of kids in California public schools were white, the state ranked second in the nation in spending for education. Today, when the majority of students are minorities, the state now ranks forty-eighth in spending! How come we still can't be the second? We're worse off today than some of the southern states that have never paid much for public education. This really tells you something.

And the discussion about vouchers is a sham, a *pendejada* (stupidity). Vouchers only help middle-class parents to send their kids to a private school, where tuition can be as high as $20,000 a year. Vouchers average about $1,000 to $1,500. How is that going to help poorer Latino working-class parents in L.A.? Vouchers only mean the further acceleration of white flight from inner-city schools.

Still another *pendejada* is the charter school concept. Where are they finding the money to attract teachers who have been retrained to be that ideal effective teacher we're talking about? All they are doing is spinning their wheels, bullshitting, and siphoning off precious funds from already severely strapped budgets for the normal schools.

Another current school issue has to do with so-called magnet schools, which partly are a reaction to the failures of integration and the hope that these schools, if they are of high quality, can attract both minorities and whites. In L.A., this simply hasn't happened. For one, it's because some of these schools are situated within the existing inner-city schools, and white parents won't send their kids to them. I'm not per se against magnet schools, such as the Bravo School or King Drew School, that are aimed at encouraging Latino students and others to go on to get medical and science degrees in college. But, for me, the crucial question is the attitude and commitment of the teachers in these schools. If the teachers possess those qualities and feel that all kids can achieve, then that's great. But if you've got teachers that only feel that Asian students can achieve and that you just have to tolerate Latino ones, then you haven't accomplished anything, whether it's a magnet school or not. You don't need a magnet school to insist on this type of teacher commitment. You can accomplish this in the regular schools, but only if you get committed teachers, spend the money in the schools, raise teachers' salaries, and cut down on class sizes. All these other frills don't matter.

Still another so-called innovation has been the implementation of year-round schools. One more *pendejada*. It has nothing to do with raising the quality of the schools. It's being done, and primarily only in the inner-city schools, to deal with over-enrollments. The only way these schools can accommodate this overflow of mostly Latino students is to operate year-round schools. It's also an excuse not to build additional schools. But it's a crime committed against the students and the parents and on the Latino community. First of all, the semester is shortened, depriving the kids of the full education they need. Because it's year-round, some kids are out of school in January and February or March and April. What the hell can a kid do in January and February? Are the playgrounds open for them? No. Are there jobs for them? No. The other part of the crime is that year-around schooling denies certain classes, including honors and AP classes, to some students, depending on their rotation. Some semesters don't provide these classes, so this hurts those students needing them for admission to a good college, including the UC system.

The only way to get rid of year-round schooling is to build new schools. The current L.A. school administration is building some, although primarily elementary schools, but there is just as much, if not more, need for new junior and senior high schools. The crisis is especially huge at the high school level. New schools will also eliminate the large amount of busing of Latino students today due to overcrowded schools. We've got kids being bused for two hours each day on dangerous freeways. One of the problems in building new schools is where to build them. As more and more box stores like Wal-Mart and Target are built, they take up prime lands where new schools could be constructed. To add to this problem, many people think that if they sell their property to Target, for example, they'll get a better price than if they sell to the school district. They don't realize that Target isn't going to give them any more than the district. What's worse is that the school district refuses to exercise its right of eminent domain, so that it can compete with these box stores for choice property. It's a major crisis.

My President

I had the honor of addressing this crisis in Latino education at the White House when I attended a one-day meeting in 1996 hosted by President Bill Clinton. I think they invited me because I have a big nose like him. Here I was an East L.A. kid in the Blue Room of the White House. It wasn't an educational conference but a gathering of Latino leaders from different walks of life. I had never met the president before, and when he walked in I was impressed with how tall and big he is. He could have been a tight end for the University of Arkansas—*alto el vato* (he's a big dude).

The other thing I noticed was that he had a big smile on his face. Now you have to remember when this was. I didn't see Monica Lewinsky, but Clinton sure had a big smile.

During the course of the discussion, no one was talking about the crisis in

President Bill Clinton and Sal Castro, with United Farm Worker president Arturo Rodríguez in the background, White House Blue Room, May 3, 1996. Courtesy Sal Castro Personal Collection.

education, so I spoke out. I had seen many years before the film *Viva Zapata*, with Marlon Brando in the title role. In one scene, Zapata meets with President Francisco Madero and addresses him as *Mi señor presidente*. So probably influenced by this, as well as my own respect for President Clinton, I used this *zapatista* salutation. "My President," I said to Clinton, "we have a crisis in Latino education. We lead the nation in high school dropouts, in college dropouts, and we have the dubious distinction of leading in teen pregnancy. There's no magic bullet to solve this crisis. But, in my opinion, we need educators who will appreciate and accept our children and recognize that they are capable of achieving their fullest potential. We need teachers who like our kids and want to be in the classrooms with them and in our barrios. Yes, we need more funding for our schools and to build new ones, but above all we need good and supportive teachers and administrators who believe that our students can succeed. That's basic Education 101. I hope you can help us, sir."

Clinton responded positively and said he really wanted to help and that he would get back to others and me on this issue. Unfortunately, he got diverted by something called an impeachment, but I think his heart was in the right place. They say that Clinton was successful as president, especially with minorities and the poor because he seemed to feel their pain. I think he did, with what I said and with Latinos. That hasn't been the case with President George W. Bush. We'll need new presidential leadership on Latino issues and especially on education in the future. I hope we will get this from President Barack Obama.

When I tell this story about meeting President Clinton in the White House to students and to educators, I also kid them about how the FBI and the CIA gave me a secret clearance and briefing on the whereabouts of Osama Bin Laden. I say that they gave me a map as to where he might be. On this map, which I show to my audience, there are the different provinces in Afghanistan where Bin Laden might be hiding. "These are the provinces," as I point to my map: "There's *Aquí no están* [He isn't here]; *No están* [He's not here]; *Tampoco están* [He's not here either]; *No se si están* [We don't think he's there]"; and then my favorite—"*Que gaucho están?* [Where the hell is he?]" I have fun with this play on words in Spanish. This is humor, but the reality is, why hasn't the United States captured Bin Laden? We can send space ships to Mars, but we can't locate Bin Laden on earth?

Superintendent Castro

Sometimes I'm asked, especially at Latino education conferences, "What would you do if you were Superintendent of Schools in L.A.?" That's a good question, but, of course, I would never be appointed to this position, given my history. But here's what I tell these audiences:

If I were to become superintendent, I would do immediately three things. First, I'd get together with the state legislature real fast and talk to them about teacher retraining and a new kind of credential based on cultural sensitivity. We need, as I told President Clinton, teachers that want to teach our kids and always have high expectations of them and that know where our students come from so that they can better relate to them and to their parents. As part of this emphasis, I'd check on teachers who fail to do this, because a failure in the classroom is a teacher's failure and not the student's.

The second thing I would do is address the Latino parents. I'd bring them in and raise hell with them as much as I could. "I'm not going to give your kid a report card," I'd tell them, "unless you come in and get it." To facilitate this interaction between the school and the parents —which doesn't exist today—I'd hold teacher conferences with parents on Sundays. The unions would raise hell with me, but again I wouldn't care. In fact, these conferences would follow noon Mass, and I'd even have mariachis and other Latino music, as well as *antojítos* (snacks) available. All this would get the parents there. Sundays are the only days that Latino parents have time for other than working. The schools need to be aware of this and take advantage of it. I'd go even further and also have Sunday classes for the parents, to teach them English and prepare many of them to become U.S. citizens.

The third thing I would do is that every administrator I would hire, including my own staff, would have to be innovative change agents and risk takers.

I'd do a lot of new things if I was superintendent, but I'd start with these three.

I've also more recently been asked about what my reaction is to Mayor Antonio Villaraigosa's attempt to move control over the L.A. school district to the mayor's office. A state court blocked that attempt, and the mayor has abandoned the legal recourse, especially after candidates he favored won in the 2007 school board election, effectively giving him majority influence on the board. I feel good about Tony being the first Chicano mayor since the late nineteenth century. I call him Tony because I've known him since he was a sixteen-year-old student at Cathedral High, my alma mater, as a participant in one of our Hess Kramer camps back in the 1970s and in trying to get him into UCLA. His election as the first Mexican American mayor of L.A. is historic. It marks the coming to political power of Latinos in this huge metropolis, which is becoming predominantly Latino. At the same time, I have to say that I don't agree with his idea of the mayor running the school district. This has nothing to do with Antonio but with my belief that this would only politicize educational issues even more than they are today. Antonio, I'm sure, would do the best for the schools, but I would be worried about successors, who might not do this.

To me, the most immediate reform rather than what Antonio wants to do is to change the school board and make it more responsive to its constituents by making the board full time. As full-time members, they should also be paid as much as city council members, who are full time. Many people are not aware that a school board member only serves part time. This is ridiculous in a large school district such as the L.A. one. Board members under this current setup don't have the time or staff to spend time with their constituents and listening to what parents are saying about the schools. Right now the school board is inaccessible to the public. You have to first of all try to find parking close to the board's offices, and you usually wind up parking several blocks away. You then go into a thirty-story building, all the way to the twenty-fifth floor. This has to change.

Legacies

In 2003, I retired from teaching in the L.A. school district and at Belmont. However, I'll never retire as a teacher. Teaching is in my blood and soul. Still, it isn't easy to stop getting ready each fall for a new school year and the anticipation of welcoming a new class of students. I miss this—and even all the ups and downs of any school year. I started at Belmont in 1963, and I finished and retired from Belmont forty years later.

I probably retired early; I didn't have to. However, there were three basic reasons why I decided to move on in 2003. First, I had been working for the construction of a new Belmont school, and it became clear to me that this wasn't going to happen. I realized that I'd be a pretty old *viejito* (old man) if I waited for this. Secondly, I also kept waiting for new Latino teachers who would come and replace me and carry on the work I had dedicated my life and teaching career to—the positive reinforcement of Latino students that comes with awareness of their identity and the recognition that I, as the teacher, believe in them. I didn't see this in many of the new teachers. I kept waiting and waiting, but they didn't appear. I couldn't wait forever. And, finally, I decided that it was important that I dedicate myself full time to the revitalization of the Camp Hess Kramer conferences. This had been floundering for lack of support by the school district. Previous superintendents over the years had provided me with funds to hold the annual gatherings, but under then-superintendent Roy Romer, this wasn't happening. When cowboy Roy, who had previously been governor of Colorado, became superintendent a few years ago, he didn't know us from a hole in the ground. I figured that in order for the conference not to die, I'd retire and work full time to try to keep it afloat.

I formally resigned from the school district, but my continued association with kids and speaking on college campuses keeps me alive as a teacher. This *testimonio* is a continuation of my teaching. I want my tombstone to read: "SAL CASTRO—A TEACHER."

I felt very honored recently when in 2010 the school district named the former Belmont Middle School the Sal Castro Middle School.

Reviving Camp Hess Kramer

Since my retirement, I've devoted almost all of my time and energy to reestablishing the historic Camp Hess Kramer conferences, which are now called the Chicano Youth Leadership Conferences (CYLC), although informally I also refer to them as the Latino Youth Leadership Conferences. It's interesting how, since the first conference in 1963, we've evolved, with respect to identity, from Mexican American to Chicano to Latino. This reflects changing ethnic and political consciousness as well as demographics. With so many Central Americans and other Latino students in the schools, we no longer can refer to only Mexican Americans and Chicanos. The county of Los Angeles had originally sponsored the conference, and we held consecutive gatherings until about 1975. By then, the county no longer supported it, and funds dried up. Since then, I pretty much had to fill in the gap by becoming the director and trying to raise funds, but this proved to be difficult. As a result, from 1975 to 2003, the conferences were held sporadically, and for several years none took place.

The funding has been the most difficult aspect of holding the conferences. The teachers' unions for awhile helped, but that didn't last very long. Some of the former alumni of the conferences stepped in for a short time, but this also didn't last. I remember, in 1988, when we held a twentieth reunion of the blowouts, some discussion of revitalizing the conferences.[2] Moctesuma Esparza, now a movie producer, had a grandiose idea of developing a war chest to contribute money to encourage Latinos to run for the school board and make changes that way. I said to him and others, "Well that's all good and well, but let's look at what we already have. What are we celebrating today? What got us to the blowouts? What helped turn you on politically? What gave you that last push to go to college? Yeah, it was the Hess Kramer conferences. Why don't we get monies to continue that?"

This rang a bell with all of the alumni. Since then, we receive help from alumni, in the form of money or by coming to spend time with the kids. I know I can always count on them. However, what the conference needed was sustained and permanent support by the superintendent's office. I did secure some of this, but not very much, and not on a permanent basis. Yet, by constantly going back for support and with help from some of the elected Latino officials, since 2003 we've been on a stronger footing, and we're able

Sal Castro at Chicano Youth Leadership Conference, Camp Hess Kramer, December 2007. Mario T. García Personal Collection.

to now host two conferences each year, one in the spring and one in the fall, with an average of about 100 students per conference. We're part of what is called the Beyond the Bell Program, which is the after-school program of the district. Our budget comes from that program. It's not much, but we make do. We put on each conference for about $35,000. Unfortunately, the recent economic recession/depression has severely affected educational budgets in California, which, in turn, has affected our ability to hold the conferences. I think the only long-range solution is for our older and professional conference alumni to step in even more and create an endowment to fund the conferences.

I don't get paid for my work on the conferences and wouldn't accept a salary anyway. I wish, however, that the district would provide a salary for my longtime assistant, Elsa Cisneros, who dedicates so much time to helping put together the conferences and being a liaison with the schools and with the parents of the kids to reassure them of the program and that their children will be safe. The district does provide us an office and pays the bills for the conferences, including renting the facilities at the historic Camp Hess Kramer in Malibu. The kids and the participating schools don't need to pay a dime. I could arrange to hold the conferences elsewhere, but I want to maintain that historical connection with the initial ones in the 1960s that led to the blowouts.

My whole philosophy about the conferences has never changed. It's an opportunity to encourage the Latino students to stay in school, graduate, go to college, graduate, and become responsible leaders in the community —who will look back and give a helping hand to others. The most gratifying thing about the conferences is how these three days change many, if not most, of the students who attend. They come out feeling more secure about themselves and determined to go to college. I couldn't ask for anything more.

We organize the conferences primarily as we did back in the 1960s. The kids are divided into small groups headed by college students, who serve as their facilitators or counselors. We give indigenous names to these small groups, such as the Aztecas, the Olmecas, the Navajos, the Apaches, the Hopis, among others. The role of the college facilitators is still a crucial one, because they spend more of the time with the kids and engage in the dialogues with them. When I speak on college campuses and encourage students to sign up as counselors for our camp, I say to them:

> We ask you to come looking like a college student so the kids will look up to you and be in awe of you. But I also want you to lie a little bit, but positive lies. Tell them that college is easy if you work hard. Give them a positive view of college life. Don't discourage them by saying that it's hard or boring or that you feel marginalized there. I'm sure that's not true for you, but my point is that as facilitators I need you to encourage the kids to go to college and not discourage them. Don't spook them.

Besides the dialogues in the small groups, the students, as in the past, are exposed to a variety of adult speakers. Now that we have so many more successful role models in education, politics, and the arts, to name just those areas, it's much easier to arrange for speakers, many of whom are alumni of the conference, such as Moctesuma Esparza, Susan Racho, and Judge Carlos Moreno. The high school students have never been exposed to so many college graduates and Ph.D.s and artists. Their role models, especially for the boys, have been their brothers and cousins in the military. We provide them with other possibilities.

To further encourage the kids to go to college, we also invite a number of college recruiters to talk about their schools and to distribute literature. We do all this because, even though, as in the past, these high school students are the cream of the crop in their schools, many of them still aren't sure whether they'll go to a four-year college.

We also expose the kids to various forms of Mexican and Latino culture. We hold a dance on Saturday night, but no hip-hop or that kind of junk. We have a formal Mexican dance, just like in a wedding. We teach the kids to dance to Mexican polkas, boleros, cha-cha-cha, mambo, and salsa. This is a really high-class occasion, almost like a cotillion ball, although the kids don't have to get all dressed up for it. In addition, we bring mariachis to play the polka. We even take away the students' I-Pods and cell phones so that they won't be distracted. We isolate the kids to focus on what they're there for: to learn about themselves, their culture, their history, and their community and to dedicate themselves to go to college and help their communities. I believe that we've succeeded in doing this.[3]

But we need continued support. The recent budget crisis in California has meant that the Hess Kramer conferences are on hold. This is a shame. We need either the school board to step up to the plate and fund us or to have the Latino community leadership, including alumni of Hess Kramer, to reach into their deep pockets and give back to the conference what it gave to them.

SONIA SALAZAR note to Sal Castro: "I still remember when I went to CYLC as a junior in high school, 2003. The camp changed my life and it was after the camp that I started to call myself a Chicana! I do so because I have love for my people, because I believe that our struggles as students still continue, and because I know that the Chicano/a Movement still exists! I know I haven't told you this, but you are my inspiration and motivation, along with my parents, in everything I do. . . . I give motivation speeches on higher education to 'at risk' labeled students. I follow your model, 'Don't be a pendejo, go to college and graduate.' Thanks for taking the blindfold off my eyes."[4]

Mestizaje

At the Hess Kramer conferences and throughout my career as a teacher, I've tried as a key part of my educational philosophy to convey to young Latinos that they should be aware and proud of their own historical legacy. They come from a rich and proud history, and this, in turn, should make them feel good about themselves. I try not to romanticize history, but I do believe that Chicanos/Latinos need to know the historical contributions that their ancestors made to this country. In translating this history to students, I also have attempted to impress upon them the significant and special and rich mixtures of ethnicity and cultures that they represent. Chicanos/Latinos are the composite of an evolving *mestizaje*, or mixing of genes and cultures. As such, they can and should take the lead in furthering racial tolerance.

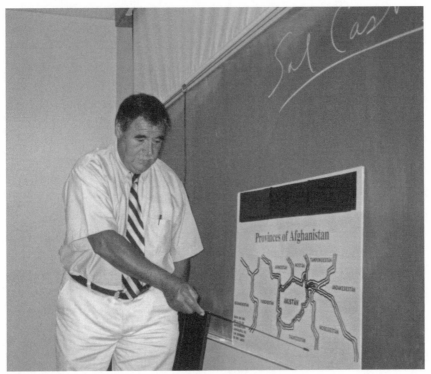

Sal Castro lecturing in Professor Mario T. García's class, University of California, Santa Barbara, 2007. Courtesy Mario T. García Personal Collection.

When I speak to a college audience today, for example, I give my little lecture on all of this. I say of Latinos:

> We're descended from people who came to this continent thousands of years ago, probably through the Bering Straits. Where did they come from? They came from China. We're *chinitos*. We're Asian. If you go to the anthropological museum in Mexico City and then go to those in China, you see the similar artifacts and images. The indigenous in Mexico and the ancestors of the Chinese look alike and their cultures are similar. If you go to a Chinese wedding today and stay long enough, people come out with chile. Where the hell did the chinos get chile? They eat chile. Go check it out and you'll see in Chinese restaurants big bottles of chile with Chinese writing on it. I swear. And if you stay longer, they'll come out with a tray that's circular and it goes round and round. They've got flour tortillas! If you listen to Mexican ranchero music, you'll find songs such as "Las Manañitas," which begins with

the words *"chinita de mis amores."* Then there is the figure of *"la china poblana."*

We're the first people of the Western Hemisphere. American history doesn't start with Plymouth Rock; it starts with our ancestors. Others might call us "wetbacks," but we've had 40,000 years to dry out.

But then there's another part of us from the Iberian Peninsula. We derive from the *vatos* inside of caves. They were the first taggers. *Orale!* If you go inside those caves, you see all of this writing on the walls. We were inside caves. Then these other *vatos* came over to Spain from a southern continent and brought us out of the caves. They pulled us out and gave us education, a form of government, our architecture, and even part of our language. Have you noticed that we use words like *ojalá, oiga, alfombra, vitrina,* and many others. Where did we get these words? What are these words? These are words from Africa. The *negroes* or Moros came to Spain from Africa. They civilized us. They took over much of Spain and brought few women. That's why some of us are *bien prietos* (very dark). When you blend this whole thing, that's what we are: *"Somos chinos, negroes, y blancos."* That's why we're such a beautiful people. That's why we're called *"la raza cósmica* [the cosmic race]." We're a mixture of all this. So we as Latinos can't be racist. How can we be, since we're a mixture of all races? Can we really look at ourselves in the mirror and say, "I hate you black! I hate you chino! I hate you *gavacho!*" We can't, because we're all this and more. That's why I say we're such a beautiful people. Give yourself a hand!

The Mexican in American History

I usually say many more things about history, such as how Mexicans have played significant roles in American history that most Americans, including Latinos, are totally unaware of. This includes the support that Spanish/ Mexicans gave to George Washington during the American Revolution by taking on the British in Florida, New Orleans, Natchez, and Baton Rouge, which allowed Washington to have his Valley Forge. It further included how during the Civil War, Mexicans in the United States fought on both sides and even were officers in the Union Army. In fact, when I speak to Chicano/ Latino students in Professor García's class at the University of California, Santa Barbara, for example, I tell them to go down to the Veteran's Building on Cabrillo Boulevard right alongside the waterfront and see the plague honoring those from Santa Barbara who fought in the Civil War. There's only two names, and guess what? Both are Mexicans! How many teachers know this?

Actually, there were many more Mexicans from California who fought in the Civil War. They were sent all the way across the country. "There's Mexican blood at Gettysburg!" I tell students.

Then there's the story of Mariano Vallejo from northern California, who owned large amounts of land and who came up with the idea of building a railroad from Sacramento to San Diego. He decided to go to Washington and sell his idea to President Abraham Lincoln. Unfortunately, this was just as the Civil War broke out.

"It's a great idea, Mariano," Lincoln told him, "but my hands are tied right now."

"Thank you, Mr. President," Vallejo said, "but this gives me an opportunity to visit my son, Platón Vallejo, who's a captain and a surgeon in the Union Army."

Mexicans were fighting in the Civil War.

"It also gives me a chance," Vallejo further told Lincoln, "to visit my brother, Salvador, who's an officer in the artillery stationed here in Washington."

How many teachers know this? In fact, 29,000 young Mexican Americans fought in the Civil War on both sides. Why aren't our kids learning this? Don't we think this would give our students a sense of their American identity?

And, of course, other plaques there include the large number of Mexicans who fought bravely and died for this country in World War I, World War II, Korea, Vietnam, the Gulf War, and now Iraq and Afghanistan. I cried when I visited the Vietnam War Memorial in Washington, D.C., and cried when I saw the names of former students I knew from Lincoln High who died in that war.

This is only a portion of Mexican American and Latino history in the United States that needs to be known by everyone, and certainly by Chicano and Latino kids so that they can feel that they too are Americans, and that's why we need to integrate this history so that these kids can also say, "I too am American."

The Legacy of the Blowouts

I have often been asked, "What's the legacy of the blowouts?"

In my opinion, there are several aspects to this legacy. First of all, it put the urban Mexican on the map. Up until 1968, the only thing the country knew about Mexicans was César Chávez and the farmworkers. Others thought Mexicans only existed in the agricultural areas. They didn't realize that millions of Mexicans lived in the cities throughout the Southwest, but also in other areas as well. They lived in Chicago, Detroit, St. Paul, Milwaukee, Cincinnati, and Atlanta, among other places. Yet the rest of the country overlooked this urban Mexican. The blowouts changed this false impression. They told the rest of the country that there were tons of Mexicans in the cities. All you had to do was open your eyes. The blowouts, in many ways, as Dr. Carlos Muñoz, one of our college students involved in the walkouts, says in his book, *Youth, Identity, Power: The Chicano Movement*, represented the start of the urban Chicano Movement, and Los Angeles, as Raul Ruiz, another of our college students in the walkouts, adds, represented the political capital of the Movement. The blowouts started all of this.

PROFESSOR RODOLFO ACUÑA: "It [the blowouts] was a definite break with the past. Before the walkouts all through the civil rights movement . . . Chicanos didn't do things the way the blacks did. But when they [Chicanos] saw the results of the blowouts there was no turning back."[5]

The walkouts also, of course, brought dramatic attention to the educational problems faced by Mexican Americans in the public schools that, in turn, were the legacy of the Mexican schools in the history of the Southwest and California. The kids who had the courage to walk out did what their parents and Mexican American leaders had been unable to do: dramatize through civil disobedience and direct action the failures of these schools and the damage they had caused to millions of Mexican American children. The blowouts forced the majority community to begin to realize that changes had to occur in the educational system and in the approach to the Chicano child in order to make education meaningful to them.

One of the key legacies of what the students accomplished in 1968 involves the thousands of Chicanos and Latino kids who have been able to go on to college since then. The legacy is in the college kids that I speak to today at UC Santa Barbara, UCLA, USC, Cal State, L.A., and many other schools. These students are living legacies of the blowouts. Call them blowout legacies. The fact is that the walkouts forced the colleges and universities to begin to open the door for Chicanos and later Latinos as well. Sure, other factors helped as well, but the walkouts, certainly in L.A., forced the issue. Statistics prove this. In 1967, for example, only about 200 Spanish-surnamed students studied at UCLA. Two years later, after the blowouts, close to 2,000 of these students were at UCLA. You could see similar changes throughout the state. How did

Sal Castro and Paula Crisostomo, May 2006. Courtesy Mario T. García Personal Collection.

they get there? By osmosis? *"No, mis hijos* [No, my children]," I tell students today, "the blowouts opened the doors to let Chicanitos in." Not only that, but also soon Harvard and Yale and other Ivy League schools, along with Stanford, started recruiting Chicano students from Lincoln, Roosevelt, Garfield, and other Eastside schools. This wasn't coincidence or some kind of new enlightenment on the part of college administrators. It was the Chicano Movement and especially the effect of the blowouts.

In the end, perhaps the most powerful legacy of the blowouts has to do with the changes in the students who walked out, the Walkout Generation, as John Ortiz refers to them. These were the *niños héroes* (child heroes) of the Chicano Movement. They were willing to put their careers and perhaps even their lives on the line to change the schools. They knew that these changes might not affect them, but they did this for their younger brothers and sisters. They walked out for millions of Chicano and Latino kids whom they didn't know who in the future might inherit a better education and more educational opportunities. The walkouts proved for many of the students in 1968 to be the most profound educational experience of their lives. That action taught them about the schools and about conditions in the country as they affected Chicanos more than anything else. They also learned about themselves and that they had the power to change not only their own lives but society as well. This inner change may well be the ultimate legacy of the blowouts. In the film *Walkout* (2006), the character of Paula Crisostomo, one of our student leaders at Lincoln, best sums this up. Asked what changes the walkouts brought about, she says with powerful conviction: "The schools might not have changed, but we did."[6]

Finally, I would say that the legacy of the blowouts and certainly the future of this legacy has to do with students today knowing about what happened in 1968 and making sure that they themselves struggle to continue to keep the doors open for others behind them, who deserve not only better elementary, junior high, and senior high schools, but the opportunity to go to four-year colleges. The final legacy is a continuation of Chicanos and Latinos at the colleges, who, in turn, provide a helping hand to other young people to achieve their dreams and their highest potential. This is what the blowouts were all about. When veteran reporter Frank del Olmo of the *Los Angeles Times* interviewed me on the tenth anniversary of the blowouts, he quoted me as saying—and I believe this: "We did what had to be done, and I feel at peace with myself."[7]

I'm honored that the story of the blowouts will be preserved and told by the HBO film *Walkout*, produced by one of my students, Moctesuma Esparza, and directed by Edward James Olmos. This film—perhaps along with this *testimonio*—will hopefully keep alive the legacy of what occurred in 1968. I'm especially proud that Esparza, who lived through the experience, did the film with care and sensitivity. It was a labor of love for him. Of course, in the mid-1990s, Susan Racho, another of our college students in 1968, produced the documentary *Taking Back the Schools* as part of a four-part PBS series on the Chicano Movement. In my estimation, Susan's segment is the best of the whole series. It was also a labor of love for her.

Esparza's film took several years before it was shown, in 2006. As far back as 1995, he approached me about it. I said, "Go for it." He went through a number of writers to produce a script. Some of them interviewed me, including the final writers, Marcos De Leon and Ernie Contreras, and I escorted some to Camp Hess Kramer so that they could get a feel for what happened. Finally, a script was written that Esparza liked. I had nothing to do with it and had no control over it.[8]

Then Esparza began to get actors for the different roles, including who would play me.

"Who would you like to play you?" he asked me.

"You get Martin Sheen to play me old and one of his sons, Charlie Sheen or

Emilio Estevez, to play me young. But get Salma Hayak to play the love interest. If you do this, I'll approve the film."

Of course, I was only kidding with Esparza, especially about Salma Hayak. But I could tell that I freaked him out, because he must have started thinking of how he could come up with the money to afford such big stars.

Instead, he threw up other names to play my role.

"How about Marc Anthony?"

"Marc Anthony? He's way too *flaco* [skinny]."

He later came up with Benjamin Bratt. I told my students about this, and the girls all sighed. But this didn't work out either.

I told Esparza that it didn't matter to me whether the actor was a Chicano or not. "Whoever you select, you send him to me and I'll set him straight about the blowouts. But whoever you select, I want him to be a guy that plays the role with dignity and feels it."

Finally, Esparza settled on a young Mexican American actor, Michael Peña. I met with him and approved. Mike spent a good deal of time with me and really got into the role. He did a great performance, as did all the other actors. The one thing I stressed to Mike was for him to play me with dignity.

At first, Esparza hoped to film the movie in Albuquerque, New Mexico, because Governor Bill Richardson, a Latino, offered him a good financial deal if Esparza filmed in that state. However, this didn't pan out, and finally and logically they filmed in L.A., with a budget of about $10 million, which isn't a lot to make a film. I spent some time with both Esparza and Eddie Olmos on the set, especially the scenes at Hess Kramer, and really enjoyed it. It's interesting and moving to see yourself being portrayed by an actor. Olmos did a terrific job in directing the film and even played a small role in it. They played a bit with the story to make sure it would be of interest to a mass audience. They did this by highlighting the love interest of the character of Paula Crisostomo, played by Alexa Vega. I didn't mind this. You have to be able to pull the audience in, especially the younger kids. In fact, millions watched it on HBO. The character of Paula is actually a composite of several of the young women involved in the walkouts.

But, on the whole, the film captures the essence and drama of the blowouts and translates this to the audience, although the actual story, as I have tried to convey, was much more complex. The one area where more could have been done involves the critical role played by the college students and those involved in the community, such as working on the Chicano alternative press. I fought like hell for this inclusion, but the producers felt they couldn't include everyone, due to a limited budget.

People who have seen it on HBO, or where I've been asked to go and show the film, all come up and say they really enjoyed it and learned from it. That makes me feel good, and I know that it does the same to Esparza, Olmos, and everyone associated with the film.

I was especially impressed with Alexa Vega and her commitment to preparing herself for her role. One day, I got a call from Eddie Olmos, who was filming his science fiction series in Canada.

"Sal, would it be possible for Alexa Vega to spend time at the next Hess Kramer conference so she can understand what goes on?"

"That's fine, Eddie, but she has to go through the whole thing. I don't want her just there as a visitor. Can you promise me that?"

"Well, I don't know."

"No, she has to do this just like one of the other students. That's your commitment to me and my commitment to you."

So she did. Alexa, herself a high school student at a Catholic high school in L.A., was picked up by the bus just like everyone else and taken to Camp Hess Kramer. There she stayed in the dorms with the other students, attended the lectures, participated in the small group dialogues, and enjoyed the entertainment provided. None of the other students knew that she was an actor and that she would be in the film about the blowouts. However, at the end of the conference, at our last group meeting, I decided to blow her cover.

"You're in for a surprise," I announced to the other students and counselors. "The lead actress in the movie being made about the walkouts is one of your fellow conference participants. She's graduating with you from this conference. I want her to come up and share some of her experiences with us. Alexa Vega, come up here."

She did, but before she could get a few words out, she started crying. She was filled with emotion. She did tell the students that the conference had really gotten to her and made her rethink many things about herself and about her ethnic identity. All of this would help her in the role. She was great, and the kids really responded to her.

I turned to someone and said, "She's either a hell of an actress or we really did get to her." I think it was a bit of both.

Olmos also attended the conference and with his crew shot some background scenes.

LOS ANGELES TIMES: "*Walkout* communicates the thrill of being swept up in something bigger, and a young person's first inklings of belonging to a point in history, a history that might be changed. Such early convictions often fade, but not—to

Sal Castro with sons Gilbert (left) and James (right), May 26, 2006. Courtesy Mario T. García Personal Collection.

judge by the moving, brief interviews that run along the closing credits—with many of the people portrayed here."[9]

HARRY GAMBOA, former student at Garfield and writer/artist: "I think what the film captured was the enthusiasm of the students."[10]

To me, the importance of the film is that it sends a message that there were a lot of sacrifices in the blowouts and that it involved the greatest generation of students, very heroic and unselfish kids who spearheaded the way for changes. Some of these changes have been accomplished, although I wish more had. However, what changes did take place were all done because of the courage of the students. That's what the film pays tribute to, and rightfully so. What's also important about the film is that it stresses education and that it's the key to success. The kids in 1968 understood this, and that's why they fought for it. We have to pass this legacy on to newer generations.

In finishing this *testimonio*, Professor Mario García asks me: "Sal, what do you think is your own personal legacy?"

This isn't easy to answer, and the question takes me off guard. But, spontaneously, this is what I said and this is where I'll conclude my story:

I don't know that I could tell you. I really don't know. I know that I encouraged the kids. I was there for them. I know that I never wanted to do anything else but be a teacher because I never wanted the blow-outs to be tainted. I had offers to go teach at some universities and even offers to run for Congress, but I turned them all down. I never wanted anyone to say, "That's the reason this guy did it; he wanted personal gain." When the blowouts happened, I was a high school teacher, and when I retired thirty-five years later, I was a high school teacher. That was it, and that's what I wanted. I did what I did in 1968, in part, to hopefully get kids to go into teaching as an honorable profession. That's why I'm a teacher.

Que Dios los bendiga y que la virgen morena los proteja. (May God bless you and may the Virgin of Guadalupe protect you.)

PAULA CRISOSTOMO CHARACTER and others in the conclusion of the film *Walkout*: "Thank you, Sal."[11]

The Camp Hess Kramer Spirit

Mario T. García

I arrive at Camp Hess Kramer early Saturday morning on a cold late May day in 2007. The foggy overcast that I awoke to in Santa Barbara has followed me all the way to Malibu. The drive was shorter than I had remembered from three years ago when we picked up my son Carlo, who attended the Chicano Youth Leadership Conference directed by Sal Castro. Carlo had a good time and, according to Sal, proved to be quite a dancer at the big Saturday night dance. This time it's only me, and, finally, after promising Sal for a few years that I would spend time at the camp and also give a talk, I've managed to do so. I find the cutoff to Hess Kramer right off of Pacific Coast Highway and park. I locate the cafeteria where the students are still having breakfast and catch sight of Sal chatting with Professor Rudy Acuña, who is scheduled to speak that morning. They greet me with *abrazos* and welcome me. Thus begins my day and a half at the historic Camp Hess Kramer conference. I cannot tell you what an experience this was. I enjoyed every minute of it and learned much of how Sal, over the years, with the help of his staff, including many college facilitators or counselors as well as blowout veterans such as Mita Cuarón and Paula Crisostomo, make the over 100 Chicano/Latino high school juniors go through a marvelous experience and even transformation. Three basic things happen that weekend: (1) the kids are made to feel safe and protected about exploring their ethnic identity and about feeling good about themselves; (2) the idea and commitment that they will go on to college is heavily promoted and accepted by the students; and (3) in a short period of time they form a strong bond with themselves and with Sal and the staff. When they board their buses to return home, they are Chicanos/Latinos in the best and wholesome meanings of these terms and they are committed to changing the world.

This is the way it has been at Hess Kramer since 1963. I came to try to feel that spirit, as I walked through the campgrounds, attended the different sessions, caught some of the dialogues when the students gathered in their small discussion groups, called "nations," all with indigenous names such as Aztecas, Olmecas, and Apaches. I felt that spirit at the meals and at the campfire on Saturday evening. By that evening and especially by the campfire, with a great Chicano musical *conjunto* Alma Grande singing in both English and Spanish and mixing the two together and with the kids joining in and dancing around the campfire, I could sense everything coming together. Exhausted after such a long day, I wound my way down to the salsa dance that closes the events of that day. I don't know where the kids get all their energy to dance until past midnight. I stay for only three tunes and again am moved by the energy in that room. But I am too tired to stay there much longer. I retire for the evening, inspired by what I have experienced that day. By the time I'm ready to leave, later on Sunday, I have attended early morning Mass, had breakfast, and given my talk to the students. I focus on the theme of leadership and tell them about how this topic has influenced much of my research, including this project, the life story of Sal Castro. I feel animated and empowered by what I have gone through, and I can see and feel the kids react positively to me. I feel gratified when Sal comes up to me with tears in his eyes to thank me. I depart after lunch, finally having witnessed and undergone the Camp Hess Kramer experience. I am pleased, and as I drive back to Santa Barbara I feel good about my work on Sal's story. In that short time at Hess Kramer, I know why Sal's story and that of the blowouts has to be told and preserved. I feel honored and privileged in being a part of this. I can't think of a better thing to leave to the future.

This epilogue brings us full circle to where we started by noting the significant leadership of Sal Castro to the Chicano struggle for educational justice. I hope that readers appreciate that leadership, the role of the individual in history, and who makes history. This is what Sal Castro did. The early chapters of this *testimonio* were to provide the reader with an understanding of Castro's early experiences as he came of age, as well as his family and school socialization, which help explain his emergence as a leader. The middle chapters saw Castro in full bloom as the indispensable teacher who galvanized, organized, and inspired thousands of Chicano students to participate in the historic blowouts or walkouts from their East Los Angeles schools, as well as the persecution that Castro experienced, in his arrest and, later, reprisals by school officials. Finally, the concluding chapters tell of Castro returning to many more years of teaching, guiding and empowering Chicano/Latino students, until his retirement in 2003. And even then, Castro has continued to be an activist, through his revival of the Camp Hess

Sal Castro and Mario T. García, February 20, 2008. Courtesy Harry Gamboa Jr. Personal Collection.

Kramer student conferences as well as his numerous speaking engagements in schools and in the community.

What should readers come away with in reading Sal Castro's story? First and foremost, that individuals can make a difference. Second, that Castro's leadership role, especially in the 1968 blowouts, has to be contextualized within the history of the Chicano Movement, the most widespread Chicano empowerment and civil rights movement in U.S. history. Third, that Castro's struggle to empower students and to challenge the school system that discriminated against Chicano students is also within the context of the historic nature of the so-called Mexican schools, which originated in the early twentieth century—segregating Mexican American students and providing an inferior education. The substance of this type of education was what Castro struggled against. Fourth, that Castro in his story comes across as an important educational critic of American education as it relates to minority communities such as in Los Angeles. As an educational muckraker and as a subversive teacher, Castro, through his praxis—observe, reflect, and act—exposed the criminality of the school system toward Chicanos. Finally,

I hope that the reader is convinced by my argument—that Sal Castro through his leadership must be considered one of the significant figures of the Chicano Movement and, indeed, one of the most important educational leaders in the United States in the twentieth century. Above all, through telling his personal story via oral history, I hope that readers, including students and teachers—of all ethnic backgrounds—will be inspired to carry on Sal Castro's struggle for educational justice.

Pedagogy of Chicano Power

Sal Castro, Paulo Freire, and the Mexican American
Youth Leadership Conferences, 1963–1968

Mario T. García

"Blowout, blowout," one high school student began to call out on a sunny spring day in 1968. Soon thousands more echoed the call. This began what came to be called the blowouts. These Chicano high school and junior high school students walked out of the East Los Angeles public schools and demanded better education after years of unequal and inferior schooling in segregated so-called Mexican schools. Standing in the halls on the first full day of the blowouts, teacher Sal Castro looked on with pride and emotion as his students took up the call to take their future into their own hands. Tears streaked down from his eyes. These were his kids, and he was proud of them.

There is no question in my mind that the blowouts would not have occurred without the galvanizing and inspiring figure of Sal Castro, one of the few Mexican American teachers in the Eastside schools and in the Los Angeles school district at the time. It was Sal (as he is popularly referred to) who came up with the idea of the walkouts and, through his leadership and that of the students, pulled it off. The blowouts were a defining moment for him and for the students who participated. As Carlos Muñoz correctly notes, the walkouts inaugurated the urban Chicano civil and cultural rights Movement.[1]

But were the blowouts the result of the spontaneity that 1960s New Left political culture favored or was it something else? The blowouts were definitely not spontaneous. Much planning had gone into this dramatic action. For weeks, Sal, working with the high school student leaders and with some of the Chicano college students (most of whom had attended the East L.A. schools), had been organizing for the walkouts. Yet the origins of one of the most important episodes in the history of the Chicano Movement had even deeper roots. Those roots were planted in what came to be known as the

Chicano Youth Leadership Conferences (CYLC) during the 1960s, which led up to the blowouts. I argue that in these conferences Sal Castro, along with the Chicano students who attended, engaged in the type of conscious-ness-raising dialogues that are identified with the work of the progressive Brazilian and Latin American educational philosopher Paulo Freire. It was these dialogues, unconsciously employing Freireian strategies and con-cepts, that created the *conscientización* that led to the blowouts. Sal Castro was not aware of Freire. Indeed, Freire and his work were not well known in the United States in the 1960s. His most famous book, which would inspire many liberationists throughout the world, *Pedagogy of the Oppressed*, was not published until 1970. Nevertheless, as I will suggest, many of Freire's concepts of how to achieve a liberating and humanistic education that will achieve progressive social change can be seen in the dialogical relationship between teacher Sal Castro, on the one hand, and the Chicano student par-ticipants at the leadership conferences, on the other.

The concept or theory of dialogue as proposed by Freire is important, it seems to me, as a means of analysis for three basic reasons. First, it helps us to understand the dynamics of what seemed to be occurring at the youth lead-ership conferences during the 1960s and how Sal Castro's and the students' version of dialogue led to a growing political Chicano consciousness that in time erupted into political protest. Second, the youth leadership dialogues in this heavily political period in U.S. history suggest that what was happen-ing at these conferences was very much in tune with the culture of protest of that era rather than in isolation from it, and not only within the country but internationally as well. What was happening at the conferences was also happening in other locations, including Latin America, where Freire initi-ated dialogue with peasants and urban workers. Sal Castro and the students may not have been aware of some or all of these connections, but the fact is that they were influenced by the protest and even revolutionary politics of their time, and, I would propose, they contributed to it. This would support Jorge Mariscal's recent revisionist view of the Chicano Movement as being less nationalistic and more internationalist than earlier thought.[2] Finally, examining the relationship of Freire to the youth leadership conferences and the progressive role that the process of dialogue played can make us reflect today on how we are approaching education and whether our praxis is also liberating and humanistic.

IN *PEDAGOGY OF THE OPPRESSED*, Freire defines dialogue in the following manner: "In order to understand the meaning of dialogical practice, we have to put aside the simplistic understanding of dialogue as a mere technique. . . . On the contrary, dialogue characterizes an epistemological (or learning) relationship. Thus, in this sense, dialogue is a way of knowing and should never be viewed as a mere tactic to involve students in a particular task. We have to make this point very clear. I engage in dialogue not necessarily because I like the other person. I engage in dialogue because I recognize the social and not merely the individualistic character of the process of knowing. In this sense, dialogue presents itself as an indispensable component of the process of both learning and knowing."[3]

Although this definition does not include all of the different aspects of Freireian dialogue that we will explore in relationship to Sal and the youth leadership conferences, it does emphasize two key points. One is that dialogue is not just an educational strategy—it is a philosophy of liberation, or what Stanley Aranowitz calls a "secular liberation theology."[4]

Dialogue not only frees the mind; it frees the human being. But, and this is the second point, this liberation is not only an individual one but also a social one. Dialogue presupposes community and the liberation of that community through a praxis of critical consciousness and social action.

One of the initial tenets of Freire's pedagogy of dialogue is the role of individual and group experience in shaping that dialogue. Dialogue does not occur in a vacuum. Each person involved brings his or her baggage of experiences that, as Freire suggests, are transferred into knowledge.[5] These experiences lay the foundation for discussion, analysis, understanding, and action. This is clearly the case with Sal Castro. "The concrete situation of individuals conditions their consciousness of the world," Freire observes; "in turn this consciousness conditions their attitude and their way of dealing with reality."[6]

Thus, one needs to understand Sal's life experiences prior to the youth conferences in order to better appreciate his role in those gatherings of Mexican American students. Sal did not just appear at those meetings ready to motivate the students to participate in a dramatic action such as the blowouts. Like all of us, Sal went through a process of becoming who he was by the 1960s. The process, of course, continued, as it continues even today. None of us, including Sal, ever stop becoming. We constantly change.

What Sal brought to these early conferences was a history of experiencing discrimination against Mexicans in Los Angeles. This profoundly affected his identity and political consciousness.

Sal was born in Los Angeles on October 25, 1933, a child of immigrant parents from Mexico who settled in the Boyle Heights barrio of East Los Angeles. Sal was too young to fully comprehend at the time the meaning of the mass deportation of Mexicans from L.A. during the Great Depression, but he knew that it affected him personally. His father became one of the deportees after his temporary visa expired and he became an undocumented immigrant. He returned to his native Mazatlán. Sal's mother had a valid visa but had to return to Mexico every six months to renew it. Sal recalls the train trips as a child that he took with his mother to visit his father in Mazatlán and for his mother to renew her visa. The stress on Sal's parents eventually led to a divorce.[7]

Because he spoke only Spanish at home, although his mother was bilingual, and because he started his education in Mexico due to his mother's visits to Mazatlán, Sal knew very little English when he began his U.S. education at Belvedere Elementary School. As a result, he encountered discrimination at the hands of his teacher. "My English wasn't so hot," he notes. "I knew much more Spanish. I remember distinctly how the teacher would put me down because of my lack of English. 'Sit in the corner until you learn English,' she scolded me."[8]

Still other acts of discrimination against him and other Mexican Americans followed that Sal remembers. But he also was affected by how his mother stood up to some of this prejudice. For example, when Sal's mother requested that her son be allowed to leave school early in order to study for his First Communion at their Catholic Church, Sal's teacher refused and threatened to suspend Sal if he did. Sal's mother was outraged and saw it as discrimination against Mexican American Catholics. "Sal's my son," she told the teacher, "and he's going to his First Communion class. And if you don't accept him back, I'm going to speak to your boss!" The teacher relented, and Sal, no doubt with admiration, witnessed his mother's courage and leadership.[9]

When Sal was ten years old and shining shoes to earn some money on the corner of 7th and Broadway in downtown L.A., in 1943, he experienced the Zoot-Suit Riots, in which U.S. Navy personnel randomly attacked Chicanos wearing the infamous zoot-suit, popular at the time. They also assaulted, according to Sal, other Chicanos who were not wearing "drapes," all of this symptomatic of wartime racial tensions, ironically during a war against fascist racism. Sal remembers all hell breaking loose and seeing police just stand by while the sailors beat Chicanos. He also recalls the curfew that local authorities imposed due to the riots and a tragic consequence that affected him personally.

"One kid that I knew from Belvedere Elementary," he told me, "went to get a loaf of bread and went through the alley, thinking he could avoid the curfew. The cops shot him in the back and killed him. He was twelve years old."[10]

As a young boy, Sal, along with other Mexican Americans, had to further live the indignity of not being allowed to attend public swimming pools, such as the one on Vermont, except on Wednesdays, the day reserved for Mexicans, blacks, and Asians—the day before they cleaned the pool.[11]

Sal continued his education in Catholic rather than public schools, but this did not mean that he was exempt from additional discrimination. At the all-boys Cathedral High School run by the Christian Brothers, he, along with most other Mexican American students, were tracked into what was referred to as the Spanish track, as opposed to the Latin track, with mostly Anglos. The Spanish track signified that these students studied Spanish and not Latin, and, further, this curriculum was less college oriented. As a result, Sal observed that most Mexican Americans, in addition to regular although less advanced basic classes, also took industrial arts, such as auto shop.[12]

After he was drafted into the army, in 1953, a year after high school graduation, Sal witnessed even more discrimination against blacks, Latinos, and Mexican Americans. Stationed in the South, he encountered the apartheid system of that region. "I was in a state of shock when I got off the plane in Atlanta," he remembers. "Both at the airport and at the bus station, they had four separate bathrooms: colored men, colored women, white men, white women. And they had two drinking fountains. This was all brand-new to me."[13]

He also observed similar discrimination against some of his black Puerto Rican buddies in the army, who were not served in restaurants but had to go to the back of these establishments to get food. "So I witnessed Jim Crow firsthand," Sal says, "and I thought it was chicken shit."[14]

Sal himself, although light-skinned, was not spared such racism, especially in Texas. On a flight from Los Angeles to Jackson, Mississippi, he had a layover in Dallas, where he went into an airport restaurant to eat. "I had my uniform on," Sal tells the story. "When you come out of basic training, you look like a general. I go over to the airport restaurant and those sons of bitches wouldn't serve me. They still remember the Alamo. This was in 1954. I was in the U.S. Army uniform—not the Mexican Army, the U.S. Army!"[15]

Despite these encounters with discrimination and despite his own rebellious nature, Sal, through this period in his life, did not have a developed political awareness of the reasons for this discrimination. These experiences were leading him to questions about this problem, questions that would lead to his later and greater understanding, but he had to first struggle against what he and W. E. B. Du Bois called a "double consciousness." Of this Sal notes: "I knew there was discrimination and racism. I had pride in who I was, but at the same time I was self-blaming. The reason why all this is happening to us is our fault. Sort of a weird mind-set in those days."[16]

By the late 1950s, however, Sal began to overcome this duality as he worked at public playgrounds, where he learned from the Mexican American kids about the problems that they were experiencing in the schools. At the same time, after enrolling at Los Angeles State College (later called Cal State, L.A.), Sal decided to study to become a teacher. After receiving his BA in history/education in 1961, he entered the credential program in education, for which he wrote a thesis comparing Mexican American student performances with those of Mexican immigrant students. He discovered that the immigrant students performed better than the Mexican Americans, despite the fact that English was not their native language. Sal concluded that the reason was that many of the immigrant students had been exposed to better earlier education in Mexico and that they as *mexicanos* possessed a certain confidence in who they were, as opposed to the Mexican Americans, who, like himself, were more ambivalent and less secure in their identities. As Sal, through his college classes, began to ask questions in the tradition of Paulo Freire that would lead to a more liberating consciousness, he began to have a better understanding of the structural basis for the discrimination that Mexican Americans experienced and that prevented their greater mobility.[17]

This growing awareness and political consciousness, in addition to his increasingly outspoken personality, led Sal to confront his own education professors, who, in Sal's opinion, had negative and stereotypical views about Mexican American students when they addressed the problems of these students. Sal challenged these views and corrected them, based on his own experiences, his working with kids in the playgrounds, and his own research. "By then," Sal notes of his evolution, "I started feeling that some of the things they [his professors] were telling us about [Mexican American] kids were not necessarily true. They stereotyped the kids too much, and they were not really getting into how to motivate them. They saw all kids as white kids, and that wasn't really the facts. I remember one professor saying that what you saw in *West Side Story* [the movie] was the way [Latino] gang kids were. I said, 'That's bullshit. First of all, *West Side Story* is the figment of the imagination of a white guy. Second, if there really was a "West Side Story," the Puerto Ricans would never dance to that kind of music they played in the damn movie anyway. That's a myth.'"[18]

It was these experiences and others that Sal Castro brought with him as he embarked on a teaching career, beginning in 1963 in the Pasadena public schools, then at Belmont High School, and finally at Lincoln High School, where he would organize the 1968 blowouts. Sal's encounter with discrimination and racism at a personal level and his evolving political consciousness that would lead to *conscientización*, to use the Freireian term, led him to understand that Mexican Americans had to shed what Sal calls "self-hatred" and begin to understand that it was the system that had to be attacked as the source of the educational, as well as the social, problems faced by Mexican Americans and other minorities in the United States. This is what Sal would bring to the table in his encounters with Mexican American students at the youth leadership conferences during the politically tumultuous decade of the 1960s. But, to further the Freireian connection, this encounter would not be a monologue on the part of Sal; it would be a dialogue with the students, who also brought their experiences and evolving identities to the conferences. Out of this dialogue—a changing dialogue, involving new students each year—would come a more critical consciousness on the part of both Sal and the students. These dialogues would involve a praxis, again borrowing from Freire, that included not only reflection but action. That action would culminate in the blowouts.[19]

In this section, I want to note some of Sal's memories—a collective memory—of the initial conferences that led up to the blowouts. Little research has been done on the youth leadership conferences, and my oral history with Sal is a way of bringing light and attention to their importance.

The initial conference took place in 1963, over the Palm Sunday weekend. The conference was initially called Spanish Speaking Youth Leadership Conference—changed to Mexican American Youth Leadership Conference in 1965, the name it would carry into the early 1970s, when it was changed to Chicano Youth Leadership Conference (CYLC).[20] The change in names clearly underscores the evolving ethnic and political identities of the participants. The conference was organized by the Los Angeles County Commission on Human Relations, due to growing concerns of some public officials, some educators, and some Mexican American leaders about the myriad problems that Mexican American students seemed to be facing in the public schools, including high drop-out rates and low college matriculation. The conference was an effort to encourage students to stay in school, to do well, and to continue on to college. Tobias Kotzin, who owned a trouser factory in Los Angeles with mostly Mexican American employees and who served on the Human Relations Commission, provided the initial funding for the conference. Arrangements were made to hold the conference at a Jewish recreational camp called Camp Hess Kramer in the Malibu Mountains off Pacific Coast Highway. The date available for the first conference and subsequent ones was the Palm Sunday weekend.[21]

Sal became aware of the conference when he read an announcement asking for adults with experience working with youth to apply to be counselors at the camp. With his background as a playground supervisor and his initial teaching at Washington Junior High in Pasadena, Sal applied and was accepted. The staff selected was small and included a few teachers, such as Sal, along with social workers, police and sheriff personnel, and those already working for the county. The students themselves were selected by their schools or by members of the Human Relations Commission. Students, for the most part working class in origin, came not only from the predominantly Mexican American schools of East Los Angeles but also from other county schools as well. About 100 students, all high school juniors, attended the first conference.[22]

At the initial conferences, Sal first encountered what Freire also had noticed: the lack of self-esteem and even feelings of inferiority on the part of some of the students and staff. Freire notes that this is partly the result of what he calls the "antidialogical" nature of public education, whereby students are not allowed to possess a voice or positive identity. They are told what to think rather than encouraged to think. This one-way pedagogy Freire terms "cultural invasion." "For cultural invasion to succeed," he notes, "it is essential that those invaded become convinced of their intrinsic inferiority." To compensate for this, the students and oppressed assume a form of "false consciousness," where they take on the views of the oppressors. They have no consciousness of their oppressed status. They possess what Freire calls a "fear of freedom."[23]

Sal recalls, for example, that most of the other staff members did not have much of a critical perspective on education or the schools. Some, according to him, were "self-haters" who blamed Mexican Americans for their problems. They were not "change agents" or risk takers. The conferences themselves were structured in a very traditional and assimilationist format.[24] Topics discussed at the early conferences included education, civic awareness, acculturation, marriage, and employment.[25] Sal also discovered that some of the students had low opinions of themselves and of their community. Sal found himself, from the very beginning, having to counter these views and offering a different interpretation to the students.[26]

TO SHIFT FROM an antidialogical process to a dialogical process, Freire observes that certain steps must be taken. First is the role of the teacher. He/she must not be afraid to enter into a dialogue with the students on the basis of trust. The teacher also should not see himself/herself as possessing the truth or all knowledge and certainly not as the liberator of the students. Very important, the teacher must work not *for* the students but *with* the students. "Revolutionary leaders," Freire observes, "cannot think *without* the people, nor *for* the people, but only *with* the people."[27] But to work with the students, the teacher must begin the dialogue by meeting the students at their level, based on their experiences and knowledge. He/she must first come to them, rather than the students coming up to the teacher's level. Of this, Freire stresses: "Revolutionary teachers do not go to the people in order to bring them a message of 'salvation,' but in order to come to know through dialogue with them both their *objective situation* and their *awareness* of that situation—the various levels of perception of themselves and of the world in which and with which they exist. One cannot expect positive results from an educational or political action program which fails to respect the particular view of the world held by the people."[28]

To achieve a liberating dialogue, the teacher must further develop an effective communication with the students. This, in turn, leads to cooperation, or what Freire terms "authentic thinking," that is, the dialogical synthesis of both teacher and students. "The teacher cannot think for her students," he cautions. "Authentic thinking, thinking that is concerned about *reality*, does not take place in ivory tower isolation, but only in communication."[29] This does not mean that the teacher necessarily takes a backseat to the students, but only that the teacher does not dominate the dialogue. The teacher initiates the dialogue and helps to direct it by his or her "critical intervention," a term that Freire borrows from Georg Lukács.[30]

In this dialogue, the students play a critical and equal role with the teacher. They bring their experiences and knowledge to the process. Discarding their passivity, they get the chance, as Freire puts it, to name the world.[31] "The important thing, from the point of view of liberation education," Freire stresses, "is for the people to come to feel like masters of their thinking by discovering the thinking and views of the world explicitly and implicitly manifest in their own suggestions and those of their comrades."[32]

This cooperative dialogue, in turn, results in both teacher and students exercising their subjectivity. They are both historical subjects and what Freire calls "co-investigators." They both learn from each other. The teacher becomes student and the student becomes teacher. This is what Freire refers to as "co-intentional education." "Through dialogue," he points out, "the teacher-of-the students and the students-of-the-teacher cease to exist and a new term emerges: teacher-students with students-teacher. The teacher is no longer merely the-one-who-teaches, but one who is himself taught in dialogue with the students, who in turn while being taught also teach."[33] The end result is what Freire refers to as a "cultural synthesis" between teacher and students.[34]

These Freireian concepts of liberation education can be detected in the relationship of Sal Castro with the Chicano students at the Camp Hess Kramer conferences in the 1960s. Sal shared his experiences with the students, but he did not impose his views on them. He worked to establish a dialogue with them so that they could teach themselves and so that he would also learn from them.

Although some perhaps have the view that Sal Castro, from the very beginning, was the key director of the conferences, in fact, as he explains, he was always behind the scenes in working with the kids, at least in the 1960s. He did his work with them and dialogued with them in the small group discussion sessions, in informal "buzz sessions," and in table hopping at mealtimes, where he could reach other students.[35] In the small group encounters, Sal did not do all of the talking. That went against his pedagogy. He didn't need to talk, because many of the students took the lead in discussing and sharing school problems. "I would throw out something and let it spin," he says. "They talked about problems in the schools, and they all had the same problems," he adds. "They felt free to open up."[36] The format of these discussion groups aided such student participation by stressing that counselors such as Sal prioritize student discourse and provide a "safe" place for students to open up.[37] When the students asked his views or if they diverted from the main points only then would Sal reinforce the dialogue and try to put it in an even-more-critical perspective. Guiding Sal's pedagogy was his overall philosophy about the conferences. "What I wanted out of these conferences," he emphasizes, "was a positive self-image and self-confidence for the students so they would go on ahead and know who the real enemy was and go on to achieve and go on to college despite the lack of encouragement by the schools." He also hoped and expected that the Camp Hess Kramer graduates would later in life provide leadership for the Mexican American community as a way of giving back to it, but all this not as apologists of the system but as critics of it. In a way, without knowing it, Sal was adopting a Saul Alinsky philosophy of "not working with the system but within it."[38]

The dialogues at Camp Hess Kramer in the years before the blowouts consisted of the shared experiences between Sal and the students. Some of the key issues involved the following:

Sal and the students recognized the low number of Chicano students matriculating in college. Very few applied to college, and even fewer were accepted. This was not because students did not want to go to college or might have entertained the idea if encouraged to do so. The problem was the lack of encouragement on the part of both teachers and counselors.[39]

The low number of students going on to college was further linked to the lack of college counselors in the East L.A. high schools. Each counselor carried a workload of about 500 students. Most, according to Sal, just told the kids to graduate and get a job. "A Mexican kid had to really shine in order for the counselors to go out of their way to counsel them to go to college," Sal observes.[40] Students at the conference complained that they were lucky to see a counselor once a semester, and then usually for only five minutes.[41]

The lack of college counseling in turn was the result of the low expectations of the mostly Anglo teachers and counselors for the academic abilities of Chicano students. They believed that the students were low achievers, and so teachers aimed at the lowest common denominator. "They're going to forget everything and go back to Mexico," some teachers would tell Sal. At Lincoln High School, some of the students only took morning classes and then were taken to the auditorium to watch films and, in fact, were charged twenty-five cents to raise funds for the school.[42]

Further limiting the education of Chicano students was the notorious tracking system, which Sal himself had faced in his high school years. Most Chicano students, based on so-called achievement tests, were tracked into vocational classes with only limited academic ones. Sal and the students at Camp Hess Kramer shared their stories about this tracking. Counselors and teachers tracked the boys into auto body shop, electrical shop, and wood shop. "They were making coffins," Sal recalls of the boys at Lincoln High. In turn, the girls went to secretarial "science" classes, business education, and, of course, home economics. In cooking classes, Sal notes that they learned how to cook Anglo food. "Nobody was teaching them to make tamales, healthy tamales," he says. "It was hotcakes and all that other good stuff."[43] One female student added: "They assume that you can't take anything more than homemaking or family planning."[44]

Students also discussed the low reading levels of many of the Chicano students and how little teachers did to correct this. Sal did what he could in his own classes but couldn't compensate for the lack of attention to this problem by other teachers. "It was bad," he observed. "You had to make sure they [the students] had a dictionary right next to them so they knew what the hell the word meant."[45] Students at the youth conferences likewise came to understand that this problem had to do with the low quality of their education rather than their own intelligence. "All these Mexican kids are not stupid," Tanya Luna Mount, a student at Roosevelt High, asserted. "You can't tell me that these kids are stupid. You can't."[46]

Overcrowded conditions in the schools were still another complaint voiced by the students. It was not unusual, Sal remembers, for forty or more students to be in a classroom. This obviously limited the ability of any teacher to be effective.[47]

The lack of bilingual education, in addition, affected the progress of some of the students who entered high school after arriving from Mexico. "It was taboo," Sal says about bilingual education. The schools prohibited the use of Spanish for any form of communication. Sal complained that the few other Mexican American teachers in the schools were intimidated into not using Spanish to speak to the kids. Did Sal use Spanish in the school? "Hell, yes," he says. "My ideas in teaching were different. I was always hearing a different drummer."[48]

Students also complained about corporal punishment in the schools, and Sal corroborated their stories of such abuse. At Lincoln High, for example, teachers swatted the boys with a paddle with holes in it so it could swing with more force. "I could hear the whack," Sal recalls. Administrators did not hit girls but instead suspended them for the day and sent them home.[49]

Adding to the insecurity and low-esteem of the students, Sal believes, was the total absence in history and social science classes of the historical and cultural contributions of people of Mexican descent in the United States. Sal, himself, had not learned about this in his own educational experiences. However, while attending L.A. City College, he came across Carey McWilliams's *North from Mexico*, first published in 1948 and the first substantive history of Mexican Americans. Reading McWilliams significantly affected his historical consciousness and his evolving critique of U.S. society, especially regarding the treatment of minorities. Taking a U.S. history class at City College from a socialist professor further provided Sal with a critical perspective. This view of history, including the integration of Mexican American history into his own classes later in the 1960s, undoubtedly extended into his dialogues with students at Hess Kramer in Sal's efforts to promote ethnic and cultural pride among them. Vicki Castro recalls that she learned about Chicano and Mexican history at the conferences.[50]

Reflecting this critical perspective, one female student at the 1967 conference exclaimed at the general assembly: "How can we as Chicanos find out who we are when our textbooks label Pancho Villa a criminal?"[51] And still another at the same conference provided a form of internal colonial interpretation, remarkable in this pre–Chicano Studies period, by rejecting a suggestion that Mexican Americans were immigrants to the United States when she added: "When you say we came to America, that's not right because America came to us because Mexicans were here first."[52]

As part of his critique of U.S. history, Sal, both in his classes and at Hess Kramer, encouraged the students to discuss the black civil rights movement, as well as the Vietnam War. Sal and the students saw the linkages between the struggle of African Americans and Chicanos. In the case of Vietnam, Sal discussed with the students the injustice of many white kids being able to avoid the draft by going to college while Chicano boys could not, since many were not encouraged to do so. "It bothered me that so many Chicano kids were being killed in Vietnam, and I told the kids this." He and the students reflected on the toll that the war was having on Chicanos by discussing the Wall of Honor at Lincoln High. This was a monument to the boys who went to Vietnam. One side listed the names of all those who went to the war while the other side listed those who died in the conflict. Both sides, according to Sal, were about equal. "That bothered me," Sal said. Sal and the students were likewise critical of the heavy emphasis placed on ROTC in the Eastside schools, which only further steered Chicano boys into the military and on to Vietnam.[53]

The dialogues at Hess Kramer focused not only on the schools as the causes of the educational problems of Chicano students but also on bad decisions made by the students themselves. Here, the issue of teenage pregnancy was of significance. It was recognized that part of the problem, of course, was that the schools failed to address the issue. But students also had to be held responsible. "Your parents didn't send you to school to find a wife or a husband," Sal discussed. "It's ridiculous—once you do get pregnant," he told the girls, "it's all over. You can't go back to school."[54]

Because of all of these problems in the schools, Chicano student drop-out rates were exceedingly high. In some of the Eastside schools, such as Lincoln, the dropout rate was 50 percent. Most dropped out by the ninth grade. Sal and the students at Hess Kramer examined the causes of this condition. They concluded that the problem lay in the schools' inability to relate to the

Chicano student. Education was geared to white, middle-class students and not to minority ones. As a result, Chicano kids felt alienated and insecure in a school setting. Teachers, counselors, and principals did not respect who they were and what they represented. Their cultural and historical backgrounds were not taken into consideration, and their parents—mostly poor, working class, and Spanish speaking—were looked down upon. As a result, Chicano students did not so much drop out as they were "kicked out."[55]

These disturbing conditions in the schools no doubt also encouraged a sense of victimization. However, Sal, both at Hess Kramer and at Lincoln, intervened to discourage a culture of victimization. He encouraged the students to work hard to overcome these obstacles and to believe that they had the agency and ability to do so. The dialogues were not intended to just decry conditions; they were intended to raise the kids' consciousness as to the sources of the problems and to motivate them to take their lives into their own individual and collective hands. "I expected them to achieve," Sal stresses. "There was no reason why they couldn't. I had high expectations of them. I constantly and positively motivated them. . . . As far as I was concerned, they were going to college. . . . Nothing says you can't do it, because you are. And that's the way it's going to be. . . . The way you fight back is by a book. Salvation is getting an education."[56]

AS PART OF THE PEDAGOGY of the oppressed, Freire advanced the concept of "problem-solving education." By this, he meant that traditional education that upheld the ideology of the oppressors had to be challenged by an education that focused on "the problems of human beings in their relations with the world."[57] Problem-solving education further consisted of what Freire called "thematic investigation," which involved examining not just a part of the problem but also the totality of it. In this process, the people—or, in this case, Sal and the students—through dialogue, would be able to, as Freire puts it, name their oppressor. Naming the oppressor meant understanding the causes of their problems and not just the symptoms. As a result, they would, as Richard Shaull asserts in his foreword to *Pedagogy*, "realize that the educational system today—from kindergarten to university—is their enemy."[58]

This shift to a problem-solving education characterized the Hess Kramer conferences. Through dialogue, the students, with Sal's critical intervention, came to name the source of their problems: the educational system. Sal stresses that by arriving at a positive self-image of themselves and self-confidence as a result of the conferences, the Chicano students "would go on ahead and know who the real enemy was and go on to achieve and go on to college despite the lack of encouragement by the schools."[59] Sal, in addition, notes: "The reason why kids were aware is because of the Hess Kramer camp. They knew what the problems were and they knew that sooner or later something was going to happen."[60] Former conference participants interviewed by Professor Dolores Delgado Bernal corroborate Sal's conclusion. "I think that [the conference] was the first I have any memory of seeing on a big scope that what I was experiencing in school," Vicki Castro recalls, "was happening all over, and to a higher degree of open racism."[61] And Rosalinda Méndez González remembers: "These youth conferences were the first time that we began to develop a consciousness that we were all a people and that everywhere we were suffering the same experiences, being discriminated against, that we had a history in this country, that we worked the fields, that we have contributed a lot. We had not been acknowledged for what we had contributed, we were American citizens and had been denied our rights."[62]

It is through the pedagogy of dialogue, according to Freire, that a critical consciousness or *conscientización* is arrived at. Freire defines *conscientización* as "learning to perceive social, political, and economic contradictions and to take action against the oppressive elements of reality."[63] Such critical awareness is "real consciousness."[64] *Conscientización*, in the case of education, leads to the conclusion that education is not neutral. It reflects the dominant ideology and perpetuates what Freire calls the "culture of silence" among students.[65] To counter this, liberating education through critical consciousness needs to be transformative, subversive, and "de-ideologizing" of the ideology of the oppressors.[66] *Conscientización* is both self-affirming of the students and critical of the system, with the intent to reconstruct it. This is what Freire labels a "cultural revolution,"[67] or what Dolores Delgado Bernal in her pioneering study of the role of Chicanas in the blowouts calls "transformative resistance."[68]

This *conscientización* is reflected among some of the participants in the Hess Kramer dialogues. Through this process, the students began to realize that their complaints about the schools had to do with the larger educational system. To redress their complaints, they had to challenge the system itself. They began to realize that the system was against them and not for them. "You could see there had been a change," Sal notes of the transformation of the students' consciousness at the end of each conference. "You could see the kids become much more aware. From the time the kids got off the bus on Friday to the Sunday when [they] were leaving, you saw . . . you had been effective in opening the kids' eyes."[69] "These youth conferences,"

Rachael Ochoa Cervera, a participant, told Bernal, "were the first time that we began to develop a consciousness. . . . It was very affirmative. That's where you began to have an identity. You could be more open. You could say what you wanted to."[70] "It changed my whole being," Vicki Castro says of the conferences. "It gave me a voice."[71]

CONSCIENTIZACIÓN THROUGH DIALOGUE, in turn, leads to the subjectivity of the people and students. They move from being objects to becoming subjects. Instead of "being for others," they become "beings for themselves."[72] As subjects, they create history. "I do not accept," Freire stresses, "history as determinism. I embrace history as possibility."[73] The result is the emergence of a "new man" and a "new woman."[74]

As historical subjects, these new men and women are moved to fulfill a praxis that Freire defines as "reflection and action upon the world in order to transform it."[75] Theory and practice are brought together. "In order to be," he adds, "it must become."[76] Through praxis, people are truly humanized. "They will not gain this liberation by chance," Freire concludes, "but through the praxis of their quest for it, through their recognition of the necessity to fight for it."[77]

As the youth leadership conferences continued into the 1960s, this subjectivity and praxis became more evident, culminating in the 1968 blowouts. The critiques of the schools mounted with every new cohort of participants, as well as with Sal's own growing frustrations at the lack of progress in the schools. He also expressed disappointment at the failure of Mexican American political and community leaders to challenge the school system—and at not even addressing the issues. He believed that Mexican Americans were falling further and further behind the black civil rights movement. Something had to be done. Sal recalls that perhaps as early as the 1966 conference he started to discuss some more dramatic action to bring attention to the educational problems. One year later, he definitely had a plan. "I had the plan in my head—that's where it was formulated," he states. The college students were ready to go. "It didn't take much to convince them," Sal remembers. "They were influenced by protests around them on free speech and Vietnam."[78] Early action included some of the students participating in supporting the election of Dr. Julian Nava to the Los Angeles School Board; organizing in Young Citizens for Community Action (YCCA), which led to the Brown Berets; and writing for early Chicano Movement publications such as *Inside Eastside*.[79] Some of the Camp Hess Kramer students on their own conducted a school survey concerning conditions in their Eastside schools.[80]

Beginning with the 1967 conference, which was organized under the theme of *Adelante* (move ahead), as suggested by student participants Isabel Arias and Rachael Ochoa, and into the rest of the year, Sal began to talk about a possible school walkout or strike that would shake the system.[81] At this conference, attended by 200 students, Sal served as chair of the Committee on Content and Format. The committee included former conference participant Vicki Castro, along with five current high school students, among them Arias, Ochoa, and David Sánchez (later the prime minister of the Brown Berets).[82] Besides talking about this at the 1967 conference, Sal also used the gathering to collect a phone bank of student telephone numbers, which would become a critical information network in organizing the blowouts. As Vicki Castro says: "The conferences created a network."[83] "This was before cell phones," Sal, with amusement, observes. Many of the 1967 student cohort would go on to become leaders in their respective schools one year later. The 1967 conference was significant because the 1968 one would take place after the blowouts. Moreover, some of the college-age counselors at the 1967 conference (many if not all of them alumni of previous conferences) would also help plan the walkouts and assist the high school and junior high school students in the historic protests of 1968.[84] A television reporter captured the zeitgeist of the conference when he concluded: "The main impression we bring back is that of a mood of impatience, a growing sense of urgency. The young Mexican American is tired of waiting for the Promised Land. As one of them told us: 'It must be today, not manana.'"[85]

"The conferences were the backbone of the blowouts," Sal concludes, "because the kids had discussed the problems there."[86] Indeed, the effects of the blowouts can be seen in the 1968 conference program, which directly addresses the walkouts and expresses much more critical perspectives, including referring to Mexican Americans as a conquered people as a result of the Treaty of Guadalupe Hidalgo following the U.S.-Mexico War of the 1840s. "The school walk-outs and rioting that has been going on in our country means that something is wrong in our society," the program reads. "Because of the walk-outs and the rioting, good leadership is needed to right wrongs and build a better society, and a healthy share of this leadership must come from Mexican American youth."[87]

LET ME CONCLUDE by saying that what I have learned about the youth leadership conferences from my interviews with Sal Castro reinforces my understanding and that of others that the conferences served to politicize a new generation of Chicano students, who participated not only in the blowouts but in the Chicano Movement as a whole. My oral history substantiates the importance of Sal Castro's role in the conferences through his work and discussions with the students, including sharing his own experiences with discrimination and his views that the educational system had to be confronted ultimately through nonviolent direct action, such as the blowouts. But I've also learned through my oral history that it wasn't just Sal and the conferences that led to this politicization and critical consciousness on the part of the students. The students themselves, through engaging in a form of Freireian dialogue, served as historical subjects in the development of a progressive and oppositional praxis. "The demands of the blow-outs were reforms," Juan Gómez-Quiñones notes. "Nonetheless they reflected opposition to cultural and national oppression."[88] Although the blowouts began a process of change in the educational system, they did not fully transform it. Many more struggles would be needed, as they still are needed. But what the Hess Kramer conferences and the blowouts changed was the consciousness of the students themselves. As the character of Paula Crisostomo says in the film *Walkout*, when confronted with the lack of change: "The schools might not have changed, but we did." It is this spirit of critical consciousness and the struggle for social justice that is the legacy of the leadership conferences and the blowouts. This is also the legacy of a remarkable individual, teacher, counselor, and leader: Sal Castro.

APPENDIX Chicano Movement Historiography

Despite the importance of the Chicano Movement, it is only recently that historians have begun to substantially study different aspects of the Movement. This is understandable—as is the case with all historical periods, a certain amount of time has to elapse for historians to begin to have a better perspective from which to study the past. The historical literature on the Chicano Movement to date consists of three basic genres or subfields: (1) scholarly researched texts; (2) autobiographies and memoirs by some Movement activists; and (3) edited collections concerning Movement subjects. Together, these areas of publications have established an important foundation or threshold for the study of the Movement and for the further advancement of Movement studies.

First, allow me to comment on the place of César Chávez and the farmworkers' struggle. Initially, I believed that Chávez and the farmworkers represented more of a precursor movement to the Chicano Movement. However, after further study, I now conclude that the "fight in the fields" in fact is an essential beginning of the Movement and a major part of it. It is César and the farmworkers' struggle for human dignity, social justice, civil rights, and labor rights and the important utilization by Chávez of Mexican cultural symbols that significantly influenced the politics and discourse (Viva La Causa!) of the urban Chicano Movement. Because César Chávez and the farmworkers captured national media attention and César became the best-known Mexican American civil rights leader, equated some times with Martin Luther King Jr., the literature on him and the farmworkers is extensive. This literature can be considered part of Movement studies, but in other respects it is a field unto itself. It also predates the development of Chicano Studies. It is, at the same time, a field that has been more characterized by journalistic writing and autobiographical texts and less based on substantive scholarship. For these reasons, I will not consider this literature here but will only refer to some of the more scholarly texts that emanate from a Chicano Studies background. These include Richard Griswold del Castillo and Richard A. García's very useful and interpretive *César Chávez: A Triumph of Spirit*; Frederick John Dalton's pioneering study of the religious and spiritual influences on Chávez, *The Moral Vision of César Chávez;* and Susan Ferris and Ricardo Sandoval's fine general history based on much oral history, *The Fight in the Fields: César Chávez and the Farmworkers Movement*. Curiously, no major biography based on archival research on Chávez has so far been published, although Professor Stephen Pitti of Yale University is working on what may prove to be the definitive study of this major American labor, civil rights, and spiritual leader. César never wrote his own autobiography, but the closest thing to it is the classic study by Jacques Levy based on extensive oral history, *Cesar Chavez: Autobiography of La Causa*.[1] See also Randy Shaw, *Beyond the Fields: César Chávez, the UFW, and the Struggle for Justice in the 21st Century*; and Miriam Powell, *The Union of Their Dreams: Power, Hope, and Struggle in César Chávez's Farm Worker Movement*.[2]

With respect to the Chicano Movement, especially in the urban areas, scholarly researched texts, although limited, can be divided into several subtopics. First, there are a few studies that document and analyze the overall ideological tenets of the Movement. One such early study is Gerald Paul Rosen's 1972 dissertation at UCLA, "Political Ideology and the Chicano Movement: A Study of the Political Ideology of Activists in the Chicano Movement," which focuses on the Movement in Los Angeles. A post-Movement analysis of *Chicanismo*, the proclaimed ideology or spirit of the Movement, is Ignacio M. García's *Chicanismo: The Forging of a Militant Ethos among Mexican Americans*. More recently, Jorge Mariscal, in *Brown-Eyed Children of the Sun: Lessons from the Chicano Movement, 1965–1975*, reassess the so-called cultural nationalism of the Movement and suggests a stronger internationalism than had previously been stressed.[3]

Students, as part of the new Chicano Generation, have been the subjects of Movement scholarship. One early overview, written by a Movement activist and intellectual, is Juan Gómez-Quiñones, *Mexican Students Por La Raza: The Chicano Student Movement in Southern California, 1967–1977*. Still another study by an activist/intellectual is Carlos Muñoz's *Youth, Identity, Power: The Chicano Movement*, which also focuses on the greater Los Angeles area. An excellent study of female students in the 1968 blowouts is Dolores Delgado Bernal's 1997 UCLA dissertation, "Chicana School Resistance and Grassroots Leadership: Providing an Alternative History of the 1968 East Los Angeles Blowouts." For the Texas Chicano student movement, an excellent study is Armando Navarro's *Mexican American Youth Organization: Avant-Garde of the Chicano Movement*. José Angel Gutiérrez, another activist/intellectual from Texas, has more recently written *We Won't Back Down: Severita Lara's Rise from Student Leader to Mayor*.[4] An excellent recent dissertation on the Chicano student movement in California is Marisol Moreno's "Of the Community, for the Community: The Chicana/o Student Movement in California's Public Higher Education, 1967–1973" (Ph.D. diss., University of California, Santa Barbara, 2009).

A third area covers specific studies of particular Movement communities. Los Angeles is the focus of two such studies: Marguerite V. Marín's *Social Protest in an Urban Barrio: A Study of the Chicano Movement, 1966–1974*; and Ernesto Chávez's very useful *Mi Raza Primero: Nationalism, Identity, and Insurgency in the Chicano Movement in Los Angeles, 1966–1978*. Denver is the focus of another activist/intellectual's work, Ernesto B. Vigil's pioneering study, *The Crusade for Justice: Chicano Militancy and the Government's War on Dissent.*[5] An even more recent and important case study, of San Antonio, is David Montejano's *Quixote's Soldiers: A Local History of the Chicano Movement, 1966–1981.*[6]

The Raza Unida Party, the Movement's independent political party, is the subject of some of the best Movement historiography, beginning with Ignacio M. García's pioneering *United We Win: The Rise and Fall of La Raza Unida Party* and followed by two major studies by Armando Navarro: *The Cristal Experiment: A Chicano Struggle for Community Control* and *La Raza Unida Party: A Chicano Challenge to the U.S. Two-Party Dictatorship.*[7] In part focusing on La Raza Unida Party but also introducing an innovative and important transregional perspective on Chicano Movement activism is Marc Rodríguez's forthcoming study, "Mexican Americanism: The Tejano Diaspora and Ethnic Politics in Texas and Wisconsin after 1960."[8]

The significant Chicano antiwar movement is the focus of Lorena Oropeza's excellent *Raza Si, Guerra No! Chicano Protest and Patriotism during the Vietnam War Era.*[9]

Biographies of key Movement leaders to date have been quite scarce. Rudy Busto's study of Reies López Tijerina, *King Tiger: The Religious Vision of Reies López Tijerina*, although not fully a biography, does cover the key periods in Tijerina's life, with a focus on his evolving religious views.[10] A short biographical study of Corky Gonzales is Christine Marin's *A Spokesman of the Mexican American Movement: Rodolfo "Corky" Gonzales and the Fight for Chicano Liberation, 1966–1972* (San Francisco: R and E Research Associates, 1977).

The role of religion in the Chicano Movement has represented a major gap in the consideration of the Movement, with the slight exception of César Chávez and the farmworkers' struggle. However, two recent texts about the role of clergy in the Movement help fill in that gap: Lara Medina's *Las Hermanas: Chicana/Latina Religious-Political Activism in the U.S. Catholic*

Church; and Richard Edward Martínez, P*adres*: *The National Chicano Priest Movement*.[11] In addition, in my own *Católicos: Resistance and Affirmation in Chicano Catholic History*, I include an extensive chapter on Católicos Por La Raza, a Chicano Movement group in Los Angeles, inspired by Catholic liberation theology, to confront the Church hierarchy about responding more positively to poverty and empowerment issues in the Chicano community. I have also attempted to bring greater attention to the role of religion and spirituality in the life and leadership of César Chávez, in my edited volume, *The Gospel of César Chávez: My Faith in Action*.[12] See also José-Antonio Orosco, *César Chávez and the Common Sense of Nonviolence*.[13]

Legal issues, primarily the prosecution of Movement activists, is the emphasis of Ian F. Haney López's excellent study, *Racism on Trial: The Chicano Fight for Justice*.[14]

The blowouts themselves are covered to some extent in some of these texts. However, the two best studies so far include Bernal's on women in the walkouts and Henry Joseph Gutiérrez's 1990 dissertation, "The Chicano Education Rights Movement and School Desegregation, Los Angeles, 1962–1970," a study of the Educational Issues Coordinating Committee (EICC), which was formed by parents and community people in the wake of the blowouts and negotiated with the board of education the demands raised by the students.[15] F. Arturo Rosales's overview text and companion piece to the mid-1990s PBS television series *Chicano! The History of the Mexican American Civil Rights Movement* has a chapter on the blowouts based on research and interviews conducted for the TV series. In the series itself, one of the four programs concerned the walkouts. Produced by Susan Racho, an activist during the blowouts, it is entitled *Taking Back the Schools* and is a major contribution to preserving the history of this historic event.[16] Although not on the walkouts, Rubén Donato's *The Other Struggle for Equal Schools: Mexican Americans during the Civil Rights Era* details the struggle for education reform, including bilingual education, by Mexican American parents in the Central Valley of California during the late 1960s and 1970s.[17]

Other useful texts that in part comment on the Chicano Movement include David G. Gutiérrez's *Walls and Mirrors: Mexican Americans, Mexican Immigrants, and the Politics of Ethnicity*, which has a chapter on CASA, the Marxist pro–immigrant rights group. This group is also featured in Laura Pulido's recent *Black, Brown, Yellow, and Left: Radical Activism in Los Angeles*.[18]

The second important genre of Movement historiography is autobiography. A few activists have now written their autobiographies, which shed light on different aspects of the Movement. These include an edited English translation by José Angel Gutiérrez of the 1978 autobiography by Reies López Tijerina, published in Spanish in Mexico. The English language version is entitled *They Called Me "King Tiger": My Struggle for the Land and Our Rights*. José Angel Gutiérrez himself, as one of the former key leaders of the Movement from Texas and one of the founders of La Raza Unida Party, has written his own autobiography, *The Making of a Chicano Militant: Lessons from Cristal*. An excellent autobiography, covering different aspects of the Movement from the perspective of a student activist and later filmmaker, is Jesús Salvador Treviño's *Eyewitness: A Filmmaker's Memoir of the Chicano Movement*. Julian Nava's *Julian Nava: My Mexican-American Journey* in part covers the blowouts from Nava's vantage point as a member of the L.A. Board of Education. My own *testimonio* of Bert Corona, *Memories of Chicano History: The Life and Narrative of Bert Corona*, also contains several chapters on the Chicano Movement. Although sometimes listed as autobiography, Oscar Zeta Acosta's *The Revolt of the Cockroach People* is mostly a fictional account of Acosta's role as a Movement attorney in Los Angeles. And Manny García has written his autobiography about his service in Vietnam, *An Accidental Soldier: Memoirs of a Mestizo in Vietnam*.

Finally, edited volumes on different aspects of the Chicano Movement represent a third genre of Movement historical studies. These include an important collection of writings by Rodolfo "Corky" Gonzales, one of the major Movement iconic leaders, edited by Antonio Esquibel, *Message to Aztlán: Selected Writings*. Rodolfo Acuña's *A Community under Siege: A Chronicle of Chicanos East of the Los Angeles River, 1945–1975* in part analyzes and documents important community newspaper coverage of the Movement in East Los Angeles. Alma M. García has edited the best collection of Chicana feminist writings during the Movement, in *Chicana Feminist Thought: The Basic Historical Writings*. F. Arturo Rosales reproduces some key Movement documents in his edited *Testimonio: A Documentary History of the Mexican American Struggle for Civil Rights*. More recently, Lorena Oropeza and Dionne Espinoza have edited the writings of a key Chicana journalist, in *Enriqueta Vasquez and the Chicano Movement: Writings from El Grito del Norte*. My own edited text, *Chicano Liberation Theology: The Writings and Documents of Richard Cruz and Católicos Por La Raza*, covers the activities of Católicos Por La Raza; and my *Dolores Huerta Reader* is the first substantive text on this iconic cofounder of the farmworkers' movement. Although not specific to the Chicano Movement, Jorge Mariscal has edited a creative volume of different writings, including fiction and poetry, concerning Chicanos and the Vietnam War, in *Aztlán and Viet Nam: Chicano and Chicana Experiences of the War.*

I am indebted to all of these studies. However, my text helps to open up a new area: the *testimonio* or oral history/life story narrative. The *testimonio* in the Latin American context is the oral history of a political oppositional activist produced from interviews by a scholar or journalist. To date, there are only two partial *testimonios* of Movement-related topics, and both do not directly deal with the Movement but very importantly with Chicanos who saw combat service in Vietnam. These include Charley Trujillo's *Soldados: Chicanos in Viet Nam: Narrative of the Viet Nam War*; and Lea Ybarra's *Vietnam Veteranos: Chicanos Recall the War.*

By contrast, my *testimonio* involving Sal Castro focuses primarily on the Movement and specifically on the struggle for educational justice, as witnessed by the 1968 school blowouts in East Los Angeles. While, as noted, there are some autobiographical texts written by Movement activists, the fact is that there are many other Movement participants whose stories will never be told unless a historian or journalist produces an oral history *testimonio*. This is certainly the case with a key figure such as Sal Castro. Until I approached Castro back in the late 1990s about doing his oral history, there was no indication that he was thinking of writing his own story. Moreover, as others have told me, Sal is too modest to do it anyway.

The same, unfortunately, is the case with many other former leaders and activists, both men and women. Hopefully, my text will inspire other similar projects. It is important to have these narratives produced. Although memory is fallible, it is still a window into history. Some have questioned the "objectivity" and "scholarlyness" of oral history, as being too dependent on memory rather than on archival documents. This is a valid question, but at the same time those with an agenda that is biased against oral history often raise it. The fact is that all research and the writing of history is biased, including historical records. Such records, in the form of newspaper accounts, correspondence, diaries, journals, government documents, including census material, and so on, are not written by "objective" computers but by subjective human beings and are fallible in telling the "truth." A letter is no less subjective than one's memory. My point here is that, although a biography of Sal Castro would be of great importance, so too is his *testimonio*. Indeed, Sal's life narrative now provides the foundation for some enterprising graduate student or professor to write that biography.

A Chicano Trilogy

My text on Sal Castro for me completes a trilogy on Chicano history. By this, I mean that my previous work has concentrated on two key periods in Chicano history. The first concerns what I call the Immigrant Generation of the early twentieth century, when thousands of Mexican immigrants entered the United States. Of course, there have been subsequent immigrant generations since then and in our own time. However, I refer to the early twentieth century as the period of the Immigrant Generation, because in no other later period have immigrants so totally dominated the Mexican experience in the United States, with the exception of northern New Mexico, bypassed by the immigrant stream. For example, my book *Desert Immigrants: The Mexicans of El Paso, 1880–1920* narrates the key importance that Mexican immigrants played in the growth of the border city of El Paso.[19] In my *Mexican Americans: Leadership, Ideology, and Identity, 1930–1960*, I helped to conceptualize the period of the Mexican American Generation, in many cases the children of the Immigrant Generation, and their particular story in adjusting and struggling in this country as U.S.-born Mexicans.[20] In both cases, I used a generational model to analyze the evolving Chicano experience. I believe that such a model helps to understand the changing nature of becoming a Chicano. Rather than rigid ethnic boundaries, as some historians apparently suggest, I see instead fluid and interconnecting generational borders. Of course, I have done other studies that expand my generational thesis, especially with respect to the Mexican American Generation. Here my work on Bert Corona, Raymond Telles, Frances Esquibel Tywoniak, and Luis Leal all add to an understanding of this key political generation—a bridge between the Immigrant Generation and the Chicano Generation.[21]

My oral history of Sal Castro now moves me more directly into the Chicano Generation and completes this generational trilogy. The Sal Castro story and that of the blowouts of 1968 takes me into this key period in Chicano history. From Mexican immigrants to Mexican Americans to Chicano Movement activists, my trilogy provides a broad and sweeping panorama of Chicano history.

NOTES

Abbreviations

Acosta Collection	Oscar Zeta Acosta Collection, Department of Special Collections, Davidson Library, University of California, Santa Barbara
Castro Collection	Sal Castro Private Collection
Taking Back the Schools	PBS documentary *Taking Back the Schools*, produced by Susan Racho and part of the four-part series *Chicano! History of the Mexican American Civil Rights Movement* (1996)
Today Not Mañana	*Today Not Mañana*, KNX TV documentary, Channel 2, Los Angeles, spring 1967, audiotape in possession of author, courtesy of Sal Castro
UCLA	University of California at Los Angeles

Introduction

1. Texts on the 1960s social protests that have influenced my view of the period include Tom Wells, *The War Within: America's Battle over Vietnam* (New York: Henry Holt, 1994); Todd Gitlin, *The Whole World Is Watching: Mass Media in the Making and Unmaking of the New Left* (Berkeley: University of California Press, 1980); Kirkpatrick Sale, *SDS* (New York: Random House, 1973); James Miller, *"Democracy Is in the Streets": From Port Huron to the Siege of Chicago* (New York: Simon & Schuster, 1987); Edward P. Morgan, *The 60s Experience: Hard Lessons about Modern America* (Philadelphia: Temple University Press, 1991); Andrew Jamison and Ron Eyerman, eds., *Seeds of the Sixties* (Berkeley: University of California Press, 1994); David Farber, ed., *The Sixties: From Memory to History* (Chapel Hill: University of North Carolina Press, 1994); and Rhodri Jeffreys-Jones, *Peace Now! American Society and the Ending of the Vietnam War* (New Haven: Yale University Press, 1999).

2. See Sale, *SDS*, 92.

3. The texts cited in note 1 for the most part mention little about the Chicano Movement.

4. See Mario T. García, *Mexican Americans: Leadership, Ideology, and Identity, 1930–1960* (New Haven: Yale University Press, 1989); and Richard A. García, *Rise of the Mexican American Middle Class: San Antonio, 1929–1941* (College Station: Texas A&M University Press, 1991).

5. See the "Plan de Aztlán" in Luis Valdez and Stan Steiner, eds., *Aztlán: An Anthology of Mexican American Literature* (New York: Vintage Books, 1972), 402–3.

6. See the appendix for my review of Chicano Movement historiography.

7. See Gilbert G. González, *Chicano Education in the Era of Segregation* (Philadelphia: Balch Institute Press, 1990); Guadalupe San Miguel Jr., *"Let All of Them Take Heed": Mexican Americans and the Campaign for Educational Equality in Texas, 1910–1981* (Austin: University of Texas Press, 1987); and Mario T. García, *Desert Immigrants: The Mexicans of El Paso, 1880–1920* (New Haven: Yale University Press, 1981), 110–26.

8. See Michael Omi and Howard Winant, *Racial Formation in the United States: From the 1960s to the 1980s* (New York: Routledge, 1986), 57, 61.

9. Ibid.

10. Rafael Pérez-Torres, *Mestizaje: Critical Uses of Race in Chicano Culture* (Minneapolis: University of Minnesota Press, 2006), 155.

11. See, for example, García, *Desert Immigrants*; Alberto Camarillo, *Chicanos in a Changing Society: From Mexican Pueblos to American Barrios in Santa Barbara and Southern California* (Cambridge: Harvard University Press, 1979); Ricardo Romo, *East Los Angeles: History of a Barrio* (Austin: University of Texas Press, 1983); and George J. Sánchez, *Becoming Mexican American: Ethnicity, Culture, and Identity in Chicano Los Angeles, 1900–1945* (New York: Oxford University Press, 1993).

12. On the Dillingham Commission, see García, *Desert Immigrants*, 33–109.

13. Ibid.; Romo, *East Los Angeles*; Sánchez, *Becoming Mexican American*.

14. González, *Chicano Education*; Paul Rabinow, ed., *The Foucault Reader* (New York: Pantheon, 1984), 8.

15. González, *Chicano Education*; García, *Desert Immigrants*.

16. See González, *Chicano Education*.

17. García, *Desert Immigrants*.

18. Ibid.

19. García, *Mexican Americans*.

20. Ibid.; Gilbert G. González, *Labor and Community: Mexican Citrus Worker Villages in a Southern California County, 1900–1950* (Urbana: University of Illinois Press, 1994); San Miguel, *"Let All of Them Take Heed"*; Charles M. Wollenberg, *All Deliberate Speed: Segregation and Exclusion in California Schools, 1855–1975* (Berkeley: University of California Press, 1976). See the documentary *Mendez vs. Westminster: For All the Children/Para Todos Los Niños*. On the *Hernández Case*, see Ignacio M. García, *White but Not Equal: Mexican Americans, Jury Discrimination, and the Supreme Court* (Tucson: University of Arizona Press, 2009); and Michael A. Olivas, ed., *Colored Men and Hombrea Aquí: Hernández v. Texas and the Emergence of Mexican American Lawyering* (Houston: Arte Publico Press, 2006). See also the PBS *American Experience* documentary *A Class Apart: A Mexican American Civil Rights Story* (2009).

21. Jonathan Kozol, *Savage Inequalities: Children in America's Schools* (New York: Harper Perennial, 1992; originally published 1991), 4.

22. Ibid.

23. Ibid., 80.

24. Rabinow, *Foucault Reader*, 22.

25. Kozol, *Savage Inequalities*, 233.

26. Neil Postman and Charles Weingartner, *Teaching as a Subversive Activity* (New York: Delta, 1969).

27. Ibid.

28. As quoted in Henry Giroux, *Theory and Resistance in Education: Toward a Pedagogy for the Opposition* (Westport, Ct.: Bergin & Garvey, 2001; originally published 1983), xxi.

29. Ibid., 45–46.

30. Ibid., 241.

31. As quoted in Rabinow, *Foucault Reader*, 6.

32. Giroux, *Theory and Resistance in Education*, 62.

33. Ibid., xxi.

34. See ibid. for an elaboration of these concepts.

35. See my various books cited above, as well as some of my other books, *Memories of Chicano History: The Life and Narrative of Bert Corona* (Berkeley: University of California Press, 1994); *The Making of a Mexican American Mayor: Raymond L. Telles of El Paso* (El Paso: Texas Western Press, 1998); coauthored with Frances Esquibel Tywoniak, *Migrant Daughter: Coming of Age as a Mexican American Woman* (Berkeley: University of California Press, 2000); *Luis Leal: An Auto/Biography* (Austin: University of Texas Press, 2000); my edited volume, Ruben Salazar, *Border Correspondent: Selected Writings, 1955–1970* (Berkeley: University of California Press, 1995); my edited volume, *The Gospel of César Chávez: My Faith in Action* (Lanham, Md.: Sheed & Ward, 2007); *Católicos: Resistance and Affirmation in Chicano Catholic History* (Austin: University of Texas Press, 2008); my edited volume, *A Dolores Huerta Reader* (Albuquerque: University of New Mexico Press, 2008); and my manuscript in progress, "Chicano Power: Testimonios of the Chicano Movement in Los Angeles."

36. See the sources cited in note 35.

37. See Stokely Carmichael with Ekwueme Michael Thelwell, *Ready for Revolution: The Life and Struggles of Stokely Carmichael (Kwame Ture)* (New York: Scribner, 2003). I want to thank Professor Jorge Mariscal for bringing to my attention how this text also uses inserts.

38. See Nell Irvin Painter, *The Narrative of Hosea Hudson: His Life as a Negro Communist in the South* (Cambridge: Harvard University Press, 1979).

Chapter One

1. For the Mexican American Generation, see Mario T. García, *Mexican Americans: Leadership, Ideology, and Identity, 1930–1960* (New Haven: Yale University Press, 1989); and Mario T. García, *Memories of Chicano History: The Life and Narrative of Bert Corona* (Berkeley: University of California Press, 1994).

2. *La Opinión*, February 27, 1931.

3. *Los Angeles Times*, January 27, 1931, A4.

4. For these deportations, see Abraham Hoffman, *Unwanted Mexican-Americans in the Great Depression: Repatriation Pressures, 1929–1939* (Tucson: University of Arizona Press, 1974); and Francisco E. Balderrama and Raymond Rodríguez, *Decade of*

Betrayal: Mexican Repatriation in the 1930s (Albuquerque: University of New Mexico Press, 1995).

5. On the White Russians in East Los Angeles, see García, *Memories of Chicano History*, 87–107; and George J. Sánchez, *Becoming Mexican American: Ethnicity, Culture, and Identity in Chicano Los Angeles, 1900–1945* (New York: Oxford University Press, 1993).

6. *Los Angeles Times*, June 7, 1943, A1. For the Zoot-Suit Riots and tensions between Chicanos and military personnel and the police during the war, see Edward Escobar, *Race, Police, and the Making of a Political Identity: Mexican Americans and the Los Angeles Police Department, 1900–1945* (Berkeley: University of California Press, 1999); Edward Obregón Pagán, *Murder at the Sleepy Lagoon: Zoot Suits, Race, and Riot in Wartime L.A.* (Chapel Hill: University of North Carolina Press, 2003); and Luis Alvarez, *The Power of the Zoot: Youth Culture and Resistance during World War II* (Berkeley: University of California Press, 2008). Zoot-suits, or drapes, refers to the particular attire worn by zoot-suitors, which included long, tailored coats and high-waisted pants. The term *pachuco* refers to Mexican American street dudes who constructed their own counterculture.

7. Sal Castro to Mr. Steven Spielberg, March 15, 1999, in Castro Collection. See also Frank del Olmo, "Saluting Our Latino Soldiers," *Los Angeles Times*, April 2, 1999; Raul Morín, *Among the Valiant: Mexican Americans in WWII and Korea* (Alhambra, Calif.: Borden Publishing Company, 1966); Maggie Rivas-Rodríguez, ed., *Mexican Americans and World War II* (Austin: University of Texas Press, 2005); and Maggie Rivas-Rodríguez and Emilio Zamora, eds., *Beyond the Latino World War II Hero: The Social and Political Legacy of a Generation* (Austin: University of Texas Press, 2010).

8. *Eastside Sun*, January 17, 1952, cited in Rodolfo F. Acuña, *A Community under Siege: A Chronicle of Chicanos East of the Los Angeles River, 1945–1975* (Los Angeles: Chicano Studies Research Center, UCLA, 1984), 281.

Chapter Two

1. Other county playgrounds included Hollywood Playground, Normandie Playground, Toberman Playground, and St. Anne's Playground. L.A. School District playgrounds also included Solano Avenue School, Elysian Heights School, and Hollenbeck Junior High School. See Sal B. Castro résumé, in possession of author.

2. See Carey McWilliams, *North from Mexico: The Spanish-Speaking People of the United States* (New York: Praeger, 1990; originally published 1948).

3. On Chávez Ravine, see Don Normark, *Chavez Ravine, 1949: A Los Angeles Story* (San Francisco: Chronicle Books, 1999).

Chapter Three

1. On the López campaign and the founding of MAPA, see Mario T. García, *Memories of Chicano History: The Life and Narrative of Bert Corona* (Berkeley: University of California Press), 195–97.

2. Kennedy's schedule is included in Castro Collection. On the Viva Kennedy movement, see Ignacio M. García, *Viva Kennedy: Mexican Americans in Search of Camelot* (College Station: Texas A&M Press, 2000).

3. *Los Angeles Times*, November 2, 1969.

4. Ibid. Kennedy's speech was scheduled for 9 P.M. Various Hollywood figures participated in the rally, including Milton Berle, Debbie Reynolds, Louie Prima, Keely Smith, Stan Freberg, Jeff Chandler, and Jo Stafford and Paul Weston's orchestra. These celebrities entertained prior to Kennedy's speech.

5. See *Los Angeles Times*, November 2, 1960, 1.

6. One of the few Mexican American appointees was Raymond L. Telles, the mayor of El Paso, who was appointed ambassador to Costa Rica, the first Mexican American to serve as a U.S. ambassador; see Mario T. García, *The Making of a Mexican American Mayor: Raymond L. Telles of El Paso* (El Paso: Texas Western Press, 1998), 133–59.

Chapter Four

1. For the early relationship between the FEPC and Mexican Americans, see Clete Daniel, *Chicano Workers and the Politics of Fairness: The FEPC in the Southwest, 1941–1945* (Austin: University of Texas Press, 1991).

2. Interview with Albert Valencia, Belmont student in the early 1960s, May 8, 2007. Valencia graduated in 1964 and recalls that most Chicanos were automatically put in vocational classes such as print shop, wood shop, and metal shop. He was one of the few Chicanos in the more advanced academic track. He remembers with some humor how Chicano students printed the school newspaper in their print shop classes and how they often subverted the text by placing certain Chicano words or symbols in the paper. "Benign neglect—we weren't given any regard," Valencia remembers. "Acknowledgments were always given to white students, no matter how well Chicanos did on our SATs, athletics, or in other areas. We were not given encouragement, appreciation, or recognition."

3. Valencia interview, May 8, 2007.

4. Valencia observes, "The first thing I noticed about Sal when I met him was how intense he was. He was on a mission. He was fearless." Ibid.

5. Valencia notes that at first the students met at lunchtime in a classroom, until the administration refused to let them meet on campus. He further remembers that Castro didn't attend the meetings on campus but was always talking informally to the students. Ibid.

6. Ibid.

7. Valencia notes that the song "Our Day Will Come" became the anthem of the TMs. Ibid.

8. Valencia adds: "I was a monitor there [at the school assembly]. I knew that some of the TMs were going to speak in Spanish. María was one of them. It was wonderful. They were really good speakers. Then they added some words in Spanish and I felt so good. It was uplifting. We were all looking at each other and smiling. I saw the principal and vice principal and they were livid. After that Sal was a marked man." Valencia

also recalls that many of the other teachers regarded Sal as an "outside agitator." Ibid.

9. Valencia further notes that sometime after the cancellation of the rally some of the TMs staged a partial walkout to protest how they were being treated. Ibid.

10. See Ruben Salazar, "New School Plan Sees Bilingualism as Asset," *Los Angeles Times*, February 25, 1964, 1, 3.

11. Valencia interview, May 8, 2007.

12. As early as 1953, the Community Service Organization (CSO) had protested the giving of ethnically biased IQ tests to Mexican American students; and in 1958 the Council of Mexican-American Affairs called for various educational reforms, including bilingual instruction. See Marguerite V. Marín, *Social Protest in an Urban Barrio: A Study of the Chicano Movement, 1966–1974* (Lanham, Md.: University Press of America, 1991), 72–73.

13. See Ruben Salazar, "Chicano Leaders Troubled by School Dropouts," *Los Angeles Times*, October 22, 1962; reproduced in Ruben Salazar, *Border Correspondent: Selected Writings, 1955–1975*, ed. Mario T. García (Berkeley: University of California Press, 1995), 68–72.

14. Report of the Ad Hoc Committee on Equal Educational Opportunity, September 12, 1963, in Castro Collection. For additional information on this report, see Marín, *Social Protest*, 73–74.

15. Vicki Castro, a student at Roosevelt High who attended the initial conference in 1963, recalls that her mother worked as a seamstress for Kotzin; interview with Vicki Castro by Mario T. García, November 12, 1998.

16. See the various programs for the conference from 1964 to 1991, in Castro Collection.

17. Videotape interview with Sal Castro by Dr. Carlos M. Haro, October 6, 2005, UCLA, Chicano Studies Research Center. I thank Dr. Haro for the use of this interview.

18. Vicki Castro, later elected to the school board, remembers being one of the initial students selected to attend the first conference, in 1963, from Roosevelt High School. She was one of five students selected by the principal, based on leadership roles—she was vice president of her class. She recalls that five students were selected from each high school in the county and that about 200 attended the first conference; Vicki Castro interview, November 12, 1998.

19. Program for Second Annual Camp Hess Kramer Spanish-Speaking Youth Leadership Conference, in Castro Collection.

20. See conference programs in Castro Collection.

21. A former student participant at Hess Kramer later stated: "It was very strange, because it was a very new experience because everybody that was there was Mexican. People who ran it were Mexican and the program was entirely devoted to education, or enlightening. . . . The theme of the program . . . was always one of identity. They were asking us to talk about our identity, who are we?" As quoted in Marín, *Social Protest*, 75.

22. Vicki Castro interview, November 12, 1998.

Chapter Five

1. Officially, East L.A. is a patch of unincorporated territory east of Boyle Heights; however, historically and symbolically, the area east of the Los Angeles River is generically referred to as East L.A. See Ricardo Romo, *East Los Angeles: History of a Barrio* (Austin: University of Texas Press, 1983); George J. Sánchez, *Becoming Mexican American: Ethnicity, Culture, and Identity, 1900–1945* (New York: Oxford University Press, 1993); and William Deverell, *Whitewashed Adobe: The Rise of Los Angeles and the Remaking of Its Mexican Past* (Berkeley: University of California Press, 2004).

2. See Gilbert G. González, *Chicano Education in the Era of Segregation* (Philadelphia: Balch Institute Press, 1990); Guadalupe San Miguel Jr., *"Let All of Them Take Heed": Mexican Americans and the Campaign for Educational Equality in Texas, 1910–1981* (Austin: University of Texas Press, 1987); and Mario T. García, *Desert Immigrants: The Mexicans of El Paso, 1880–1920* (New Haven: Yale University Press, 1981).

3. Dolores Delgado Bernal, "Chicana School Resistance and Grassroots Leadership: Providing an Alternative History of the 1968 East Los Angeles Blowouts" (Ph.D. diss., UCLA, 1997), 84.

4. In the mid- to late 1960s, some 138,000 Latino students attended Los Angeles public schools but less than 3 percent of the teachers had Spanish surnames; see Rodolfo F. Acuña, *A Community under Siege: A Chronicle of Chicanos East of the Los Angeles River, 1945–1975* (Los Angeles: Chicano Studies Research Center, UCLA, 1984), 157.

5. See also interview with Luis Torres, July 4, 2007, by Mario T. García. Torres was a senior at Lincoln in 1968.

6. Tanya Luna Mount, a former student at Roosevelt High School, recalled: "We had the statistics of reading and arithmetic. . . . And it was, I mean we were appalled. It was enough to make you angry and it was like, you know, that's bullshit. I mean, all these Mexican kids are not stupid. You can't tell me that these kids are stupid. You can't. Now those teachers are there just doing time collecting money. I don't believe it. . . . And neither did a lot of other people[;] that's why they, the walkouts, really took off[;] it's like, 'We're not stupid.'" As quoted in Bernal, "Chicana School Resistance," 107.

7. See "The Inside," in *Chicano Student News*, February 16–March 1, 1968, 3. According to this article, the library at Garfield had room for only 40 students out of 4,000.

8. Luis Torres, a senior at Lincoln in 1968, notes: "It's hard to generalize, but most teachers regarded us with condescension." Torres interview, July 4, 2007.

9. As quoted in Bernal, "Chicana School Resistance," 136–37.

10. See Marguerite V. Marín, *Social Protest in an Urban Barrio: A Study of the Chicano Movement, 1966–1974* (Lanham, Md.: University Press of America, 1991), 77–78.

11. "The Inside," *Chicano Student News*, February 16–March 1, 1968, 3.

12. See "Drop-Out Derby," *Inside Eastside*, November 24, 1967, 4.

13. See Bernal, "Chicana School Resistance," 83.

14. Henry Gutiérrez interview in *Taking Back the Schools*.

15. Acuña notes that Chicanos represented 10 percent of L.A. County but 21 percent of war casualties; Acuña, *Community under Siege*, 171.

16. Interview with Harry Gamboa by Mario T. García, July 1, 2007.

17. Alicia Escalante, a parent, protested teacher abuse: "I have three children attending [Lincoln]. . . . I have constantly heard my children complain (and others too) of teachers there that are always criticizing the Mexican student. I personally know a Mr. Gordon who used a choking method . . . on my son. (An example of what goes on there!) When I confronted the so-called vice principal, I was sarcastically and hypocritically brushed off. I am a Mexican mother involved in community work, *intending* to encourage my children and all Mexicans to *demand*, to protest, and to organize for better treatment, more capable teachers, and a better education." See Alicia Escalante's letter to the editor, in *Chicano Student News*, January 5–19, 1968, 2. Escalante was the head of the East Los Angeles Welfare Rights Organization.

18. Gamboa interview, July 1, 2007.

19. Torres interview, July 4, 2007.

20. Interview with John Ortiz by Mario T. García, June 13, 2010.

21. See Raul Ruiz, "Tragedy of Lincoln High," *Inside Eastside*, December 8–21, 1967, 7.

22. "Moctesuma Esparza: Revolucionario Por Vida," oral history paper by Roberto Soto in Mario T. García's class on the history of the Chicano Movement, University of California, Santa Barbara, March 11, 1998, 1. Paper in possession of author.

23. Torres interview, July 4, 2007.

Chapter Six

1. On César Chávez and the farmworker struggle, see Richard Griswold del Castillo and Richard A. García, *César Chávez: Triumph of Spirit* (Norman: University of Oklahoma Press, 1995).

2. On Tijerina and Gonzales, see Rudy V. Busto, *King Tiger: The Religious Vision of Reíes López Tijerina* (Albuquerque: University of New Mexico Press, 2005); and Ernesto B. Vigil, *The Crusade for Justice: Chicano Militancy and the Government's War on Dissent* (Madison: University of Wisconsin Press, 1999).

3. Rudolph Chávez, a teacher at Roosevelt High School, later testified before a grand jury that on October 5, 1967, at a Mexican American Student Association meeting, he heard Sal Castro say: "The only way you are going to impress the kids and the Board of Education is to get the kids to walk out"; see testimony in Summary of Grand Jury, Acosta Collection, box 4, folder 8, p. 9. Moctesuma Esparza recalls that as early as fall 1967, he and other college and high school students were talking about a walkout; interview with Moctesuma Esparza by Mario T. García, June 29, 2010.

4. Vicki Castro was the initial president of the Young Citizens for Community Action and Sánchez was the vice president. Castro, who was several years older and a college student, remembers being one of the adults who signed the lease; she also remembers the Piranya as being "half hippie and half intellectual." Because she was in her early twenties at the time of the walkouts, Moctesuma Esparza would affectionately call her the "grandmother of the blowouts"; interview with Vicki Castro by Mario T. García, November 12, 1998. Father John Luce, the pastor of the Episcopal

Church of the Epiphany in Lincoln Heights, testified later before a grand jury that he arranged with his church officials to help pay the rent for the Piranya until January 1968, when he felt there was not sufficient adult supervision; Father Luce testimony, Summary of Grand Jury, Acosta Collection, box 4, folder 3, p. 398.

5. Paula Crisostomo notes that the owner of the building was a former highway patrolman named Tripp. The kids wanted to call the coffeehouse "Mr. Tripps," but the owner did not let them; interview with Paula Crisostomo by Mario T. García, April 27, 2007.

6. A former Chicano high school student told Marín for her study that the idea of the walkouts developed at one of the discussions at Piranya; Marguerite V. Marín, *Social Protest in an Urban Barrio: A Study of the Chicano Movement, 1966–1974* (Lanham, Md.: University Press of America, 1991), 76. Historian Acuña refers to Sal Castro as a "charismatic speaker"; see Rodolfo Acuña, *Occupied America: A History of Chicanos* (New York: Harper & Row, 1981), 357.

7. Crisostomo interview, April 27, 2007.

8. *Time*, April 28, 1967, 24–25.

9. Vicki Castro interview, November 12, 1998.

10. According to Acuña, Congressman Edward Roybal did criticize the article, and other Mexican Americans sent letters of complaint to *Time* and threatened a boycott of the magazine. In response, *Time* stated that it had not meant to offend Mexican Americans; see Rodolfo Acuña, A *Community under Siege: A Chronicle of Chicanos East of the Los Angeles River, 1945–1975* (Los Angeles: Chicano Studies Research Center, UCLA), 161.

11. Paula Crisostomo recalls that her dialogue group of about a dozen students also discussed whether marijuana should be legalized. Her group counselor was Richard Alatorre, who would later become a major Latino politician. She also remembers that the high school boys still tended to speak out more than the high school girls, although this wasn't the case with the college female students, who were more outspoken; Crisostomo interview, April 27, 2007.

12. *Today Not Mañana*.

13. Dolores Delgado Bernal, "Chicana School Resistance and Grassroots Leadership: Providing an Alternative History of the 1968 East Los Angeles Blowouts" (Ph.D. diss., UCLA, 1997), 110.

14. Interview with Paula Crisostomo by Mario T. García, May 25, 2007.

15. Vicki Castro interview, November 12, 1998.

16. Interview with Paula Crisostomo, April 27, 2007.

17. Acuña notes that this survey, apparently in a thirty-page proposal, was submitted to the school board in February 1968 and that it threatened a walkout of the schools if the recommendations were ignored; see Acuña, *Community under Siege*, 166.

18. See *Taking Back the Schools*. Vicki Castro recalls that the students met with Stuart Stengel, the regional supervisor for the Eastside schools; Vicki Castro interview, November 12, 1998.

19. The Reverend James Jones became the first black elected to the school board; see Henry Joseph Gutiérrez, "The Chicano Education Rights Movement and School

Desegregation, Los Angeles, 1962–1970" (Ph.D. diss., University of California, Irvine, 1990), 10. Nava won in a runoff by 50,000 votes; see Acuña, *Community under Siege*, 158–59.

20. Interview with John Ortiz by Mario T. García, June 13, 2010.

21. Acuña observes that, in the fall of 1967, Chicano Movement newspapers such as *Chicano Student Movement* and *La Raza* called for walkouts; Acuña, *Community under Siege*, 166.

22. See *La Raza Yearbook*, September 1968.

23. Juan Gómez-Quiñones recalled that sometime in January or February 1968 Castro and some of the high school students went to UMAS at UCLA to ask the college students to serve as monitors for a possible action; see Gómez-Quiñones testimony, Grand Jury Proceedings, Acosta Collection, box 4, folder 2, p. 94. Carlos Vásquez, a junior at UCLA, recalls that at the meeting Sal's words were: "I want to use your heads to write, to get translations if we need them, to get good flyers and to stop the billy-clubs whenever they come. That's your job." Vásquez further remembers he and the other college students being very impressed with Castro's energy and commitment. Vásquez characterizes Castro as *"puro corazón* [all heart]." He also notes that Castro did already discuss the possibility of a walkout by the high school students. Interview with Carlos Vásquez by Mario T. García, June 10, 2008.

24. See Leo Grebler, Joan Moore, and Ralph Guzmán, *The Mexican-American People: The Nation's Second Largest Minority* (New York: Free Press, 1970).

25. Ralph Guzmán, "Brown Power: The Gentle Revolutionaries," *West Magazine, Los Angeles Times*, January 26, 1969. Guzmán borrowed the term "gentle revolutionaries" from a statement by Senator Robert Kennedy, who, after meeting with some Brown Berets in 1968, stated: "These fellows have a deep anger which they have trouble expressing. They are not sure of their goals. Compared to others that I have heard they are really gentle revolutionaries."

26. Rosales contends that the Brown Berets represented the main planners of the walkouts, but no evidence exists to substantiate this claim; see F. Arturo Rosales, *Chicano! The History of the Mexican American Civil Rights Movement* (Houston: Arte Publico Press, 1996), 189. In fact, Rosales barely mentions the role of Sal Castro.

27. See interview with Sal Castro by Juan Gómez-Quiñones in Acosta Collection, box 4, folder 3, p. 454.

28. As quoted in Dolores Delgado Bernal, "A Reconceptualization of Female Leadership: An Alternative History of the 1968 East Los Angeles School Blowouts," unpublished paper, 16. Crisostomo and Tanya Luna Mount, a student at Roosevelt, both wrote articles for these papers. Crisostomo also notes: "I typed and did layouts, and wrote ghost articles about the schools. I would also go to the [Whittier] Boulevard to sell *Chicano Student Movement* or *Inside Eastside.*" See Dolores Delgado Bernal, "Grassroots Leadership Reconceptualized: Chicana Oral Histories and the 1968 Los Angeles School Blowouts," *Frontiers: A Journal of Women Studies* 2 (1968): 128.

29. Interview with Luis Torres, July 4, 2007, by Mario T. García.

30. Ian F. Haney López, *Racism on Trial: The Chicano Fight for Justice* (Cambridge: Harvard University Press, 2003). Tanya Luna Mount, a student at Roosevelt, and Mita Cuarón, a student at Garfield, both had access to mimeograph machines through

their parents and used these to run off leaflets and flyers about conditions in the schools, which they distributed on the high school campuses; see Bernal, "Grass-roots Leadership Reconceptualized," 128. Paula Crisostomo recalls that about ten students at Lincoln constituted the strike committee; Crisostomo interview, April 27, 2007. Cuarón further notes that the Garfield Strike Committee consisted of about six students, including herself; interview with Mita Cuarón by Mario T. García, June 10, 2007. Harry Gamboa, another student at Garfield, adds that the origins of the Garfield Strike Committee lie in a few students from his school regularly meeting with Ralph Cuarón. Cuarón was the father of Mita Cuarón and a longtime community and political activist who operated an apartment complex on Princeton near the Plaza Community Center, which was, according to Gamboa, owned by the Episcopal Church. There Cuarón provided offices for various community groups. The students would often attend meetings of these groups besides being mentored by Cuarón; interview with Harry Gamboa by Mario T. García, July 1, 2007.

31. Videotape interview with Sal Castro by Dr. Carlos M. Haro, October 6, 2005, UCLA, Chicano Studies Research Center, courtesy of Dr. Haro.

32. Bernal, "Chicana School Resistance," 133. For the development of the larger Chicano student movement, see Carlos Muñoz Jr., *Youth, Identity, Power: The Chicano Movement* (New York: Verso, 1989), 47–98. See also interview with Raul Ruiz by Mario T. García conducted in early 1990s and in author's possession.

33. As quoted in Bernal, "A Reconceptualization of Female Leadership," 9. Crisostomo does not remember that she and other students believed that they were part of a bluff; Crisostomo interview, April 27, 2007. Luis Torres from Lincoln notes, "We communicated effectively through rumors"; see Torres interview, July 4, 2007. According to Gerald Rosen, a few days prior to the walkouts, *La Raza* printed slogans such as "Turn On, Join In, Walkout"; as referenced and quoted in Marín, *Social Protest*, 77.

34. See Jesús Salvador Treviño, *Eyewitness: A Filmmaker's Memoir of the Chicano Movement* (Houston: Arte Publico Press, 2001), pp. 1–2; *Chicano Student Movement* 1, no. 6: 9.

35. See *Chicano Student News*, April 25, 1968, 2, which noted that about 500 students protested at Wilson. Paula Crisostomo recalls that the Wilson walkout took her and students from the other schools by surprise but that they realized that they now had to follow suit: "Our hand was dealt." See Crisostomo interview, April 27, 2007.

36. As noted in Marín, *Social Protest*, 80. Susan Racho, a student at UCLA, recalls that everything at the time felt spontaneous and that the high school students met often on their own and asserted a certain independence from the college students and even from Sal Castro. Interview with Susan Racho, April 28, 2007; see also Cuarón interview, June 10, 2007. Harry Gamboa, a student at Garfield, notes that the key leader and most articulate spokesman for the Garfield Strike Committee was John Ortiz, who, according to Gamboa, was the "Mario Savio of East L.A." Savio was the charismatic leader and spokesperson for the free speech movement at Berkeley in 1964. Gamboa interview, July 1, 2007.

37. See *Chicano Student News*, special issue on the blowouts (n.d.). Principal Reg-

inald Murphy at Garfield testified later before the grand jury that before noon on March 5 a false fire alarm had taken place, along with an anonymous phone call concerning a bomb threat. According to Murphy, about 500 students walked out around 12:30 P.M. Murphy testimony, Grand Jury Proceedings, Acosta Collection, box 4, folder 2, pp. 153–56.

38. Sal Castro interview with Gómez-Quiñones, Grand Jury Proceedings, Acosta Collection, box 4, folder 3, p. 463.

39. Harry Gamboa, a student at Garfield, recalls: "We printed 5,000 fliers and put them in all the student lockers and nearby homes. This was not a spontaneous walkout; we were organized." Gamboa interview, July 1, 2007. Gamboa adds that the Garfield walkout was planned for Tuesday. Although the students knew a walkout was imminent, they didn't know it would be that day.

40. Cuarón interview, June 10, 2007. Harry Gamboa disputes that it was the fire alarm that triggered the walkout—instead it was the members of the strike committee, who went around to the classrooms calling for the students to walk out. Gamboa interview, July 1, 2007.

41. See testimony of Sheriff Deputy Dan Castrellon at Grand Jury Proceedings, Acosta Collection, box 4, folder 2, pp. 52–53.

42. Gutiérrez, "Chicano Education Rights Movement," 72–73. According to county sheriff Donald L. Stiver, thirty sheriffs and fourteen highway patrolmen descended on Garfield that afternoon. See Stiver testimony, Summary of Grand Jury, Acosta Collection, box 4, folder 2, pp. 156–57.

43. Mita Cuarón interview in *Taking Back the Schools*.

44. Vicki Castro interview, November 12, 1998.

45. See also "Moctesuma Esparza: Revolucionario Por Vida," oral history paper by Roberto Soto in Mario T. García's class on the history of the Chicano movement, University of California, Santa Barbara, March 11, 1998, 4. Paper in possession of author.

46. Ortiz interview, June 13, 2010.

47. Juan Gómez-Quiñones noted that he and other UCLA students made some of the picket signs and that he personally distributed some at Roosevelt High for the March 6 walkout. Gómez-Quiñones testimony, Grand Jury Proceedings, Acosta Collection, box 4, folder 2, pp. 93–94.

48. Carlos Vásquez believes that he was not arrested or indicted for his role in the blowouts because he was very careful to avoid having his picture taken by the police during the walkouts. Vásquez interview, June 10, 2008.

49. Crisostomo interview, April 27, 2007. Luis Torres, a senior in 1968 at Lincoln, recalls that he and most other students knew the walkouts were going to happen but not when. Torres interview, July 4, 2007.

50. See *Taking Back the Schools*.

51. Vicki Castro, on the other hand, notes that the college students were well organized and apparently on their own had obtained maps of the schools showing the different floors of each school and the different exits. Vicki Castro interview, November 12, 1998. Robert Kladifko, the registrar at Lincoln, later testified before the grand

jury that on March 6 at 9:45 A.M. he saw Carlos Montes, one of the Brown Berets, in one of the hallways telling students to walk out. See testimony in Summary of Grand Jury, Acosta Collection, box 4, folder 7, p. 8. Another teacher at Lincoln, Jessie Gómez Franco, also testified that she encountered Joe Razo in one of the hallways and asked him if he had a permit to be there. According to Franco, Razo answered, "Come on, get off it. You are a Chicano. You know what's going on." Franco stated that Razo continued down the hall shouting, "Walkout, walkout." Franco testimony in Summary of Grand Jury, Acosta Collection, box 4, folder 8, p. 8.

52. Principal George Ingels testified to the grand jury that the walkouts occurred at 9:50 A.M. and that about 800 students participated. He also stated that at the time of the demonstration Sal was teaching his government class, Contemporary American Problems; Ingles testimony in Summary of Grand Jury, Acosta Collection, box 4, folder 2, pp. 123, 128, 133. In his interview with Gómez-Quiñones a few days after the walkouts, Sal Castro stated that the March 6 walkouts at Lincoln commenced between 9:50 A.M. and 9:55 A.M. See Sal Castro interview, Acosta Collection, box 4, folder 3, p. 464.

53. Ruiz interview, early 1990s.

54. Sal Castro interview in *Taking Back the Schools*.

55. Crisostomo interview, April 27, 2007.

56. Videotape interview with Sal Castro by Dr. Carlos M. Haro, October 6, 2005.

57. Principal Ingles testified to the grand jury that after the students walked out of the school he went to the front gate and there encountered Joe Razo, whom he identified as a Brown Beret (although whether this was true is not clear) and that he told Razo to leave the school and then was physically threatened by Razo. Ingles also testified that he filmed the walkout with a Super 8 camera. See testimony in Summary of Grand Jury, Acosta Collection, box 4, folder 2, pp. 129–34. Moctesuma Esparza notes that when he realized his mistake about not informing the media about the correct time of the walkout he quickly called some of the media and they arrived around 10:30 A.M.; Esparza interview, June 29, 2010.

58. Paula Crisostomo's mother waited for her daughter outside the school and picketed along with Paula and the other students; Crisostomo interview, April 27, 2007.

59. One teacher, Jessie Gómez Franco, later testified before the grand jury that a few days after the March 6 walkout, in which she had not participated, she talked to Castro, who, according to her, said: "If you are a real Mexican, you should have walked out with those kids too." Summary of Grand Jury, Acosta Collection, box 4, folder 8, p. 8. Castro does not recall the incident but believes that it's very probable that he said this to Franco. Interview with Sal Castro, May 23, 2007.

60. For a fictionalized account of the blowouts, see Oscar Zeta Acosta, *The Revolt of the Cockroach People* (New York: Vintage Books, 1989; originally published 1973), 37–42.

61. Moctesuma Esparza interview in *Taking Back the Schools*.

62. See Gutiérrez, "Chicano Education Rights Movement," 73.

63. Ibid., 79. Principal Thomas Dyer at Roosevelt later testified before the grand

jury that the students walked out around noon and that he saw between 400 and 500 students at one of the gates that was opened. Dyer testimony, Summary of Grand Jury, Acosta Collection, box 4, folder 2, pp. 144–45.

64. As quoted in *Taking Back the Schools*.

65. Somers testimony in Summary of Grand Jury, Acosta Collection, box 4, folder 8, p. 11. Somers also testified that he saw Brown Berets distributing paper bags to students and that the students obtained eggs from the Berets to throw at the sheriffs.

66. Videotape interview with Sal Castro by Dr. Carlos M. Haro, October 6, 2005. Rodney King was the African American in the early 1990s who was severely beaten by Los Angeles police, with their actions captured on videotape.

67. Tom Dyer interview in *Taking Back the Schools*.

68. See *Chicano Student News*, special issue on the blowouts. Tanya Luna Mount, a student at Roosevelt, recalls: "They [the police] were treating us like we were rioting and tearing everything up, which we weren't. We weren't breaking, destroying anything. . . . And we were told to disperse, we had three minutes. Everybody kept yelling that we had a right to be there. . . . All of a sudden they [the riot squad] started coming down this way. They start whacking people. Now they're beating people up, badly. . . . Now people, administrators are inside yelling, 'Stop, my God. What are you doing?' They couldn't even open the gate and tell the kids to run inside because the police were telling them, 'Remove yourself from the fence and go back, mind your own business.' That's when all of a sudden they [the administrators] realized, 'My god.'" As quoted in Bernal, "Grassroots Leadership," 121. The *Los Angeles Times*, on March 14, 1968, reported: "Police action one afternoon to clear crowds off 4th St. in front of the school [Roosevelt] was 'unfortunate.' While some of the teachers thought the police exercised restraint [Principal] Dyer remarked, 'I felt they overreacted and I think they did too.'" Vicki Castro remembers the violence and that some students broke glass doors and threw bottles at the police. She also notes that the following day she witnessed, at Evergreen Park on Fourth Street, close to Roosevelt, a virtual "police camp," with tents, police cars, and motorcycles. Vicki Castro interview, November 12, 1998.

69. See Gutiérrez, "Chicano Education Rights Movement," 71.

70. Principal Ingles testified to the grand jury that Castro returned to school around 1 P.M.; Ingles testimony, Summary of Grand Jury, Acosta Collection, box 4, folder 2, p. 133.

71. In 1968, only 1.9 percent of school administrators were Spanish surnamed. See Gutiérrez, "Chicano Education Rights Movement," 87.

72. Crisostomo interview, April 27, 2007. Years later, in an interview for the writing of the script for the HBO film *Walkout*, Avila, who was a career member of the L.A. police, confessed that he had originally been assigned to Wilson to catch drug dealers as an undercover narcotics agent. However, when, in one of his weekly reports, he noted rumors of a possible mass walkout of students, his superior officers instructed him to report on this as well. In this interview, he stated that he understood the problems of the students but that he had a job to do. According to Paula Crisostomo, Avila was older than the other high school students but looked young. Crisostomo fur-

ther notes that Avila died in the early 2000s of cancer. Finally, she observes that she and the other students became aware that he was a cop later in the spring of 1968. Crisostomo interview, April 27, 2007. *Chicano Student News* one year later still called attention to the undercover role of Bobby Avila when it wrote: "Wanted: Look closely at the face inside the black square, you may have seen him. You may have seen him during the Walkouts, on picket lines, or as a trusted member for more than a year of the Brown Berets. Many of you have rapped with him, marched with him, worked with him. But you better think carefully now about all the things you might have said to him or done with him because he is a cop. . . . He was planted as a student at Wilson by the LAPD [Los Angeles Police Department] to infiltrate the walkout movement there, and then joined the Brown Berets. Since that time he has been feeding information to the man about all those who have been his friends and who have trusted him. Robert Avila is a traitor. He has betrayed his friends, his Raza [people], and himself; because in selling out to the Man he has become something less than a human being. . . . Remember his name, and remember his face, and remember that the Man will stop at nothing." A photo of Avila picketing with others was published with the article. See *Chicano Student News*, March 1969, 8.

73. Bernal, "Grassroots Leadership," 129. Of this outreach effort, Paula Crisostomo recalls: "We were also doing speaking engagements. I remember we spoke to the B'nai Brith in West L.A. And we went to Hamilton [High] and they had a rally for us in a park. During that week we were hot items, and a lot of groups were asking us to come and speak, and we were getting more support." As quoted in Bernal, "A Reconceptualization of Female Leadership," 13.

74. William Stupin, a teacher at Lincoln, testified later before a grand jury that on Thursday, March 7, at 9:30 A.M., he heard Sal Castro tell a student: "Screw 'em. They are not going to do anything anyway. We are going to have to go out again!" Stupin testimony, Summary of Grand Jury, Acosta Collection, box 4, folder 8, p. 9.

75. Principal Ernest Naumann of Belmont testified later that he saw signs that morning reading "Walkout, 12:30 today" posted at different locations on the campus. Naumann testimony, Summary of Grand Jury, Acosta Collection, box 4, folder 2, p. 233.

76. Ibid., p. 238. Naumann stated that about 800 students walked out (p. 239).

77. Ibid., box 4, folder 8, p. 10.

78. *Chicano Student News*, special issue on the blowouts. The paper reported: "At Belmont High School on Thursday, March 7, students tried to walk out. Before they could move in the same direction of protest as their fellow students at Garfield, Lincoln, and Roosevelt, they found their school invaded by police. Helmeted cops with nightsticks moved through the halls, from classroom to classroom grabbing students as they went and hustling them roughly, either to the principal or to jail."

79. According to Henry Gutiérrez, this news conference was held at All Nations Center in Boyle Heights with about 150 people attending. See Gutiérrez, "Chicano Education Rights Movement," 79–80. He also notes that the PTA presidents from Garfield and Roosevelt also opposed the walkouts (ibid., 88).

80. The Garfield High School Strike Committee on its own did issue, on that Thursday, March 7, a list of demands calling attention to some of the problems at Garfield.

See Gerald Paul Rosen, "Political Activity and the Chicano Movement: A Study of the Political Ideology of Activists in the Chicano Movement" (Ph.D. diss., UCLA, 1972), 258–59.

Chapter Seven

1. Ingles testimony in Acosta Collection, box 4, folder 2, pp. 135–36. Ingles also testified that about 500 students walked out and returned around 1 P.M. (137–38).

2. Paula Crisostomo recalls that along the march there were people hanging from their porches or windows expressing anger at the students and making ugly faces. Crisostomo interview, April 27, 2007. Robert Thoms, an L.A. police officer, later testified that he saw Sal Castro in front of Lincoln at 9 A.M. directing students to picket, and that at 9:40 A.M. he saw Castro walking at the rear of students on their way to Hazard Park, and that about 400 to 600 students participated in the march. See testimony in Summary of Grand Jury, Acosta Collection, box 4, folder 8, p. 13.

3. Sal Castro interview with Gómez-Quiñones, Acosta Collection, box 4, folder 3, p. 475.

4. Harry Gamboa recalls that about fifty students from Garfield made the long walk from their school in Boyle Heights to Hazard Park and that these students represented the most committed of students. Gamboa interview, July 1, 2007.

5. See *Taking Back the Schools*; and *Los Angeles Times*, March 9, 1968, part 3, pp. 1, 3.

6. *Taking Back the Schools*.

7. Crisostomo interview, April 27, 2007.

8. For the Venice High walkouts, which by the next week involved almost 1,000 mostly white students, see *Los Angeles Times*, March 15, 1968, 3.

9. Ibid., March 9, 1968, part 3, pp. 1, 3. That Thursday, March 7, almost 200 black students from Jefferson High School confronted the school board, demanding that there be black administrators, including a black principal, at their school and preventing the board from conducting its regular business. See *Los Angeles Times*, March 8, 1968, 1.

10. Ibid., March 13, 1968, 1, 3.

11. See Marguerita V. Marín, *Social Protest in an Urban Barrio: A Study of the Chicano Movement, 1966–1974* (Lanham, Md.: University Press of America, 1991), 81. The *Garfield High School Striker*, a newsletter by the Garfield High School Strike Committee, on Thursday, March 7, 1968, carried this headline: "Walk Out Now or Drop Out Tomorrow!" See copy in Acosta Collection, box 4, folder 7.

12. Cuarón interview, June 10, 2007.

13. Crisostomo interview, April 27, 2007.

14. Harry Gamboa interview in *Taking Back the Schools*. Gamboa also recalls that at the time he had long hair, which was hard to keep out of his face. When Kennedy met him, Gamboa remembered, "he touched my hair, and said, 'We have the same problem.'"

15. See *Chicano Student Movement*, April 25, 1968, 8. Besides printing the picture of Kennedy with the students, the *Chicano Student Movement* stated: "We reprint this picture of Robert Kennedy and add the telegram which he later sent. The *future*

president of the U.S. is telling us that he supports Blowouts as an excellent method of getting reforms for education. Now are we going to let some 2 bit mayor, police chief, racist administrators and teachers and a ridiculous Vaudeville team that poses for a Board of Education say we are wrong? It is quite possible that when Kennedy is president, we might expect Federal troops on *our side* and then maybe these honkie racist L.A. cops and Sheriffs will get a few knots on their ugly heads. So let's not give up. We are right, right, right, with or without the future president's approval."

16. Vicki Castro notes that sometime later that spring she and other Chicano college students met with Kennedy at a breakfast at El Adobe Restaurant on Melrose Avenue organized by the Kennedy people. Vicki Castro interview, November 12, 1998.

17. Henry Joseph Gutiérrez, "The Chicano Education Rights Movement and School Desegregation, Los Angeles, 1962–1970" (Ph.D. diss., University of California, Irvine, 1990), 74. On the meeting with the school board, the Garfield High School Strike Committee proclaimed: "We must show the Board, the principals, our parents and the people of Los Angeles that we the students can no longer tolerate the conditions that make us educational and cultural cripples by the time we leave high school. We must continue this strike! The more of us striking, the better our chances of winning our fight!" See statement in appendix 2 in Gerald Paul Rosen, "Political Activity and the Chicano Movement: A Study of the Political Ideology of Activists in the Chicano Movement" (Ph.D. diss., UCLA, 1972), 259.

18. *Los Angeles Times* clipping in Castro Collection.

19. Ibid.

20. See ibid., March 13, 1968, 1, 3. On March 12, about twenty-five Mexican American parents and community leaders protested at the district attorney's office to get charges against students arrested dropped. Bert Corona, state chair of MAPA, threatened a sit-in if charges were not dropped. See also Cuarón interview for repercussions against her at Garfield, including her arrest along with her father and aunt when they went to see the principal a week or so after the walkouts to discuss these events; the principal refused to talk with them and called the police to arrest them.

21. *Los Angeles Times*, March 12, 1968, 1, 3.

22. Interview with Sal Castro by Mario T. García, June 28, 2007.

23. For a listing of the thirty-eight demands, see *Los Angeles Times*, March 17, 1968, 1, 4, 5. According to Henry Gutiérrez, one set of the thirty-eight demands was distributed at the time of the walkouts, apparently by some of the college students. See Gutiérrez, "Chicano Education Rights Movement," 76.

24. See *Chicano Student News*, March 15, 1968, 7. On March 9, 1968, the American Federation of Teachers sponsored a forum on the walkouts with some of the student participants. On March 13, Antonio Hernández, president of the Mexican-American Unity Council, organized a meeting between police officials and the Mexican American community, including students. See Marín, *Social Protest*, 82.

25. Jesús Salvador Treviño, *Eyewitness: A Filmmaker's Memoir of the Chicano Movement* (Houston: Arte Publico Press, 2001), 11. According to Rosales, the Educational Issues Coordinating Committee (EICC) originated from the Emergency Support Committee (ESC), which was formed by about twenty-five parents to raise bail for

those students arrested during the walkouts; see F. Arturo Rosales, *Chicano! The History of the Mexican American Civil Rights Movement* (Houston: Arte Publico Press, 1996), 191.

26. For a listing of other organizations, see Marín, *Social Protest*, 87–88.

27. Ibid., 90.

28. Treviño, *Eyewitness*, 11–12. See also film clip of Mardirosian making this statement, in *Taking Back the Schools*. The Treviño quote is slightly different. The EICC issued the following statement: "The purpose of the EICC is to invite all responsible opinion[,] including students, parents, community groups, etc., in an assertion of human dignity to create a program of suggested changes in the school system that will enable the educational establishment to more adequately, justly, and effectively meet the needs of the Mexican-American school population. We endeavor to respond to the educational needs of our community through creative and positive action in order to enrich the life of the community and we commit our efforts to pave a more viable way for the fulfillment of life in the total community." See EICC Minutes, March 23, 1968; and quoted in Marín, *Social Protest*, 87.

29. Marín, *Social Protest*, 95.

30. See Rosen, "Political Activity and the Chicano Movement," 147. Marín writes: "Women, usually concerned parents, were always present at the group's activities, as were college students and senior citizens." The group's directory listed more than 200 members. EICC minutes were distributed in both English and Spanish. Marín, *Social Protest*, 91–92.

31. Gutiérrez, "Chicano Education Rights Movement," 81.

32. The student demands were edited and presented as "proposals" by the EICC to the school board at the Lincoln meeting; see this list in Castro Collection. See also Gutiérrez, "Chicano Education Rights Movement," 82–83.

33. According to Gutiérrez, at a certain point in the meeting, the board asked to hear from additional members of the audience. The EICC leaders, however, objected because they did not want opponents to speak or the board to conclude its deliberations before agreeing to concessions. Unable to prevent this, EICC adherents and supporters walked out as the meeting continued, and, indeed, some opponents of the walkouts did voice opposition. The meeting went into the evening hours. See Gutiérrez, "Chicano Education Rights Movement," 84.

34. The East L.A. walkouts inspired students in other locations throughout the Southwest to use the same tactics to bring attention to the problems with the Mexican schools. Indeed, at that same time in March 1968, on March 20, Chicano students walked out of Denver's Westside public schools to demand the resignation of a racist teacher. The walkout lasted three days and resulted in police violence against the students and the arrest of twenty-five, including Corky Gonzales, the leader of the Crusade for Justice; see Rosales, *Chicano*. In November 1968, sixty Chicano students walked out of the Mar-Vista High School in San Diego to protest the treatment of Chicano students; see *Chicano Student Movement*, November 1968, 10. One year later, in Pomona, 450 Chicano students walked out of their classes, demanding better education and more attention to their culture, part of a general southwestern walkout by Chicano students, on September 16, 1969, Mexican Independence Day;

see *Los Angeles Times*, San Gabriel Valley edition, April 30, 1970. In the fall of 1969, school walkouts in Crystal City, Texas, by Chicano students were the beginning of La Raza Unida Party, a Chicano independent political party led by José Angel Gutiérrez, and the takeover by the party of the educational and political system in that area. La Raza Unida would go on to become a significant part of the Chicano Movement throughout the Southwest; see José Angel Gutiérrez, *The Making of a Chicano Militant: Lessons from Cristal* (Madison: University of Wisconsin Press, 1998). See also Armando Navarro, *The Cristal Experiment: A Chicano Struggle for Community Control* (Madison: University of Wisconsin Press, 1998). Acuña notes additional walkouts in other southwestern areas inspired by the East L.A. blowouts, such as Denver, San Antonio, Santa Clara, California, and Phoenix. See Rodolfo Acuña, *Occupied America: A History of Chicanos*, 2nd ed. (New York: Harper & Row, 1981), 358. For excellent surveys of the blowouts, see Heather E. Hays, "A Cry for Change: The 1968 East L.A. Blowouts," and Raquel Acosta, "Educational Reform in Response to the Chicano Movement," undergraduate research papers for my class on the Chicano Movement, University of California, Santa Barbara, spring 1997, in possession of Mario T. García.

35. Vicki Castro interview, November 12, 1998.

36. Cuarón interview, June 10, 2007.

Chapter Eight

1. See Gerald Paul Rosen, "Political Activity and the Chicano Movement: A Study of the Political Ideology of Activists in the Chicano Movement" (Ph.D. diss., UCLA, 1972), 147. The demonstration occurred on April 4, 1968.

2. As quoted in Marguerite V. Marín, *Social Protest in an Urban Barrio: A Study of the Chicano Movement, 1966–1974* (Lanham, Md.: University Press of America, 1991), 96.

3. See *La Raza Yearbook*, September 1968. Davis was transferred the following school year. See Rosen, "Political Activity and the Chicano Movement," 148.

4. According to Marín, these "walk-throughs" also helped to recruit new members to the EICC. Marín, *Social Protest*, 92–93.

5. An anonymous former EICC member recalls: "One of them [undercover police] came up to me and said, 'It's time to take action. I have some dynamite.'" As quoted in ibid., 98.

6. Julian Nava, *Julian Nava: My Mexican-American Journey* (Houston: Arte Publico Press, 2002).

7. According to Jesús Treviño, school officials had been secretly testifying to the grand jury against Castro and others. See Jesús Salvador Treviño, *Eyewitness: A Filmmaker's Memoir of the Chicano Movement* (Houston: Arte Publico Press, 2001), 49. Gutiérrez adds that the grand jury proceedings were the result of a three-month investigation by a special task force of intelligence detectives from the LA police, the county sheriff's office, and the district attorney's office. The grand jury proceedings lasted three days and more than fifty witnesses testified, including police officers, school administrators, teachers, and others. See Henry Joseph Gutiérrez, "The Chicano Education Rights Movement and School Desegregation, Los Angeles, 1962–

1970" (Ph.D. diss., University of California, Irvine, 1990), 90. Carlos Muñoz, one of the college students and one of those arrested, notes that Younger probably was reacting to a directive by FBI director J. Edgar Hoover in early March 1968, calling on local law enforcement officials to engage in intelligence gathering to undermine ethnic nationalist movements in minority communities in the country. See Carlos Muñoz Jr., *Youth, Identity, Power: The Chicano Movement* (New York: Verso, 1989), 67–68. See copy of Grand Jury Proceedings, "The People of the State of California vs. Salvatore B. Castro, et al.," Acosta Collection, May 21, 22, 23, 28 (1968), box 4, folder 2. Castro notes that, when arraigned, he was listed as Salvatore, even though he explained that his full name was Salvador. Interview with Sal Castro, May 23, 2007.

8. For Gómez-Quiñones testimony, see Grand Jury Proceedings, Acosta Collection, box 4, folder 2, pp. 68–100. The radio interview took place on March 14, 1968. The full transcript of the interview is in Acosta Collection, box 4, folder 3, pp. 450–81.

9. Moctesuma Esparza notes that he never testified before the grand jury; interview with Moctesuma Esparza by Mario T. García, June 29, 2010. Oscar Zeta Acosta, *The Revolt of the Cockroach People* (New York: Vintage Books, 1973), 54.

10. The indictments for Sal Castro and others were issued on May 28, 1968, by the grand jury. See copy of indictment in Acosta Collection, box 4, folder 9.

11. See Oscar Zeta Acosta's description of the Glass House in Acosta, *Cockroach People*, 51.

12. Ian F. Haney López observes that at the time Acosta had little experience as a trial lawyer. See Ian F. Haney López, *Racism on Trial: The Chicano Fight for Justice* (Cambridge: Harvard University Press, 2003), 30.

13. Gutiérrez, "Chicano Education Rights Movement," 91.

14. See *La Raza*, June 7–13, 1968.

15. Acosta, *Cockroach People*, 52.

16. See *Open City* (Los Angeles), June 7–16, 1968, in Castro Collection; see also Marín, *Social Protest*, 101. Moderate Mexican Americans, such as Dr. Francisco Bravo and the League of United Latin American Citizens (LULAC), criticized the arrests and pledged support for those arrested. See Rodolfo Acuña, A *Community under Siege: A Chronicle of Chicanos East of the Los Angeles River, 1945–1975* (Los Angeles: Chicano Studies Research Center, UCLA, 1984), 169. See also Rosales, *Chicano! The History of the Mexican American Civil Rights Movement* (Houston: Arte Publico Press, 1996), 193.

17. As quoted in Gutiérrez, "Chicano Education Rights Movement," 91. In his novel, Oscar Zeta Acosta claims that he was the principal organizer of the demonstrations; references in Chicano Movement newspapers about the demonstrations do not substantiate Acosta's claim. See Acosta, *Cockroach People*, 58.

18. Acosta, *Cockroach People*, 60.

19. Muñoz describes his arrest in *Taking Back the Schools*.

20. "Chicano Prisoners of Liberation: Conspiracy for Better Education," n.d., in Castro Collection. According to Gutiérrez, the media at first referred to all of the thirteen as Brown Berets, although only four were actual members. Gutiérrez, "Chicano Education Rights Movement," 91. Esparza and Cruz Olmeda were arrested while picketing in front of the Hollenbeck Police Station; Risco and Razo were arrested at

La Raza offices and police confiscated some of their materials; David Sánchez was arrested at the Brown Berets office and police confiscated some of the Berets' materials; Muñoz was arrested at home; López, Vigil, Gómez, and Pat Sánchez voluntarily turned themselves in. Clipping in Acosta Collection, box 4, folder 1.

21. See *Chicano Student Movement*, June 12, 1968, 1.

22. Ruiz interview in *Taking Back the Schools*. For police–Chicano Movement tensions in Los Angeles, see Edward J. Escobar, "The Dialectics of Repression: The Los Angeles Police Department and the Chicano Movement, 1968–1971," *Journal of American History* 79, no. 4 (March 1993): 1483–1514. See also Armando Morales, *Ando Sangrando/I Am Bleeding: A Study of Mexican American Police Conflict* (La Puente, Calif.: Perspectiva Publications, 1972). *La Raza* wrote: "Atmosphere in the 8th floor Hall of Justice was tense and expectant as the SRO [standing room only] spectators filed in for the [morning] session. The tension was broken by Sal Castro who raised an arm above his head and made the familiar 'V' sign with his fingers. Immediately hands shot into the air responding to the gesture and smiles broke out on the faces of girlfriends, parents, and relatives of the prisoners." See *La Raza*, June 7–13, 1968.

23. *La Raza*, June 7–13, 1968. Michael Hannon at the time was also the candidate of the Peace and Freedom Party for district attorney, opposing Evelle Younger. See Gutiérrez, "Chicano Education Rights Movement," 90.

24. *Open City* (Los Angeles), July 1968, 1. The bail of David Sánchez of the Brown Berets, however, was reduced to $1,000 because the district attorney argued that he posed a greater bail risk. Moctesuma Esparza recalls that he was released on his own recognizance; Esparza interview, June 29, 2010.

25. According to Acuña, the Kennedy people contributed $10,000 to the walkout defendants' defense. Acuña, *Community under Siege*, 171.

26. *Open City* (Los Angeles), June 7–16, 1968, in Castro Collection.

27. On the harassment of the students, the *Chicano Student News* reported: "In the aftermath of the blow-outs many high school students are being subjected to unnecessary, continuous, and sometimes cruel harassment by teachers and administrators. In one case, a leader was suspended from school for circulating sheets of paper announcing a march from the Placita to the Board of Education. . . . Before the suspension the parents of this leader received several derogatory letters claiming that their child would be jailed for participating actively in something so beautiful that it made the Chicano student come to grips with himself. . . . Leaders were given low grades by teachers who are against the blow-outs. . . . Leaders are being kept after class and 'talked' to. They're being told to forget about the scholarships that were offered them before the blow-outs." See *Chicano Student News*, May 18, 1968, 2. Paula Crisostomo recalls that she was threatened with not graduating and that counselors withheld college entrance and scholarship information from her. See Dolores Delgado Bernal, "Chicana School Resistance and Grassroots Leadership: Providing an Alternative History of the 1968 East Los Angeles Blowouts" (Ph.D. diss., UCLA, 1997), 139.

28. *Los Angeles Times*, June 5, 1968.

29. Crisostomo interview, April 27, 2007. Paula Crisostomo was a commencement speaker, but instead of giving the usual type of speech she chose to talk about a

"dream deferred," which was her way of indirectly bringing the subject of the walk-outs into the graduation ceremony. By "dream deferred" she meant that there were still many problems in the schools and that the blowouts brought attention to the fact that many Chicano graduating seniors would never have a chance to achieve the mythical American Dream. She also notes that there were no visible symbols at the commencement ceremony about the blowouts. On the other hand, the 1968 Lincoln High yearbook did publish a two-page spread on the blowouts with several photos of the protests. I thank Paula Crisostomo for sending me a copy of these two pages.

30. "The Chicano Legal Defense Committee is a committee that was formed as a result of the police malpractices that occur daily in our barrios. . . . In the past two years Mexican-Americans have intensified their efforts to achieve dignity, equality and justice. This struggle, in disfavor by those in authority, has recently claimed 13 Chicanos in East Los Angeles. They are charged with conspiracy to commit a misdemeanor, which is a felony. The legal defense of a conspiracy charge is very costly since the question of the constitutionality of the conspiracy law has to be tested. What those 13 Chicanos that have incurred punishment have done is in behalf of the collective interests of our community. The least that you and I can do is contribute our personal and financial support. In doing so we will not only be helping to decide the fate of the 13 Chicanos but also our own." As quoted in *Chicano Student Movement* 1, no. 5 (n.d.): 3. See also *East Los Angeles Tribune*, July 4, 1968. The Chicano Legal Defense Committee established the Chicano Legal Defense Fund to raise money for the defense of the East L.A. 13. Sponsors included César Chávez, Bert Corona, and Rodolfo Acuña, as well as Anglo and black politicians such as Edmund G. Brown and Tom Bradley. See López, *Racism on Trial*, 31. Richard Alatorre, later an elected official, served as the initial president of the committee. See Marín, *Social Protest*, 85.

31. *Los Angeles Times*, October 6, 1968; see also "Castro, Davis Not at Lincoln This Semester," newspaper clipping, in Castro Collection.

32. "Castro, Davis Not at Lincoln This Semester," newspaper clipping, in Castro Collection.

33. See *Los Angeles Herald-Examiner*, September 30, 1968. Treviño, a member of the EICC, remembers about 300 people protesting. See Treviño, *Eyewitness*, 66. See also Rosen, "Political Activity and the Chicano Movement," 254.

34. Treviño, *Eyewitness*, 69.

35. Raul Ruiz, "Sal Castro," *Chicano Student News*, April 25, 1968, 2.

36. Rosalinda Méndez González recalls her testimony before the school board: "I remember also the testimony that I gave about Sal. I talked about the conditions at Lincoln and how he had gone to the board. I talked about what a wonderful teacher Sal Castro was, how he inspired us, and how he got us to think about going to college." As quoted in Bernal, "Chicana School Resistance," 137.

37. Rosen, "Political Activity and the Chicano Movement," 149.

38. The actual date of the beginning of the sit-in was September 26, 1968. See Treviño, *Eyewitness*, 71.

39. See Ralph Guzmán, "The Gentle Revolutionaries: Brown Power," *Los Angeles Times West Magazine*, January 26, 1969; Treviño, *Eyewitness*, 73; and *Chicano Student*

Movement 1, no. 6 (n.d.): 5. Carlos Vásquez recalls that the sit-in was more spontaneous than planned and that it was not so much about Sal as it was about a good teacher being persecuted. See interview with Carlos Vásquez by Mario T. García, June 10, 2008.

40. Treviño, *Eyewitness*, 70. According to Treviño, it was Mardirosian who spontaneously proposed the sit-in (71). Rosen adds that the idea of a sit-in was actually a compromise between those who wanted a more militant action and those who wanted to negotiate with the school board. See Rosen, "Political Ideology and the Chicano Movement," 158. Gutiérrez adds that the original protest was to be some form of civil disobedience on the Lincoln school grounds. See Gutiérrez, "Chicano Education Rights Movement," 95–96.

41. Treviño participated in the sit-in and mentions that 100 people were involved in the protest. Treviño, *Eyewitness*, 73.

42. Castro's recollection of people being able to enter the auditorium conflicts with a *Los Angeles Herald-Examiner* account that only those leaving on an emergency basis or to get food were allowed back in by security officers; anyone leaving for other purposes was not allowed back. See *Los Angeles Herald-Examiner*, September 29, 1968.

43. *Chicano Student Movement* 1, no. 6 (n.d.): 4.

44. Ibid., 5.

45. Ibid., 4.

46. *Los Angeles Herald-Examiner*, October 2, 1968, A-4.

47. According to Gutiérrez, the school board, at a special meeting that Wednesday, October 2, voted to approve a new policy, that teachers who were indicted would be entitled to a hearing before being reassigned to a nonteaching position, with the exception of a morals charge or other serious criminal indictment; the adoption of this policy convinced Mardirosian and others of the EICC to end the sit-in with the expectation that this new policy would reinstate Castro to his teaching position at Lincoln. Gutiérrez, "Chicano Education Rights Movement," 99.

48. See *Los Angeles Herald-Examiner*, October 3, 1968; see also *Los Angeles Times*, October 3, 1968. Those arrested posted bail, which was raised by other Chicano activists, apparently mostly EICC participants, including attorney Oscar Zeta Acosta, and were released that evening. See Treviño, *Eyewitness*, 81; and Rosen, "Political Activity and the Chicano Movement," 150. According to Gutiérrez, Father Luce and Father Wood led the group in prayer prior to the arrests. Gutiérrez, "Chicano Education Rights Movement," 100. One of the women arrested was Alicia Escalante, a mother and head of the Eastside welfare rights movement. See *Chicano Student Movement* 1, no. 6 (n.d.): 5.

49. Gutiérrez notes that some fifty people signed up to address the board on behalf of Castro. Gutiérrez, "Chicano Education Rights Movement," 100.

50. See sign in *Taking Back the Schools*.

51. See Mardirosian statement to board of education, in ibid.

52. See headline of *Los Angeles Times*, October 4, 1968. Following the decision by the school board to reinstate Castro, 40 teachers out of 170 at Lincoln High threatened to request transfers if Castro resumed teaching at the school; it is not clear how many actually transferred. See *Los Angeles Times* clipping in Castro Collection. Alicia

Escalante, one of the thirty-five arrested, stated: "For you who may not think it was a just cause, do you think if it wasn't Castro would have been reinstated? As the Pledge of Allegiance states, 'One nation under God with liberty and justice for all.' This is all we asked for and justice was done." As quoted in *Chicano Student News* 1, no. 6 (n.d.): 5.

Chapter Nine

1. See letter to the editor, *Chicano Student Movement*, August 1969, 2. See also "Lincoln High Invites Public to Its Weekend Latin Fiesta," *Los Angeles Times* clipping, in Castro Collection.

2. As quoted in *Los Angeles Herald-Examiner*, October 6, 1968.

3. See letter, October 24, 1969, in Castro Collection.

4. According to Acuña, bilingual classes were started at Roosevelt and some Mexican American studies classes were started at Lincoln in the 1968–69 year. Rodolfo Acuña, *A Community under Siege: A Chronicle of Chicanos East of the Los Angeles River, 1945–1975* (Los Angeles: Chicano Studies Research Center, UCLA), 170.

5. Of the thirty-six members, twenty-six were chosen by the EICC; the rest were chosen by the school board. See Gerald Paul Rosen, "Political Activity and the Chicano Movement: A Study of the Political Ideology of Activists in the Chicano Movement" (Ph.D. diss., UCLA, 1972), 150. See also Henry Joseph Gutiérrez, "The Chicano Education Rights Movement and School Desegregation, Los Angeles, 1962–1970" (Ph.D. diss., University of California, Irvine, 1990), 103.

6. For a list of initial members, see appendix E in Marguerite V. Marín, *Social Protest in an Urban Barrio: A Study of the Chicano Movement* (Lanham, Md.: University Press of America), 255–56. Marín notes that there were forty initial members.

7. According to Marín, some of the reforms initiated by the commission included the elimination of IQ tests during the first three years of elementary school; a bilingual-bicultural curriculum; and new teacher training for Eastside teachers. Ibid., 108–9.

8. See *Chicano Student Movement*, February 1969, 1. The Roosevelt walkout and protests occurred January 10–13, 1969.

9. *Los Angeles Times* clipping, n.d., in Castro Collection.

10. See *Chicano: Mexican-American Heritage Series*, vol. 1, KNBC, in Castro Collection.

11. See *Chicano: Mexican Heritage*, in Castro Collection.

12. Ibid.

13. See *Los Angeles Times* clipping, n.d., in Castro Collection. According to the *Times*, the two teachers voted in the minority.

14. *Chicano Student Movement*, August 1969, 6. See also *Eastside Sun*, December 11, 1969. In an open letter to George Ingles, the principal at Lincoln, Joseph Eli Kovner, the editor and publisher of the *Eastside Sun*, appealed to Ingles to reinstate Sal Castro at Lincoln: "You can achieve harmony among faculty, students and community involved persons interested in the retention of this much maligned teacher, who is only one of some excellently trained Mexican Americans in the art of instruction,

but who stands out because he is courageously trying to right what is wrong with educational procedures and facilities here."

15. *Eastside Sun*, August 28, 1969, A-6. The *Eastside Sun* referred to Castro as "The Brown Socrates," "An Eastside Hero," and "A Southwest Legend."

16. *Los Angeles Times*, October 8, 1968. See the motions to quell the indictments in Superior Court posted on August 6, 1968, in Acosta Collection, box 4, folder 4. The motion challenged the exclusion of Mexican Americans from the grand jury system and read: "The Grand Juries for Los Angeles County for the year 1959 through 1968, and specifically the 1968 Grand Jury . . . have been illegally constituted in that there has been, and to the present still exists, an unconstitutional and underrepresentation of American citizens of Spanish Surname on these Grand Juries, all in violation of the due process and equal protection clause of the 14th Amendment to the United States Constitution and Article I Section 11, 13, and 21 of the California Constitution." For a transcript of the hearings concerning the lack of Spanish-surnamed people in the grand jury pool, see Acosta Collection, box 5, folder 2.

17. See Ian F. Haney López, *Racism on Trial: The Chicano Fight for Justice* (Cambridge: Harvard University Press, 2003), 91.

18. See *Regeneración* 1, no. 5 (1970): 1. The case of the East L.A. 13 was dismissed on July 24, 1970. See Acosta Collection, box 4, folder 9.

19. For an excellent examination and analysis of the initial appeal by the East L.A. 13, see López, *Racism on Trial*. López in particular focuses on the role of Oscar Zeta Acosta in the initial appeal and his questioning of the process whereby Mexican Americans were excluded from the grand jury over the years. In this stage of the legal process, Acosta stressed the violation of the Fourteenth Amendment rather than the Bill of Rights issues. In the end, the latter defense vindicated the East L.A. 13.

20. Rodolfo "Corky" Gonzales, *I Am Joaquin: An Epic Poem* (Denver: Crusade for Justice, 1967).

21. See *Arcade* (from North Hollywood High), March 12, 1971, 1, in Castro Collection. See also *Los Angeles Times*, February 19, 1971, part 2.

22. All thirty members of the Mexican American Education Commission resigned in protest of Castro's transfer to North Hollywood High. See *Los Angeles Times*, February 19, 1971, part 2.

23. Sal Castro, in an interview with *Arcade* of North Hollywood High, compared it to Lincoln High: "I make an observation to you that I'm here contrasting Lincoln to North Hollywood High. But at Lincoln High School there are gun-toting security guards. I haven't seen one chain on your panic bars. I haven't seen your toilets closed, yet at Lincoln they close them. You still have an open campus; you don't have to climb fences to get out. Kids over there have to climb fences." See "Mr. Castro Gives Views on Chicano Problems," *Arcade*, March 12, 1971, 2, in Castro Collection.

24. See Lorena Oropeza, *Raza Si! Guerra No! Chicano Protest and Patriotism during the Viet Nam War* (Berkeley: University of California Press, 2005).

25. Ruben Salazar, *Border Correspondent: Selected Writings, 1955–1970*, edited by Mario T. García (Berkeley: University of California Press, 1995).

26. See photocopy of photo in Castro Collection.

27. *Los Angeles Times* clipping, October 10, 1969, in Castro Collection.

28. See Gutiérrez, "Chicano Education Rights Movement," 7.

29. In 1979, voters in California passed Proposition One, which ended mandatory integration strategies, such as busing, in the public schools; see ibid., 10.

30. *Los Angeles Times*, November 11, 1973, part 4, pp. 1–3.

Chapter Ten

1. See clipping from *Northwest Leader*, October 3, 1974, in Castro Collection.

2. See my chapter "¡Presente! Father Luis Olivares and the Sanctuary Movement in Los Angeles—A Study of Faith, Ethnic Identity, and Ecumenism," in Mario T. García, *Católicos: Resistance and Affirmation in Chicano Catholic History* (Austin: University of Texas Press, 2008), 207–50.

3. See, for example, Haki R. Madhubuti, ed., *Why L.A. Happened: Implications of the '92 Los Angeles Rebellion* (Chicago: Third World Press, 1993).

Chapter Eleven

1. Frank del Olmo, "Back to the Most Basic Basic: Teachers' Expectation Levels," *Los Angeles Times*, June 17, 1983, part 2, p. 7.

2. For the tenth anniversary of the blowouts, see Frank del Olmo, "'68 Protests Brought Better Education, Most Believe," *Los Angeles Times*, March 26, 1978, part 2, pp. 1, 5. For the twentieth anniversary, see Frank del Olmo, "'60s 'Blowouts': Leaders of Latino School Protest See Little Change," *Los Angeles Times*, March 7, 1988, part 2, pp. 1, 2.

3. See the folder given to each student participant in the Chicano Youth Leadership Conferences, in Castro Collection.

4. Sonia Salazar to Sal Castro, May 23, 2007, courtesy of Sal Castro and with permission of Sonia Salazar.

5. As quoted in Frank del Olmo, "No Regrets, Chicano Students Who Walked Out Say," *Los Angeles Times*, March 26, 1978.

6. See HBO film *Walkout*.

7. Frank del Olmo, " No Regrets, Chicano Students Who Walked Out Say."

8. Sal Castro served as a technical adviser on the film. See film credits for HBO film *Walkout*.

9. *Los Angeles Times*, March 18, 2006, 16.

10. Gamboa interview, July 1, 2007.

11. See HBO film *Walkout*.

Afterword

1. Carlos Muñoz Jr., *Youth, Identity, Power: The Chicano Movement* (New York: Verso, 1989).

2. See Jorge Mariscal, *Brown-Eyed Children of the Sun: Lessons from the Chicano Movement, 1965–1975* (Albuquerque: University of New Mexico Press, 2005).

3. Paulo Freire, *Pedagogy of the Oppressed* (New York: Continuum, 2005; originally published 1970), 17.

4. As quoted in ibid., 25.

5. Ibid., 19.

6. Ibid., 130.

7. Interview with Sal Castro, May 15, 2001, tape 1–2.

8. Ibid.

9. Ibid.

10. Ibid.

11. Interview with Sal Castro, July 25, 2001, tape 5–6.

12. Interview with Sal Castro, July 24, 2001, tape 1–2.

13. Ibid., tape 3–4.

14. Ibid.

15. Ibid.

16. Interview with Sal Castro, July 25, 2001, tape 5–6.

17. Ibid. See also Freire, *Pedagogy of the Oppressed*.

18. Interview with Sal Castro, July 25, 2001, tape 5–6.

19. Freire, *Pedagogy of the Oppressed*.

20. See copies of initial conferences provided by Sal Castro.

21. Interview with Sal Castro, April 20, 2006.

22. Ibid.

23. Freire, *Pedagogy of the Oppressed*, 46, 140, 153.

24. Dolores Delgado Bernal, "Chicana School Resistance and Grassroots Leadership: Providing an Alternative History of the 1968 East Los Angeles Blowouts" (Ph.D. diss., UCLA, 1997), 80.

25. Program for Second Annual Camp Hess Kramer Spanish Speaking Youth Leadership Conference, in Castro Collection.

26. Freire, *Pedagogy of the Oppressed*, 46, 140, 153.

27. Ibid., 131.

28. Ibid., 95; see also 39, 48.

29. Ibid., 77.

30. Ibid., 53.

31. Ibid., 33.

32. Ibid., 124.

33. Ibid., 80; see also 69, 72.

34. Ibid., 181.

35. Camp Hess Kramer programs, Castro Collection.

36. Interview with Sal Castro, July 25, 2001, tape 9–10.

37. Camp Hess Kramer programs, Castro Collection.

38. Interview with Sal Castro, July 25, 2001, tape 9–10.

39. Interview with Sal Castro, July 26, 2001, tape 11–12.

40. Ibid.

41. *Today Not Mañana*.

42. Ibid.

43. Ibid.

44. Ibid.

45. Ibid.

46. Bernal, "Chicana School Resistance," 107.

47. Interview with Sal Castro, July 26, 2001, tape 11–12.

48. Ibid.

49. Ibid.

50. Ibid.

51. *Today Not Mañana.*

52. Ibid.

53. Interview with Sal Castro, July 26, 2001, tape 13–14.

54. Ibid.

55. Ibid., tape 11–12.

56. Ibid.

57. Freire, *Pedagogy of the Oppressed*, 79.

58. Ibid., 34; see also 21, 47, 107.

59. Interview with Sal Castro, May 14, 2002, tape 16.

60. Ibid.

61. Bernal, "Chicana School Resistance," 110.

62. Ibid.

63. Freire, *Pedagogy of the Oppressed*, 34.

64. Ibid., 113.

65. Ibid., 30, 34.

66. Ibid., 25, 29, 173.

67. Ibid., 36, 158–59.

68. Bernal, "Chicana School Resistance," 3.

69. Interview with Sal Castro, July 25, 2001, tape 9–10.

70. Bernal, "Chicana School Resistance," 80.

71. Vicki Castro interview, November 12, 1998.

72. Freire, *Pedagogy of the Oppressed*, 25.

73. Ibid., 26; see also 32, 84, 67.

74. Ibid., 49.

75. Ibid., 51.

76. Ibid., 84; see also 19.

77. Ibid., 45.

78. Interview with Sal Castro, July 26, 2001, tape 13–14.

79. Bernal, "Chicana School Resistance," 81–82.

80. Interview with Sal Castro, July 26, 2001, tape 13–14.

81. Camp Hess Kramer programs, Castro Collection.

82. Ibid., 1967 program. See also *Today Not Mañana.*

83. Vicki Castro interview, November 12, 1998.

84. Interview with Sal Castro, July 26, 2001, 13–14.

85. *Today Not Mañana.*

86. Ibid.

87. Camp Hess Kramer program, 1968, Castro Collection.

88. Juan Gómez-Quiñones, *Mexican Students Por La Raza: The Chicano Student Movement in Southern California, 1967–1977* (Santa Barbara, Calif.: Editorial La Causa, 1978), 31.

Appendix

1. On Chávez, see Richard Griswold del Castillo and Richard A. García, *César Chávez: A Triumph of Spirit* (Norman: University of Oklahoma Press, 1995); Frederick John Dalton, *The Moral Vision of César Chávez* (Maryknoll, N.Y.: Orbis Books, 2003); Susan Ferris and Ricardo Sandoval, *The Fight in the Fields: César Chávez and the Farmworkers Movement* (New York: Harcourt Brace, 1997); and Jacques Levy, *Cesar Chavez: Autobiography of La Causa* (New York: W. W. Norton, 1975).

2. Randy Shaw, *Beyond the Fields: César Chávez, the UFW, and the Struggle for Justice in the 21st Century* (Berkeley: University of California Press, 2008); Miriam Powell, *The Union of Their Dreams: Power, Hope, and Struggle in César Chávez's Farm Worker Movement* (New York: Bloomsbury Press, 2009).

3. Gerald P. Rosen, "Political Activity and the Chicano Movement: A Study of the Political Ideology of Activists in the Chicano Movement" (Ph.D. diss., UCLA, 1972); Ignacio García, *Chicanismo: The Forging of a Militant Ethos among Chicanos* (Tucson: University of Arizona Press, 1997); Jorge Mariscal, *Brown-Eyed Children of the Sun: Lessons from the Chicano Movement, 1965–1975* (Albuquerque: University of New Mexico Press, 2005).

4. Juan Gómez-Quiñones, *Mexican Students Por La Raza: The Chicano Student Movement in Southern California, 1967–1977* (Santa Barbara, Calif.: Editorial La Causa, 1978); Carlos Muñoz Jr., *Youth, Identity, Power: The Chicano Movement* (London: Verso Press, 1989); Dolores Delgado Bernal, "Chicana School Resistance and Grassroots Leadership: Providing an Alternative History of the 1968 East Los Angeles Blowouts" (Ph.D. diss., UCLA, 1997); Armando Navarro, *Mexican American Youth Organization: Avant-Garde of the Chicano Movement in Texas* (Austin: University of Texas Press, 1995); José Angel Gutiérrez, *We Won't Back Down: Severita Lara's Rise from Student Leader to Mayor* (Houston: Arte Publico Press, 2005).

5. Marguerite V. Marín, *Social Protest in an Urban Barrio: A Study of the Chicano Movement, 1966–1974* (Lanham, Md.: University Press of America, 1991); Ernesto Chávez, *"Mi Raza Primero!" Nationalism, Identity, and Insurgency in the Chicano Movement in Los Angeles, 1966–1978* (Berkeley: University of California Press, 2002); Ernesto B. Vigil, *The Crusade for Justice: Chicano Militancy and the Government's War on Dissent* (Madison: University of Wisconsin Press, 1999).

6. David Montejano, *Quixote's Soldiers: A Local History of the Chicano Movement, 1966–1981* (Austin: University of Texas Press, 2010).

7. Ignacio M. García, *United We Win: The Rise and Fall of La Raza Unida Party* (Tucson: Mexican American Studies & Research Center, University of Arizona, 1989); Armando Navarro, *The Cristal Experiment: A Chicano Struggle for Community Control* (Madison: University of Wisconsin Press, 1998); Armando Navarro, *La Raza Unida Party: A Chicano Challenge to the U.S. Two-Party Dictatorship* (Philadelphia: Temple University Press, 2000).

8. See Marc Rodríguez, "Mexican Americanism: The Tejano Diaspora and Ethnic Politics in Texas and Wisconsin after 1950" (currently under consideration by University of North Carolina Press).

9. Lorena Oropeza, *Raza Si! Guerra No! Chicano Protest and Patriotism during the Vietnam War Era* (Berkeley: University of California Press, 2005).

10. Rudy V. Busto, *King Tiger: The Religious Vision of Reies López Tijerina* (Albuquerque: University of New Mexico Press, 2005).

11. Lara Medina, *Las Hermanas: Chicana/Latina Religious-Political Activism in the U.S. Catholic Church* (Philadelphia: Temple University Press, 2004); Richard Edward Martínez, *PADRES: The National Chicano Priest Movement* (Austin: University of Texas Press, 2005).

12. See Mario T. García, *Católicos: Resistance and Affirmation in Chicano Catholic History* (Austin: University of Texas Press, 2008); and Mario T. García, ed., *The Gospel of César Chávez: My Faith in Action* (Lanham, Md.: Sheed & Ward, 2007).

13. José-Antonio Orosco, *César Chávez and the Common Sense of Nonviolence* (Albuquerque: University of New Mexico Press, 2008).

14. Ian F. Haney López, *Racism on Trial: The Chicano Fight for Justice* (Cambridge: Harvard University Press, 2003).

15. Bernal, "Chicana School Resistance"; Henry Joseph Gutiérrez, "The Chicano Education Rights Movement and School Desegregation, Los Angeles, 1962–1970" (Ph.D. diss., University of California, Irvine, 1990).

16. See F. Arturo Rosales, *Chicano! The History of the Mexican American Civil Rights Movement* (Houston: Arte Publico Press, 1996), 173–96. See also *Taking Back the Schools*.

17. Rubén Donato, *The Other Struggle for Equal Schools: Mexican Americans during the Civil Rights Era* (Albany: State University of New York Press, 1997).

18. David G. Gutiérrez, *Walls and Mirrors: Mexican Americans, Mexican Immigrants, and the Politics of Ethnicity* (Berkeley: University of California Press, 1995); Laura Pulido, *Black, Brown, Yellow, and Left: Radical Activism in Los Angeles* (Berkeley: University of California Press, 2006).

19. Mario T. García, *Desert Immigrants: The Mexicans of El Paso, 1880–1920* (New Haven: Yale University Press, 1981).

20. Mario T. García, *Mexican Americans: Leadership, Ideology, and Identity, 1930–1960* (New Haven: Yale University Press, 1989).

21. See Mario T. García, *Memories of Chicano History: The Life and Narrative of Bert Corona* (Berkeley: University of California Press, 1994); Mario T. García, *The Making of a Mexican American Mayor: Raymond L. Telles of El Paso* (El Paso: Texas Western Press, 1998); Frances Esquibel Tywoniak and Mario T. García, *Migrant Daughter: Coming of Age as a Mexican American Woman* (Berkeley: University of California Press, 2000); and Mario T. García, *Luis Leal: An Auto/Biography* (Austin: University of Texas Press, 2000).

INDEX